"He who knows not the world,

knows not his own place in it."

MARCUS AURELIUS

The Unicorn
BOOK of
1954

Prepared under the Editorial Direction of

JOSEPH LAFFAN MORSE, Sc.B., LL.B.

Editor in Chief

THE NEW FUNK & WAGNALLS ENCYCLOPEDIA

UNICORN BOOKS, INC., NEW YORK

iv

STAFF

Joseph L. Morse, Editor in Chief
Richard M. Gordon, Executive Editor
Clayton Rawson, Art Director
John Hackett, Consultant

WRITERS: Val Adams • Charles H. Brown • Leonard Engel
David Dempsey • Stanley W. Page • Samuel T. Williamson
John T. McAllister • Gordon C. Hamilton • Morris Weeks, Jr.
Martin Fass • Emory Lewis • Lois Pearson • Jesse Zunser
S. A. Schreiner, Jr. • Sherwin D. Smith • Barbara Yuncker

RESEARCH: Pictures — Bea Danville • Marilyn Lukashok
Text — James Allen • Natalie Raymond • Marjorie Rose

PRODUCTION: Breton Morse • Annabelle Nemser

Preface

THE MOST PORTENTOUS EVENT OF 1954 WAS the death of a humble Japanese fisherman. His name was Aikichi Kuboyama, and he was the first victim of a hydrogen bomb. Kuboyama was fishing in the Pacific Ocean when he heard "the sound of many thunders" and saw "flashes of fire as bright as the sun itself". What he heard and saw happened 80 miles away. Nonetheless, he was fatally burned by a fallout of radioactive ash carried by the soft sea breezes.

For every adult in the world, the death of this simple man dramatized the H-bomb's terrifying power and the unspeakable possibilities of a hydrogen-era war. Pondering them, British scientist and philosopher Bertrand Russell predicted: "War with hydrogen bombs is quite likely to put an end to the human race."

So staggering a prospect set the best brains of the free world struggling to avert it. Throughout the year statesmen met in London, Paris, Brussels, Geneva, Berlin. But what was being thought behind the Iron Curtain no one could say for sure.

Adaptable man, however, has always found ways of living constructively, comfortably, and even gaily on the slopes of volcanoes, and, hydrogen era or no, there were signs that he was doing so again. The year saw the invention of a solar battery, designed to do nothing less than convert the sun's limit-less energy into power. The year saw also the near-final conquest of tuberculosis, an old man-killer, and the promising mass trial of a vaccine against polio, another one.

Wherever one looked, what could not be done was done. No man could run a mile in less than four minutes, but in 1954 two men did, and then for the fun of it did it again. No Negro child in the South could be educated in a school with Whites, but after the 1954 Supreme Court ruling against segregation thousands were.

As 1954 drew to a close, for the first time in nearly twenty years there was no major war, although Israelis and Arabs, Chinese Reds and Chinese Nationalists were still dying by gunfire and were just as dead as the dead of Belleau Wood, Okinawa, and Heartbreak Ridge. World peace might be a dream in the hydrogen era, as in eras before, but dreams were being realized.

And America was still America. To the delight of the whole world, the best-known woman in the United States — with the possible exception of Eleanor Roosevelt—was the product of a hospital charity ward, an orphan asylum, eleven foster homes, and a glowing personality: actress Marilyn Monroe.

Thus the Hydrogen Era's Year 1.

RICHARD M. GORDON
Executive Editor

vi

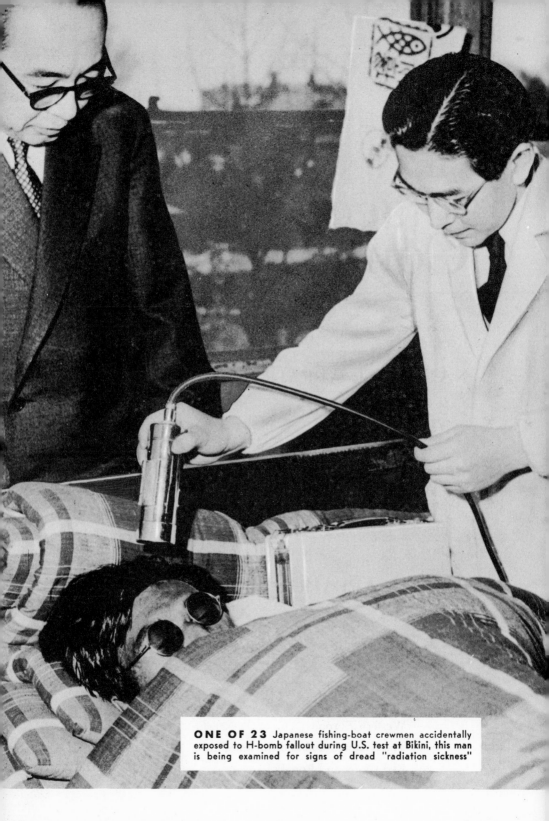

ONE OF 23 Japanese fishing-boat crewmen accidentally exposed to H-bomb fallout during U.S. test at Bikini, this man is being examined for signs of dread "radiation sickness"

Contents

THE UNICORN

BOOK OF 1954

EISENHOWER
BANDWAGON
FOR U. S. S
CITIZENS
FOR
EISENHOWER
BIG JOB
LET'S BACK IKE

Official ISENHOWER BANDWAG
ACCOMPLISHMENTS
CRACKDOWN
ADMINISTRA

NATIONAL AFFAIRS

The PRESIDENT

"SMILE, MR. PRESIDENT!" is photographers' standard plea at press conferences. Ike offers his usual response

AFTER TWO YEARS IN THE PRESIDENCY, Dwight D. Eisenhower in 1954 was still not entirely reconciled to his complete loss of privacy.

"I'm not complaining," he said. "I just never thought people would be so interested in me. I can't even have a bellyache in private."

Yet to many of his fellow citizens, the President, despite the spotlight, remained an enigma.

Publicly, Eisenhower was still the warm, friendly figure whose grin invited people to call him "Ike". Officially, he encouraged no one to do so, not even the closest members of his Cabinet.

"There's nothing casual about the President," said a White House aide. "Nothing informal even in Cabinet meetings."

Some critics lambasted Eisenhower as another bumbling Ulysses Grant incapable of dealing responsibly with the problems of office. Some enthusiasts hailed him as a crusader who was delivering America from enemies at home and abroad.

Eisenhower himself still regarded his job with self-effacing reverence, and often spoke of himself in the third person. "The President feels . . ." or "It seems to the President . . ." were frequently heard at his press conferences.

When asked about the trials of office, he chuckled and answered: "Well, I've not grown any hair."

Public Relations

During 1953, the President's relations with the press had been stiff. Said one veteran newsman: "Eisenhower approached his job like a rookie pitcher with the bases loaded."

In 1954, the President was more at ease, better informed, more responsive. He also talked more freely. The press conference, once a major ordeal for him, had become an opportunity to put across his ideas.

Some reporters felt that Eisenhower had adjusted slowly to the presidency. Blank spots on national affairs still showed up at his meetings with the press. Said one observer: "He seems to know only partly what is going on." Often, during free-wheeling question-and-answer sessions, he would still redden angrily at the questions of even friendly reporters.

He was also apt to blow up over small matters although he was understanding about big ones. He still let loose on underlings. Any attempt to gloss over mistakes irritated him, and offending aides were told off right on the spot.

Once during the early days in office, Eisenhower ripped into Jim Hagerty, his press secretary, for a trivial error. The secretary stood by impassively and finally Ike broke off: "You don't scare easy, do you?"

"No," said Hagerty.

"We'll get along fine," said the President.

Relaxation

A trim, military figure, the 64-year-old Eisenhower was learning to live with the terrible grind that is imposed on every President. He eased up on a strict diet that had kept him at 176 pounds, and, without worrying about it, went a couple of pounds overweight.

He was still a devoted painter. Among his subjects during the year were three Cabinet members and all his grandchildren. For light reading, he still preferred Western adventure yarns.

Whenever possible, Eisenhower escaped from the Washington atmosphere.

CONCENTRATING on canvas, President and Sunday painter relaxes from the pressure of his job

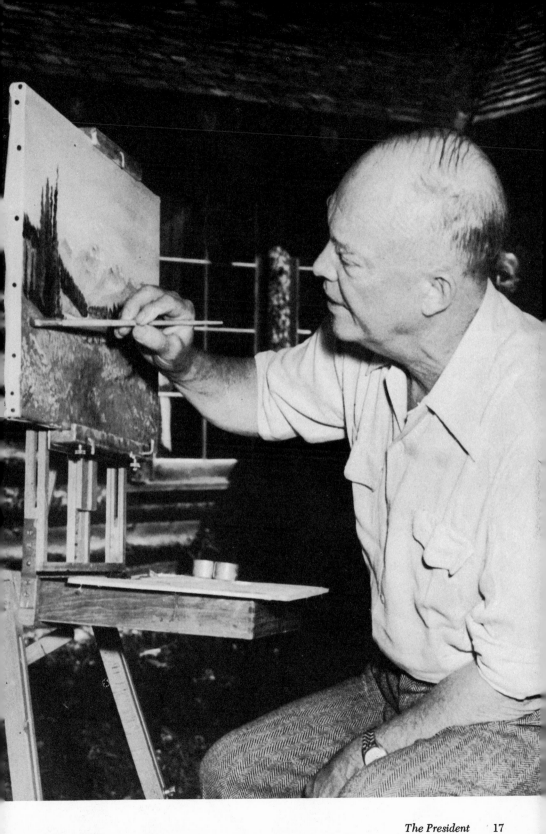

A statistical-minded columnist figured that he spent 1 day away for every 2.1 days he spent in the White House. He golfed in California and Georgia. He hunted in Ohio. He passed weekends at the presidential mountain retreat in Maryland. And in July he began a much-publicized eight-week "work-play" sojourn in Colorado.

Nonetheless, he found that the job of President is mostly work and little play. Sometimes he was able to combine business with pleasure. From time to time he issued invitations to "stag dinners" in the White House. Top business executives, government officials, sports figures, and labor leaders as well as personal friends attended, and the lively discussions covered a wide variety of subjects. The President found this a pleasant way to gather information. At one dinner, labor leader

John L. Lewis sat next to Texas oil millionaire Sid Richardson. At another, golf pro Ed Dudley was seated next to Allen Dulles, head of the government's super-secret Central Intelligence Agency.

A Big Job

When the President took office, he admitted he had a lot to learn.

To do his job properly, Eisenhower adopted a short cut he had used in the army—the military type of "briefing". Under this system, experts concentrated the most complex subjects into capsule form. Information was assembled, analyzed, boiled down, and then presented to the President in an easy-to-understand way.

Critics objected. Such briefings, they said, were superficial and gave Eisenhower a distorted, oversimplified view of

PRESIDENTIAL EXPRESSIONS: A fleeting scowl and an almost audible "Oh, my!" prove that Eisenhower's normally quiet features can change abruptly to suit his mood

important issues. "Not so," said his aides. "The President receives all the details a busy man can absorb and all a sharp executive mind needs to act on."

Aides estimated that the President worked an average sixty-hour week and signed about 200 documents a day. Twenty of those sixty hours were taken up with briefings. In other words, he spent one third of his time learning and preparing for what he had to do in the two thirds remaining.

Ike insisted on brevity. "He doesn't like to be burdened with detail," said one adviser, "so we sort out the marginal things and try to keep to the essentials."

Typical of Ike's attitude is a story told of his visit to Philadelphia during his election campaign. Politicians handed him a 25-page directive about the city. Said Ike: "It took only a 6-page directive to get me into Normandy."

Briefings prepared the President before he met with his Cabinet, congressional leaders, or the press. Even to greet a delegation from some patriotic organization or similar group, he had to be given a quick fill-in. It was not unusual for Eisenhower to be instructed on twenty or thirty major subjects in a week, or on a score of minor topics in a day. Other Presidents have used briefings to some extent, but none so much as Eisenhower.

Usually, during these sessions, Ike leans back in his chair as he listens. Sometimes he shuts his eyes for a moment. At other times, he gets up to walk around the room. Often, he interrupts to summarize what he has heard and to make sure he hasn't missed any important points. He seldom takes notes.

"Ike is not a paper and scratch man," his aides say.

A close friend and adviser gave his opinion: "The President has a panoramic mind. He grasps big, broad pictures and ideas with rapidity, but labors over details. After two years in the White House, Eisenhower, by hard work, patience, and study, has filled in most of the details."

The Program

In a series of messages to Congress in January, 1954, Eisenhower proudly presented what he called a "dynamic, forward-looking program". To his surprise, it was much criticized as well as much praised. "It was as dynamic as the dodo," said Democrat Sam Rayburn, House Minority Leader, "and as forward-looking as yesterday."

Economically, the program was conservative, though it did urge extension of unemployment insurance and social security. "In a modern industrial society," Eisenhower declared, "banishment of destitution and cushioning the shock of personal disaster on the individual are proper concerns of all levels of government."

Democrats joked. "The Eisenhower administration," said Representative Richard Bolling of Missouri, "has just ratified the New Deal."

"I thought we voted for a change," cried Republican Senator John Marshall Butler of Maryland.

"If this is the policy of the Republican Party," said Senator John W. Bricker of Ohio, "I don't know what I'm doing here."

This was hardly the unity the President had expected on his middle-of-the-road program, which he thought would attract both liberals and conservatives. It was Eisenhower's earnest desire to be considered "the President of all the people"—all 163 million of them—regardless of party or faction. The ideal fetched up against one hard reality: people do not think alike. As Mr. Eisenhower discovered, no President could be above all controversy.

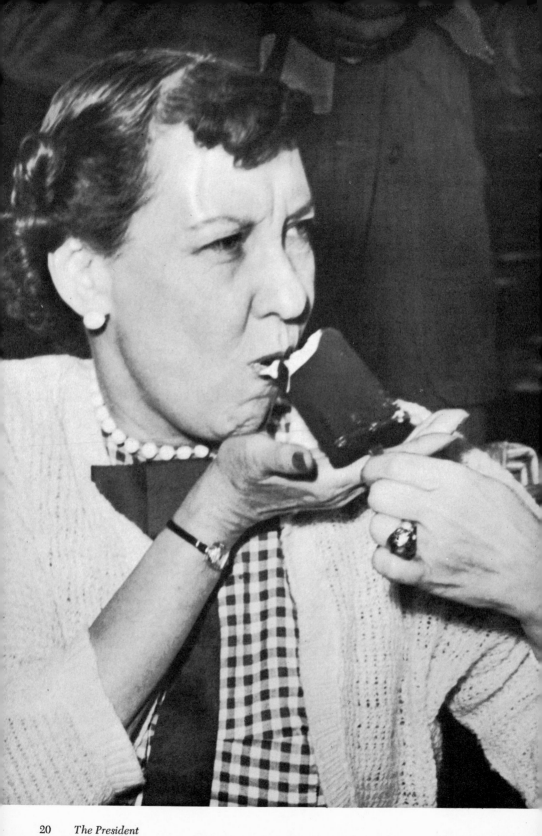

HAPPY MOMENTS: The First Lady braves a popsicle during outing at Camp David, Md., Ike's mountain retreat; the President beams as Secretary Benson's grandson Steven watches birdie

The President 21

Political Growth

After enunciating his domestic policies early in the year, Eisenhower at first pursued a hands-off-Congress program. He felt it was his job as President to recommend legislation but the job of Congress to enact it. When reporters asked about specific bills, he referred them to recommendations made by Cabinet members, adding: "Now the job is up to Congress."

He sincerely believed he could get on with "the toughest job on earth" by quiet behind-the-scenes patience. He believed that reasonable men in the executive departments and in Congress could and would work together to solve problems logically, on the basis of facts and in line with national welfare.

His friend, General George ("Blood and Guts") Patton, a careful planner as well as a dashing military leader, once pointed to a piece of boiled spaghetti on a table top.

"Suppose," said Patton, "you want to move the spaghetti across the table. If you get behind and push, you'll get nowhere, no matter how much you huff and puff. But if you get in front of it and pull gently but firmly, the spaghetti is far more likely to slide across the table in an orderly manner."

Congress moved slowly. Reluctantly, Eisenhower began to act more like a practical politician, pulling as well as pushing. He was giving "spaghetti" leadership a whirl.

Congressmen who sought patronage or government contracts for constituents received a warmer welcome at the White House than they had a year ago. Thirty new judgeships were being created and were rich prizes for those who voted right. The President controlled vast amounts of money that were being channeled into river-and-harbor funds and road-building projects, and these were powerful lures.

Bucking stiff opposition in his own party, Eisenhower whipped and cajoled recalcitrants into line. Wayward Republicans were warned to toe the mark, especially if they were up for re-election in November. Ike learned to speak the language of politics in terms of jobs, favors, and campaign funds.

The President wrote letters to key senators and representatives urging their support. He made direct appeals to the people by radio and television.

When his program emerged from a welter of ideas into a series of legislative proposals, Eisenhower grew excited. He accepted with only a mutter of protest the continuing restrictions the presidency imposed on his personal life. He appeared less bored with the daily routine of office and accustomed himself to the "state of continuous confusion" that surrounds the operation of democratic government.

"I hope he learns to like politics," said an aide. "Politics is the only kind of fun a President can really afford."

From day to day, Eisenhower followed the struggle in Congress. Five large, businesslike charts, prepared by the White House legislative staff, stood on easels in the Cabinet room through the spring and summer. Red flags, pinned to four of the charts, showed at a glance the progress of his legislative program in both Senate and House. The fifth chart—referred to with grim humor as the "Dienbienphu chart"—showed administration proposals that had been stalled or defeated.

Farm Program

Eisenhower's greatest victory was passage of a new farm program.

While debate over the program raged in Congress, the public grew familiar with such terms as "90 percent of parity", "rigid supports", and "flexible supports", though to average city dwellers they meant little.

The situation was this: Under the old law, the government had bought up surplus crops in tremendous volume to guarantee the farmer a high price for his products. Under the new law, the government would reduce its surpluses and the farmer would get less for his crops.

Secretary of Agriculture Ezra Taft Benson told the President: "The storage bill alone [for surplus crops] in round numbers runs about $700,000 per day, about $5 million a week, and a quarter of a billion dollars a year."

Economy minded, the President encouraged Benson to take his cause to the country. The Secretary often spoke to hostile, heckling audiences. Said he: "If for the last forty years we had had a high, rigid support on harness, we would still have a thriving harness business and be up to our necks in harness."

Some Republicans from farm States urged that Benson be dismissed and his program disavowed. Democrats gleefully suggested that Benson remain in the Cabinet until after the election.

Farm-belt Republican politicians warned Eisenhower that this issue would cost the Republicans heavily in the November elections. The President made public answer.

"In this matter I am completely unmoved by arguments as to what constitutes good or winning politics . . . Though I have not been in this political business very long, I know that what is right for America is politically right."

Eisenhower stuck to his guns and, despite his professed ignorance of politics, his judgment was vindicated. His party did lose some seats in the congressional elections later in the year, but in the farm districts it held up relatively well. Ike had felt the farmers would not revolt against his program, and they did not.

By late summer, Washington observers commented: "The second session of the Eighty-third Congress was as responsive to White House leadership as any in peacetime since 1936."

But the President still wasn't sure that he liked the taste of politics. One day in October, he unexpectedly dropped in at a luncheon of the West Point Association in New York's Sheraton Astor Hotel.

"I regret that I am not free these days to attend more luncheons such as this," he said. Then he paused, flashed the famous grin, and added: "But just give me a little time and I'll be back in the crowd, cheering for some other poor sucker."

Of course he was joking that day in New York, but at times the President did seem to suspect that he had been a "sucker" to take the job in the first place.

The November, 1954, elections and public-opinion polls proved that the President was still highly popular with American voters.

The Dream House

Meanwhile, Mrs. Eisenhower was busy readying a permanent home. The Eisenhowers had bought a 100-year-old brick house and 189 acres of land in the gentle southern Pennsylvania countryside beside the battlefield of Gettysburg. The local folks called it "Mamie's Dream House" and "Ike's Place".

Mamie was having a grand time, choosing the colors for interior decorations, planning where to put the furniture the Eisenhowers had acquired in years of shuttling from one temporary home to another. Most of it had been in storage so long she had forgotten what it looked like. She was impatient to move in.

"Gee whiz," said the wife of the President of the United States, "all I've ever wanted was just to be a plain old housewife."

A FORMER PRESIDENT, Truman by name, rocks the keys at an American Federation of Musicians convention as A.F.M. President James C. Petrillo hits a downbeat

CONGRESS

THE SESSION IN THE U.S. HOUSE OF REPRE-
sentatives on March 1, 1954, was dull.
Members had to be summoned to the almost empty chamber to act on a bill.
The quorum bells were answered by 243
congressmen, who entered slowly, chatting.

Suddenly, shots slammed out. Congressmen dived for cover behind chairs
and tables.

"Freedom for my country!" screamed a
woman's shrill voice.

"Those are blanks!" one congressman
shouted.

"The hell they are," cried Representative George S. Long of Louisiana (whose
brother had been killed by an assassin).

Representative Alvin Bentley stag-
gered. Blood stained his white shirt and
he fell to the floor, a bullet just below his
heart. Judd of Minnesota, once a medical
missionary in China, rushed to his side to
give him first aid.

Dozens of bullets were drilled into
walls, floor, and furnishings—and into five
congressmen—as four young Puerto Rican
terrorists, three men and a girl, emptied
their Lugers from the ladies' gallery.

The terrorists were members of the
fanatic Independence-for-Puerto Rico organization that had once plotted the assassination of President Truman and also
had designs on President Eisenhower.
They had bought one-way tickets from
New York, expecting to be shot down by

CAMPAIGN HAZARD in Chicago: a G.O.P. worker nervously tries
to offer peanuts to an elephant rented
to help promote Senate candidate
Joseph T. Meek. (He was defeated.)

Capitol guards. Instead, they were captured alive and got sentences of sixteen to seventy-five years. All five congressmen survived.

Wheel Horses on Capitol Hill

Until March 1, the day of the shootings, the make-up of the Eighty-third Congress promised nothing more exciting than a stalemate. Many members of the Grand Old Party, conditioned by twenty years of "that man in the White House", were opposing Eisenhower almost as firmly as they had opposed his Democratic predecessors.

There were several reasons for this conduct, among them failure to understand party responsibility and discipline. One veteran Republican senator expressed his sentiments cynically: "The first business of a politician is to get elected. The second business is to get re-elected."

For some congressmen, the President's program was too liberal. Representative Noah Morgan Mason of Illinois reflected their thought processes: "I'm not voting against the administration. But I'm against the program the Truman administration wanted and, since it's the same program, I am still against it."

Other congressmen, like Senator George Wilson Malone of Nevada, believed the White House had usurped powers that belong to Congress. Said Malone: "The fight is whether the legislative branch is going to be a satellite just like it's been for twenty years."

A few legislators complained of poor liaison between the White House and the Capitol. Milton Young, junior Senator from North Dakota, had seen the President a total of five minutes in more than a year. "You don't feel like a Republican," he complained. "You feel like an outcast."

Pulling these disparate Republican elements together was the job of three men.

In the Senate, the Republican leader was William F. Knowland, a blunt, 46-year-old Californian who was the hand-picked choice of his mentor, patron, and predecessor, the late Senator Robert A. Taft. Essentially, Knowland was more Senate man than administration leader. He did not dictate the President's program to the Senate; he was more a negotiator between two powers. Although he was the administration's worst tormentor in the field of foreign policy, fortunately for the President he was a strong and effective supporter of much of the administration's domestic program.

In the House the task of conciliating Republicans was undertaken by Speaker Joseph Martin Jr. of Massachusetts and Indiana's Charles A. Halleck, Majority Floor Leader. By cajolery, dickering, and pressure, they eventually pushed much of Ike's program through.

Speaker Martin, an amiable, easy-to-meet veteran of thirty years in Congress, planned the Republican strategy. President Eisenhower once exclaimed: "I can't understand how Joe Martin knows what's going to happen in the House months before it happens. It's uncanny."

Martin decided when to fight for legislation and when to compromise. In a party that included every shade of political opinion, he managed to avoid the strong statements and the animosities so common in politics. As a result, he earned the respect and affection of his colleagues and even reporters who differed with him liked him.

The son of a Scottish Presbyterian blacksmith and an Irish Catholic mother, Martin started working on a paper route at the age of 6. By the time he was 24, he had saved a thousand dollars. With this money and investments by townspeople, he bought the North Attleboro *Evening Chronicle*.

Three years later, his well-established

capacity to win friends helped him to be elected to the Massachusetts House of Representatives. Election to the U.S. Congress followed.

Martin once boasted: "I know my district so well that if a postmaster writes in for a new canceling machine I probably know whether he needs it or not."

A 69-year-old bachelor, he lived in a small, quietly distinguished Washington hotel which caters to a permanent clientele of sober habits. He is a stocky man with a broad, placid face and thinning black hair. He doesn't smoke or drink. On an average day he is up at 7:15 A.M. and home again at 5:45 P.M., takes a walk after dinner, and is in bed by 9:30 or 10.

"He lives, eats, drinks, sleeps, and dreams politics," said a friend. He has never given his name to a major piece of legislation nor been identified with any idealistic cause.

Martin once summed up his philosophy: "We [Republicans] are not reformers, not do-gooders, not theorists, not the advocates of any alien philosophy or political dipsy-doo. We are just practical Americans, trying to do a practical job to reach practical goals. We do not belong to that school of political thought which has for so many years pursued the fallacious proposition that, if a little bit is good for us, ten times as much is just wonderful."

While Martin was down-to-earth, phlegmatic, usually soothing in lining up votes, Indiana's Charlie Halleck was energetic, excitable, a bit bossy. As a team, Halleck and Martin had the right combination of push and pull.

Said one White House aide: "If any man in Congress has taken the place of Bob Taft [the late "Mr. Senate"], it is Charlie."

Halleck's task as Floor Leader was to push the administration's program through the labyrinth of committees, whip recalcitrants into line, and arrange votes.

Halleck, 54, was described by a veteran news analyst as a "shrewd, resourceful parliamentary strategist" who "knows the House rules thoroughly and understands how to squeeze the last ounce of party advantage out of them".

Loyal to his party, he often supported administration measures to which he was opposed. For years he had barnstormed against public housing. Yet in 1954, at the President's request, he supported the administration's federal-housing proposal. Against strong Republican opposition, he salvaged a face-saving formula that provided for 35,000 public-housing units—not many—in one year.

Halleck graduated *cum laude* from the University of Indiana in 1922, and became top man in his class at law school.

For ten years a prosecuting attorney in Indiana, he was elected to Congress in 1935. He was a man in a hurry. An observer reported that he "constantly gives the impression that he is five minutes late and is trying to catch up". But for a man-in-a-hurry, he produced results. The President often soothed White House worriers by telling them: "Charlie's guaranteed it."

Asked how he reconciled his own views with the White House program, Halleck explained: "To be a leader, you've got to follow." He could hardly ask his colleagues to support the President if only a few weeks before he had opposed the administration's proposals himself.

The Inland Sea

Both parties hailed the passage of the St. Lawrence Seaway bill as the greatest single piece of legislation to come out of the Eighty-third Congress.

Extending 1600 miles across the top of the United States from the Atlantic Ocean to Duluth, Minn., at the western tip of

Lake Superior, is a great inland waterway. The Seaway bill calls for the dredging of a 27-foot channel in this waterway to open the inland ports of the Great Lakes to ocean navigation. One result: cheaper transportation. Two huge dams also are to be built to generate power for a vast area.

For more than forty years Presidents had dreamed of initiating this great waterway. All of them had failed. Railroad magnates as well as port cities of the Atlantic and Gulf coasts had fought against it. Private utilities had lobbied against a seaway that could generate cheap public power for the Northeast.

In addition, U.S. steel firms and coal-mine owners had opposed the plan, which would afford easy access to rich, undeveloped mine fields in Canada. But Admiral Radford, Chairman of the Joint Chiefs of Staff, pointed out that access to Canadian ore might be a decisive factor in any future war.

A middle-of-the-road Republican administration in 1954 accomplished the seemingly impossible. The White House mustered as many Democratic as Republican votes, and, in the name of national defense, it was done.

Tax Law Remade

Of more immediate importance to Americans was the tax law passed by this session of Congress. The U.S. Internal Revenue Code had been patched and amended by every Congress for generations, but had not been thoroughly reworked for three quarters of a century. Its complete revision was the life ambition of stubborn Dan Reed. A conservative up-State New York Republican, old Dan drove the House Ways and Means Committee for more than a year to get the new tax bill ready. It proposed so many changes that tax experts moaned they

would have to relearn their lifework.

One expert called it "nothing less than a revolution in federal tax philosophy", and added: "The 1000 pages of the new law provide more special benefits and concessions for . . . business than any previous measure in history."

Treasury Secretary George Humphrey testified that the new law "will encourage investment so that big business can expand and create more jobs. America needs big business. It requires big business, big enterprise to do all the things in big ways that a big country has to have."

In a televised speech to the nation, the President told his listeners: "These tax reforms and reductions have saved you 7 billion 400 million dollars a year. This is money you spend for yourself now instead of the government spending it for you."

Disagreeing profoundly with this viewpoint, Democratic Party statisticians estimated that, for every dollar of tax reduction, 64¢ will go to corporations, 30¢ to the 26 percent of U.S. families with incomes of over $5000 a year, and 6¢ to the 74 percent of families with annual earnings of $5000 or less.

The charges and countercharges, the claims and counterclaims, were on record. But in the final analysis the individual taxpayer, struggling over his new tax forms in April, 1955, would decide where lay the truth.

The Bill No One Liked

By midsummer, the atmosphere in the Senate was inflamed. Democrats, exhausted by the unusually long congressional session, were stung by repeated Republican charges that they had "coddled" Communism.

VICTOR BY A STRAW in Senate race, Democrat Richard Neuberger beams over headlines

FOILED in their attempt to further cause of Puerto Rican independence by killing congressmen, three of the four terrorists involved are shown being taken to jail

Not only reckless but even conservative, highly respected elements of the G.O.P. had uttered such charges. Thomas E. Dewey, Governor of New York, advised an audience to think of treason and the blood of our boys in Korea "whenever anybody mentions the words Truman and Democrat".

Violently the Democrats struck back. One day in August, Senator Hubert H. Humphrey of Minnesota arose in the Senate and said: "I am tired of reading headlines about being soft toward Communism. . . . I will not be lukewarm. I do not intend to be a half-patriot."

That was the preamble to one of the strangest pieces of legislation ever to be proposed by a stalwart Democratic liberal, a leader of the organization of citizens known as Americans for Democratic Action, a group composed mainly of Roosevelt New Dealers and Truman Fair Dealers.

Humphrey sponsored a Communist Control Act which would have labeled every Communist a criminal, not for any overt acts he might have committed, but solely because of his beliefs. He proposed that the Communist Party be outlawed and that every member be subjected to a $10,000 fine or five years in jail. His bill would have put out of business any labor unions found to have leaders who within the previous three years had lent support to any organization listed as a Communist front by the Department of Justice.

The Justice Department called the Humphrey proposal a "legal catastrophe".

The administration, which had an anti-Communist measure of its own, wanted no part of it. Many lawyers said it was unconstitutional.

Even the late Senator Pat McCarran of Nevada, an extreme conservative who boasted that he had never been left of center since his college football coach shifted him from left tackle to right guard, argued that the proposal violated "the conception of innocence until guilt is proven".

One newsman reported that Humphrey thought it a good joke to put Republicans in the position of seeming to be opposed to a bill against Communists. But Republicans were not in a joking mood and neither were most Democrats—it was just before election.

Causing chaos on the floor, senators of both parties rushed to get on the anti-Communist band wagon. Some voted for clauses without hearing them read. Spessard Holland, Florida Democrat, ran to the Senate door with shaving cream on his face to shout "Yea".

Kicked from Senate to House and back again, the bill was a political football. At one point Attorney General Brownell, a Republican, pleaded with Humphrey, a Democrat, to support the administration. His clinching argument: Each Communist prosecuted would have to be identified in open court by a competent witness. For each Communist tried, therefore, the F.B.I. would have to sacrifice one of the undercover agents planted in the party. Soon it would run out of agents and still there would be Communists uncaught. Wouldn't it be better to concentrate on the leaders?

Humphrey gave in and changes were made in the bill—the party would be "outlawed", but membership in it would not be a crime. The Humphrey bill passed the Senate unanimously. In the House,

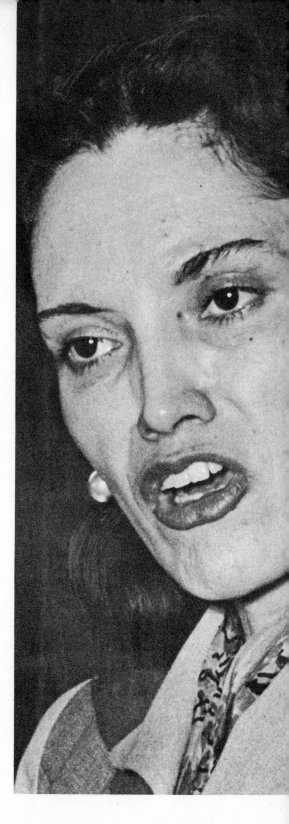

RINGLEADER of the terrorists (left), Lolita Lebron, admits to newsmen: "I am a sinful woman"

only two votes were cast in opposition.

"If this law is not strong enough to do the whole job," shouted Humphrey, "I will come back next year to help make it stronger—if I am re-elected."

The two representatives who held out to the end against the bill were a New York Democrat, Abraham Multer, and a North Dakota Republican, Usher Burdick.

Multer warned: "Putting any group out of business this way is basically wrong in principle; it is the way a Fascist would use." Burdick declared himself opposed to "any form of tyranny over the mind of man".

The bill needed "further study", said President Eisenhower, though he signed it. The Justice Department said it would go slow on enforcing it until its constitutionality had been determined.

Hastily drawn, patched, and endlessly amended, the law was not printed in an official version until weeks later. When it did emerge from the Government Printing Office, its most eager readers were congressmen who wanted to find out what it was they had passed.

For the Record

In 1954 Democrats in Congress tended to support Ike on the liberal, humanitarian parts of his program, Republicans on the conservative economic measures. When the congressional session ended, a major portion of Eisenhower's "must" legislation was an accomplished fact.

Bills passed covered a wide range of subjects. Ten million people previously uncovered by Social Security were put on the rolls. Unemployment insurance was extended. Approved bills provided for road-building projects and for a 5 percent raise in salary for government workers.

In late August, when the record was being totted up for campaign purposes, Democrats, who recognized Eisenhower's personal popularity, were beginning to say: "Ike wouldn't have gotten far except for us."

"But we voted for him more consistently than you did," Republicans retorted.

The Elections

When Congress adjourned, legislators scurried home to devote themselves to one of the bitterest congressional campaigns in an off-year election.

For two years, by a razor-thin margin, Republicans had controlled both House and Senate, but all 435 seats in the House and 37 in the Senate were at stake in November. And when the tumult and shouting ended, the Democrats were the new rulers of Congress.

Vice-President Nixon set the tone for the Republican election campaign. In a marathon speaking tour, covering more than 25,000 miles in thirty-one States, he repeatedly identified the Democrats with foreign agents and Communists. Stanch Republicans called it good aggressive campaigning. Democrats called it a campaign of "smut, smear, and slander".

Republican speakers reminded voters that this was a nation of "peace and prosperity". Democrats urged them to "vote Democratic; the job you save may be your own".

On election day, most political seers made two broad predictions. First, the vote would be light. Second, because sentiment traditionally swings against the party in power during off-year elections, the Democrats would win control of Congress by a wide margin. Univac, the electronic thinking machine employed by the Columbia Broadcasting System to forecast elections, joined the human analysts by predicting a landslide Democratic victory.

But both human and mechanical prophets went astray. The balloting was heavy —41 million Americans trudged to the polls in history's greatest off-year turnout. And the vote was the closest ever recorded.

If there was any obvious trend, it was that those candidates who had been subjected to the most violent personal attacks fared best.

In California, for example, James Roosevelt, son of the late F.D.R. and a Democratic nominee for the House, ran with a political albatross around his neck. In a lurid divorce trial, his estranged wife had accused him of a dozen instances of adultery. Despite the sensational charges, Roosevelt won.

Some contests ended early and decisively. Others hung in the balance for hours and even days after the ballot counting began.

In New Jersey, a popular vote getter, former Representative Clifford Case, was hand-picked by administration Republicans to run for the Senate against Democratic Representative Charles Howell.

Tall, soft-spoken, and a Phi Beta Kappa from Rutgers University, Case was an "egghead" Republican—an independent thinker whose special interests were in the fields of social legislation and civil liberties.

While Howell had the solid backing of his party, Case faced a revolt from the G.O.P.'s ultraconservative wing, led by former Representative Fred Hartley (co-author of the Taft-Hartley labor law).

Anti-Case Republicans charged him with socialism, and a whispering campaign spread rumors that Adelaide Case, his sister, was a Communist. The story finally burst into national headlines.

Case denied the charge. Before the television cameras, he made an emotional reply: "I have just one thing to say to those character murderers: Adelaide Case is not running for the Senate of the United States. Clifford Case is the candidate. Smear me if you can. Leave my sister alone."

When the last ballot had been counted, Case had squeaked through to win by 3507 votes, one fifth of 1 percent of the nearly 1,800,000 ballots cast in New Jersey.

The New Congress

No Democrat from Oregon had won a seat in the U.S. Senate in forty years. Richard L. Neuberger, 41, decided it was time for a change. Energetic, a dynamic speaker, a clever publicist, free-lance writer and news reporter Neuberger stumped the State for a year. His principal charge: Guy Cordon, the Republican Senator from Oregon, had aided the administration's "giveaway" of the nation's natural resources.

More than a half million voters went to the polls in Oregon. In the afternoon of Nov. 3, the day after election, Neuberger led by only 100 votes. Now the whole nation's attention was focused on Oregon. This one race would determine which party would control the upper house of Congress.

Slowly the last votes were counted. In the final tabulation, Neuberger had won by 2462. The Democrats controlled both Senate and House.

Samuel Taliaferro Rayburn was once again to become Speaker of the House. A 72-year-old Texan, bald, stocky, with the dry personality of old parchment, Rayburn was the leading Democratic strategist in Congress.

The Democrats, he promised, would wage no "cold war" against the White House, but neither would they be rubber stamps for the administration. They would cooperate with the President, but only when they believed him to be right.

ADMINISTRATION

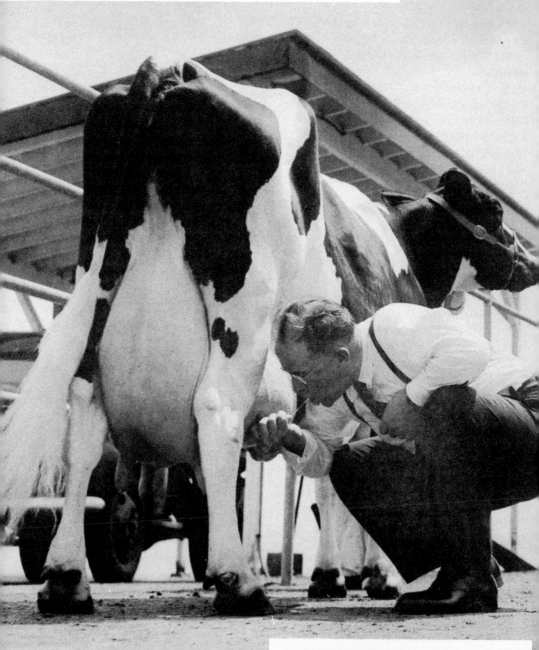

THE RURAL TOUCH is applied by Agriculture Secretary Benson at Penn State U. model farm

THE REAL GOVERNMENT OF THE UNITED States," said one important Washington official, "is the National Security Council." The statement was too broad, but there was some truth in it. The decisions of the Council touch the lives of all Americans and of countless other millions in the rest of the world. Vice-President Nixon has defined it as "the board of directors of the American government with Ike as chairman of the board".

When constituted by the National Security Act of 1947, the Council had little power or influence and was used largely as a forum to resolve jurisdictional conflicts among federal agencies concerned with problems of national defense.

But Eisenhower saw it able to perform other, more important functions, and turned it into a "super-Cabinet" that determined all national policy.

The Council has eight active members, among whom are the Vice-President, Secretary of State, Secretary of Defense, and Secretary of the Treasury. Attending as advisers are the Chairman of the Joint Chiefs of Staff and the Director of the Central Intelligence Agency.

Neither the deliberations of the Council nor its decisions are matters of public record. Every Thursday it meets without fanfare in the Cabinet room of the White House, with the President presiding. Seated at the oblong table are men who propose, evaluate, and discuss decisions of the most vital importance.

If ever there is a decision to wage war, it will probably originate in the Council.

Mystery Man

In 1954, the most influential individual of this innermost circle was a little-known Boston banker, Robert Cutler, chairman of the Council's Planning Board. Said one Council member: "If I wanted to be the most powerful person in Washington in affecting policy, I'd pick Cutler's job. No Cabinet post touches it in influence."

Cutler was the filter for every report funneled to the Council. Whether the Council's decisions were based on fully thought through or on incomplete appraisals depended in large degree on Cutler. He decided whether problems were to be faced or evaded; whether the Council was to look far ahead or focus intently on an immediate crisis. He worked a twelve-hour day and briefed the President before each Council meeting. At all times he had Eisenhower's ear.

With a small staff, Cutler cut through mountains of paper work. In 1954 he prepared reports for the Council on Russia's progress in the manufacture of H-bombs, on the cost of the latest U.S. jet bomber, on Communist infiltration in Latin America, on the strength of French armies in Indochina—among a hundred other crucial topics.

Cutler had been an honor student and a member of Phi Beta Kappa at Harvard. Back in the '20's, he had written two novels. When asked what they were about, he snapped: "Love, love. What else does a young man write about?"

Cutler had persuaded his friend, the novelist Owen Wister, to read his work. Wister did and gently suggested to the young man that "a novelist needs to discipline himself and I'd suggest you start by studying law". Cutler took the hint and channeled his energies into law and banking.

Essentially an organizer, he had no great political ambitions. He admired the President and wanted to serve him. Witty and a good storyteller, he was a frequent and welcome visitor at the White House after his appointment.

Cutler once defined the power of the Council. "There is no such thing," he said, "as domestic, foreign, or farm pol-

icy. There is national-security policy and, in making it, every agency and department plays a part."

At a meeting of the National Security Council, a Defense official remarked of a new directive: "That Eisenhower policy has a Boston accent."

Palace Guard

While Cutler shaped the issues that faced Eisenhower in the National Security Council, Sherman Adams, Assistant to the President, exerted a more personal kind of influence in the White House. An ex-lumberjack and an ex-Governor of New Hampshire, Adams was chief of the "Palace Guard", a group of liberal Republicans that included Representative to the United Nations Henry Cabot Lodge Jr. and Attorney General Herbert Brownell Jr.

Adams arranged appointments and channeled information to Eisenhower, and was in and out of the President's office a half dozen times a day.

"Next to the President," said one member of the White House staff, "Sherm is the boss. No one else outranks him."

Ike hated disorder and Adams was the buffer between the President and the organized chaos of government. Of a hundred matters that visitors directed to the President—letters, government memos, telephone calls—Adams diverted eighty to the proper specialized agencies, handled fifteen personally, and put five before the President for decision.

It was a thankless job and one calculated to make enemies. In 1953, senators and representatives had often come back from the White House breathing fire and muttering: "The President is a wonderful

guy, but that so-and-so Adams won't let you near him."

Inspired stories had been given to columnists: "Take it from me, Adams will be out in six months. They're getting some sort of diplomatic post in Afghanistan warmed up for him." But at the end of two years, Adams still operated out of his secluded White House office.

Coolheaded in a crisis, he took on his own shoulders the settlement of many squabbles within the administration. If one member refused to back down, Adams might say in his dry Yankee way: "We all belong to a team. We signed on voluntarily to serve our country. If you are in basic disagreement with the captain of the team, no one is holding your coattail."

When Adams said "I feel we should do this . . .", it usually meant the President felt that way. Though Adams was inclined to be aloof with strangers, Ike found him a warm and reliable friend.

"Sherm is impeccably honest and wonderful to have around," one associate said. "You sleep well at night knowing he is Assistant to the President. Nobody is going to pull any shady deals as long as the Governor is around."

At mid-year, Washington observers called Robert Cutler "The Web"—his fingers spun a thousand strands of policy— and Sherman Adams "The Rock"—no one stormed the White House portals without his consent.

Heir Designate

A more flamboyant personality than either Cutler or Adams, 41-year-old, beetle-browed Vice-President Richard M. Nixon probably exerted more political influence on Eisenhower than any other man.

"Politics with Dick," said his wife Pat, "is like a crusade, a dedication."

CLASPING HANDS, Defense Secretary Charles E. Wilson tells reporters that the monster H-bomb blasts in Pacific tests were "unbelievable"

OUTGOING GOVERNOR of New York, Thomas Dewey—a strong Eisenhower man—poses at his Pawling, N.Y., farm. He quit the governorship after three terms, returned to law practice

INCOMING GOVERNOR Averell Harriman, seen on his estate at Arden, brought Democratic rule back to New York. In party politics he is known as a New and Fair Dealer

SOME OF IKE'S TEAM: (from left) Assistant Sherman Adams; Economic Adviser Arthur F. Burns; National Security Council Planning Board Chairman Robert Cutler

An ex-officio member of the Cabinet, Nixon was the only official, except for the President himself, who knew all the time, and at firsthand, both administrative and legislative doings. He was the first Vice-President to preside, in the President's absence, over meetings of the National Security Council and of the Cabinet. He spoke for Congress in the administration and for the administration in Congress. He was a regular at meetings which the President held weekly with congressional leaders to discuss his program.

"Nixon is the best salesman Eisenhower has," said Representative Patrick J. Hillings, California Republican.

But many disagreed. Senator Wayne Morse, Oregon Independent, called Nixon "the number one smear artist of the Republican Party".

Having come out of the navy in 1946 to practice law in Whittier, Calif., Nixon rose to power quickly. Twice elected to the House and then to the Senate, he supported Eisenhower for the Republican presidential nomination and at the 1952 Republican National Convention became Ike's running mate.

A man of enormous energy, he was without doubt the busiest Vice-President

in history. He tried to be all things to all factions of the G.O.P., he was the bridge between the President and the administration's most formidable foes, and he had a hand in the administration's every major decision. Nixon's immediate goal, one approved by the President, was to keep the Republican Party from blowing apart.

When Senator Bricker sponsored a constitutional amendment to curb the President's treaty-making power, the Cabinet advised Eisenhower to denounce it.

"You'll run into a buzz saw if you do," said Nixon. He advised compromise—and the measure was compromised to death.

Nixon was used as a good-will ambassador to foreign countries. He sent up administration trial balloons to determine public sentiment on such diverse policies as American troops for Indochina and peaceful coexistence with the Communist world.

He persuaded a reluctant Eisenhower to endorse all Republican candidates for the Senate and House regardless of their views, on the ground that a Republican President needed a Republican Congress, and even to campaign for some.

MORE TEAMMATES: (from left) Henry Cabot Lodge Jr., U.S. Representative to U.N.; Attorney General Herbert Brownell Jr.; Secretary of the Treasury George Humphrey

Eisenhower admired Nixon's political flair and chose him to answer a frontal attack on the administration by Democratic leader Adlai Stevenson.

Personally ambitious, the Vice-President courted powerful friends. Republican National Committee Chairman Leonard Hall insisted that Ike would run again. "However," he said, "I'd say that the President is. very, very fond of Mr. Nixon. Life being uncertain, he feels the Vice-President should not be unprepared, should anything happen."

"The country can survive the election of Ike as long as he lives out his term," said Democrats, "but the thought of Nixon being one heartbeat from the presidency is terrifying."

Dollars and Sense

Two key figures in the administration's hierarchy were Treasury Secretary George Humphrey, who controlled the government's purse strings, and economic adviser Arthur F. Burns, who spelled out the economic facts of national life for the President. In social and political background, these men were poles apart. But in economics they thought alike.

Both were opposed to excessive government controls and both were exponents of dynamic capitalism.

Humphrey, a Republican, was a hard-headed businessman and a leading figure in coal, iron, steel, and banking circles. When he took over the M. A. Hanna Company of Cleveland in 1929, it was $4 million in debt. When he left to join the Cabinet, the firm had assets totaling more than $200 million.

An associate said of him: "If you dropped Humphrey in the middle of the Sahara, he'd come out with a newly organized corporation on a dividend-paying basis."

A stranger to politics, he had set himself two goals: balancing the budget and stabilizing the economy.

Although 1954 started in shaky fashion —more layoffs than in any of the three previous years, falling prices, and slackening of production—business later picked up. In December, Republicans were confidently predicting that, by controlling credit, they could avoid an economy of boom-and-bust. A healthy American economy, they said, was insurance that the rest of the Western world would stay prosperous.

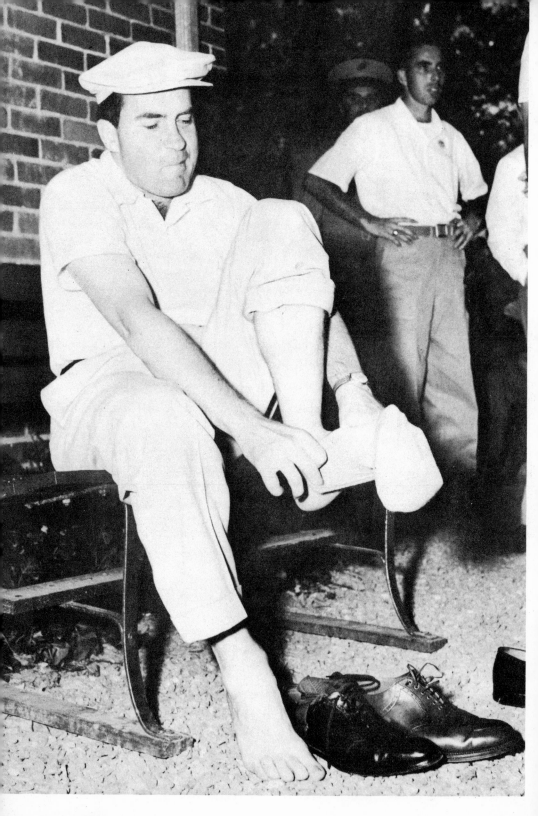

But by year's end the budget was still unbalanced and the estimated deficit for the 1955 fiscal year (July, 1954 through June, 1955) was $4.7 billion. One reason: Though the government was spending less, it was also taking in less, largely as a result of huge tax cuts.

To stabilize the economy, Humphrey lent his weight to revision of the entire tax structure with its built-in aids to big business. At the beginning of the year, he tightened credit controls. Business, unable to borrow on easy terms, did less expanding. Individuals, for the same reason, bought fewer products, from cars to refrigerators. The mild recession grew worse. But Humphrey had flexibility. When he eased credit, the economy leveled off.

On questions of government finance and domestic economics, Humphrey got virtually a free hand from the President.

"When George speaks," said Eisenhower, "all the rest of us listen."

Economic adviser Burns was a strange fish in the Eisenhower pond. A Democrat (but he voted for Eisenhower) and a college professor, he had closer contacts with the President than many members of the Cabinet.

Born in Austrian Poland, the 49-year-old Burns had been brought to the U.S. by his father in 1914. He worked his way through college and then taught economics while he wrote his doctorate thesis on "production trends in the U.S.".

As a professor at Columbia and research director of the National Bureau of Economic Research, Burns was recognized as the leading U.S. expert on business cycles—the boom and the bust.

Eisenhower, who confessed that he knew little of economics, wanted the man who knew most about depressions and

their causes to join his team. Burns was that man. The President gave him his instructions: "I want my economists to stick to economics. Don't give me political advice."

In his weekly meetings with Eisenhower, Burns stuck to economics. He analyzed business conditions in language the President could understand and he presented long-range forecasts. Burns predicted that the business dip early in 1954 would prove to be a "minor contraction", not a recession nor a depression.

Adlai Stevenson, the Democratic Party's spokesman, disagreed, saying: "The economy seems to be creeping toward G.O.P. normalcy. The administration is right when it says we are not in a depression. We are just in a rut."

Burns shaped the President's annual Economic Report to Congress, and in it he formulated the President's economic philosophy.

"The best service that the Government can render to our economy is . . . to create an environment in which men are eager to make new jobs, to acquire new tools of production, to improve or scrap the old ones, design new products and develop new markets, increase efficiency all around, and thus be able and willing to pay higher wages and provide better working conditions."

Businessman Humphrey, college professor Burns, and the other members of the administration's team subscribed to that program. Eisenhower listened to their counsel and learned. The President's attitude toward advisers was summed up well by Kevin McCann, his biographer, in *The Man from Abilene*: "If he always has relied much on others, Eisenhower, in all things decisive and critical, has stood apart from them, measuring their counsel against his own convictions."

A GOLFER like his boss, Vice-President Nixon is snapped slipping into his socks after a game

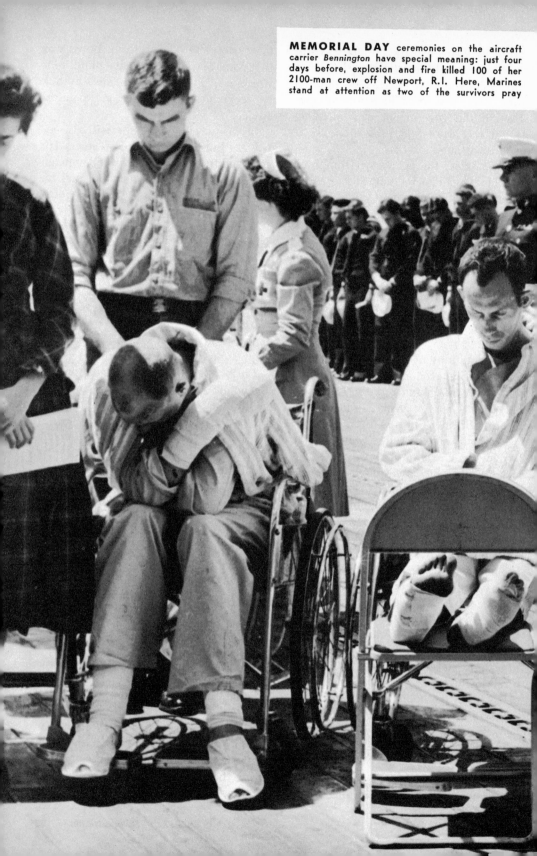

DEFENSE

BIG WHEEL comes with army's new 62-foot, 60-ton Barc (Barge, Amphibious, Resupply, Cargo)

IN 1954 AN EXTRAORDINARY EXPLOSION IN the middle of the Pacific Ocean set off an emotional chain reaction in the Japanese islands and caused repercussions of fear and confusion all over the world.

In January, a small Japanese fishing boat, the *Fukuryu Maru* (*Lucky Dragon*) *No. 5*, set sail from the port of Yaizu. Weeks later and thousands of miles to the south, the crewmen were hauling in their nets. The date was March 1.

That same day at Bikini, a tiny atoll in the Pacific, the United States tested its latest H-bomb. Some 30,000 square miles had been marked off as a danger zone no ship was to enter. Navy planes searched the area on a prestrike patrol, but missed the *Lucky Dragon*. An all-clear signal was flashed to Bikini and the explosion went off on schedule.

The simple fishermen, more than 80 miles from the test island, witnessed an awesome spectacle.

"We saw strange sparkles and flashes of fire as bright as the sun itself," said 29-year-old crewman Sanjiro Masuda. "The sky glowed fiery red and yellow. The glow went on for several minutes . . . and then the yellow seemed to fade away. It left a dull red, like a piece of iron cooling in the air. The blast came five minutes later . . . the sound of many thunders rolled into one. Next we saw a pyramid-shaped cloud rising and the sky began to cloud over most curiously. The thought of *pikadon* [Japanese slang for "atomic bomb"] flashed through my mind, I think, but we were busy and went back to our nets."

Hours later a fine ash began to fall on the *Lucky Dragon* and her unlucky crew. It was a fallout of radioactive "death ash". Unaware of their danger, the fishermen continued to throw out their nets until the boat's hold was full. Two weeks after their exposure, they returned to Japan, complaining of burns.

When Japanese medical authorities diagnosed the cause of the burns, the irradiated crewmen were hustled to hospitals. By then the 16,500 pounds of radioactive tuna and shark in the *Lucky Dragon's* hold had been sold to markets all over Japan. Hastily the government tried to track down the dangerous fish with Geiger counters. The Japanese people, at first panic-stricken, grew angry. Anti-American feeling in Japan reached its highest peak since World War II.

Five months after the explosion, Aikichi Kuboyama, the most seriously burned of the Japanese fishermen, died. He was the world's first H-bomb victim.

The Realities

In 1954 the terrifying destructiveness of an H-bomb, dramatized by the case of the *Lucky Dragon*, forced itself into the whole world's consciousness.

People began to parrot the jargon of scientists. They talked of "fallouts". They discussed the "genetic consequences of radioactivity" and the possibility of monsters being born of men. "Megaton" (denoting the equivalent of the explosive power of 1 million tons of TNT) became a household word.

The power of the explosion over Bikini on March 1 was estimated at 10 megatons, and there was now no limit to the size of future thermonuclear weapons.

Experts said that a 45-megaton bomb (2250 times as powerful as the bomb that leveled Hiroshima in World War II) dropped over Washington, D.C., would totally destroy the entire District of Columbia, reducing every government building and monument to rubble. Total destruction would extend also to suburbs in Virginia and Maryland.

Such a bomb striking New York City would demolish the entire island of Manhattan, leveling every skyscraper, and would destroy vast outlying sections as well. Further death and damage by fall-out would be incalculable.

Man was attaining the ultimate in force. It was now possible, scientists stated, to increase the radioactive after-effects of thermonuclear weapons and poison an entire country. Within the realm of probability was a cobalt bomb capable of contaminating the atmosphere of the world and hence injuring or anni-hilating all life on earth.

This power to destroy was not ours alone. The Soviet Union also possessed thermonuclear bombs and was rapidly building its own stockpile. In 1954, that was the central fact in the relations be-tween the free world and the Communist world. It might spell the destruction of either or both.

The Continuing Shock

How was the horror of the H-bomb to be coped with?

In England, headlines cried: CALL OFF THAT BOMB. Winston Churchill foresaw a possible "peace of mutual terror". Clem-ent Attlee, ex-Prime Minister of Britain, asserted: "The only way open to us seems to be to make a new approach to world problems with the consciousness of this great danger."

Russian Premier Georgi M. Malenkov warned that all-out hostilities "under con-temporary conditions of war mean the death of world civilization".

But while Malenkov spoke soberly, Nikita S. Khrushchev, First Secretary of the Soviet Communist Party, boasted: "We outstripped the capitalist class and created the hydrogen bomb before them. They think they can intimidate us. But nothing can frighten us, because if they know what a bomb means, so do we."

Prime Minister Nehru of India called for an end to hydrogen-bomb tests and

stirred anti-American sentiment in Asia.

Pope Pius XII promised that he would "tirelessly endeavor to bring about . . . proscription and banishment of atomic . . . warfare".

U.S. author and critic Lewis Mumford startled readers by writing: "Submission to Communist totalitarianism would still be far wiser than the final destruction of civilization."

The Case of Dr. Oppenheimer

The H-bomb set minds working more furiously than ever on the subject of na-tional defense—defense against security risks at home and against enemies abroad.

Some citizens argued that in the era of the H-bomb, which could obliterate U.S. cities overnight, there could be no se-curity test too severe for government em-ployees capable, by espionage or even by indiscretion, of transmitting defense se-crets to the enemy. Other citizens argued that, in this H-bomb era, the best scien-tific brains were needed in government service, even though, in the past, some of these leading scientists had shown more or less sympathy toward Communism, or were otherwise less-than-perfect security risks. According to the latter line of rea-soning, severe security tests that would exclude or expel such men from govern-ment service would be self-defeating.

The controversy was brought to a head by the case of the physicist J. Robert Oppenheimer.

During World War II, Dr. Oppen-heimer had bossed the project at Los Alamos where the atomic bomb was cre-ated. He was credited with being the man most responsible for our having the atomic bomb on time. He became adviser on atomic matters to Cabinet members, military leaders, and Presidents.

However, on Dec. 23, 1953, by direct order of President Eisenhower, he was suspended from all government duties. In April, 1954, a panel of the Atomic Energy Commission's personnel-security board started hearings to determine if the man who had helped create secrets the security regulations were designed to guard was a security risk himself.

Oppenheimer was graduated from Harvard, studied at Cambridge in England, and in 1927 received his doctorate at Göttingen, Germany. At 23, he was appointed associate professor of physics simultaneously at the University of California and at the California Institute of Technology, where, in nuclear physics, he soon established a reputation as one of the great theoreticians of our time.

In many other respects, also, Oppenheimer was an unusual man. He learned to read Sanskrit, but never read a newspaper or magazine. He had no radio or telephone. He heard of the 1929 stock-market crash only long after the event. He never voted until 1936.

Late in that year, his interests began to change. He was never himself a Communist, but he associated with men of every political opinion, Communists included. "I began to sense the larger sorrows of the great depression," he wrote later. "I began to understand how deeply political and economic events could affect men's lives."

Oppenheimer, profoundly impressed by the potential horrors of nuclear weapons and the need for peace, was the man chosen to head the most sensitive agency in the entire history of the United States —the nine-man General Advisory Committee, top scientific consultant body to the Atomic Energy Commission.

He became a spokesman for many of the nation's most influential scientists. He had a hand in every U.S. proposal for international atomic control.

On moral, political, and technical grounds, Oppenheimer vigorously opposed a speed-up program to develop the hydrogen superbomb, and by so doing he set off a debate that raged in military, civilian, and scientific circles alike.

President Truman ended the debate in January, 1950, when he ordered the A.E.C. to go ahead with the H-bomb project. In a surprisingly short time, "super" was a reality.

The majority report of the A.E.C.'s personnel-security board ruled that the United States owed Oppenheimer "a great debt of gratitude for loyal and magnificent service", but added that "if Dr. Oppenheimer had enthusiastically supported the thermonuclear program either before or after the determination of national policy, the H-bomb project would have been pursued with considerably more vigor, thus increasing the possibility of earlier success in this field".

Oppenheimer was declared a security risk and was dismissed from government service, but the controversy about his case and about internal security in general raged on—unabated and unresolved —at year's end.

The New Look

In 1954 national defense had many aspects. Not only was there the problem of security among such government employees as Oppenheimer, but there was also the complex problem of military defense against foreign foes.

Was there no way to halt an arms race that was leading to an endless spiral of bigger armies, more ships, and more airplanes? Could the U.S. afford the staggering costs of meeting Communist aggression wherever in the world it occurred? In one short year, 1954, national-defense policies traced a full circle.

Late in 1953, the National Security Council had launched a series of secret, far-reaching discussions on the questions

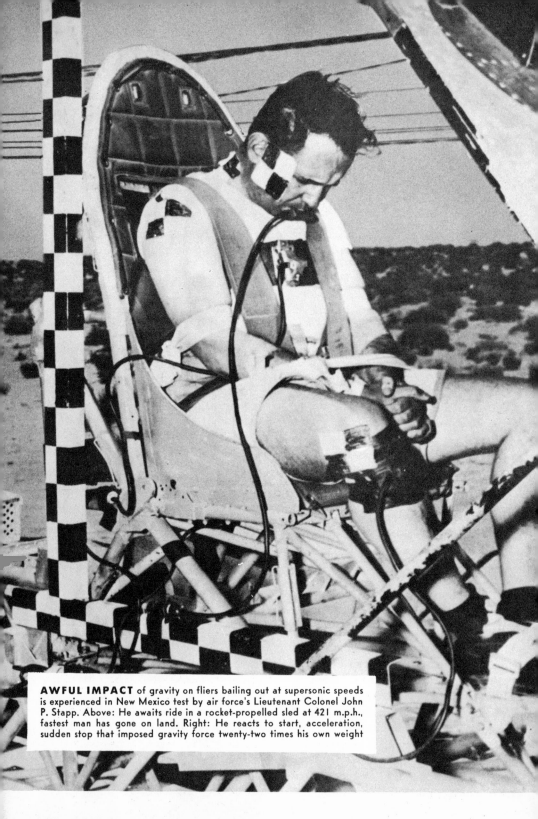

AWFUL IMPACT of gravity on fliers bailing out at supersonic speeds is experienced in New Mexico test by air force's Lieutenant Colonel John P. Stapp. Above: He awaits ride in a rocket-propelled sled at 421 m.p.h., fastest man has gone on land. Right: He reacts to start, acceleration, sudden stop that imposed gravity force twenty-two times his own weight

posed above. Out of those meetings, with the approval of the President, came the New Look for U.S. defense forces—a stern warning to enemies that the United States would rely heavily on the atomic bomb and an air force capable of dropping it at any point on the globe.

The New Look meant reductions in army manpower and navy ships, and therefore huge cuts in the budget. In January, 1954, Secretary of State Dulles spelled out its other meanings. The United States, he said, would "depend primarily upon a great capacity to retaliate instantly [against aggressors] by means and at places of our choosing".

The purpose of the New Look, said Dulles, was to reinforce local defense by "the further deterrent of massive retaliatory power".

War on the Horizon

The decision to rely largely on air-atomic power sharply split the military planners of U.S. defense, the Joint Chiefs of Staff. Admiral Arthur W. Radford, Chairman of J.C.S., was a strong advocate of the new policy, but it left Army General Matthew B. Ridgway cold.

Radford's thesis was that the alternative to toughness toward Communism—and, if necessary, use of thermonuclear weapons—was appeasement and unchecked Communist expansion.

The Admiral, a stern-faced man with thinning gray hair, tough leathery skin, and hooded eyelids, is a commanding and persuasive personality. Tall, with the stiff-backed crispness of the traditional officer, Radford asked the key question that led to the New Look: Would the White House approve the use of nuclear weapons in military planning?

Critics accused him of atom-rattling, but Radford insisted his policy was a peace policy; that the only language

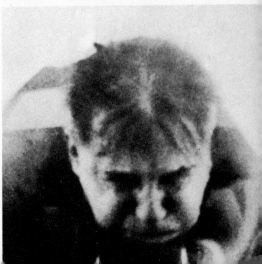

Communists understand is force—force without stint or limit—and that nothing but the threat of force would deter them from aggression.

Air Force General Nathan Farragut Twining, broad shouldered and, at 57, the youngest member of the Joint Chiefs, supported Radford. The supremacy of the air force was to a large extent his personal accomplishment and the end of a fight that spanned a quarter of a century.

Like Radford, Twining reasoned that the Communists would back away from local aggression if they understood clearly that retaliation would not be restricted to the immediate battlefield, as it had been in Korea, but that, using thermonuclear weapons, the U.S. could and would lay waste the very sources of Communist power.

General Ridgway clashed sharply with Radford. He opposed whittling down the size and strength of the army and objected to a cut in the budget.

Ridgway, like Eisenhower, was a foot soldier. More than a decade of combat had etched deep lines in his face. To his mind, war was the ultimate tragedy of man, and no matter how started, must be ended by the foot soldier. He believed that the destructiveness of hydrogen bombs, which could annihilate whole divisions in the field, would require larger —not smaller—armies, dispersed widely and in depth.

Admiral Robert B. Carney, bald, scholarly, bespectacled J.C.S. member, supported the get-tough policy, but sided with Ridgway in opposing budget cuts for the army and navy.

Throughout the nation and the world, an ominous silence followed January's public pronouncement by Secretary of State Dulles. Then rumbling objections to it became audible.

Adlai Stevenson, spokesman of the Democratic Party, asked: "Are we leaving ourselves the grim choice of inaction or thermonuclear holocaust?"

Sarcastically, Senator Richard B. Russell of Georgia asked why, if the New Look gave the nation more security at less cost, the administration did not cut military spending in half and thus get twice as much security. Jittery Europeans worried that U.S. troops would be withdrawn from the continent, leaving the people trapped in the giant pincers of Russia's massive land armies, on the one side, and America's power of massive atomic retaliation, on the other.

Canadian Foreign Minister Lester B. Pearson asked for assurances that "instant" retaliation by the U.S. would be preceded by consultation with her allies.

Questions snowballed. Would the U.S. abandon local defenses? Would it rely solely on air-atomic power? Would all little battles be turned into big wars?

The Turning Point

The administration stood firmly on its new policy until March 1, the day the H-bomb explosion over Bikini horrified the world.

Then Dulles redefined the New Look. Its main purpose, he indicated, was to warn Russia and Communist China that they would be "hit with everything we have" if they attacked the U.S. or "our vital interests". It did not mean that every little war started by the Communists would develop into a world war. It did not mean abandoning our allies.

There were other definitions of the New Look also, but many felt that its precise implications were still in doubt.

In April, the U.S. policy of massive retaliation was put to the test. Red Vietminh armies, supplied by the Chinese Communists, threatened to overrun French colonial forces and conquer all of Indochina.

In the Pentagon, Admiral Radford had anticipated French defeat and had prepared a plan for American intervention. Two aircraft carriers (the *Essex* and the *Boxer*) were deployed in the Gulf of Tonkin off the coast of Indochina. Long-range bombers in the Philippines and on Okinawa were armed for battle.

On the morning of April 28, 500 planes were to drop tactical A-bombs on the Vietminh forces. If American action brought Red China openly into the war, bombs would destroy Peking.

Radford unfolded his plan to eight congressional leaders. The U.S., he said, would never be secure so long as the Communists ruled China. If it were his decision, not another inch of territory would be yielded to Communism. The congressmen were flabbergasted.

General Ridgway raised his voice in objection. Intervention, he said, would make Indochina a graveyard for American ground forces.

When the Radford plan was presented to President Eisenhower, he vetoed it. "The only way to win World War III," he said, was "to prevent it."

Eisenhower's reshaping of American defense policy was under way. The policy was soon to be tested again.

Ordeal of Peace

One day in early September, while the Eisenhowers were vacationing in Denver, Ike bounced into his temporary White House, a stucco building at Lowry air force base, looking cheerful and rested. "Oh boy, I had a good night's sleep," he happily told his staff. Then he went out to the golf course and shot a good round in 82.

But that night three brown manila envelopes, sealed and top secret, came to Denver on the courier plane. They were given to the President shortly after he awakened at 6 the next morning. By the time Ike arrived at his office at 7:30 he was frowning. The Defense Department and the Central Intelligence Agency had advised him that things looked bad at an island called Quemoy, 5 miles off the coast of Red China. The Reds were shelling it and an all-out attack seemed to be in the cards.

The Communists might even go on to invade Formosa, seat of Chiang Kai-shek's Nationalist Chinese government which the U.S. was pledged to support. If matters worsened, the U.S. would have to decide whether or not to fight.

The President got on the "scrambler" phone—it foils wire tappers by mixing up words so that they can be sorted out only by an unscrambler at the other end—and summoned a meeting of the National Security Council. But this body of the nation's top-ranking military and civilian leaders could not meet for several days. The President was worried. He knew that, no matter how heavily he might lean on the National Security Council, the final decision on war or peace would have to be his alone.

The Council members converged on Denver. Dulles, the most traveled Secretary of State in history, was away, this time in Manila, and could not reach the rendezvous in time.

Admiral Radford argued for instant retaliation by blockading the China coast and bombing the mainland. Only Ridgway, with bitter memories of Korea fresh in his mind, opposed him.

Dulles cabled his opinion. It carried a great deal of weight, for in foreign policy the President relied heavily on his Secretary of State. The message advised immediate action. Dulles was supported by every member of the National Security Council except one. Opposed was Walter Bedell Smith, Eisenhower's Chief of Staff during World War II.

At last, the President sat alone. He had listened to counsels of war and of peace, and he vetoed the proposal to bomb China and blockade the coast. That course might lead to another world war, he reasoned, and the U.S. would not deliberately make a move that might tend in that direction.

"The great hope of mankind," he said, "is that we can find methods and means of progressing a little bit, even if by little steps, toward a true peace, and that we do not go progressively toward war."

The ordeal of finding some means of peaceful coexistence with Communism—if that were possible—continued.

MAN DOWN: Captain Edward G. Sperry, U.S.A.F., is snapped at moment of ejection by new explosive device from nose of B-47 jet bomber in flight

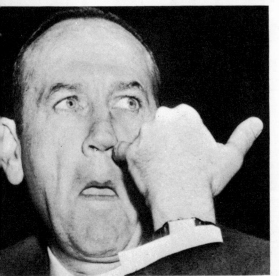

A NUMBER OF CONGRESSIONAL COMMITTEES, empowered to seek out fact to facilitate the intelligent passage of laws, probed into many aspects of American life in 1954. Most of these committees served the nation well. Some, however, turned their investigations into public trials, and treated witnesses who were merely uncooperative as though they were defendants whose guilt had been proved.

One committee weighed the influence of comic books on the minds of children; others investigated public utilities, the State Department, and the high cost of red tape in government bureaus; and three separate committees hunted Communists and subversives. Before the end

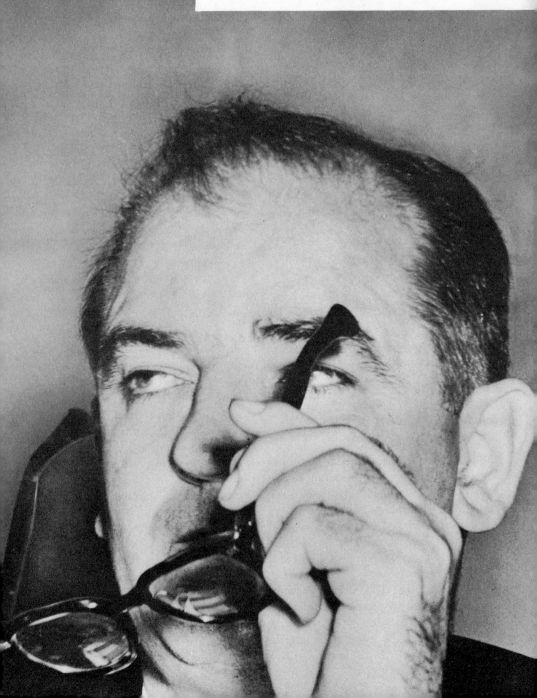

COMMUNISM

of the year, congressional investigations had gone so far that investigators were investigating the investigators.

Billionaire Socialists

A special House committee charged the billionaire Rockefeller, Carnegie, and Ford Foundations with promoting socialistic ideas. Its Republican chairman, Representative Brazilla Carroll Reece of Tennessee, believed that international agreements and social changes of the past twenty years were part of a vast and "diabolical conspiracy" to communize America, and that these changes were speeded by socialistic propaganda of the tax-exempt foundations.

Democrats on the committee angrily dissented. During the hearings Thomas M. McNiece, the committee's assistant research director, was asked his opinion about some short printed statements dealing with social inequality, the lot of the poor, and social reforms generally.

"Emotional products without one word of truth . . . closely comparable to Communist literature," he said of them, adding that they "parallel very closely . . . Communist ideals".

It was then pointed out that the selections were taken verbatim from papal encyclicals. Two had been written by Pope Leo XIII in 1891, one by Pope Pius XI in 1931.

The Reece report filled 416 pages, cost the taxpayers $115,000, won Reece much publicity, and was added to the numbers

ATTENTIVE investigators of Army-McCarthy hearings include (l. to r.) Senators Dworshak, Dirksen, counsel Jenkins, Senators Mundt, McClellan, Symington, and Jackson. Below: Senator Joseph McCarthy and former aide, Private G. David Schine, exchange handclasp

of other investigative reports noted for the record and then forgotten.

The Hunter

In a year in which congressional probes made many headlines, the most sensational of all the investigators was Senator Joseph Raymond McCarthy. McCarthy, who had become junior Senator from Wisconsin in 1947, was an obscure, conservative Republican during his first three years in office.

In 1950, the Senator created headlines with his sensational charges that the State Department, then under a Democratic administration, was a nest of Communists and subversives.

By 1954, McCarthy had become the most controversial figure in the U.S. and the most publicized Red-hunter in the world. Probably more words had been written or spoken about him in the previous year or two than about the President. By suffixing "ism" to his name a new word was coined to identify the Senator's methods and aims: McCarthyism.

The Senator made more bitter enemies and more fanatic friends in his brief, meteoric career than most politicians make in a lifetime.

Some people called him a boor and an irresponsible demagogue. McCarthyism, they said, was the technique of the "Big Lie" and the "Dirty Smear". The Senator was dubbed a charlatan armed with phony documents, faked photostats, and false official papers, using methods that reeked of Berya and Vishinsky.

Other people saw McCarthy as the polar opposite of all the foregoing. To them he was fearless, honest, brilliant, patriotic, and as indestructible as a hero in a comic strip. McCarthy, they said, was simply trying to drive subversives out of government, and all who opposed him were Communists, fellow travelers,

pinkos, or misguided liberal dupes. His friends called McCarthyism "a movement around which men of good will and stern morality may close ranks".

Between the two camps there was a middle group whose feelings were summed up in the remark: "I don't like McCarthy's methods, but I do like his objectives."

Informed observers agreed that, whatever else he might be, McCarthy was no ordinary politician. In March Richard H. Rovere, correspondent of the sophisticated *New Yorker* magazine, reported that, according to the prevailing view in Washington, McCarthy was "a political figure of the first rank, a man cast in a large, unique mold, quite possibly an authentic genius, and, at the very least, the most daring and original political innovator since Franklin D. Roosevelt".

In his rise to power, McCarthy fought with Presidents, cowed Cabinet members, humiliated generals. He campaigned against and helped to defeat Senators who had criticized him. He attacked a critical press, even tried to drive some publications out of business. He won free broadcast time from radio and TV networks to answer attacks on him. Yet, despite his power, by the end of the year McCarthy was a badly battered figure.

The Man

Not only opinions about but even descriptions of this man from Wisconsin were conflicting.

To his admirers, McCarthy seemed, in a dark and granite-jawed way, handsome. He appeared tall, with a strong neck and powerful shoulders. To critics, he seemed a heavy-bearded lout, inclined to run to fat, who created an illusion of height by wearing elevated shoes.

Actually, McCarthy is a 200-pounder, an inch under 6 feet tall. He has a big head and large hands. His features are regular, and his smile is warm and compelling. Highly emotional, he is easily moved to tears or laughter. His laugh, something akin to a high-pitched giggle, has been described by some as friendly and by others as frightening.

Nearly everyone calls McCarthy "Joe" soon after meeting him. Ingratiating, an inveterate handshaker, he enjoys sitting around holding a drink and swapping tales. Owing to a severe sinus ailment, he does not smoke and he dislikes having smokers near him. A man of tremendous physical energy, he is continuously in action. His hours are unregimented, and he is usually late to bed and late to rise. He will go far out on a limb to do a favor for a supporter.

One of seven children, McCarthy was born in the rolling farm land of up-State Wisconsin. He attended a country school and helped out in his father's fields. At 19, he moved to Manawa to manage a small-town grocery store. Encouraged by his landlady to continue his education, he completed the four-year high-school course in one year, then five years later graduated from the law school of Marquette University, a Jesuit institution in Milwaukee. He was an average student.

McCarthy worked in restaurants and a gas station to pay for his education, but still found time to act as a student boxing coach. "The moment you draw back and start defending yourself, you're licked," he advised his pupils.

From the day McCarthy was fired with political ambition, the course of his life was a stormy one.

A year after he tacked up his legal diploma, he was defeated as the Democratic candidate for district attorney of Shawano County. He never again ran as a Democrat.

In 1939 McCarthy, then 29, was elected a circuit-court judge in Wisconsin. On the bench only two years, he was rebuked by the State Supreme Court for destroying evidence in a case tried before him. The Chief Justice deemed his conduct "highly improper" and declared him guilty of "an abuse of judicial power".

On another occasion the Wisconsin Supreme Court criticized McCarthy for violating "the terms of the Constitution and laws of the State of Wisconsin".

During his career on the bench, he was accused of granting "quickie" divorces to further his political ambitions.

The voters of Wisconsin obviously placed little stock in these charges, for they re-elected him judge and ultimately sent him to the U.S. Senate.

McCarthy as a Marine

The military service of Joseph McCarthy was as controversial as his public career. Critics maintained that the portrait he drew of himself as a military man was at complete variance with the facts. In public statements and approved biographical sketches, McCarthy pictured himself as a judge who during World War II joined the Marines as a private and then was promoted from the ranks. In this version, Captain McCarthy was a dashing war hero, a wounded tail-gunner with a load of shrapnel in his leg. He was a man who left the service of his country reluctantly.

Enemies drew a less flattering portrait. McCarthy, they said, had applied for and received a commission before he joined the Marines. He was an on-the-ground intelligence officer. His wound was the result of an accident which occurred during the traditional initiation ceremony tendered to men aboard ship as they cross the equator for the first time.

When the war against Japan reached its climax, McCarthy applied for a leave of absence to resume his judicial duties.

CONTROVERSIAL PHOTO in hearings shows Private Schine and Secretary Stevens together at New Jersey air base. When McCarthy aide had picture cropped, other figures were eliminated

Denied the leave, he resigned. While the Marines fought the bloody battles of Iwo Jima and Okinawa, McCarthy as the returning war hero was laying the groundwork for his successful campaign for the U.S. Senate.

"I'll either end up in jail or in the White House," McCarthy once told a friend.

By January, 1954, the Senator stood on the threshold of almost unlimited power. His following was large and devoted; in hundreds of communities across the nation McCarthyites held important positions. McCarthy was charged with obtaining this power at the cost of splitting the nation.

He had accused the Democratic Party of "twenty years of treason". He appeared to be trying to gain control of the Republican Party. His ultimate goal may indeed have been the White House. Before

the year's end, however, he had slipped far from this pinnacle. Ironically, an obscure dentist started his decline.

This Is the Army

The dentist was Dr. Irving Peress, a slight man in his late 30's who had a harassed air and large, soft eyes. A member of the middle class, Peress practiced in New York City's borough of Queens.

During the Korean War emergency, Peress was commissioned an army reserve captain to meet the military demand for doctors and dentists. Peress, however, did not sign his loyalty oath. Instead he wrote "Federal Constitutional Privilege" on it.

In the case of Peress, the army acted as though it did not want its left hand to know what its right hand was doing. Four

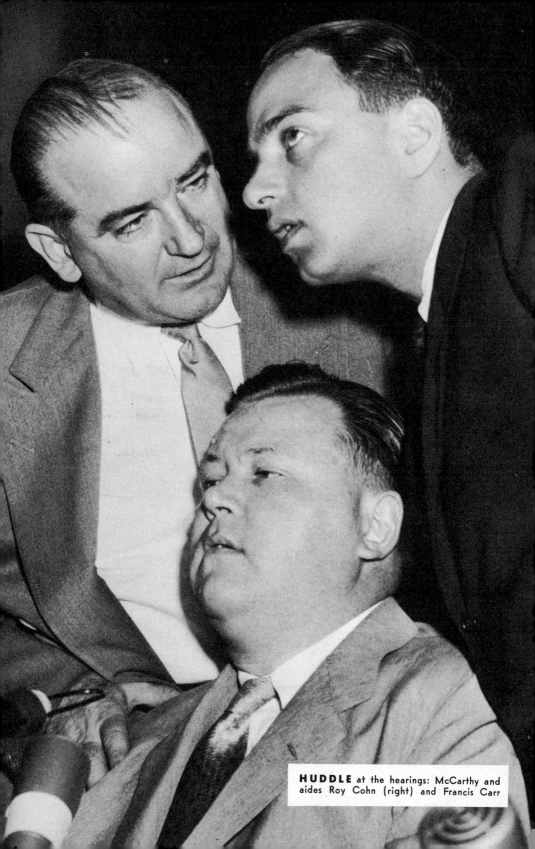

HUDDLE at the hearings: McCarthy and aides Roy Cohn (right) and Francis Carr

ANTAGONISTS are caught (above) at Army-McCarthy dispute. Left: McCarthy counsel Cohn leans forward to make a point. Right: Army counsel Adams leans back to listen to one

months after his induction, the army noticed the notation on his loyalty oath and ordered an investigation that inched slowly through channels. Meanwhile, one branch of the army granted Peress a "compassionate reassignment" to be near his sick child and wife, and transferred him to Camp Kilmer, N.J., under the command of Brigadier General Ralph Zwicker. Another branch of the army, under the provisions of the doctors' draft law, promoted him to major.

After Peress had been in service more than a year the army's investigation of his case was completed, and on Jan. 18, 1954, the Pentagon ordered his honorable discharge. On Jan. 30 the Wisconsin Senator haled Peress before the Senate's Permanent Subcommittee on Investigations in regard to his alleged Communist activities. But the Major parried all questions by pleading the Fifth Amendment. McCarthy thereupon demanded that Peress be court-martialed. By that time the Pentagon's wheels were grinding to a halt, and on Feb. 2 Peress received an honorable discharge.

To millions of ex-G.I.'s, the handling of the Peress case was typical army snafu (situation normal, all fouled up). To McCarthy, it was proof that the army was coddling Communists.

General Zwicker, summoned before Senator McCarthy's investigating subcommittee, refused to name those responsible for Peress' assignment to Camp Kilmer, his promotion, and his honorable discharge. Zwicker, a much-decorated World War II combat soldier, cited a presidential directive that prohibited army officials from revealing the details of loyalty investigations.

McCarthy labeled Zwicker a "Fifth Amendment General" and questioned his "honesty" and intelligence. He accused the General of using "double talk" and of "not being fit to wear the uniform".

Army officials were furious. Secretary of the Army Robert T. Stevens, a mild-mannered, politically naive businessman, expressed his resentment of "unwarranted abuse of our loyal officers".

The Hearings

Charges and countercharges soon boiled into a national scandal. The army accused McCarthy and his staff of trying to blackmail officials with threats in order to get preferential treatment for Private G. David Schine, a former unpaid aide on the Senator's staff. The Senator accused the army of holding Schine as a hostage so that McCarthy would call off his investigations of Communists in the military. Long lists of accusations and answers were drawn up by McCarthy and Stevens until finally the other Senators on McCarthy's investigating subcommittee opened hearings to get at the truth.

The hearings were held in the marble-columned caucus room of the Senate office building. They were nationally televised and attracted a tremendous audience. For the first time, millions of Americans saw the Senator in action.

Although the army evidently had botched the Peress case, it was obvious to the TV audience that General Zwicker, Secretary of the Army Stevens, the men in the Pentagon, and high-ranking Republican officials, all of whom had aroused McCarthy's ire, were not themselves Communists and would not be apt to coddle Communists. It seemed to many who watched the TV spectacle that McCarthy was not fighting Communism so much as he was fighting the Eisenhower administration.

During the hearings many Americans were shocked to hear the Senator call on government employees to violate their oaths of office by revealing government secrets to him. "I will receive evidence of wrongdoing, graft, corruption, treason," McCarthy shouted, "from any government employee who will give that to me."

Somewhat later the people heard the Attorney General warn that executive responsibility "cannot be usurped by any individual who may seek to set himself above the law of our land".

After thirty-six days of contradictory testimony, which yielded more than 2 million words, every major charge made by either side had been denied under oath. Every issue was clouded. The subcommittee, unable to resolve its differences of opinion in regard to the testimony, issued majority and minority reports, which were almost as confusing as the hearings. In the Republican report, McCarthy, his aides, and the army officials involved were mildly criticized. In the Democratic report, too, the army officials were mildly criticized, but McCarthy and his aides were sharply criticized. In a supplementary report Michigan's Senator Potter, a Republican, declared that the record was "saturated" with apparent perjury.

The extent to which the Republican cause had been damaged by the intra-party row was not at once apparent, but McCarthy's prestige obviously had suffered severe injury.

I Believe

In 1954, also, Senator McCarthy withdrew a $2 million libel suit against former Senator William Benton, Connecticut Democrat.

In 1952 Benton, waiving the congressional immunity that would have protected him from legal action, had accused McCarthy of "fraud . . . deceit . . . perjury . . . deception of the Senate and . . . the American people".

McCarthy explained that he dropped his libel action because his lawyers had been unable to find anyone, anywhere in the United States, who would say he believed Benton's charges. Therefore it was impossible to prove damages.

A prominent Connecticut industrialist, Walter H. Wheeler Jr., president of Pitney-Bowes, Incorporated, sent McCarthy a telegram: "Your lawyers could not have looked very hard. I would be glad to testify that I believe what Benton has said about you, and I am sure there are millions of others in this country who would be happy to do likewise."

The Watkins Committee

The stiffening of the administration attitude toward McCarthy lessened the timidity of others who had feared his power. Vermont's elderly Senator Ralph Edward Flanders denounced McCarthy and demanded that the Senate censure him. McCarthy was aping Hitler, he said. "Were the junior Senator from Wisconsin in the pay of the Communists, he could not have done a better job for them."

McCarthy roared that Flanders was "senile". "I think they should get a man with a net and take him to a good quiet place."

Finally, the Senate formed a Select Committee to hear forty-six formal charges against Senator McCarthy. Six conservatives were chosen to serve on the committee. Its chairman was a Republican, Utah's Arthur Vivian Watkins.

McCarthy hailed the committee, saying its hearings would give him a chance "to put to rest all the false, scurrilous, defamatory, irresponsible charges that have been made over the past number of years".

In striking contrast with the burly McCarthy, Senator Watkins was a frail, sickly man with snow-white hair atop a high-domed forehead. Rimless glasses added to his conservative appearance. He

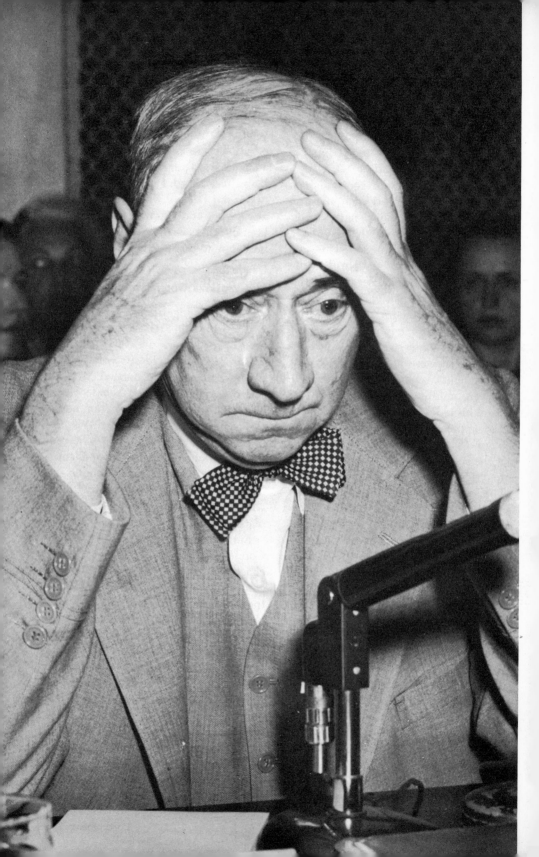

was a quiet, polite, deeply religious Mormon who hated smoking and did not touch whisky, coffee, or tea.

When running for the Senate in 1946, he promised the voters that if he were elected "the spirit of Christianity will be my guide".

Most Washington newsmen predicted that the self-effacing Watkins would knuckle under to McCarthy. He did not. Moreover, his committee's hearings, untelevised, were run with efficiency.

From the start, McCarthy was checked by a sharply rapped gavel and clear, precise rulings. McCarthy heard his own record discussed in detail. His loud, insistent "Mr. Chairman!" was silenced time and again.

In a sharply worded report, the committee recommended that the U.S. Senate censure Senator McCarthy on two counts. The first charged that, although McCarthy had been accused of using his senatorial prestige and position to feather his own nest, he had been contemptuous of a Senate committee appointed to inquire into his personal finances. The second count condemned his treatment of General Zwicker as "inexcusable".

In a special session of the Senate, the recommendation for censure set off a fiery debate. McCarthy shouted that the Watkins committee was guilty of "deliberate deception" and that the Senate session called to hear the charges was a "lynch bee". The committee had "done the work of the Communist Party . . . distorted, misrepresented and omitted".

ENNUI seems to seize army special counsel Welch (left) as Army-McCarthy hearings drag on to exhausting, inconclusive end. Senator McCarthy looks puzzled

ALMOST OBSCURED by Army-McCarthy dispute was the court-martial in Washington, D.C., of Corporal Edward Dickenson (right). Charge: collaborating with Reds while a P.O.W. in Korea

Watkins lashed back: "Continuous guerrilla warfare was waged against us by the junior Senator from Wisconsin. It was abuse heaped on abuse . . . Right here in the Senate . . . Senators have seen . . . an attack upon their representatives . . . They have heard the Senator say that I am both stupid and a coward . . . that we [the committee] are either traitors or fools . . . What are you going to do about it?"

The Final Blow

When the roll of the Senate was called, McCarthy was condemned for his conduct by a vote of 67 to 22. He thus became the fourth man to be censured in the entire history of the Senate.

Two days later, Senator Watkins visited the White House and was personally congratulated by President Eisenhower on "a very splendid job".

Furious, McCarthy denounced the President. Eisenhower, he charged, protected Communists in the U.S. government and showed weakness toward Communists abroad.

The Senate's censure and this final bitter attack on the popular President of the United States shook all but a hard core of Senator McCarthy's followers. Temporarily, at least, he went into political eclipse.

DICKENSON'S PARENTS pose in their Virginia home with his photo (right) and that of his brother Leonard, who served in Germany. Edward's sentence: ten years in prison, dishonorable discharge

REACTION to Supreme Court's ruling against school segregation varied with geography. This lad, too young to read his own placard, was recruited to publicize white sentiment in Baltimore

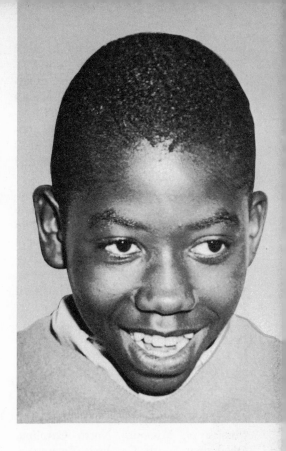

ACTION of Court in segregation issue resulted from legal suits instituted in behalf of Spottswood Bolling (right) and other children

SUPREME COURT

ON MAY 18, 1954, THE FIRST DAY OF A NEW era for America's Negroes, the air was full of radically divergent comment.

In New York City: "Little by little we move toward a more perfect democracy" —*The New York Times.*

In Jackson, Miss.: "Human blood may stain southern soil . . . but the dark red stains . . . will be on the marble steps of the Supreme Court"—Jackson *Daily News.*

In Charleston, S. C.: "We shall need wisdom and tolerance"—Charleston *News & Courier.*

In Atlanta, Ga.: "The Court has blatantly ignored all law and precedent . . . Georgia will not comply"—Governor Herman Talmadge.

What had provoked this comment? Shortly after noon on May 17, the United States Supreme Court, in a unanimous decision of spectacular simplicity, had declared: "Separate educational facilities [for Negroes] are inherently unequal" and hence unconstitutional. In other words, segregation in public schools had been outlawed. Equal rights had been granted to Negroes in education with the prospect of more gains to come in other fields.

For Negro citizens it was the greatest legal gain since Abraham Lincoln's Emancipation Proclamation in 1863.

The May 17 decision climaxed a controversy that began probably in 1619 when the first Negro slaves were landed on colonial soil.

Dramatically, it repudiated the doctrine, formulated in an 1896 Supreme Court ruling in a transport case, that Negroes could be segregated if they were given equal facilities. Now "separate-but-equal" in the field of public education was dead, and Negro lawyer Thurgood Marshall, celebrating the victory of a lifetime, could say: "Once and for all, it's decided, completely decided."

At the time of the decision, school segregation was required in the District of Columbia and seventeen States (Alabama, Arkansas, Delaware, Florida, Georgia, Kentucky, Louisiana, Maryland, Mississippi, Missouri, North Carolina, Oklahoma, South Carolina, Tennessee, Texas, Virginia, and West Virginia). It was permitted in four States (Arizona, Kansas, New Mexico, and Wyoming). Nearly 11,000,000 children, almost 40 percent of the nation's pupils, went to public schools in these areas; about 2,-500,000 of them were colored.

Surprisingly, only in the District of Columbia did Negro pupils outnumber white pupils—by about three to two. They comprised 50 percent of the school enrollment in Mississippi, less in other Southern States. In West Virginia and Kentucky, they comprised only about 6 percent. Individual school districts, however, might be as much as 90 percent or as little as 1 percent colored.

In educating its Negro pupils the South as a whole had been more concerned with giving them "separate" than "equal" facilities, although their lot was improving.

In 1952, for every dollar spent to educate a white child, the average Southern school district spent 70¢ to educate a Negro; in 1940 the latter figure had been 42¢. For every dollar put into a white school building, colored schools got 82¢; in 1940, 23¢. For every hundred books in the white child's school library, the Negro child had thirty-nine.

Now nine men in Washington had made "equal" mean equal.

One of the five cases with which the Court decision specifically dealt was that docketed as "Bolling vs. Sharpe". The widowed mother of a shy seventh-grader, Spottswood Bolling of Washington, D.C., resented the fact that he had to attend a once-condemned Negro school while there was a better white school nearby. With other Negro parents who shared her resentment, she filed suit in 1951 to open all school doors to her son.

Ironically, Spottswood, by a caprice of zoning, was attending one of the few all-Negro schools left in Washington when 1954 ended.

Needless to say, the sun did not rise on integrated schools on the day after the Supreme Court decision. At the end of the year there were still many segregated schools, but the situation had been anticipated by the Court. Aware of the emotional impact its decision would have, it had asked for new argument in October on how to put the ban on segregation into effect.

This hearing was delayed, however, by the death of Justice Robert Jackson. His death created a historical coincidence. The Justice who had dissented from the Supreme Court 1896 separate-but-equal decision was John Marshall Harlan, who had said: "The Constitution is color-blind." Early in 1955, when the Court is to meet again to put this principle into effect, one of the nine black-robed men will probably be his grandson, today's

John Marshall Harlan, who was named to fill the vacancy left by Justice Jackson's death.

Reaction in Georgia

Most observers felt that real integration would take time. They were sure of it when they noted the uproar the Court's decision created in Georgia.

It is said that Rotarians lunching in Savannah cheered the news on May 17, but Governor Talmadge's defiance was echoed on all sides, particularly by the gubernatorial candidates in the 1954 summer Democratic primary in Georgia. There were nine such candidates. One of them, Lieutenant Governor Marvin Griffin, suggested (1) that local officials be empowered to assign pupils to specific schools and (2) that residence requirements be set up to keep out "foreign agitators". "The schools," he said, "are not going to be mixed come hell or high water." He ran first.

Another candidate, Grace Wilkey Thomas, made the statement: "There doesn't seem to me to be anything to do but obey the law." She ran last.

The views of the seven other candidates were far closer to Griffin's than to Grace Thomas'. One candidate even suggested that the United States abolish the U.S. Supreme Court.

In the fall election the Georgia electorate approved, though by a small margin, a plan to abolish public schools if necessary and set up "private" segregated schools financed by the State.

But some voices were flatly dissenting. In the little town of Shellman, Ga., the Reverend Henry A. Buchanan mounted the Baptist pulpit one Sunday and told his startled congregation that the Supreme Court ruling was just and Christian and that, if his hearers did not want to comply with it, they should "secede from the United States" and turn their church into a club.

The congregation fumed for months; then in December the Board of Deacons voted 78-17 to demand the pastor's resignation. The Reverend Buchanan scratched his name and his wife's from the church roll, wrote "Cast out" beside them, and left Shellman.

With variations, Georgia's pattern was repeated in some other Southern States. In Louisiana, by four to one, voters adopted a plan to keep segregation by using State police power to protect "public health and morals".

In Alabama and Mississippi, Citizens' Councils sprang up apparently to discourage integration by exerting economic or other pressures. Meanwhile angered Southern leaders erupted with some wild words. One State legislator declared that the real goal of desegregation was "to open the bedroom doors of our white women to Negro men". Next, he said, there would be a Negro Vice-President, "and after that, what would prevent them from assassinating the President?"

Reactions Elsewhere

While all this was going on in the deep South, Kansas, Arizona, New Mexico, and the District of Columbia moved toward total integration and Missouri, Arkansas, West Virginia, Delaware, and Maryland toward integration in part.

The first threat of violence originated in the oil town of Hobbs, N.Mex., which had 400 Negro pupils and 5600 white ones. A desegregation order to Hobbs schools stirred little comment until the Reverend Bill Carter, pastor of Rock Chapel Baptist Church, began circulating anti-integration petitions.

Carter found his justification in the Bible ("God segregated the three children of Noah. He did it, not me."), and warned of violence if Negroes went to school with Whites. Police were alert, but opening day was placid.

But in White Sulphur Springs, W.Va., a pretty resort town near the Virginia border, there was overt hostility. On Sept. 18, four days after 400 Whites and 25 Negroes began to attend school together, over 300 white youngsters went out on "strike".

That evening some 700 white adults met and voted to toss bodily out of class any Negro who attended the school next day. None did. By nightfall, Greenbrier County's Board of Education had resegregated the schools.

In the next three weeks the virus of violence spread to Delaware, to Maryland, and finally to Washington, D.C.

In Milford, Del., a tree-shaded town of some 1500 Negroes and 4200 Whites, Negro children had had to travel 18 miles to Dover and back if they wished to attend high school. Following the Supreme Court ruling, Milford's four-man school board decided they could attend "white" Lakeview High if they chose.

Eleven did, and for nine days all was quiet. An interracial school dance went off without a hitch, and a Negro boy made the football team. However, when white parents learned from their children of the new state of affairs, the town was laced with angry phone calls. A protest meeting drew 2000 Whites.

Fearing violence, the local board closed the schools, then resigned. At that point Delaware's Governor J. Caleb Boggs stepped in and ordered the schools reopened without segregation.

Protest meetings continued. The school superintendent's home was stoned and he was threatened with bodily harm if he obeyed the Governor. When the schools did open, 10 Negro pupils received a police escort and two thirds of the white students were absent.

Some of the white pupils opposed the strike. "The colored kids are as good as anyone else," said one white pupil kept out against his will. But many parents shared the view of a mother who declared: "I've got to put a stop to this or else someday I'll be having colored grandchildren."

A newly appointed school board ordered resegregation. The order was reversed in court, but the decision was appealed. Pending the final decision, segregation remained.

In Baltimore, Md., the demonstrations were more tumultuous but less successful. They began at Southern High School (35 Negroes in an enrollment of about 1700) and were notable for the courage of two white women teachers.

A Negro lad reported that, as he left school, he "heard someone say they ought to take us out and hang us. Then they were all around me and my home room teacher came out and took my hand and led me through them to her car and drove me home." Another white teacher nosed her car into a jeering crowd and rescued two Negro children.

Not all white pupils were hostile. The white players of Southern's football team offered to "run interference" for a colored teammate if he would come out for practice. He did.

There were mass meetings to spread the school strike, but strict police work and fines for disorderly conduct restored calm and desegregation within a week.

Trouble in Washington

Next trouble spot was Washington, where desegregation had gone furthest. Even before the Supreme Court ruling, Washington's Board of Education (six Whites and three Negroes) had begun to plan for integration. To guide Superintendent Hobart Corning it had enunciated this simple standard: assign pupils by zone, teachers by merit.

Until then Corning had been presiding over a system rigidly divided into two divisions: Division I with about 40,000 Whites, Division II with about 60,000 Negroes. As Negro enrollment expanded, Negro schools became overcrowded and understaffed while white schools remained only partially filled.

A Negro cab driver described the reaction to this situation: "Colored folks got sore when their kids had to go past McKinley High sittin' so pretty up there on the hill half empty, then be jammed up in rackety old Armstrong."

Corning's plan was to rezone the city, send all new pupils to the schools in their zones, and arrange for transfers from the crowded schools in Division II. Integration was to be virtually complete by the fall of 1955.

Few people really liked the plan. Some foes warned that white children would be minorities of one in all-Negro classes. In a few cases that happened.

The first month passed without incident. Then trouble began. At Anacostia High School, in a racial-transition neighborhood, 400 pupils walked out. In the next few days, at 7 of Washington's 165 other schools there were similar disorders.

Most of the disorders were easily kept within bounds. At McKinley High School, for example, the principal promised to set up an interracial committee to deal with the problems. He told his strikers: "This is a new road we must travel . . . I need your help."

But even during McKinley's strike, Negroes had sat with Whites in the school cafeterias, Negro children had played with white children on playgrounds, and students had crowed about their football team's victory as the first "integrated" team to play in the South. As the year ended, integration seemed to be winning in Washington.

Handsome Rabble Rouser

Through all the troublous days, the name of Bryant Bowles cropped up repeatedly. A former drummer in the Marines, Bowles was a handsome, glib Floridian who founded what he called the National Association for the Advancement of White People (dues $5). He had had difficulties with the law regarding phony checks.

Bowles addressed mass meetings in Delaware and Maryland. (He was not allowed to speak in Washington.) He counseled against violence, but climaxed speeches by snatching up his pretty 3-year-old daughter and shouting that she would never attend school with Negroes "while there's a breath in my body or gunpowder burns".

When he left resegregated Milford, Del., he exulted: "Now the only thing black in the schools is the blackboards."

In other States, in dozens of other schools, desegregation was begun without incident. White pupils in Carthage, Mo., liked a couple of their new Negro classmates so well they promptly elected them to class office.

There were other gains in race relations in 1954. The week following the school case, the Supreme Court handed down six other opinions granting Negroes unrestricted access to college training, theaters, municipal golf courses, and public housing.

In baseball, where the player color line was so far erased that towheads in sandlot games scrapped for the privilege of "being" Willie Mays, there was now a Negro umpire. The Episcopalians took their 1955 convention away from Houston, Texas, which had Jim Crow customs, and planned to meet in Honolulu, a racial melting pot.

And in 1954 the Supreme Court itself, appropriately, got its first Negro page boy.

FACE OF VIOLENCE: Frank Cuniffe, 27, is held by officers in a New York basement after pummeling woman to unconsciousness. Police said she refused to attend movie with him

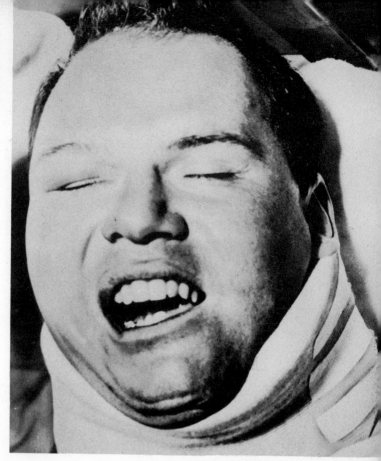

FACE OF SUFFERING is offered by Cleveland's Dr. Samuel Sheppard, hospitalized, allegedly with a broken neck, after the death of his wife Marilyn — for which he later was convicted of murder

CRIME

THE NIGHT OF AUG. 16 WAS HOT IN BROOKlyn, N.Y. Factory worker Willard Menter, homeward bound after visiting a bar, stopped to rest in the comparative coolness of a little park near the East River. He took off his shoes and socks, leaned back on a bench. Presently he slept.

When he awoke, it was to searing pain: a lighted cigarette was being pressed against his naked foot. Four strange figures loomed over him. He was dragged erect, then knocked sprawling. Again he was picked up, again knocked down. Finally, close to unconsciousness, he was walked to the river and pushed in. He could not swim. . . .

An hour later the police, alerted by a passer-by, caught up with the four who, they said, had done this monstrous thing. Soon, according to the police, the prison-

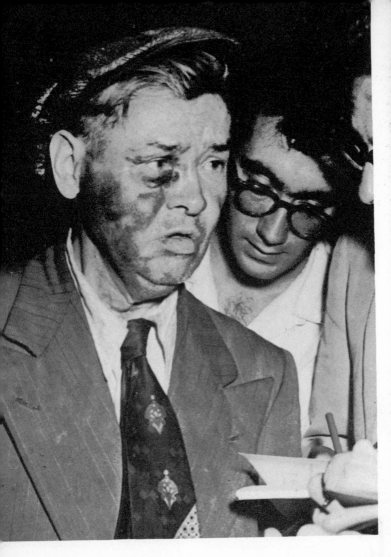

ers confessed that they had killed not only Menter but also steeple jack Reinhold Ulrickson, and that they had horse-whipped two girls and wrapped a third man's legs in gasoline-soaked cotton and set it afire.

And who were the four—gangsters, revenge slayers, sadistic maniacs? No. All were teen-age boys from respectable Brooklyn homes. None had a criminal record. And *they did not know who their victims were.*

The senseless brutality of their acts created an immediate sensation. Newspapers dubbed the youths the "Teen-age Thrill Killers". Educators, psychologists, and law enforcers had a field day second-guessing their motives. The parents of other teen-agers wondered, and worried.

These were the four:

Jack Koslow, ringleader, 18. Tall, thin, and introspective, he revealed a neurotic leadership drive and a strange admiration for the late Adolf Hitler (on whose mustache he modeled a wispy red one of his own). According to police, he beat men in parks because he had "an abstract hatred for bums and vagrants".

Melvin Mittman, 17 and 210 pounds.

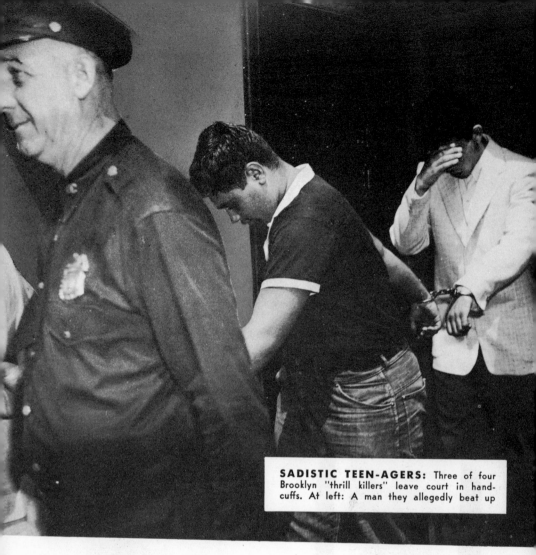

SADISTIC TEEN-AGERS: Three of four Brooklyn "thrill killers" leave court in handcuffs. At left: A man they allegedly beat up

"Muscle man" of the group, he was quoted as saying he enjoyed hitting people "to see how hard I could punch".

Jerome Lieberman, 17, and Robert Trachtenberg, 15. Caught up by Koslow's soaring ego, they followed Jack blindly toward what he reportedly called "the supreme adventure": murder.

Outwardly, all four were normal American boys. But inside them deep and dangerous pressures were at work. Koslow had been spotted as disturbed and aggressive at the age of 7. Psychiatric help had been recommended; after four treatments, however, his parents had stopped

them, feeling that they cast a "stigma" on the family.

In December, Koslow and Mittman were tried for killing Menter. A jury found them guilty and recommended life imprisonment. Young Trachtenberg, having turned state's evidence, was freed. Mittman and Lieberman still faced trial in the Ulrickson slaying (Koslow played no direct part in this killing).

Widespread Juvenile Crime

The Brooklyn case highlighted the most disturbing aspect of 1954's crime

DEATH ON TV is recorded by two Little Rock, Ark., television photographers. After holding Mrs. A. D. Lynn in her own home at gun point, escaped mental patient H. B. Long, 42, tries to use her as a shield from police (left), but is shot dead (right, below) by off-duty patrolman

news. Teen-agers, traditionally filled with excess energy, too often were releasing it in the form of violence. "Juvenile delinquency" was becoming straight-out "juvenile crime". Boys too young to shave were knocking down women, beating men, committing random vandalism. Girls still in bobby socks were forming roving gangs, robbing people, helping boys attack adults.

For boys and girls under 18, the national crime rate was up at least 8 percent over the 1953 figure (the previous postwar high), compared to only 2 percent for adults. Authorities estimated *one youngster in twenty* now was involved with the police. Most alarming of all, more and more children were following the Koslow pattern and turning killers:

In Des Moines, Iowa, a 14-year-old baby sitter confessed to shooting and killing an 8-year-old because the latter kept getting out of bed and asking to "play guns".

In Detroit, Mich., one 12-year-old basketball player stabbed another to death after a game because "[I] didn't like the way I was guarded".

In Sherburn, Minn., a boy of 15 shot his parents and grandmother dead because he had been punished for coming home late from school.

In Toledo, Ohio, a 17-year-old confessed to the rape-slaying of a girl he had overpowered with the help of a 12-year-old friend.

In Norwood, Mass., a 15-year-old boy was charged with strangling a girl of the same age. His previous avocations: altar boy, Boy Scout.

In Hunters, Wash., a girl of 10 was shot dead by a boy whom she had teased while he was trying to read a book. His age: 9.

In New York City, during the first six months of the year juvenile delinquency was greater by 32 percent than in the comparable period of 1953. When a woman of 85 surprised two lads of 17 bent on robbery, they simply killed her (and so became the youngest criminals ever sentenced to the electric chair in the United States). Another 17-year-old was convicted of manslaughter for kicking a 40-year-old man to death. After an eight-month investigation, detectives arrested two boys who reportedly killed a 58-year-old druggist during a holdup. Both boys were 14.

Not without reason did one observer comment: "This may go down as the year America began to be afraid of its teen-agers."

Many things were blamed for the growth of juvenile crime: broken homes and parental laxity, "comic" books and TV crime programs, inadequate recreational facilities and lack of child-guidance clinics, world tensions and the threat of war.

One thoughtful psychologist, Dr. Robert Lindner, suggested that today's youth, instead of rebelling against "the world" in youth's time-honored way, was striking out on an almost animal level—the level of violent crime—because humanity itself was becoming dehumanized.

The Search for Remedies

Some of these diverging views brought appropriate action. The comic-book industry hired a "czar" pledged to ban the publication of unwholesome reading. TV's impact on youth was widely debated. Cities loosened purse strings for more school sports and after-school recreation. States pondered better youth courts and rehabilitation facilities. Some communities set a curfew for children under 16.

A Louisville judge tried creating a teen-age advisory committee to help him handle young offenders. (The committee felt today's youngsters generally are treated too leniently.) A New York judge invited thirty-four seventh-graders to watch as he sentenced a 17-year-old boy to the reformatory for attempted burglary.

"You see," he said of the weeping boy, "tomorrow he won't be wearing a suit and tie. He'll be wearing a prison uniform with a number on it."

The seventh-graders seemed impressed.

At year's end, however, no one formula yet covered the cause and cure of juvenile crime. Nor was the outlook much better at the adult level.

Crime in the Cities

As usual, the biggest cities had the biggest crime problem. New Yorkers were jolted in midsummer when Police Commissioner Francis Adams said their city then averaged 327 crimes a day, including 1 murder, 1 death by criminal negligence, 3 rapes, 30 holdups, and 140 burglaries. Adams asked funds to increase the police force from 19,000 men to 28,000; while waiting, he instituted "saturation" policing of extra-tough precincts (and later reported excellent results).

Though Chicago struck one encouraging note (a modest drop in the homicide rate), in New Orleans the whole police force was accused of complicity in widespread vice operations; the mayor of Erie, Pa., admitted to links with a county-wide gambling ring; in California the governor began probing a "shocking and deplorable" mess in the field of liquor licenses.

In proportion to population, however, the year's No. 1 sin spot was little Phenix City, Ala. (23,000 inhabitants).

Located just across the Chattahoochee River from Columbus, Ga. (pop. 60,000),

and Fort Benning (infantry), Phenix City first won a name for frontier lawlessness in the early 1800's. Time erased the frontier, left the lawlessness. Thus in the 1930's, hard hit by depression, Phenix City readily broke with Alabama morality and licensed slot machines to raise tax money.

Underworld Rule in Phenix City

Then legal liquor came back. Soon honky-tonks, saloons, gambling, and prostitution were bringing in civilian and soldier trade by the carload. In their wake came fights, robberies, even killings. The majority of decent citizens, lulled by prosperity, realized too late that home-grown racketeers and hired thugs had taken over.

In the 1950's reaction finally set in. God-fearing folk (Phenix City has an exceptionally high percentage of churches) formed the Russell Betterment Association (R.B.A.), named for the county of which Phenix City is the seat. The R.B.A. persuaded the local gambling overlord to close shop. But the underworld surged back, and for two years the Association found its every move blocked by local politicians in the pay of gangsters.

As a last, desperation move the R.B.A. put up its own legal counsel for State Attorney General. An honest country lawyer, 60-year-old Albert Patterson squeaked through to a surprising victory in the June, 1954, Democratic primary—equivalent to election. On Jan. 1, 1955, he would replace Attorney General Silas Garrett, who had not run for re-election.

But someone came up to Patterson in the street and fired three bullets into him, one with the gun actually in his mouth.

Now, for once, there was action. Fort Benning put the town off limits. From Montgomery, the State capital, came 150 National Guardsmen, and racket-ridden

Phenix City was placed under martial law.

Phenix City officials and criminal big-wigs and their henchmen were rounded up; many fled town. A "clean-up" grand jury subpoenaed some 1000 persons and, in its first report alone, returned 545 indictments against 59 individuals—for everything from possession of gambling equipment to murder. It also indicted Attorney General Garrett on a charge of election fraud.

Meanwhile, the National Guard was sworn to stay until Albert Patterson's killing had been solved. In December the grand jury evidently felt a solution was in sight; it indicted Silas Garrett and two Russell County officials for murder.

And Patterson's memory lived on. In Phenix City, the honky-tonk district he had fought was marked for razing and replacement by a modern shopping center. In Hollywood, his good work was being re-created in a screen version of *The Phenix City Story*. Best of all, Alabama Democrats named his son John to succeed him as Attorney General.

Headlined Murders

Elsewhere, crime had its usual rich diversity. There were more killings. In New York's Greenwich Village, "Bohemian" novelist-poet Maxwell Bodenheim, 63, literary darling of the 1920's who long since had descended to cadging drinks and sleeping in doorways, was shot (along with his third wife) by a new acquaintance named Harold Weinberg. The deed sent Weinberg to an institution for the criminally insane.

In Cleveland, an oversize 15-year-old named Raymond Kuchenmeister apparently became carried away by his devotion to "Western" stories and movies. Just as a big commercial plane was about to take off for St. Louis, he forced his way into the cockpit waving a .38 at the pilot. "Fly to Mexico or be shot!" he ordered. Pilot William Bonnell, alarmed for his fifty-three passengers, tried to laugh the boy off; when Raymond persisted, Bonnell drew his own revolver and shot him dead. The boy's gun, it developed, was unloaded.

Cleveland saw the year's most headlined killing: the Sheppard case. On July 4, in a comfortable suburban home, police found pretty Mrs. Marilyn Sheppard, 31, beaten to death, and her handsome husband, osteopath Samuel Sheppard, 30, injured. Sheppard said he had been clubbed by "a bushy-haired man" as he tried to protect his pregnant wife. Police, however, suggested that his injuries were self-inflicted. An attractive hospital technician, termed by Sheppard a casual friend, admitted intimacies with him.

The case aroused unusual interest. When Sheppard actually went on trial for murder, so many reporters descended on Cleveland that the ordinary citizen was crowded out of the courtroom.

The trial did not quite live up to its advance billing. The prosecution offered 31 witnesses and 244 exhibits designed to prove the guilt of Dr. Sam; the defense countered with 38 witnesses who indicated that he was, at least, not the only possible suspect. After nine weeks of this the jury deliberated five days, finally reached a verdict of second-degree (unpremeditated) murder. Sheppard, sentenced to life imprisonment, would be eligible for parole in ten years.

At year's end public interest was waning, but Sheppard's lawyers were working hard for a new trial.

Another much-headlined murder involved John Francis Roche, 27-year-old plumber's helper who in June gave New York's East Side a brief taste of pure terror. The terror struck when Dorothy Westwater, 14, was found raped, hacked,

IRONY: In checked suit and brandishing cap gun, former New Jersey Governor Harold Hoffman clowns at Circus Saints and Sinners luncheon. Three months later he died, leaving a confession of embezzlement

FIVE DOWN is the visible score as lunatic Howard Ellis, 64, holed up in his home with two guns, resists capture by Indianapolis police. He shot down eight before tear gas, shotguns, submachine guns finally killed him

and beaten (apparently with a saw and a blunt instrument) in a walk-up apartment building. For several days American Legionnaires patrolled the area and most residents stayed home after dark. Then, in another part of the city, John Roche was picked up for driving the wrong way on a one-way street. Police soon found that 1) he had no driver's license, 2) his car was a stolen one, 3) in it were a kitchen saw and a length of pipe. That same night Dorothy Westwater died.

At his trial it was disclosed that Roche had been born with the odds against him. Both his parents became alcoholics and deserted the family; he grew up antisocial, a poor student, soon turned to petty crime. His lawyer defended him on grounds of inability to tell right from wrong. Roche, he said in one of the year's memorable quotes, had "a mind like a scrambled egg". Experts, however, ruled Roche sane. Verdict: death.

The case developed one unexpected side light. When Roche was picked up, one Paul Pfeffer was serving a jail sentence for the 1953 killing of a seaman named Edward Bates. Roche "confessed" to murdering Bates (along with four other persons, including Dorothy Westwater) and Pfeffer was released on bail. A sympathetic public watched as (for fees) Pfeffer proclaimed his innocence on television. The TV appearances stopped when the Bates case was reopened and Pfeffer was reindicted for manslaughter.

One more slaying made big headlines. The victim was 37-year-old William Remington, onetime $10,000-a-year Commerce Department economist. In 1953 he was convicted of perjury (for denying he had given classified data to a Russian spy ring) and sentenced to three years in the federal penitentiary at Lewisburg, Pa. Late in 1954, when Remington's term was half served, someone killed him with a brick wrapped in a stocking. Three fellow convicts were indicted for the murder. A possible motive was robbery.

Coincidentally, three days after Remington's death another convicted perjurer, Alger Hiss, was released from Lewisburg.

Big-Time Embezzlement

Politics also made crime news, following the sudden death of Harold G. Hoffman, Republican Governor of New Jersey from 1937 to 1939.

Hoffman had been a small-town boy with big ideas. Born in 1896 in South Amboy, N.J., he grew up to organize a local bank, become mayor of the town, represent the district as a U.S. congressman. After his term as Governor he was named head of the $600 million State unemployment fund, a $13,500-a-year job he kept right into 1954. Meanwhile he lived comfortably, raised a family, was active in fraternal and veterans' organizations, and boasted a legion of friends in politics, business, and entertainment.

Typical was Hoffman's free-wheeling participation in the famous New York men's club, the Circus Saints and Sinners. This semicharitable group long has held monthly luncheons at which men of national prominence—so-called "fall guys"—are needled by some of Manhattan's sharpest wits for the amusement of the hundreds of assembled guests.

Behind Hoffman's healthy extroversion, however, lay a canker of self-knowledge. Its presence first was hinted at in March, 1954, when New Jersey's incumbent Governor Robert Meyner suspended Hoffman for "misconduct in office". Few knew that Meyner, a Democrat, had begun a sweeping probe of Hoffman's official actions. When the Republican ex-Governor dropped dead in a New York hotel room three months later members of both parties accused Meyner of hounding him to his grave.

Then the truth began to emerge. Hoffman had left a letter for his daughter, Mrs. Ada Hoffman Leonard, to be read only in the event of his death, then destroyed. Mrs. Leonard read it and destroyed it; then with heavy heart she went to Meyner and told him what the letter had said.

Harold Hoffman had not been the carefree politico he seemed. Between 1926 and 1938, he confessed, he had embezzled $300,000 from his own bank in South Amboy (its chief depositor was the State of New Jersey). Half the money had gone for his own expenses ("No poor man should ever get into the field of elective politics," he wrote), half to silence an official, now dead, to whom he admitted his wrongdoing.

The letter paved the way for new revelations. Investigation showed that Hoffman's first embezzlement had led to more and more juggling. The trail led from South Amboy to the State capitol at Trenton, from banks to State offices to various firms that had done business with the State.

Hoffman had favored certain companies; he had kept detailed records of some transactions, none at all of others; he had falsified statements, refused to let his books be examined, involved lesser employees in highly suspect transactions. All told, it appeared that he had played fast and loose with perhaps $16 million in State funds.

Thus in 1954 crime maintained its pace as a growing, and ugly, part of life in America.

STARK DRAMA: James Killimayer, brought to a Long Beach, Calif., police station for questioning in regard to a brutal attack on 3-year-old Mickey Daniels, suddenly is confronted by Mickey herself, who whispers: "He can't hurt me any more now, Mama"

WORLD AFFAIRS

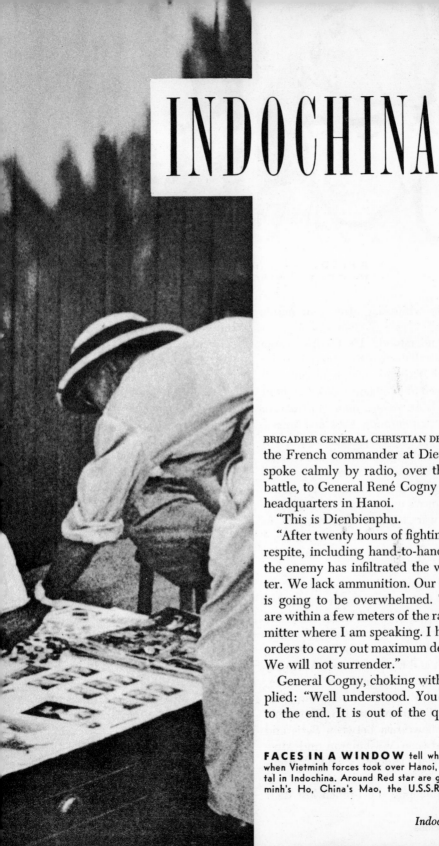

INDOCHINA

BRIGADIER GENERAL CHRISTIAN DE CASTRIES, the French commander at Dienbienphu, spoke calmly by radio, over the roar of battle, to General René Cogny at French headquarters in Hanoi.

"This is Dienbienphu.

"After twenty hours of fighting without respite, including hand-to-hand fighting, the enemy has infiltrated the whole center. We lack ammunition. Our resistance is going to be overwhelmed. The Viets are within a few meters of the radio transmitter where I am speaking. I have given orders to carry out maximum destruction. We will not surrender."

General Cogny, choking with tears, replied: "Well understood. You will fight to the end. It is out of the question to

FACES IN A WINDOW tell what happened when Vietminh forces took over Hanoi, French capital in Indochina. Around Red star are grouped Vietminh's Ho, China's Mao, the U.S.S.R.'s Malenkov

A HERO to his wife (right)—as he is to all the French—General de Castries
kept in touch with her by radiotelephone until just before the fall of Dienbienphu

run up the white flag after your heroic resistance."

"Well understood," De Castries came back. "We will destroy the guns and radio equipment. The radiotelephone link will be destroyed at 1730 hours. We will fight to the end. *Au revoir, mon général. Au revoir, mes camarades. Vive la France.*"

The fall of Dienbienphu, on May 7, was the decisive development of 1954 in international affairs and a turning point in post-World War II history. It undermined France's will to continue its eight-year-old war against Communism in Indochina and caused it to accept a cruel armistice at Geneva, Switzerland, on July 21.

The only major war anywhere in the world was thus ended. But it was ended not in stalemate, as the Korean War had been a year earlier, but in surrender. This was not just a colonial conflict between the French and the pro-French Vietnamese on the one side and, on the other, the pro-Red Vietminh led by the Moscow-trained Communist Ho Chi Minh. It was a showdown between Paris and Peking, between Washington and Moscow, between Democracy and Communism.

At Dienbienphu the French lost their second war within fourteen years and suffered the rudest shock to their morale since their collapse in 1940.

At Dienbienphu there was set in motion a series of events that weakened the alliance of Western nations, bared the defenselessness of Southeast Asia, boosted Red China's prestige sky-high, and, in full view of all the world's fence-sitting neutralists, dealt the democracies their worst blow since the Communist conquest of China.

Doom of Dienbienphu

It was the French rather than the Red-led Vietminh ("League for the Independence of Vietnam") that chose Dienbienphu as the decisive battlefield of the Indochina war. Situated far off in the northwest corner of Vietnam, 180 miles from Hanoi, the metropolis of northern Indochina, it was accessible only by air. The French grabbed the red-mud valley, ringed by jungle-clad hills, on Nov. 20, 1953, in the biggest paratroop landing of the war.

The motto of the French commander in chief, General Navarre, was: "Victory is a woman. She does not give herself except to those who know how to take her."

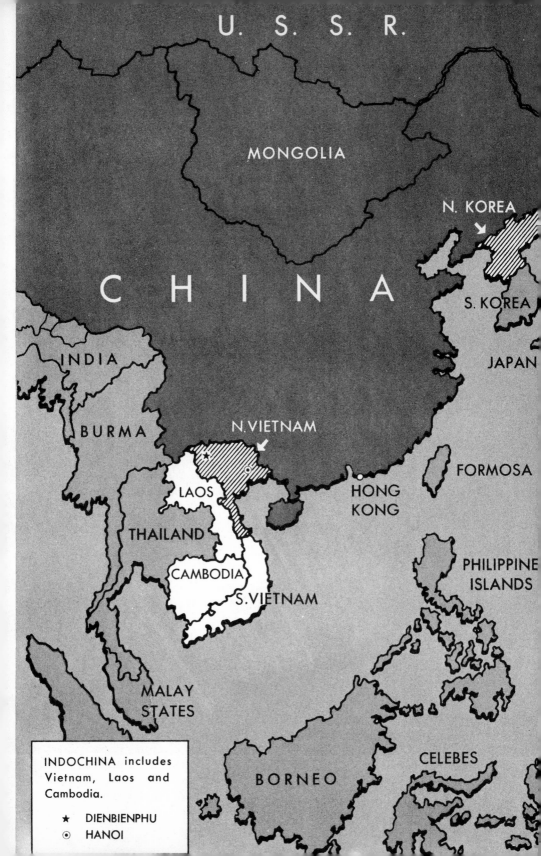

U. S. S. R.

MONGOLIA

N. KOREA

C H I N A

S. KOREA

JAPAN

INDIA

BURMA

N. VIETNAM

FORMOSA

LAOS

HONG
KONG

THAILAND

CAMBODIA

S. VIETNAM

PHILIPPINE
ISLANDS

MALAY
STATES

CELEBES

BORNEO

INDOCHINA includes
Vietnam, Laos and
Cambodia.

★ DIENBIENPHU
⊙ HANOI

MOVING OUT before the Red advance in Indochina, a Catholic peasant pushes two children and worldly goods. Smoke behind him marks bridge burned to slow the enemy

MOVING IN, Vietminh (Communist) veterans of Dienbienphu brandish
bouquets and clap hands in rhythm as they swing triumphantly down Hanoi street

Was the Dienbienphu strategy the way to take her? Some French military men argued that Dienbienphu blockhouses, like Maginot lines, could not assure victory.

Dienbienphu was designed as a padlock to hold the door to the jungle trails forming the Red invasion route to nearby Laos, the least populous of the three Associated States of Indochina. But by hacking out new trails, the Reds bypassed it as easily as the Nazis had bypassed the Maginot Line in 1940.

Dienbienphu was to be a point of leverage from which the French could apply guerrilla tactics against the Vietminh. But the Vietminh were masters of such tactics, and, by laying siege to Dienbienphu, they changed the point of leverage into a place of imprisonment.

Dienbienphu, moreover, was intended to goad the Vietminh into a frontal assault against a supposedly impregnable stronghold. In this it was spectacularly successful. But the wrong side won.

The Reds' boyish-faced commander, General Vo Nguyen Giap, picked up the gauntlet. Through December, through January, through February, he moved four of his six regular divisions—40,000 men—on foot from the Hanoi delta area to the Dienbienphu perimeter. Antlike swarms of coolies kept them supplied. French bombers, although unchallenged in the air, could not cut the columns of men marching over the jungle trails.

Stripping the rest of Indochina of crack troops, the French flew into Dienbienphu the cream of their army—all nine of their paratroop battalions, one third of their Foreign Legionnaires (mostly Germans), tough Moroccan *goumiers*, jet-black Senegalese, lithe Vietnamese—15,000 men in all. But air transport could not compete with the Reds' foot transport.

The United States, heeding French pleas, rushed 250 air force technicians to Indochina for the noncombatant task of repairing France's American-built aircraft. Red guerrillas gave them plenty of work. One drizzling night, twelve C-47 transports were time-bombed at Hanoi's airport.

On Feb. 18, the Big Four conference of American, British, French, and Soviet Foreign Ministers meeting in Berlin agreed to discuss "the problem of restoring peace to Indochina" at Geneva beginning April 26. Before April the Dienbienphu battle had been joined. Seeking peace with honor, Premier Joseph Laniel laid down France's war aim: "Negotiation". Seeking victory by force of arms, the Vietminh aimed to crush Dienbienphu and thereby make the war-weary French accept peace at any price.

The Battle Begins

Round One began on March 13.

General Giap unleashed the Reds' biggest artillery bombardment of the war. Commanding high ground surrounding Dienbienphu, they rained one shell every five seconds down onto the saucer-shaped valley, only 6 miles long by 4 miles wide.

Their firepower caught De Castries by surprise. Battery upon battery of anti-aircraft artillery and 105- and 155-mm. howitzers had been brought down from China by 1000 Soviet-supplied Molotova trucks, driven by Chinese Army personnel, over a new road hacked out by Vietminh coolies. Many of the guns had been captured from the U.S. in Korea.

Advised by a score of Chinese Communist technicians, the Vietminh sought to submerge the French garrison in a human sea. Red suicide troops pushed up explosives in carts or strapped explosives to their bodies to blast through the French fortifications. "The barbed-wire entanglements disappeared under heaps of corpses," one French officer said. The whole valley smelled of death.

From outpost Béatrice (De Castries named his strong points after his old sweethearts), a Foreign Legionnaire reported: "We had trouble angling our guns low enough to hit them. We threw grenades down, but they kept on climbing like monkeys." Finally the Legionnaires ordered their supporting artillery: "Fire on top of us." Béatrice was gone. So was Gabrielle.

"Surrender or die," Red loud-speakers ordered in French, German, Arabic, and Vietnamese. "Come and get us," the French forces yelled through megaphones.

By March 17—four days later—Dienbienphu's two airstrips were useless. Their artillery-spotting planes were gone. Henceforth the French could supply their stronghold only by parachute, and the Reds' radar-controlled antiaircraft, operated by Chinese Communist troops, made even parachute drops hazardous. Many of the parachuted supplies fell into Communist hands. No longer could the French evacuate their wounded, including hundreds of amputees. They just lay in open trenches.

The Angel of Dienbienphu

The Reds even fired at ambulance planes. Thus they marooned at Dienbienphu a lone woman—Lieutenant Geneviève de Galard-Terraube. Nurse, parachutist, and pilot, she sent this radio message to her mother: "The boys have invited me to stay for the siege."

Geneviève de Galard spent her 29th birthday under fire and was nicknamed the "Angel of Dienbienphu". Just before the end, De Castries pinned the Legion of Honor on her blood-stained uniform. He kissed both her cheeks, saying: "The entire garrison wishes it could do the same."

Round Two began on March 30.

Again the Reds threw huge and terrible masses of manpower and firepower against the shrinking stronghold. "I am still the master of the situation," De Castries radioed Hanoi. "The morale of the men is magnificent."

But Dienbienphu's situation was soon desperate. De Castries was reported to have ordered: "I expect all the troops to die at the positions assigned to them rather than retreat an inch."

The French government promoted De Castries from colonel to brigadier general, as it had been needled to do by ex-General Dwight D. Eisenhower.

The Commander at Dienbienphu

General de Castries was as much a soldier of fortune as were most of his men. If he wore all the eighteen citations to his Croix de Guerre, his ribbon would hang as far as his knees. In the middle of battle he calmly radioed Hanoi, where his blond second wife Jacqueline was nursing the wounded: "If you see my wife, give her a kiss for me." Again he radioed her: "Send me razor blades and shaving cream. Everything is *formidable*."

A swashbuckling fighting man of 51, De Castries was said by his Moroccan troops to have *baraka* (heavenly protection). A distant kin to Lafayette, the eagle-beaked general liked wine, women, and horses. He once held the world equestrian records for both broad and high jumps. Captured by the Germans when badly wounded during World War II, he three times tried and failed to escape. The fourth time he got away, went back into battle, and was again wounded.

Now there was no escape from Dienbienphu. General de Castries tried to break out of the Red trap. It was too

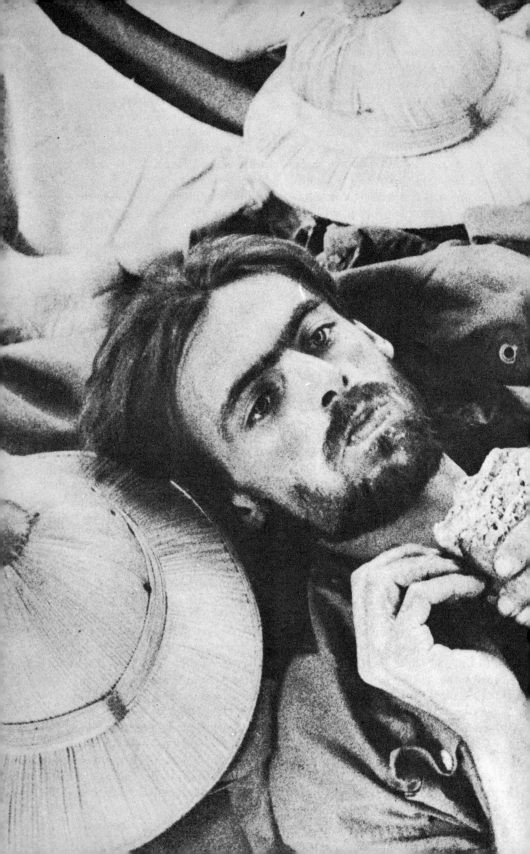

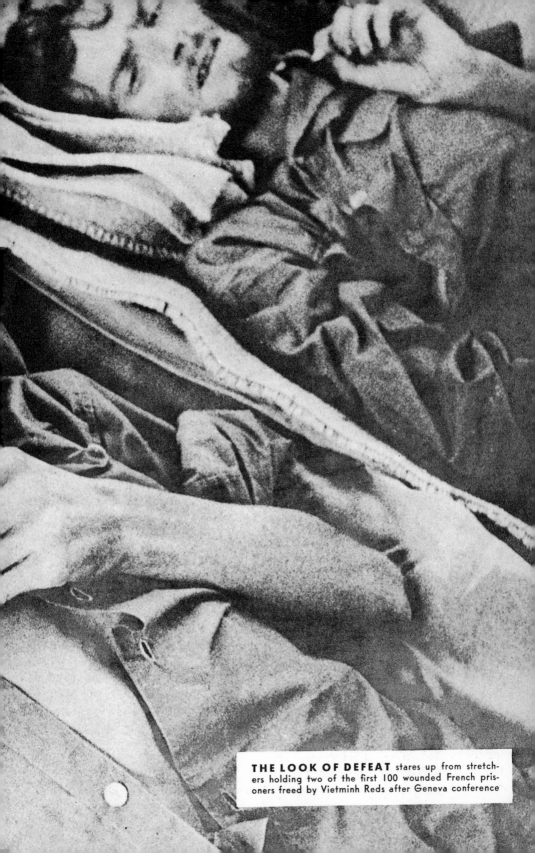

THE LOOK OF DEFEAT stares up from stretchers holding two of the first 100 wounded French prisoners freed by Vietminh Reds after Geneva conference

tight. Still he vowed: "I'm going to kick General Giap's teeth in."

Soon his garrison was squeezed into a single square mile, his remaining tanks bogged down in the mud, half of his artillery knocked out, his airpower blinded by the rains. He got a few reinforcements, who volunteered to jump into battle although they had never parachuted before. A U.S. airlift of French paratroopers in C-124 Globemasters from France and North Africa, forced by Prime Minister Jawaharlal Nehru's objections to bypass India, was both too little and too late.

The U.S. rushed 9000 armored vests from Korea. The French did not drop them on Dienbienphu, lest they be worn by more Vietminh than French soldiers.

So deadly was the Red attack that two American civilian pilots were killed when their supply-dropping C-119 Flying Boxcar was shot down. They were James B. McGovern Jr., a fabulous 250-pounder known as "Earthquake McGoon", and Wallace A. Buford. Both were on the payroll of the Civil Air Transport outfit headed by U.S. Major General Claire Chennault, World War II commander of the Flying Tigers in China.

Was it too late to save Dienbienphu?

French S.O.S.

On the eve of the Geneva conference, General Navarre notified Paris, which in turn notified Washington and London, that the stronghold would soon collapse—and with it the whole French position in Indochina—unless it was saved by massive air attacks, such as only the U.S. and Britain could mount.

In the U.S., such air attacks would require an OK from Congress. Secretary of State John Foster Dulles had been calling for "united action" in Southeast Asia, but on April 25 the British Cabinet, in its first Sunday session in seven years, de-cided that nothing now could save Dienbienphu. Without Britain's partnership, the U.S. felt that it could do little.

Round Three began a week later.

Before long it was being fought in the monsoon rains on a sodden battlefield no bigger than Yankee Stadium. For the coup de grâce, the Reds used Russian-made "Stalin Organ" rocket launchers. The French strong points were crushed in turn—Huguette, Dominique, Claudine, Elaine, and the isolated Isabelle to the south.

One of De Castries' subordinates asked: "We can keep on fighting for only ten more minutes—should we surrender?" The General replied: "Keep on fighting for ten more minutes."

After radioing farewell, De Castries instructed Isabelle's only two remaining guns to shoot at his own sand-bagged command post Junon. From the air, French pilots saw the end: A flash of knives, a burst of grenades, a flailing of iron and wooden clubs, "like a spectacle of wild beasts in a Roman amphitheater".

The rest was silence—the silence of the graveyard. Some 5000 French Union troops lay dead; 9000 men and the lone woman were taken prisoner. The Reds lost perhaps 8000 killed and 12,000 wounded. But General Giap's Red headquarters boasted: "The victory is complete. The French garrison and its commander are captured."

General Navarre issued this Order of the Day: "After 56 days of continuing combat, submerged by numbers, by odds of 5 to 1, the garrison has had to end its fight . . . The enemy, thanks to Chinese Communist assistance, was suddenly able to start a form of modern warfare entirely new to Indochina.

"**ANGEL**" of Dienbienphu, Geneviève de Galard —still wearing a parachutist's suit—is "crowned" during a post-truce reunion with former comrades

"The defenders of Dienbienphu have written an epic. . . . The fight continues."

Collapse of the Delta

How long would the fight continue? In terms of military strategy, the French had lost a battle but had not lost the war. In terms of the will to win, the French had lost everything.

The Vietminh moved in for the kill. Hardly waiting to flesh out their own decimated divisions, they about-faced from Dienbienphu toward the Hanoi delta. Over Route Coloniale 41, they shuttled spearhead troops by Molotova trucks. They blackmailed the French into calling off air attacks in order to permit them "to evacuate our wounded and your own healthy prisoners of war".

The P.O.W.'s had to walk. Their death march stretched 500 miles, lasted 56 days. Five hundred died of dysentery, malaria, and starvation.

General Paul Ely, France's Chief of Staff, flew to Indochina to see what, if anything, could save the situation. His top-secret report was that more Dienbienphus, bigger Dienbienphus, were threatening. The best French troops were lost. The rest were demoralized. The pro-French Vietnamese troops were shaky.

All France could do, Ely said, was to pull back its dispersed forces and try to defend only the Red River delta around Hanoi and the Mekong River delta around Saigon. Otherwise, the French troops would be massacred. He asked Paris to rush 40 to 50 battalions of reinforcements and, for the first time, to send draftees to fight in Indochina. He also urged that General Navarre be replaced as commander in chief by Marshal Alphonse Juin, the Central European commander for the North Atlantic Treaty Organization. Juin refused to take the job.

Ely himself became Indochina's eighth commander within eight years. He was soft-spoken and shy. His face was painfully lined. Now 56, he had been wounded twice in World War I and again in World War II. In the latter, he fought as a colonel in the French underground, shuttling back and forth across the English Channel. A bullet had cut nerves in his right arm. He had to salute with his left.

Vietnam also got a new Premier to try to instill some vigor into its apathetic people, many of whom preferred Communism to French colonialism. Fun-loving Chief of State Bao Dai, who was sunning himself on the far-off Riviera, replaced his cousin, Prince Buu Loc, with an unquestionably nationalistic leader, Ngo Dinh Diem (pronounced *no din zim*).

Premier Diem, an ascetic bachelor of 53, was a devout Catholic. For four years he had exiled himself from Indochina. He had lived at times at a Maryknoll Seminary in New Jersey, at a Benedictine monastery in Belgium, and most recently in an obscure Paris hotel. He had never collaborated with either Communists or French colonists. Now he flew home to take over. His policy: Only full independence, without partition, for all of Vietnam could save his country. However high his principles, he proved inexperienced and ineffectual.

Too Little and Too Late

It was already too late. Although General Ely ordered an all-out defense of the Hanoi delta, it was as soggy as its paddy fields. The French had only 65,000 frontline troops to defend this vital area, one of the most densely populated in the world, against the 100,000 Vietminh guerrillas inside their 250-mile perimeter.

Of the delta's 6400 villages, 3300 were known to be held by the Reds, and only

1200 by the French. The rest were held by either or neither side or by both.

Even Hanoi's 60-mile lifeline to its port of Haiphong, along Route Coloniale 5 and a parallel railroad, was mined and ditched every night. By day French convoys had to fight their way through.

To safeguard this lifeline, the French had to give up one third of the delta without a fight, without even burning bridges or blowing up mill machinery. In this "strategic retreat", they surrendered to Communism, not a worthless dust bowl like Dienbienphu, but 1500 square miles of rice-rich lands, the key fortress of Phuly, the delta's third-largest city, Namdinh, and 3,000,000 people—including 1,000,000 Catholics, the most anti-Communist of all the Vietnamese.

Cease-Fire at Geneva

At 3:50 A.M. on July 21, in the far-off Palais des Nations at Geneva, two obscure generals, one representing France, the other the Vietminh, signed a 5000-word document. It put an end to the Indochinese war, a war that had been going on since Dec. 19, 1946, and that had lasted longer than World War II and twice as long as the war in Korea.

The war's cost in casualties on both sides totaled 800,000. The French Union suffered 234,000 casualties—92,000 dead (19,000 from France itself), 114,000 wounded, and 28,000 prisoners.

The war's cost in money and matériel was equally staggering. It cost the French $5 billion. By the end the United States was defraying 78 percent of the expense. It had long since delivered 175,000 rifles and machine guns, 1400 tanks and armored vehicles, 21,000 trucks, 360 aircraft, 390 warships—in vain.

But the cost of peace was even higher. The peace treaty signed at Geneva turned over half of Vietnam to Communism, sur-rendered the Hanoi area, and as scant consolation left Laos and Cambodia free. In detail, the treaty provided for:

(1) The partition of Vietnam at roughly the 17th parallel.

Thus the Iron Curtain fell over Vietnam's richer northern half—over 12,000,000 people, over 77,000 square miles, over the Red River's rice bowl, over the biggest coal mines in Southeast Asia, over vast resources of iron, tin, tungsten, manganese, and phosphates. The 17th parallel was hardly a line defensible against future Red drives.

(2) The regrouping of all French forces south of the 17th parallel and all Vietminh forces north of it, together with the transfer of all civilians who wished to move north or south. The French had to evacuate Hanoi within 80 days and Haiphong within 300.

Not all the troops commanded by the French went south with them. As many as 800 Vietnamese soldiers, sometimes whole companies, deserted to the Vietminh in a single day. Many of the civilians who moved south were Red agents in disguise.

Not all the Vietminh forces went north. Many were ordered to bury their weapons and go underground.

(3) The prohibition against sending into Vietnam any reinforcements in men or matériel and against building new military bases there.

These clauses blocked the creation of an anti-Communist bastion in the French half of Vietnam.

(4) The holding of free elections for an all-Vietnamese government before July 20, 1956.

Barring a miracle, the vote probably would turn over the entire state to the Vietminh. For South Vietnam was defeatist and demoralized, its people apathetic, its government disorganized, its army riddled by disloyalty.

"It is an anguished peace," General Ely admitted. "Many deaths for nothing."

On his release by his Red captors, General de Castries, haggard and half-starved, dissolved into tears. "Excuse me, it's foolish," he blurted. "But I cannot control my emotion."

In obedience to the armistice terms, a single French bugler sounded taps in Hanoi on Oct. 8 as the French bade farewell to this brightest jewel of their colonial empire. In the pouring rain, the Tricolor was lowered for the last time after 81 years. Soldiers wept. A French colonel observed: "We shall never come back. My heart is heavy as I think of the great heritage we are abandoning."

As French tanks pulled out, green-clad Vietminh troops paraded in—in sneakers—while Molotova trucks hauled in U.S.-made artillery pieces captured at Dienbienphu.

Everywhere the Vietminh's red flags with golden stars were broken out. One Red flag was flown over a statue of the Virgin Mary in front of the Roman Catholic Cathedral. Photographs of Red leaders Ho Chi Minh (North Vietnam), Mao Tse-tung (China), and Georgi M. Malenkov (Soviet Union) appeared. So did Communist doves of peace. Banners read: "President Ho for 10,000 Years!" Ho himself moved into the French governor general's palace.

By the end of 1954, the Red grip was unshakable. The Vietminh even made the clocks run on Peking time. It also doubled its armed forces in defiance of the armistice terms. Although half a million Vietnamese fled from Communist control to the French half of their unhappy land, no one could tell how long even South Vietnam would remain free.

THE WAR IS OVER, but in Indochina military cemetery, where French and Vietnamese are buried side by side, widows and children still weep

CONFERENCES

THE DIPLOMATIC STORY OF 1954 WAS A tale of six cities—Berlin, Geneva, Brussels, Manila, London, and Paris.

At Berlin, a "Siberian cold" from the Soviet steppes brought swirling snows and 9.5° temperatures on Jan. 25, 1954. It also brought a frigid atmosphere to the seventh session of the Big Four Council of Foreign Ministers—the first held since 1949 and the first in the era of the H-bomb. The West expected no settlement with the Soviets. It obtained none.

The Big Four's task was to try to unite Germany, which was still divided into Western and Soviet zones, and to make formal peace with Austria, which their troops still occupied. They met alternately in West and East Berlin.

In West Berlin, the American, British, French, and Soviet Foreign Ministers assembled in the 500-room Hohenzollern Palace beneath a garish painting of the Last Judgment. There the Angel Gabriel trumpeted doom as death sentences were pronounced on the Germans who plotted to assassinate Adolf Hitler during World War II.

East Berlin Sessions

In East Berlin, the Big Four met in the spanking new Soviet Embassy. Some Western diplomats were so cold in the building that they turned up their collars. They were also so afraid of hidden microphones that they did not discuss secrets, even in private. Instead they swapped written notes and pocketed these to burn later.

Soviet Foreign Minister Vyacheslav M. Molotov gallantly guided Janet Dulles, wife of the U.S. Secretary of State, through the Embassy's Hall of Mirrors, with its pink marble columns and circular pine table.

"This, madam, is where your husband gives me so much trouble," Molotov said.

"I am sure you can hold your own," Mrs. Dulles rejoined.

Her host protested: "After all, I am alone against three of them."

Molotov's manner, for once, was mellow. He even let his poker face relax into a smile. No longer did he live up to the nickname "Stone Bottom" that his Soviet colleagues used behind his back.

Molotov's aim was to split French Foreign Minister Georges Bidault from Secretary Dulles and British Foreign Secretary Anthony Eden. He wanted to wreck the North Atlantic Treaty Organization (N.A.T.O.) and to kill the European Defense Community (E.D.C.). E.D.C. was to embody an intricate plan for a European Army containing rearmed West German as well as French, Italian, Belgian, Netherlands, and Luxembourg units.

On the issue of Germany, Molotov ridiculed the West's plan for German unification based on free all-German elections. Instead he asked for a united but neutralized Germany, which would not be allowed to conduct genuinely free elections.

He proposed an "all-European system of collective security" to replace both E.D.C. and N.A.T.O. Along with Communist China, the United States would be relegated to the role of "observer". At this preposterous idea, one American diplomat laughed. The other Americans, Britons, and Frenchmen joined in. The Soviet Foreign Minister grew "redder".

On the issue of Austria, Molotov even rejected the West's acceptance of the Kremlin's own long-standing terms for a formal peace treaty. He insisted on keeping Soviet troops in Austria indefinitely pending the realization of his often-expressed "wish" for a German peace treaty. Dulles likened this idea to "a rather peculiar sandwich", with tasty words enclosing "some poisonous proposals".

Thus the Berlin conference proved that the Kremlin had no intention of relaxing its grip on Germany and Austria or of thawing out the cold war. As Dulles put it: "We brought Mr. Molotov to show Russia's hand. It was seen as a hand that held fast to everything it had . . . and also sought to grab some more."

France's Bidault, planning strategy with Dulles and Eden before many of the meetings, helped his Anglo-American allies block Molotov's move to split the Western alliance. But once the issue of Indochina came up, Bidault was caught. In view of the French yearning for peace, he had to consent to meet again, this time with Red China represented, to discuss Far Eastern problems.

The Berlin conference broke up on Feb. 18. Its only agreement: to take up, on April 26 at Geneva, "a peaceful settlement of the Korean question" and "the problem of restoring peace in Indochina".

Geneva Debacle

The Palais des Nations, overlooking Lake Geneva in Switzerland, stood as a gleaming white monument to the pre-World War II futility of the League of Nations and to its inability to stop aggression. As the world's eyes turned again to the Palais in April, 1954, its maroon-carpeted chambers were darkened by the shadow of doomed Dienbienphu.

What the Communists sought at Geneva was unconditional surrender in Indochina.

What the West wanted there was peace —as honorable as possible.

By the time the conference opened, the West's front, united at Berlin, had disintegrated. The French had made an eleventh-hour bid for Anglo-American air strikes to save Dienbienphu. But their allies had shied away. The U.S. and Britain had pressed France to ratify E.D.C.

before Geneva. But Paris had procrastinated.

Now came what *The London Economist* called "the first full-scale incursion into the diplomatic world of the new species of Peking man".

Communist China's Premier and Foreign Minister, Chou En-lai, flew into Geneva like a conqueror. His entourage was the biggest of all. He was prepared to stay, if necessary, the full six months of his lease at Montfleury, a twenty-room lakeside villa ringed by magnolias and barbed wire. Even Molotov took notes when Chou spoke.

"The United States is isolated here," a Chinese Communist spokesman boasted. Secretary Dulles never spoke to the Red Chinese, whom Washington refused to recognize. Neither did he shake hands with Chou nor look at him. He joked that he would meet the Chinese Premier only if their autos crashed. After a single week at Geneva, he flew home. Under Secretary of State Walter Bedell Smith took over.

The Reds stalled and stalled, pending the collapse of Dienbienphu. They cold-shouldered Bidault's desperate pleas for a mercy truce to evacuate the French wounded. In the first dozen days, they agreed on nothing more than to seat the delegations counterclockwise in French alphabetical order.

When Dienbienphu fell on May 7, cases of wine were trucked into the Vietminh delegation's Geneva headquarters. Glasses were clinked to toast the Red victory. The laughter was raucous.

The Vietminh, with their Chinese mentors, sought French surrender of all Indochina. On June 8 Molotov made it plain that that was the Kremlin's aim also.

The Soviet Foreign Minister was savage. He taunted the French government on its "still increasing losses". He scoffed:

IN LONDON, British Foreign Minister Anthony Eden leaves 10 Downing Street with his boss, Prime Minister Churchill, and an American caller, State Secretary John Foster Dulles

"The defense of Dienbienphu was in the main carried out not by the French but by all kinds of foreigners."

Molotov's words in Geneva proved that the Reds would not make peace with the existing French government in Paris. As a result, Premier Joseph Laniel's Cabinet fell. Laniel was replaced by a peace-minded Premier, Pierre Mendès-France.

Amid all the commotion over Indochina, the simultaneous peace talks on Korea were scarcely noticed. After getting nowhere, they were broken off by the sixteen United Nations allies on June 15. The reason: The Reds were no more willing in Korea than in Germany to agree to free elections to unite a divided land.

What really revived Geneva's prospects was the pledge of the new Premier Mendès-France to obtain a cease-fire by July 20 or resign. He invited Chou to join him over orange juice at the French Embassy in Bern, Switzerland. His conclusion: "This conversation gives reason for hope that the Geneva conference can produce happy results."

Four weeks of tough bargaining fol-

IN NEW DELHI, Indian Prime Minister Jawaharlal Nehru (left) shares ice cream— and some high-level conversation — with Red China's visiting Premier Chou En-lai

lowed before an armistice agreement was signed at Geneva.

The U.S. refused to honor the Geneva debacle with its signature. But it promised to refrain from the threat or use of force to disturb the cease-fire.

Brussels Blow

On the battlefield of Waterloo, on the outskirts of Brussels, capital of Belgium, lay buried the wreckage of Napoleon's drive to unite Europe under the leadership of France. Now, at a new international conference beginning on Aug. 19, Brussels became the graveyard for the dream of uniting France and Germany within a six-nation European Defense Community.

This conference rang the death knell on two years of diplomacy that had begun with the signing of the E.D.C. treaty in Paris on May 27, 1952. The treaty had been conceived by French diplomats, but it had never been ratified by France. Now, knowing that it would never be ratified in its existing form, Mendès-France came up with twenty-nine pages of amendments to make it acceptable to the French Assembly. His would-be allies preferred to see it dead rather than crippled.

"The only regulation really missing," West Germany's *Düsseldorfer Nachrichten* editorialized, "is one requiring German soldiers to turn in their rifles every evening."

"I could have put E.D.C. as it stood to a vote," Mendès-France said at Brussels. "But I am convinced it would have failed. The fact that I have re-examined the problem proves, I hope, that I am a European and a partisan of European union."

France's five E.D.C. partners felt the Mendès amendments were "a stab in the back of European unity". The U.S. told the French Premier they meant the end of E.D.C. The State Department cabled the British Foreign Office: "France cannot be counted on as a reliable partner able to reach decisions."

For three days the Brussels debates raged. After the military catastrophe in Indochina, a weakened France simply was not willing to submerge its uniformed forces in a supranational European army.

The sole agreement that the six-nation communiqué could report on Aug. 22 was this: "Despite a long discussion [we] were unable to reach agreement."

The Brussels deadlock made it inevitable that the French Assembly, as Mendès predicted, would kill E.D.C. It did so on Aug. 30. "A gigantic victory for Soviet diplomacy," said one European diplomat.

Manila Comeback

The sultry city of Manila, which still wore the scars of World War II, became the birthplace of the first collective-security system against Communist imperialism in the Far East.

On Sept. 6, eight "like-minded" nations, from both East and West, sent Foreign Ministers or deputies to Manila to find some way of saying to Moscow and Peking: "This far and no farther."

Within three days, they agreed upon a unique alliance. On Sept. 8 they signed with gold pens in alphabetical order: Australia, France, New Zealand, Pakistan, the Philippines, Thailand, the United Kingdom, and the United States.

The official title of the alliance was Southeast Asia Collective Defense Treaty. But the initials S.E.A.C.D.T. were unpronounceable. Over cocktails, Secretary Dulles suggested: "Why not call it the Manila Pact?" The label stuck.

The Manila Pact pledged each member to regard an armed attack in Southeast Asia as endangering "its own peace nd safety". However, this pledge was less binding than the N.A.T.O. formula of automatic action against any aggressor. One Pentagon official debunked it as "a nonmilitary alliance". Another confessed: "We cannot do much more than paste a Band-Aid across the gaping wounds of Asia."

An unusual pledge, against Red subversion from within as well as Red attack from without, also was included. It bound the Manila powers, in case of a subversive threat, to "consult immediately".

The Manila powers agreed, furthermore, to regard a threat to Indochina as a threat to themselves.

A Pacific Charter also was signed. This document pledged the Manila powers to "strive by every peaceful means to promote the self-government and to secure the independence of all countries whose people desire it and are able to undertake its responsibilities".

Secretary Dulles hailed the Manila Pact as an Asian "Monroe Doctrine". Radio Peking called it an "elaborate hocus-pocus" and a "U.S.-made yoke". Prime Minister Jawaharlal Nehru of India thought it "very unfortunate" that "Asian problems, Asian security, and Asian peace" were being taken care of "chiefly by non-Asian powers".

But both the Communists and the neutralists now felt that the free world would not bury its head in the sand in case of new Red threats in the Far East.

London Success

In the same majestic room in which Chopin had played mazurkas for Queen Victoria, the Foreign Ministers of nine Western powers sat down on Sept. 28 around a hollow oblong table covered with blue felt.

Anthony Eden, who had convoked the conference at Lancaster House in Lon-

don, opened it by saying: "This is a conference which must succeed." Its job was to find a workable substitute for the dead E.D.C.

There was real hope for action, largely because of Eden himself. Following the breakup of the Brussels conference, he had made a 2000-mile flying tour to visit the Foreign Ministers of the six E.D.C. nations. He had sold them on the idea of refurbishing the 1948 Brussels Alliance, linking Britain, France and the Benelux nations (Belgium, the Netherlands, and Luxembourg), and using it as an E.D.C. substitute.

Although the original Brussels Alliance was designed for collective defense against Germany, Eden's idea was to include both West Germany and Italy in the new alliance for collective defense against Russia.

Britain's Pledge

To put over his plan, Eden came up at London with a precedent-shattering pledge not to pull Britain's powerful land and air forces from the Continent, where they acted as a shield against the Red army, without the OK of the Brussels Treaty allies.

"Britain's guarantee will rejoice the heart of France," Mendès-France said jubilantly.

An agreement in principle was embodied in the Final Act of London, signed on Oct. 3. The three epoch-making decisions, although made necessary by France's rejection of E.D.C., were in many ways much more advantageous to West Germany than E.D.C. would have been.

(1) N.A.T.O.: West Germany, which would have been barred from N.A.T.O. under the old E.D.C. formula, now would be admitted. Bonn would contribute the same 12 divisions, 1500 aircraft, and 500,-

WORLD TRAVELERS: British Labourite leader Clement Attlee—a 1954 visitor to Red China—absorbs a reporter's question. Right: Chou is festooned with flowers in New Delhi during his triumphal tour of Asia while Geneva conference meetings are in recess

000 men as it would have done under E.D.C. These forces, like all other N.A.T.O. continental units, would be placed under the command of U.S. General Alfred M. Gruenther, as Supreme Allied Commander in Europe.

(2) W.E.U.: The Brussels Alliance (to be called Western European Union or W.E.U.) would be empowered to limit each member's national army to a maximum size and to prevent Britain's withdrawal from the Continent.

(3) Sovereignty: West Germany would be granted full sovereignty, instead of limited sovereignty under E.D.C. The U.S., Britain, and France would end the occupation. West Germany was pledged not to employ force to change its borders and not to manufacture "ABC" (atomic, bacteriological, and chemical) weapons.

Paris Clincher

The Château de la Celle-St.-Cloud near Versailles was a onetime royal love nest. There King Louis XV had dallied with the Marquise de Pompadour. To that historic mansion, now owned by the French Republic, Premier Mendès-France invited West Germany's Chancellor Konrad Adenauer on Oct. 19. One French diplomat said "it should provide the right atmosphere" for Franco-German rapprochement.

The Mendès-Adenauer get-together was designed to remove the last big stumbling block—a Franco-German dispute over the Saar—to be surmounted before the London agreement was put into the precise form of diplomatic contracts.

But the château's atmosphere worked no wonders. For the Saar basin, with its coal-rich 900 square miles and its 1,000,-000 German-speaking and beer-drinking people, was an age-old barrier between France and Germany.

It had been detached from Germany after World War I and placed under the League of Nations. It had voted to rejoin Hitler's Germany in 1935. After World War II, it had been made a self-governing territory, economically united with France.

Mendès' Warning

Before an open fire in the small château Mendès warned that, unless Germany gave up all claims on the Saar, he would not approve any of the pending documents to implement the Final Act of London. No Saar, no signature.

All week long the French and Germans haggled over the Saar. One Mendès-Adenauer meeting lasted until 3 A.M., amid piles of scattered paper on the floor and mounds of cigar and cigarette ashes overflowing from the ash trays.

Only one hour before the scheduled signing of all the various documents on Oct. 23 was a Saar settlement reached. Chancellor Adenauer made most of the concessions. In essence, he agreed that,

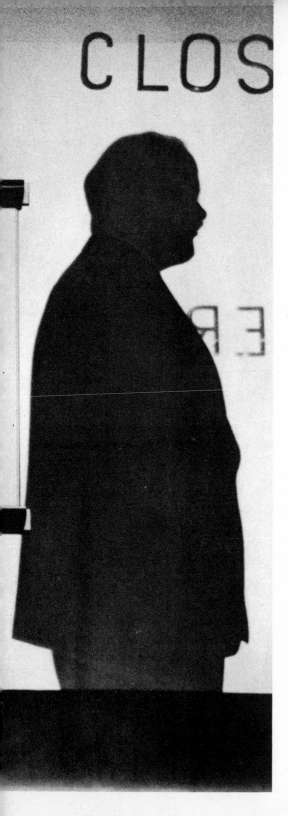

subject to plebiscite, the Saar should remain an economic province of France and become a political ward of the new Western European Union.

Thus was the go-ahead given for a whole series of autographing ceremonies. In the baroque "Clock Room" of the Quai d'Orsay, as attendants moved the bulky papers to and fro with the sort of rakes used by Monte Carlo croupiers, were signed the documents creating the Western European Union and restoring Germany's sovereignty.

At N.A.T.O. headquarters in the modernistic Palais de Chaillot, in the shadow of the Eiffel Tower, were signed the papers making West Germany the fifteenth member of N.A.T.O.

"Everything, including the Saar, has been signed, sealed, and delivered," Secretary Dulles cabled President Eisenhower.

Now the Western allies pushed the Paris protocols through to ratification despite political opposition in both France and West Germany. Before the end of the year, the all-important lower houses of the British, German, Italian, and French parliaments had signified their approval of the documents.

Thus the diplomatic story of 1954 proved to be the story of how, united at Berlin, the Western diplomats stood up to the Kremlin; of how, divided at Geneva and Brussels, they scuttled their position in Indochina and scrapped their defense plan for Western Europe; and of how, just when they appeared to be losing the cold war against Communism, they saved the day at Manila, London, and Paris by forging a new alliance in Southeast Asia and by inviting a rearmed West Germany into the North Atlantic alliance.

OMINOUS SHADOW of Russian Foreign Minister Molotov looms in Geneva as he walks to join French-Chinese talks that ended Indochina war

LAST CASUALTY in Indochina,
a corporal killed by machine-gun fire,
lies in a military cemetery under the
French flag, guarded by Legionnaires

FOURTEEN NATIONS in the North Atlantic Treaty Organization are represented in Paris' Palais de Chaillot at meeting to admit Germany to N.A.T.O. At right: Britain's Eden, America's Dulles. Background: The Eiffel Tower

Belgium   Canada   Denmark   France   Iceland   Italy

mbourg   **Netherlands**   **Norway**   **Portugal**   **Turkey**   **United Kingdom**   **United States**

FRANCE

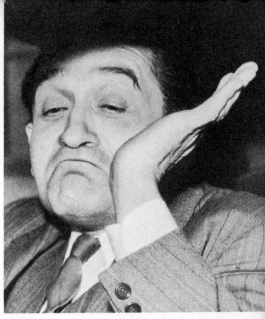

FRANCE'S MAN OF 1954 was Premier Pierre Mendès-France. Even though he prefers milk to wine (note bottle on his desk at Foreign Office, left), Mendès won French hearts through his courage, determination, and industry. Constantly on the move, he kisses his wife at airport, greets the press (above), and sleeps, while the Anthony Edens chat, on plane returning him to Geneva conference

ANGRY VETERANS of Indochina fighting riot against bareheaded Defense Minister René Pleven after popular Marshal Alphonse Juin was removed from his post for criticizing European Army plan

AS THE FRENCH MOTTO GOES, WATER IS FOR washing, milk is for infants, tea is for invalids, coffee is for Americans, but wine is for Frenchmen.

The French live by that motto. They consume more alcohol per capita than any other nation. Their alcohol industry takes 10 percent of the national income, supports 14 percent of the people, and is blamed, directly or indirectly, for 40 percent of both accidents and deaths.

France's 1954 man of change, Premier Mendès-France, although not a teetotaler, drank milk. He drank milk at the rostrum of the National Assembly, at his desk in the French Foreign Ministry, at a steak lunch with President Eisenhower, at a white-tie dinner with Secretary Dulles. When he drank milk at his Radical Socialist Party's convention, he urged everyone to do the same.

This untypical Frenchman, brought to power by the disaster at Dienbienphu, lived by this slogan: "To govern is to choose." He chose to end the Indochina war, to grant new freedom to France's North African empire, to revolutionize the French economy, even to stem the alarming rise in alcoholism. Instead of E.D.C., he chose another means of re-arming France's traditional enemies, the Germans.

Laniel: *Immobilisme*

Over France's head, as 1954 opened, hung Secretary Dulles' threat of an "agonizing reappraisal" of America's policy of defending Western Europe if France did not ratify E.D.C. But the policy of Joseph Laniel, then Premier, was *immobilisme*. His purpose was to stay in power as long as possible. Dodging an E.D.C. showdown helped. A wealthy, stolid Norman, he was a conservative Independent. Left-wing opponents dubbed him "Mr. Interim".

Months passed. E.D.C. not only was not ratified, it did not even come to a vote.

Too many Frenchmen balked at E.D.C.'s curbs on France's sovereignty, or shied away from provoking the Kremlin lest it block a cease-fire in Indochina, or distrusted or hated the Germans, or simply did not want to choose.

The impetuous Alphonse Juin, at 65 France's only living Marshal and its most respected soldier, brought the issue into sharp focus. After a secret tête-à-tête with France's World War II hero, General Charles de Gaulle, Marshal Juin, although slated to command the European Army as N.A.T.O.'s commander for Central Europe, openly proposed that E.D.C. be scrapped.

Laniel summoned Juin to the Hôtel Matignon, the Premier's residence, to explain. The Marshal did not appear. The Premier sent another summons, in writing.

"Another day," the Marshal replied. "I will not be called on the carpet like a simple bugler."

Instead, the seven-starred Marshal, fond of fancy uniforms, decked himself out in red epaulets and red vest to address a cavalry banquet.

"I will not say Mass twice for deaf people," he sneered. "Explain my speech to whom? The state? First there has to be a state. We have only an administration which has neither ears nor guts and which does only routine bookkeeping."

Just before midnight that March 31, the Cabinet met in emergency session. "Either he goes or I go," Defense Minister René Pleven raged.

"I always claimed we should only name marshals posthumously," Vice-Premier Paul Reynaud quipped.

By 1 A.M. the Cabinet had sacked the Marshal as its top adviser on military matters and as vice-chairman of the Supreme Council of War. N.A.T.O., how-

FRENCH ENTERTAINERS were as entertaining as ever in 1954. Below: Dancer Leslie Caron tries an amusement-park ride. Opposite: Singer Maurice Chevalier (top) "mugs" in his own distinctive way for a Paris cameraman, while a great continental clown, Grock, retiring at 74 after sixty years of circus life, weeps at the end of his last appearance ever, let him keep his Central European command.

But *l'affaire Juin* was not so easily ended. On Sunday, April 4, Laniel and Pleven drove to the Arc de Triomphe to honor the fallen defenders of Dienbienphu. Gaullist hotheads shouted "*Vive Juin!*" and "Resign!" and showered the hallowed spot with leaflets. The Premier was kicked in the shins. The Defense Minister was slapped in the face.

General de Gaulle, breaking a self-imposed political silence, assailed the Laniel government's "unspeakable mediocrity". Approval of E.D.C., he said, would "dissolve France by merging her with vanquished Germany".

But what would have happened if General de Gaulle, when wartime chief of state, had been disobeyed, even by a Marshal of France? He thundered: "I

was France. I was the state, the government. I spoke in the name of France. I was the independence and sovereignty of France . . . That is why everybody obeyed me!"

At long last, the Laniel government set May 18 as the date to debate the date for the debate on E.D.C.

But before May 18 even Laniel's ludicrously tentative timetable was scrapped. On May 7 Premier Laniel plodded up to the Assembly's rostrum and read these words: "After 20 hours of uninterrupted fighting, Dienbienphu has fallen . . . France will have the virile reaction which befits a great nation." The non-Communist deputies rose in tribute to the dead of Dienbienphu. The Reds stayed seated.

France was left stunned. Its will to fight on was shot. Theaters were closed. Communist Party headquarters were stoned.

Laniel's Plea

Premier Laniel pleaded to the Assembly: "Our heroic fighting in Indochina must not end in shameful capitulation." If his Cabinet fell, he said, France would be left "without friends and without honor". He was insulted even inside the French Parliament, but by a hairbreadth two-vote margin won a 289-287 "vote of confidence". The neutralist newspaper *Le Monde* editorialized: "A two-vote majority may be sufficient to make peace. It is certainly not sufficient to continue the war."

At this point, within the Assembly, a cold, calculating economist named Pierre Mendès-France spoke plainly: "It is possible to end the disorder [in Indochina] immediately. But it is not this government that can do it." His speech, on top of Molotov's warning at Geneva that the Reds would make no concessions to the Laniel regime, turned the Assembly's majority against the government.

On June 12 the Laniel Cabinet was overthrown. It was beaten by a curious coalition including Communists, Socialists, and right-wing Gaullists—whose fear was that the Cabinet might somehow succeed in getting E.D.C. ratified. The Laniel Cabinet, France's nineteenth postwar government, had lasted fourteen days less than one year. Even so, it ranked second in longevity.

Mendès: Man of Change

Mendès-France, given first chance to form a new government, was not personally popular; he had no political following; he was only 47. But he was fresh, vigorous, ambitious, and self-confident. He had ideas. He faced the facts.

No Premier-designate had ever spoken so bluntly as he did on June 17 in demanding the Assembly's confidence. "Our rule," he said, "will be never to make promises that we cannot keep, but to keep those that we do make, no matter what the cost." His three key promises set deadlines and he substantially met all three:

(1) Indochina: Mendès-France promised to end the war by July 20 or to resign, saying flatly: "Peace is required by the facts."

(2) E.D.C.: He promised to break the stalemate by the end of summer.

(3) Economic reform: He promised "a coherent and detailed program" by July 20.

Of the Communists who said they would vote for him "to restore peace in Indochina", Mendès-France was disdainful. He said he would not count such votes.

His outspoken words won the Assembly. By 419 to 17, Mendès-France was confirmed as Premier. Not since 1947 had any of his predecessors won such a victory. Even without counting the Communists' votes, he would have had ten more than the 314 votes he needed.

Promptly he chose France's youngest postwar Cabinet. Its average age was 47. Its members were mostly centrist and rightist unknowns. Mendès-France dropped such hardy perennials as René Pleven, Paul Reynaud, and Georges Bidault. He himself became Foreign Minister.

Who was this precedent-breaking politician? "I hate politics," Mendès-France insisted. "I am not a politician." But he proved that to violate every political shibboleth was the best politics. He was a leader. He was what the French had been awaiting ever since the wartime days of General de Gaulle. He was bigger news in France than André Dubois, the Paris police prefect who forbade the honking of automobile horns, or Christian Dior, who flattened the bust.

Mendès-France aimed at *le New Deal Français*. He vainly tried to find an equivalent label in French. He sold his New Deal by resorting to the press conference and the fireside chat. To stress the F.D.R. analogy, his brain trust called him P.M.F.

The name "Mendès" (pronounced *mahn-dess'*) is often used alone. The "France" had been adopted in the 14th century to identify the members of the Mendès family who had settled in France after being ousted from Portugal because they were Jewish.

A prosperous clothing manufacturer's son, Mendès was married to Lily Cicurel, an Egyptian-born painter, whose family owned Cairo's best store. She was chic and piquant, wore dazzling gowns, and weighed only 108 pounds. Their sons were aged 20 and 18.

Mendès-France customarily looked sleepy, unshaven, and rumpled. His nose had been bashed in during his university days by less intellectual royalists. His leg was broken when he insisted on learning to ski, as "a study in will power". Once France's youngest lawyer, at 25 he became its youngest deputy, and at 31 its youngest government member.

During World War II came the boy prodigy's big test. At the collapse of France, he railed at his nation's "moral abdication, lack of honor, treason". He made his way to a Moroccan airfield and reported for duty.

Vichy French authorities arrested him for desertion and convicted him without giving him a chance to defend himself. Although Mendès insisted on appealing the decision after the war's end, it was not until June, 1954, the same month he became Premier, that his conviction was upset.

Mendès-France had not served out his six-year prison sentence. He stole a hack saw, cut through his window bars, lowered himself on a rope of knotted bed sheets, and entered the Resistance. Eventually, he escaped to Britain and joined a Free French bomber group.

After serving as De Gaulle's Minister of National Economy in 1944 and as Minister of Finance in 1946, Mendès quit in disgust at all the politicking. Refusing to serve in any succeeding French Cabinet, he argued that none was courageous enough in dealing with France's stagnant economy. He quipped: "You cannot cauterize a wooden leg."

After long years as a prophet of doom, Mendès-France got his first chance to form a government in June, 1953. In seeking the Assembly's confidence, he summed up the philosophy that was to guide him in 1954: "France must limit her objectives, but attain them; establish a policy which is perhaps less ambitious than some would desire, but hold to it. Our aim must not be to give the illusion of grandeur, but to remake a nation whose word will be heard and respected."

Mendès missed becoming Premier that

time by a scant 13 votes. But he had only twelve more months to wait.

Installed in office in 1954, he wasted no time. He became the first Western Premier to meet face to face and to come to an agreement with Communist China's Premier Chou En-lai.

Yet Mendès-France convinced Secretary Dulles that he was not selling out Indochina. He insisted he would quit if he did not get the "honorable" settlement he wanted.

The Cease-Fire

Mendès missed his July 20 deadline by two hours. But he got his cease-fire without capitulation. "It is after 2 A.M.," he joked to Molotov. "I have lost my bet. Do you think I should resign?"

"You mustn't do that," Molotov replied.

"Thank you," Mendès said. "May I tell the French Parliament that I stayed in office at your insistence?"

"I don't think that would help you," Molotov observed.

The French Premier, flying home to Paris from Switzerland, ordered that he get no hero's welcome because he had no triumph to report. When he landed, Mme. Mendès hugged him. "Pierre has no joy in his heart," she said.

Within six hours, Mendès was frankly confessing to the Assembly: "The texts [of the agreements settling the Indochina war] are cruel because they consecrate facts which are cruel."

He admitted: "I have no illusions, and I want no one else to have illusions." But he said: "Blood will cease to flow, and we will no longer see our youth decimated over there. This is the end of a nightmare."

By a unique vote of 462 to 13, the Assembly applauded "the cessation of hostilities in Indochina" and "the decisive action of the Premier".

From there on, Mendès raced ahead with his "timetable politics".

The Assembly voted him semidictatorial powers until March 31, 1955, to give the shock treatment to France's archaic economy: to free trade from the shackles of protectionism, to trim spending on uneconomic production (of alcohol, for example), to make sense out of the social-security system, to drive inefficient factories out of business.

The Assembly also OK'd his sweeping plan for greater home rule in France's riot-torn North African protectorates.

Then his timetable politics collided with the E.D.C. roadblock. The result was shattering—to E.D.C. The Premier proposed to drive through the Assembly a watered-down version of the plan.

"We must say yes or no," he insisted. The Assembly said "no". Mendès himself did not vote, nor did his Cabinet, which had split 50-50.

Death of E.D.C.

Among E.D.C.'s foes was beloved elder statesman Édouard Herriot, too ailing at 82 even to climb the rostrum. He summed up from his Assembly seat: "The treaty, and I say this at the end of my life, would be the end of France." .

By 319 to 264, E.D.C. was defeated. Had it not been for the "no" vote of the 99 Communists, the treaty would have won.

As soon as E.D.C.'s death was announced, the Communists roared forth the "Marseillaise" on the floor of the Assembly.

E.D.C.'s partisans were bitter. Ex-Premier Paul Reynaud accused Mendès-France of "killing a French idea which restored French prestige ".

For once the Premier's own prestige was shaken, due to his failure to make a choice himself for or against E.D.C.

TROUBLE IN MOROCCO: Students in Fez demand return of ex-Sultan, banished by French

Nonetheless he again won a vote of confidence, 418 to 162.

"We were paralyzed by our indecision," Mendès summed up. "Now we must act quickly . . . If there is a division, it is on the means of organizing Western defense. Our policy is unchanged: that of the Atlantic alliance and the organization of Europe, which should be founded on Franco-German reconciliation."

Mendès did act and quickly. After the London conference, he reported back to his people: "German rearmament has already been decided upon. The only question is whether it will be with us or in spite of us . . . France and Germany need each other."

By then Mendès was proving to be France's most popular, most powerful, and most controversial Premier since World War II. His popularity grew from the grass roots.

Advised not to stake his government's future on German rearmament, he rejoined: "No, I will do it. You wait and see. You have been talking to the parliamentarians. But this is Friday, and they don't like me on Friday. But they will like me on Tuesday, after they have returned from a weekend in their constituencies." With his unique ability to feel the Frenchman's pulse, the Premier proved to be correct.

He finally won Washington's confidence in late November when, during a triumphant good-will tour, he promised to support German rearmament. On Dec. 30 he persuaded the French Assembly to

LAWBREAKER: Gaston Dominici, 77-year-old French farmer on trial for the 1952 murder of three members of a titled English family, shows mixed emotions as prosecuting attorney talks

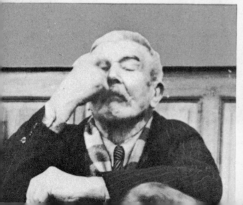

LAW ENFORCER: A Paris gendarme, walking his beat, passes night club called Gate of Hell

STREET SIGHTS in Paris include U.S. dancer Rose Hardaway strolling in a bikini and ample lady (right) dispensing ice cream at a stand close to the Eiffel Tower

do likewise, although it did so reluctantly and grudgingly.

The milk-drinking Mendès then turned to an equally tough target. By decree he cut the alcoholic content of *apéritifs*, curtailed liquor advertising, cracked down on the home-brewing of Calvados (applejack), shut all bars one day a week, and even banned the sale of hard liquor between 5 and 10 A.M., when French workers get an eye opener. He planned to levy heavy taxes on liquor and send drunks to jail.

If Mendès could indeed cure France's alcoholism, he would go down in history as one of the country's greats. He himself was confident of the success of his policies.

"Now we have the certainty of a great future for the Republic," he said. "The wind is rising, morning is here; we are at the dawn of a new France."

GLACES
Pur Sucre.. Pur Fruit
·10·15·20·
·Vanille·
·Framboise·
·Chocolat·

INDUSTRIAL HEALTH of West Germany in 1954 is symbolized by these railway rails forming a massive pattern in a Ruhr steel mill

GERMANY

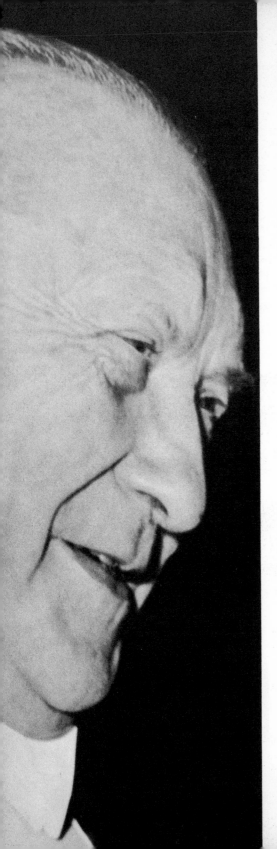

A 25-YEAR-OLD BERLIN MODEL NAMED Christel Schaak (bust 38, waist 22, hips 38) strutted in a 1954 beauty contest at Vichy, France. Already "Miss Germany", she also walked away with the title "Miss Europe". It was only nine years after V-E Day.

But Miss Europe turned out to be a Mrs. The judges discovered that Frau Schaak had been widowed two years earlier. She was therefore stripped of her title in favor of the runner-up, France's Danielle Genot. For the sake of international harmony, however, Frau Schaak was named "Honorary Miss Europe".

The incident was symptomatic—in none of the affairs of our time, small or large, could Germany any longer be denied.

As the industrial heart of continental Europe, it was now so phenomenally prosperous that its erstwhile enemies were asking: "Who won the war, anyway?" Although still partitioned into Western and Soviet zones, it was the great prize in the cold war.

A Vacuum

When the Big Four conference in Berlin in January and February, 1954, killed whatever hope had existed for an East-West agreement to unite Germany, Chancellor Adenauer broadcast a message of cheer to his 17,000,000 captive countrymen in Red-run East Germany: "Be alert, be hard, be patient. Today we in the Federal Republic [of West Germany] are developing our economic and political powers for the future benefit of all Germany, for you."

He developed Bonn's economic power by cutting taxes an average of 25 percent

CHANCELLOR ADENAUER: a facial study (left). Right: In Washington in October, he beams on Mrs. John Foster Dulles and the Secretary of State

NAZI ECHOES: Steel-helmeted West German border guards revive memories of Hitler's once mighty *Wehrmacht.* Right: Hitler's prewar Foreign Minister, Baron Konstantin von Neurath, at 81, is freed eight years after conviction as a war criminal

—the biggest postwar slash by any Western nation. His object: the encouragement of business initiative. Already West Germany's business was booming 80 percent above the prewar peak.

The Kremlin countered these moves in West Germany by springing in East Germany what Bonn called a "booby trap". It granted "full sovereignty" to its puppet state. By so doing it unmasked East Germany's so-called "People's Police" and revealed a full-fledged army: 600 tanks, 2000 guns, 200,000 men. The British Foreign Office gibed that East Germany now was "completely free to obey Moscow".

That East Germany really remained a Kremlin satellite was soon indicated. Its monocled Foreign Minister, Georg Dertinger, was railroaded to jail as a "Western spy". Dertinger, an unprincipled ex-Nazi propagandist who called himself not a Communist but a Christian Democrat, was given fifteen years at hard labor. One of his mistresses got eleven years. Another got three.

Chancellor Adenauer worked ceaselessly for real sovereignty for West Germany, but gradually his people, still disarmed, grew disillusioned with his pro-French and pro-European policies.

Dr. Heinrich Brüning, the pre-Hitler Chancellor who taught at Harvard University during World War II, told pow-

erful industrialists that Germany should return to its old policy of neutrality.

The tip-off to Adenauer's declining popularity was provided by the June 27 local election in North Rhine-Westphalia (including the Ruhr), West Germany's largest State. In vain did Adenauer stump for his party's candidates. Votes polled by his Christian Democrats fell sharply from 49 percent of the State's total in 1953 to 41.2 percent. Adenauer estimated that France's failure to ratify E.D.C. had cost his party a million votes.

It was in July that the Adenauer regime was most gravely shaken, this time by the defection of Dr. Otto John.

Dr. John, "the man with a thousand secrets", was chief of Bonn's Federal Office for the Protection of the Constitution. As such he was charged with ferreting out espionage, sabotage, treason.

When he was picked for the post in 1950, one top American intelligence man remarked: "You can't trust him. He drinks too much. When he drinks, he talks."

Blond, stocky, 44, John spoke English fluently though with a heavy German accent. In World War II he had been a double agent, for both German intelligence and the British secret service. Both he and his brother Hans had played major parts in the July, 1944, plot to assassinate Hitler. Hans was caught, tortured by the Gestapo, and murdered. Otto, being legal adviser to the German air lines, was able to escape to Lisbon and thence to London. Thereafter he helped interrogate top German prisoners and prepare war-crimes cases.

In 1954, to celebrate the tenth anniversary of the anti-Hitler plot, Dr. John flew to West Berlin. There was plenty of reminiscing and plenty of drinking. John seemed nervous and depressed.

About 8 P.M. he left his wife in their hotel room and went out, supposedly to get a beer. Actually he sought out Dr. Wolfgang Wohlgemuth, a gynecologist, trumpet player, and known Communist. Dr. Wohlgemuth left a note: "The fact is that Dr. John will not return to the Western sector." Then they drove off toward East Berlin.

A customs guard stopped their Ford and warned: "You are now crossing into the Soviet sector."

"That's exactly where we want to go," Dr. John replied.

Over the East German radio, on the night of July 23, came this announcement: "At the microphone, Otto John."

The security chief's voice was firm and readily recognizable: "I have on the anniversary of July 20 taken a decisive step and have entered into connection with the East Germans." His reasons: "West German policy has entered a blind alley . . . Nazis are reappearing everywhere in political and public life".

Dr. John's defection was the first ever by the chief of a national-security agency. It stunned Bonn and shocked Washington. "Everything and everyone is compromised," one intelligence officer said. Only a few weeks earlier, Dr. John, as a guest of the U.S. government, had conferred with both F.B.I. Director J. Edgar Hoover and Allen Dulles, Director of the supersecret Central Intelligence Agency.

East German authorities boasted that John's defection enabled them to nab hundreds of secret agents for the West. Wolfgang Hoefer, a German-born American who said he had been ordered by U.S. Army intelligence to spy on his old schoolmate Dr. John, committed suicide.

In vain did Bonn assert that Dr. John had been "lured" to East Berlin. In vain did it offer a $119,000 reward for the solution to his "abduction". Dr. John was photographed sipping coffee on the terrace of a plush café in East Berlin. He broadcast "sincere thanks" for his Communist sanctuary. He held a press conference for 200 newsmen, Western and Eastern. Only then did Bonn brand him a traitor.

"Terrible," Chancellor Adenauer said of Dr. John's defection. But he countered John's basic charge by saying: "There is no revival of National Socialism in Germany, and it will not revive."

"I beg my listeners to believe," Adenauer said, "that the damage which he can do is not so great as many thought at first." The Chancellor insisted that the security chief had had "absolutely nothing to do with military matters".

Nonetheless the Adenauer regime had been shaken by its worst scandal. Almost immediately it was followed by the defection of Karl Franz Schmidt-Wittmack,

a Bundestag deputy belonging to Adenauer's own Christian Democratic Party.

A Hamburg businessman, Protestant layman, "almost a royalist", Schmidt-Wittmack had known the Bundestag's secrets as a member of two key committees. Now he broadcast fanciful charges that Bonn was plotting to create, not the twelve divisions called for by E.D.C., but four times as many.

A Tired European

To a photographer at the Brussels conference in August, Chancellor Adenauer suggested a caption for his picture: "Underneath it you can write: 'A tired European'." At 78, "The Old Man" saw his pro-E.D.C. policy crashing.

From Brussels the Chancellor, suffering from insomnia, went to his favorite retreat in the Black Forest. There, with a distant view of the Rhine and of France, he watched E.D.C.'s death in the French National Assembly on the news teletype. "Well, that's the way it is," the Chancellor commented.

Despite the body blow dealt his policy and his prestige, the Chancellor still sought to head off both ultranationalism and neutralism in West Germany. Friendship between France and Germany, he said, was "absolutely necessary".

The growing anti-French feeling in West Germany was reflected when a N.A.T.O. jet-fuel tank at Bitburg, in the French zone, exploded as the French were testing fire-fighting equipment. Some thirty Frenchmen and Germans were charred to death. A German reporter voiced the common reaction of his countrymen: "This proves the French can do nothing correctly."

Chancellor Adenauer arrived at the London conference resolved that it had to succeed. He read a message in which the phonetic English pronunciation was spelled out in blue ink: "Ai houp sset see London Konfernss will bi seksessful."

His statesmanlike concessions there won the promise that his nation, rearmed and restored to sovereignty, though still divided, would take its place with its erstwhile enemies in the North Atlantic and Brussels alliances.

So worried was the Kremlin by this new deal for West Germany that Soviet Foreign Minister Molotov popped up in East Germany on Oct. 6 to celebrate that puppet state's fifth anniversary. Seeking to block the London agreement, he warned that, if West Germany were rearmed, "the restoration of German unity would become impossible".

But Chancellor Adenauer shrugged off the Soviet warning. On Oct. 7, he won such overwhelming approval in the Bundestag for the London agreements that nobody even bothered to call the roll. "Fifty million brave, industrious, diligent people are now returned to freedom," the Chancellor rejoiced.

Above all else, Chancellor Adenauer's new defense force was to be a "citizen's army". The goose step was banned. So were the Prussian *Kommiss* (spit and polish) and other symbols of extreme militarism. Even the name was changed from the Nazis' *Wehrmacht* (War Machine), "because of its past associations", to the safer-sounding *Die Streitkräfte* (The Military Forces).

Late in 1954 Adenauer, the antimilitarist architect of Germany's military comeback, flew the Atlantic to confer with Eisenhower, the soldier-statesman who had destroyed Germany's military might ten years earlier. Together the Chancellor and the President pledged that West Germany's entry into N.A.T.O. would lead toward "freedom and unity".

MISS GERMANY won the Miss Europe ribbon in 1954, but she turned out to be a widow

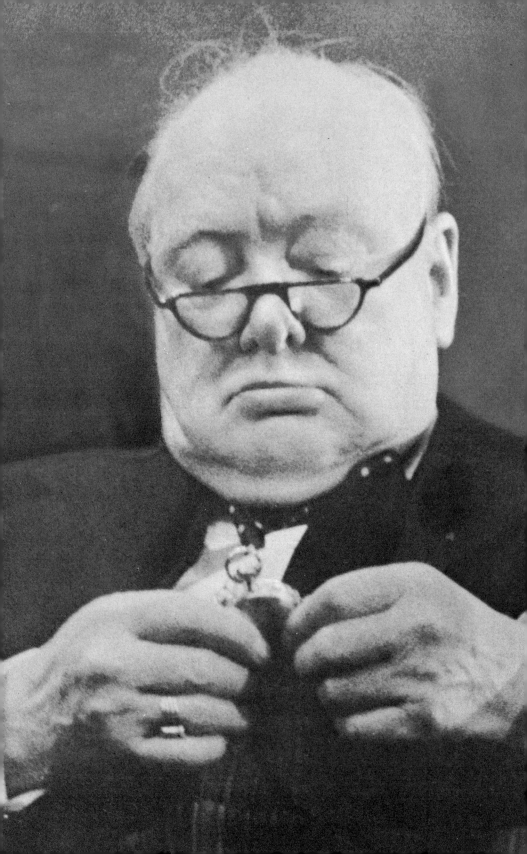

HEIR APPARENT to the job of 80-year-old Sir Winston Churchill (left), Foreign Minister Eden in 1954 was the British Premier's good right arm

GREAT BRITAIN

BRITAIN'S BIG STORY THROUGHOUT 1954 WAS the story of Churchill and Eden. Prime Minister Sir Winston Churchill and Foreign Secretary Sir Anthony Eden became convinced that their nation could no longer sit smugly behind the English Channel. Britain, they felt, now must do everything possible to save Europe from the further spread of Communism. Otherwise, they feared, their island would be defenseless against the appalling destructiveness of the hydrogen bomb.

Churchill's Conservative government

VISITING AUSTRALIA, Queen Elizabeth, husband, and party are amused by native "wallaby" dance. Spear carrier apes hunter seeking wallabies (small kangaroos)

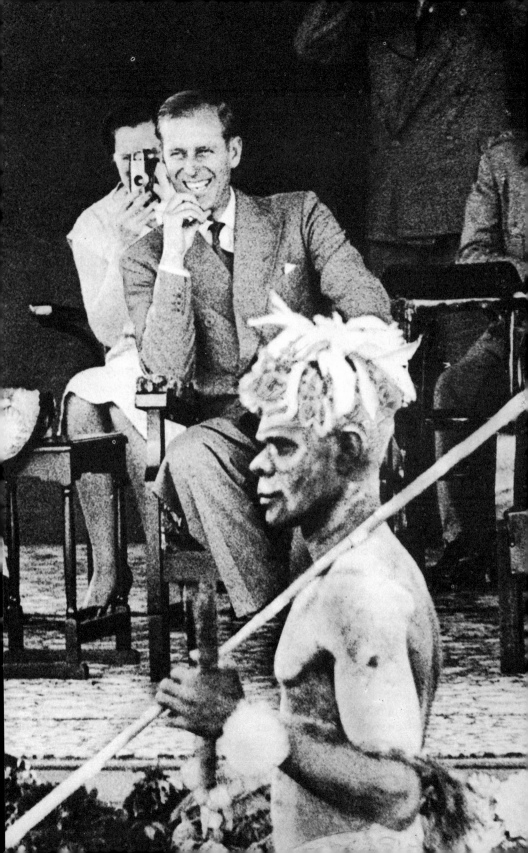

therefore made a historic break with Britain's 300-year-old policy of "splendid isolation". Eden pledged Britain not to withdraw its four crack divisions of ground forces and its jet-equipped tactical air force from the Continent "against the wishes of the majority" of the six continental nations in the new Western European Union.

For his nation, Eden said, this was "a very formidable step . . . We are still an island people in thought and tradition, whatever the modern facts of weapons and strategy may compel." The Eden pledge capped a whole series of successes for his diplomacy and boosted his prestige to its highest peak. There was now no real question as to whether he would succeed Churchill as Prime Minister. The only question was when.

Churchill and Eden

"One does not leave a convivial party before closing time," Sir Winston often told close friends. As 1954 opened, the "Old Man" had staged a remarkable comeback from his 1953 stroke.

Privately he confessed that American admirers were sending him "pep pills" to rejuvenate the elderly. "Do you take them?" he was asked. Smiling, he replied: "I don't think it would be fair to Anthony."

Sir Winston was aged, bowed, enfeebled, only fitfully at his best. The pro-Labourite tabloid, *The London Daily Mirror*, flatly called the Conservative Prime Minister "too old, too ailing, too tired . . . a disaster to his party and to the country".

As if to confound his critics, the old warrior spent one wintry half hour on the rifle range, testing Britain's newly adopted Belgian FN .30-caliber automatic rifle. He reported to the House of Commons: "It has a butt—remember that.

It is very important when one has no ammunition left."

Eden, well again after his gall-bladder operations of 1953, was more than ever the Prime Minister's right arm. Already Foreign Secretary, Deputy Prime Minister, and Sir Winston's nephew-in-law, he was also elected president of the National Union of Conservative and Unionist Associations (a national league of Conservatives and their political allies). Almost every night, B.B.C. news announcers brought the name they pronounced "Miss Treeden" (Mister Eden) into every British home. Still debonair at 57, he even made himself into something of a backslapper to offset his reputation for arrogance and aloofness.

Together Churchill and Eden had led the 1938 battle against Prime Minister Neville Chamberlain's appeasement of Hitler at Munich. Now, early in 1954, they themselves were accused of seeking to appease the Chinese and Russian Communists with regard to Indochina. They were profoundly worried that some spark might set off a third world war and turn their island home into atomic ashes.

The British policies of recognizing Red China, of seeking to trade with the Russians, of cultivating the neutralist Indians, of peace at almost any price in Indochina, all ran counter to Washington thinking. Out of these policies arose a sharp split in the Anglo-American alliance.

To patch it up, Churchill flew to Washington with Eden. But twenty-four hours earlier Eden had widened the breach by telling Commons that he was acting at Geneva as an intermediary between East and West. He paid "personal tribute" to Molotov, rejoiced at the "opportunity" to meet Chou En-lai, and did not once mention Secretary Dulles.

"Someone had to provide a channel of communication [between the free and Communist worlds], even at the risk of being called a Municheer," said the old-time enemy of Munich.

Arriving in the U.S. on June 25, Sir Winston, with British understatement, announced: "I have come to talk over a few family matters, and to try to make sure that there are no misunderstandings."

The Churchill-Eisenhower conference produced full agreement on sharing atomic secrets insofar as permitted by American law, and on bringing West Germany into the Western alliance. But it produced only "generalized" agreement on the necessity for a security system for Southeast Asia and produced specific disagreement on doing diplomatic business with Communist China.

To the Washington press, the Prime Minister expressed his philosophy: "We ought to have a try at peaceful coexistence [with the Communist world], a real good try." On returning to Britain, he admitted, more frankly than ever before, that Britain's diplomatic moves now were influenced by the threat of H-bomb devastation.

The Eden diplomacy marched on from one tension-relaxing triumph to another —settling the Suez base dispute with Egypt, breaking the oil deadlock with Iran, helping to mediate the Italian-Yugoslav feud over Trieste.

By the end of summer, Eden was plainly ready to take over from Churchill. But when? The question inspired a song written for a London revue:

Thirty-one years in the business,
Years of unselfish devotion;
Nearly twenty years in the same old job
With hardly a hope of promotion . . .
Thirty-odd years of frustrated desire
Waiting for senior men to retire.
Assistant, adviser, consultant, and guide.
Always the bridesmaid—never the bride!

The Lord Chamberlain, as "Keeper of the Queen's Conscience", censored the song just before the show's opening. But if Eden was bothered by it, he gave no sign. He was too busy anyway. In the bathtub one day, he got the idea of expanding the Brussels Alliance as a substitute for E.D.C. The adoption of this plan sent his prestige soaring.

"The Greatest Man . . ."

In October, 4100 Conservatives convened for their seventy-fourth annual conference in the Winter Garden at Blackpool, a British Coney Island. Normally decorous, the Tory convention gave Eden a tumultuous ovation. Eden, in turn, introduced Churchill as "the greatest man upon this earth".

Sir Winston applauded Eden's "energy and boldness", his "knowledge, experience, tact, and skill", his "influence and distinction", which had produced the Brussels Alliance agreement, "a monument and a milestone in our march toward peaceful coexistence".

The Prime Minister spoke slowly, haltingly, to an audience that felt he should and probably would retire. Nonetheless he fascinated them with his oratory and with his puckishness. Fully aware of his brandy-fancying reputation, he downed a glass of water and wisecracked: "I only do it to show you that I can."

But was the Prime Minister ready to let Eden inherit his mantle? Sir Winston said: "There is quite enough for both of us to do at the present time."

Soon thereafter he shook up the Tory Cabinet, for the fifth time since the Conservatives regained the reins in 1951. No fewer than twenty-four shifts were made. Seven ministers, averaging 61 years in age, were retired. Seven newcomers, averaging 41, were promoted to ministerial rank.

ROYAL RETURN: Home with their children after a 44,000-mile Empire tour, Queen and Duke arrive at Buckingham Palace. The first to enter is Princess Anne

"EXILED" to British Embassy in Brussels in 1953 because of his attentions to Princess Margaret, Colonel Peter Townsend looks forlorn at Belgian race meet

IN FAVOR with the Princess—at least temporarily—is Colin Tennant. Unlike Townsend, he is of noble birth, son of the landowning Lord and Lady Glenconner

But on the topmost level there was, once again, no change. Eden remained merely the heir apparent. He was summoned to Buckingham Palace, however. There, while he knelt, Queen Elizabeth touched him on each shoulder with a shiny sword and said: "Arise, Sir Anthony." Thus Sir Anthony Eden joined Sir Winston Churchill as a Knight Companion of the Most Noble Order of the Garter—the highest honor a British political leader can receive and still remain in the House of Commons.

On Nov. 30 Sir Winston Churchill also was honored, at what he called "the most memorable public occasion of my life". It was the Old Man's 80th birthday.

In the ancient Westminster Hall, after the Grenadier Guards drummed out the rhythm of "V for Victory", the Prime Minister was presented by his fellow Commoners with an ornate book inscribed with this quotation from John Bunyan: "You have been so faithful, and so loving to us, you have fought so stoutly for us, you have been so hearty in counseling of us that we shall never forget your favor towards us."

Sir Winston also was presented with a bulldog portrait of himself painted in chalky orange and white tones by Graham Sutherland. Impishly the Prime Minister, himself an amateur artist known for his dislike of modernistic painting, commented: "A great example of modern art." Privately he confided: "It makes me look half-witted, which I ain't."

With his sense of history and mastery of the English language, Churchill then put his own finest hours—in World War II —into personal perspective: "I have never accepted what many have said, namely that I inspired the nation . . . It was the nation and the race dwelling all 'round the globe that had the lion's heart. I had the luck to be called upon to give the roar. I also hope that I sometimes suggested to the lion the right place to use his claws."

Queen and Family

Queen Elizabeth II during 1954 proved her right to reign as sovereign not only of Britain but of her world-wide Commonwealth. She made a grueling 173-day, 44,-000-mile, round-the-world tour for the purpose of seeing and being seen by as many of her subjects as possible. She spent the bulk of her time in three of the Commonwealth's independent nations: New Zealand, Australia, and Ceylon.

Her welcome was "almost overwhelming", she admitted. She lost 7 pounds.

The tour ended on May 15 when, just 28, she stepped ashore in London as forty-one guns boomed in salute. Her return touched off typically British rejoicing at having the Queen back in the family homestead.

Once again the British people were treated to the remorseless coverage of the Queen's every gesture that they had doted on while she was away. They were told how a 4-year-old girl had climbed into her lap and tried to kiss her in Brisbane, Australia; how Melbourne students had hazed the Duke of Edinburgh by unrolling a moth-eaten carpet and handing him a pair of crutches; how the Queen's microphones had failed and her elevator had stuck as she was opening the Owen Falls hydroelectric dam at the Nile's headwaters; how Prince Charles and Princess Anne had joined their parents in time to watch their athletic father score a goal at polo in Malta; how the Queen, like any mother, had kept a tight grip on her wriggling son as they sailed up the Thames; how the Queen had told both her children, as they drove off to Buckingham Palace: "Sit up straight in your seats."

During the rest of 1954, Queen Elizabeth called upon other members of her family to share the royal responsibilities.

The smiling Queen Mother Elizabeth visited President Eisenhower at the White House, received an honorary degree from Columbia University, and turned just plain tourist in New York–gazing at the skyline from atop the Empire State Building, seeing *The Pajama Game* on Broadway, and shopping along Fifth Avenue. Princess Margaret, still unmarried, danced with British troops in West Germany and prepared to tour the British West Indies in 1955. She also won $8.82 worth of sports books by submitting the first correct solution in a crossword puzzle contest.

In the future, the Queen was expected to make short flying trips to the various parts of the Commonwealth rather than to be subjected again to the endless overwork of a world-wide tour. For it was undeniable, as one British official observed, that "that young girl has done more to solidify the Commonwealth than all the conferences we have ever had".

COMFORTING a crying boy whose lunch her visit (and popping flash bulbs) interrupted, the Queen Mother has pleasant chat at N. Y. day-care center

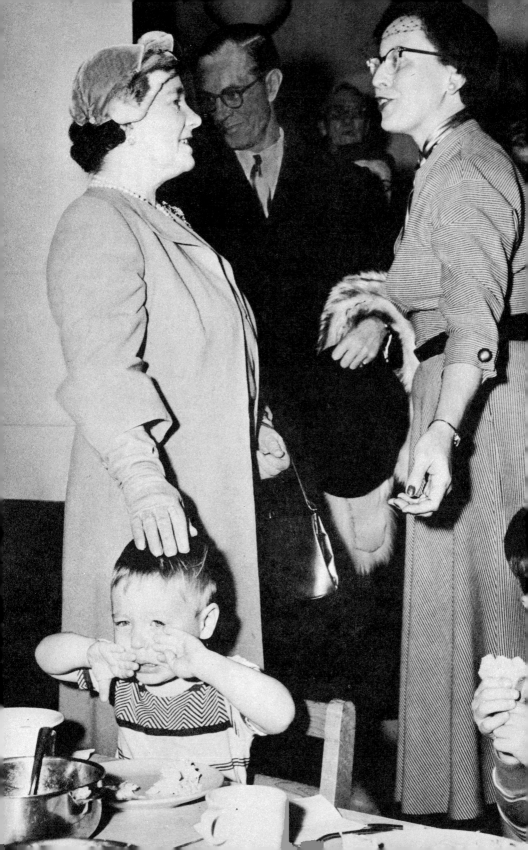

WESTERN EUROPE

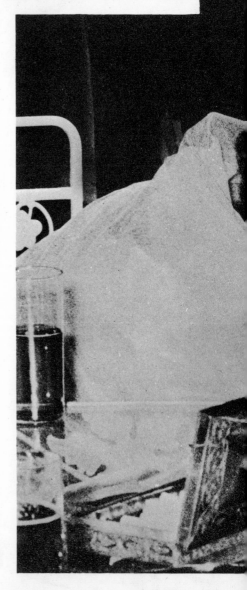

ON OCT. 26, 1954, A DRENCHING GALE SWEPT the great port city of Trieste at the head of the Adriatic Sea. It ripped red, white, and green bunting from the buildings and washed out the scheduled ceremonies. But it could not dampen the spirits of the Italian-speaking people of Trieste. For on that joyous day, the Italian Alpine Division, which had liberated Trieste in 1918 from more than five centuries of Austrian rule, again rolled into the city, this time to take it over from Anglo-American occupation.

All patriotic Italians rejoiced at the recovery of Trieste, which had become a colony of ancient Rome back in the days of Emperor Augustus. Trieste's return to Italy, Premier Mario Scelba (pronounced *shell'-ba*) gloried, "represents one of the greatest demonstrations of Italy's recovery following the tragic days of the War". It also represented a great success for Anglo-American diplomacy, especially for the U.S. Ambassador to Rome, Clare Boothe Luce.

The Trieste settlement had been signed in London on Oct. 5. Under its terms, the so-called "Free Territory of Trieste" was split between Italy and Yugoslavia. Most

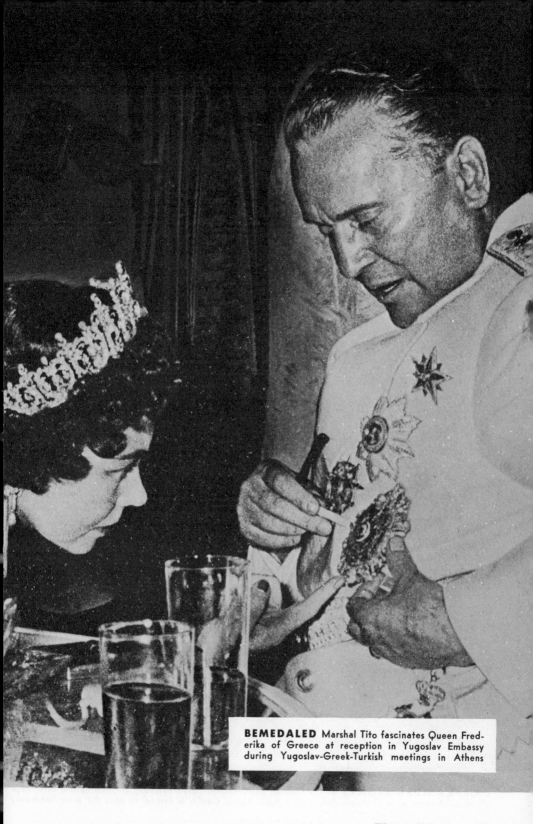

BEMEDALED Marshal Tito fascinates Queen Frederika of Greece at reception in Yugoslav Embassy during Yugoslav-Greek-Turkish meetings in Athens

CAMERA HIGH LIGHTS of the Montesi case. Above: Italy's Attorney General hurls a brief case full of documents at a photographer. Right: Anna Maria Caglio is forced to pose for other lenshawks

of Zone A's 86 square miles and 310,000 people, including the city itself and its shipyards and oil refineries, were transferred from Anglo-American occupation to Italy. Zone B's 199 square miles and 75,000 people, already under Yugoslav rule, were certified as part of Yugoslavia. In addition, the Yugoslavs were given a small slice of Zone A and promised port and minority rights there.

Thus was settled a bitter Italian-Yugoslav feud which had hampered the West's efforts to build up a solid front against the Kremlin.

The Trieste settlement was just what Premier Scelba needed to reinforce his regime. For Italy had been shaken to the foundations of the Colosseum by a scandal of orgiastic debauchery. This scandal gave the Communist cause the greatest fillip it received all year.

On April 11, 1953, the body of a lush brunette of 21, clad in silk panties embroidered with Teddy bears, had been

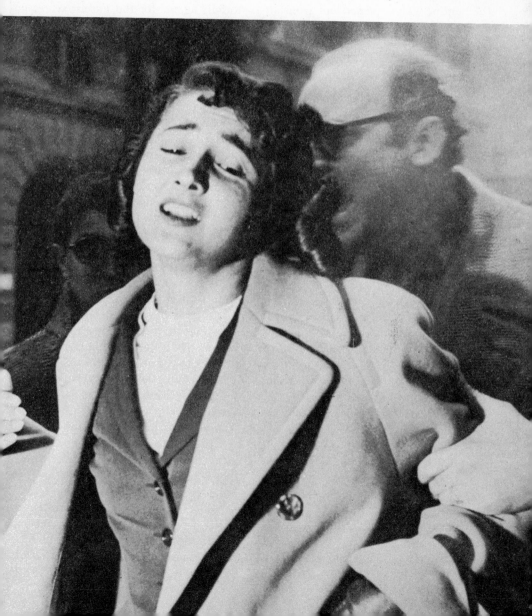

found on a deserted beach near Ostia, Rome's Coney Island.

She was identified as Wilma Montesi, a carpenter's daughter. She was reported to have been caught in the undertow while washing an eczema-infected foot. A postmortem concluded: "Asphyxia by drowning."

Silvana Muto, the 24-year-old editor of a sensational magazine named *Attualità*, did not agree. That October he wrote that Wilma Montesi had gone to wild orgies at a hunting lodge, passed out from an overdose of opium, and been tossed on the beach to drown. The lodge's manager, Muto wrote, was Ugo Montagna di San Bartolomeo, a Roman aristocrat who called himself *"Marchese"* ("Marquis") and supposedly masterminded a dope-smuggling ring.

The editor was charged with spreading "false and adulterated news to disturb the public order" and in January, 1954, was put on trial. To defend himself, he produced as star witness Anna Maria Moneta Caglio, the stage-struck, 23-year-old daughter of a wealthy Milan lawyer.

Star Witness Testifies

Signorina Caglio testified she had been Ugo Montagna's $800-a-month mistress. But she had been jilted, had retired to a convent, and had made up her mind to tell her story. She testified that her lover had acted strangely at the time of Wilma Montesi's death. When she mentioned it, "Ugo became simply furious and told me I knew too much."

The Caglio girl went on: "Montagna told me he had to go to the chief of police [Tommaso Pavone] to hush up the affair, since they were trying to link Piero Piccioni [the jazz-pianist son of Italy's Foreign Minister Attilio Piccioni] with the death of Wilma Montesi.

"Ugo drove me to police headquarters.

A few minutes later Piccioni arrived. They went inside and stayed more than an hour. 'Now everything's fixed up'," she quoted Montagna as saying. She also said that Montagna had obtained a $50,000 apartment for the police chief.

After splitting with Montagna, she testified, she had gone to the local police with her story, only to be advised to mind her own business. Instead she went to the rival Carabinieri, the national police. They reported Montagna had been a "notorious agent" for the Fascist secret police, a Nazi spy, a procurer of women of "doubtful morality" for high-ranking personages (whether Fascist, Nazi, American, or British), a tax evader, a passer of bad checks—and a close associate of young Piero Piccioni, Pavone, government big shots, and high Vatican lay officials.

Signorina Caglio produced a letter she had left with her landlady, to be opened if she did not return from dinner at Montagna's hunting lodge. It read:

"Who knows what will happen to me? I have too many Christian scruples to commit suicide. But knowing both Montagna and Piccioni, I am afraid to disappear without leaving a trace of myself. Unfortunately for myself, I have learned that Ugo is the chief of a dope ring responsible for the disappearance of many women. He is the brains of this organization. Piero Piccioni is its assassin."

These sensational charges rocked the Italian government. But Premier Scelba acted quickly to keep the Communists from riding to power on the Montesi case.

"I promise to do all in my power to clear away this shady, suspicious atmosphere that is hanging over us," he pledged. He forced Pavone, whom he had originally named as police chief, to resign. He ordered a probe into Montagna's finances and the lifting of the passports of Montagna, Piero Piccioni, and others. The trial of editor Muto was called off in favor of a no-holds-barred government inquiry.

The inquiry was no whitewash. It resulted in the arrest of Montagna and Piero Piccioni for manslaughter. Attilio Piccioni resigned as Foreign Minister "to defend my son and my family's good name".

Scelba and Friends

Premier Scelba needed to act resolutely to save his middle-of-the-road regime. He sought to offset the Montesi case with progressive and anti-Communist policies.

On taking over as Premier in February, Scelba had only a 300-to-283 edge in the Chamber of Deputies. But he had courage. The 53-year-old son of a Sicilian sharecropper, he had been grabbed by the Nazis in World War II for putting out an underground periodical. In the postwar era, the Communists called him "assassin" when, as Interior Minister, he created the jeep-borne Speed Brigade which broke up Red riots with rubber truncheons. Scelba's pet peeves were Bikini bathing suits and classical nude statues.

"We do not agree with those who write that democracy in Italy is heading toward its doom," Scelba insisted. Quickly he headed it in the direction of more public housing and more public works, of less tax evasion and less timidity toward the biggest and wealthiest Communist Party outside the Iron Curtain. "Death to Scelba!" raged Red billboards.

The Premier moved to oust the Communists from all the many government-owned office buildings, resorts, printing establishments, gymnasiums, and the like which they had taken over after Fascism's collapse; to clean the Reds out of the government-subsidized movie industry, where eight of the fourteen top directors were Communists or fellow-travelers; to choke off the Communist-controlled trading companies which, out of profits on commerce with the Soviet bloc, supposedly paid $50 million a year into the Red's coffers.

But the Scelba government's intentions were better than its achievements. During 1954 it was unable to get any of its grandiose plans enacted into law. For Scelba's Christian Democratic Party was not only challenged from without by the huge Communist Party but also split from within into feuding factions led by Scelba's two predecessors as Premier.

On the Christian Democrats' right wing stood ex-Premier Giuseppe Pella, longtime Treasury Minister, known as the government's "economic conscience". A redheaded Piedmontese, he was a hardheaded businessman—even while serving as treasurer of the underground during World War II. Pella had resigned as Premier on Jan. 5.

On the party's left wing trotted ex-Premier Amintore Fanfani. An ascetic Tuscan, he lived by the Sermon on the Mount, subsisted on an inevitable bowl of apples on his desk, and in his days as an economics professor walked barefoot and slept in a monastery cell. His government, succeeding Pella's, had lasted eleven days.

Fanfani is "as dead as a sad smoked herring", Pietro Nenni, the pro-Communist Socialist leader, had gloated. But at 46, winning election as secretary-general of the Christian Democrats, Fanfani came back to become his party's ideological leader.

Thus challenged from left and right, Premier Scelba sorely missed his middle-of-the-road mentor, Alcide de Gasperi, Italy's greatest postwar statesman, who had resigned in 1953 after eight years as Premier. In August, after suffering a heart attack, De Gasperi had drawn upon his last reserves of energy and emotion to telephone Scelba from his Alpine chalet. He pleaded his favorite cause of European unity: "Europe and the fatherland

PRIVATE GRIEF at bier of Alcide de Gasperi shows in expressions of three of his four daughters (in black stockings). The fourth, a nun, could not be present

must be saved. If the European Defense Community is not accomplished, only God knows what will happen." Then he broke down in tears.

Undoubtedly De Gasperi knew that he might not live to attain his overriding ambition—to become the first President of a United States of Europe. Not many hours after telephoning Scelba, he gasped: "I am dying." He suffered a second heart attack and then a third. "*Gesù! Gesù! Gesù!*" the devoutly Catholic De Gasperi said. On Aug. 19, at 73, with these words on his lips, he died.

An Actress and Yugoslavia

AROUND A YUGOSLAV PIN-UP GIRL REVOLVED Yugoslavia's bitterest internal feud since the rebel Communist Marshal Tito broke with the Kremlin in 1948.

A 21-year-old brunette actress named Milena Vranjak, newly married to Colonel General Peko Dapcevic, the army chief of staff, found herself socially ostracized by the wives of many Titoist big shots. Reason: She had not fought as a partisan in World War II.

Milovan Djilas (pronounced *jee'-las*), President of Parliament and a Vice-President of Yugoslavia, rushed, with pen drawn, to Milena's defense. On twenty pages of the magazine *New Thought* he used the most lurid phraseology to describe the premarital misadventures of some of the ex-partisan wives. Djilas pointed out that the pretty actress was only 13 at the time of V-E Day and thus too young to have served with the partisans.

At that Djilas was black-listed from Titoism's social register. Publication of a

PUBLIC MOURNING for the late Italian Premier is symbolized by this man bending to kiss De Gasperi's coffin as his body lies in Rome's St. Jesus Church

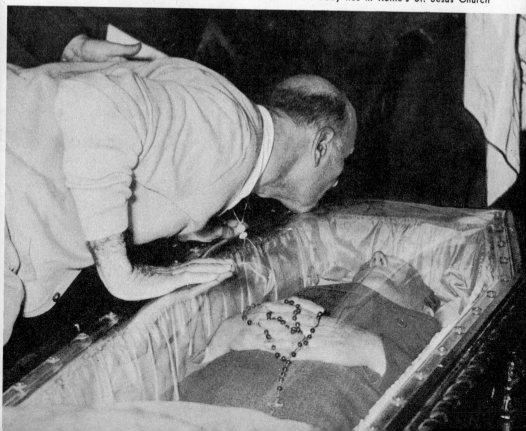

series of articles by him in *Borba*, the Titoist organ, was halted. In them, Djilas urged less "Stalinist" discipline and "more democracy" within Yugoslavia's Communist Party.

Marshal Tito, whose third wife had been a partisan major, called a showdown session of the Communist Central Committee in Belgrade. Djilas arrived on foot, pallid and shaken. But unlike heretics in the Soviet Union, he was allowed to broadcast his defense over the radio. "My attitude was wrong," he said, but "I am still a true Marxist."

It was up to Tito to settle the issue. He castigated his onetime protégé for seeking "the restoration of capitalism."

Djilas was shorn of his position as president of Parliament and of all of his party posts, but remained a free man. However, in December, while Tito was away visiting India and Burma, Djilas called for a new "democratic-socialist" party to challenge the one-party "totalitarian" rule. At that, together with his strapping friend Vladimir Dedijer, Tito's official biographer, he was formally accused of "a criminal act".

While not renouncing his heretical variety of Communism, Marshal Tito meanwhile was tightening his foreign-policy ties with the West. At a once-royal villa in the mountain resort of Bled, the Yugoslav President on Aug. 9 linked his Communist dictatorship with the kingdom of Greece and the republic of Turkey in a twenty-year "treaty of alliance, political cooperation, and mutual assistance".

It stated that an attack on one would be "a mortal danger for the other partners and for world peace". Since Greece and Turkey were already N.A.T.O. members, the new Balkan alliance indirectly linked

RECOGNITION: In Lausanne, Switzerland, Charlie Chaplin and wife are amused (left) by circus acrobat doing Chaplin imitation (right)

Yugoslavia to N.A.T.O. and thus plugged the biggest gap along the Iron Curtain.

A Queen and Spain

"DEATH TO QUEEN ELIZABETH! BRITAIN, GET out of here!" Spanish students shouted outside the British Embassy in Madrid as Falangist (Fascist) youth stoned the Embassy, broke a British bank's windows, and bombarded the British Consulate in Seville with oranges. The Falangist organ *Arriba* roared that the British-occupied Rock of Gibraltar was Spain's "sovereign territory".

Thus Generalissimo Francisco Franco's regime thundered against Queen Elizabeth's scheduled stopover at Gibraltar on the way home from her globe-trotting tour. It was feeling its oats following the signing in 1953 of a twenty-year defense agreement with the U.S.

But the Spanish protests got out of hand. The Madrid students rioted more vehemently than their government intended, and turned their passions against their police state. As they moved on the British Embassy, they were clubbed with rubber truncheons wielded by Franco's police. The students fought back with paving stones and tree branches.

They dared to insult the Franco regime, yelled "Murderers!" outside police headquarters, and built bonfires out of *Arriba*. Like the rest of the Spanish press, that newspaper made no mention of the anti-police brawls. Twenty police and 80 students were injured and 100 students were jailed before hot heads cooled off.

Only after Elizabeth had visited Gibraltar on schedule did Franco dismiss the troubles with Britain as "small talk".

In his first press conference in fifteen years, the Spanish dictator frankly admitted: "I do not believe in freedom of the press." He held out no hope, either, for free elections.

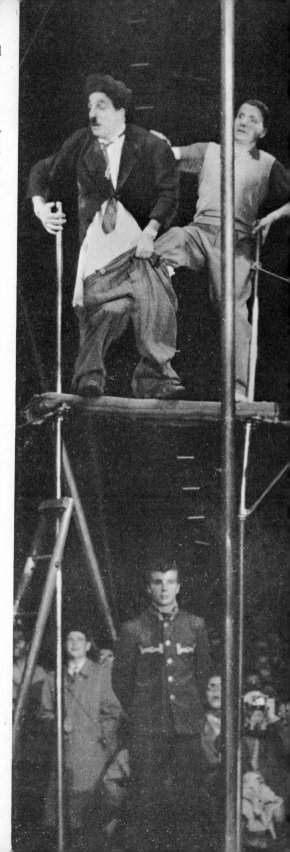

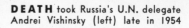

DEATH took Russia's U.N. delegate Andrei Vishinsky (left) late in 1954

The SOVIET UNION and SATELLITES

THE LONG YEARS OF STALIN'S RULE, WHICH ended with his death in March, 1953, had been a constant preparation for war by way of all-out industrialization. Guns, tanks, and planes had multiplied, but not watches, refrigerators, nylons, or perfumes.

The Soviet worker returning to his crowded home after a day's assembly-line labor had had the choice of reading prop-aganda in a Communist Party newspaper, tuning in on a war-scare broadcast, or attending a factory lecture on the joys of Communism.

With Stalin's death things eased up.

From bottom to top, there were changes. Bureaucrats, geologists, railroad men, and others, who for years had worn uniforms, were ordered into "civvies".

Premier Georgi M. Malenkov's brown,

LIFE went on as ever in Moscow — including the annual battle with winter. Here, women street sweepers push away wet snow with crude brooms

SPORTS FOR PROPAGANDA continue to be a Communist preoccupation. Here, Soviet women parade in Moscow (above), Chinese women in Peking

double-breasted, two-piece suit, the jacket several inches shorter than average and the trousers "of a length which displays several inches of sock", aroused the admiration of London's *Tailor and Cutter*. It hinted that Malenkov might someday be voted one of the world's ten best-dressed men.

Both Malenkov and Communist Party boss Nikita Sergeyevich Khrushchev, through the summer, wore light-weight suits and white fedoras, in marked contrast to Stalin's severe military dress.

There was an amnesty for criminals, a softening of police restrictions, and, notably, a dip in the price of vodka out of proportion to other reductions.

By 1954, an old plague of Czarist Russia was back in force—unrestrained drinking. Harrison E. Salisbury, Moscow correspondent of *The New York Times*, reported that drunks "sleeping it off" were common sights, whether in the center of Moscow or around the farms on holidays. Saloons flourished in the capital. In front of one of them, said Salisbury, a typical wee-hour drunken brawl resulted in a contestant's neck being deliberately broken by one man who bent his head back while two others pinioned his arms and legs. A policeman standing nearby steadily looked the other way.

Commenting to a resident of Yakutsk, Siberia, on the excessive drinking of miners and lumber workers, Salisbury was asked: "What else is there for them to do?"

Juvenile delinquency was growing. In February, the newspaper *Izvestia* reported nationwide instances of teen-age boozing, vandalism, and sadism. In Koktail Khall, Moscow's plushest bar, the *Moscow Consomol*, official gazette of the young Communists, was shocked to note 16-year-old lads, past midnight, imbibing drinks bought for them by elderly admirers. The boys wore "foreign-style jackets"

(zippered windbreakers) and zoot suits. Their hair was done Tarzan style. They spoke English and addressed each other as "Mister", not as "Comrade". In Moscow young people deliberately provoked arguments by refusing to speak Russian, and would speak only English or Latin.

Other countries behind the Iron Curtain were having similar troubles with teen-agers. A Romanian commentator cited "jitterbugging, boogie-woogie, Bikiniism, and hooliganism" as features of American imperialism "designed to destroy the creative intelligence of our youth".

In satellite Poland, the "American" fever ran high. "From the Samba to the Gallows" was the headline in one newspaper on a story which drew moral lessons from the death sentence given to a young man for "hooliganism and Bikiniism".

The principal of a Polish school cracked down hard. He sent his schoolboys to the barber, a class at a time, and ordered that no boy's hair be longer than one and a quarter inches.

Time for a Change

Reports from visitors to Red Europe revealed disheartening ways of life, despite the new effort of officials to make living conditions more pleasant. During his ten weeks in the U.S.S.R., American attorney Marshall MacDuffie could recall only two clean toilets, and only four men who wore white shirts.

Workers lived in cramped quarters, their bedrooms full of narrow iron beds and cribs. *Life* reporter Emmet John Hughes wrote of "a society scraped clean of every ornament", and of fashion shows displaying seventy-five attractive dresses and coats of which none was for sale.

In satellite Czechoslovakia, William R. Mathews, publisher of the *Arizona Daily Star*, found running water in Prague's famous Alcron Hotel unreliable, store windows empty, except for propaganda, streets jammed with people "because there is nothing left to do but walk".

In Warsaw, Poland, at the state department store, Mathews found "very shabby men's clothes that you couldn't sell for five dollars on New York's Lower East Side going for 1000 zlotys a suit", a month's wages for the average worker.

Yet in 1954 the Soviet government did much to give grubby Russia a brighter appearance. A housing program went into high gear. Big metropolitan hotels were refurbished. For the ladies, the cosmetics trust marketed dozens of new creams, with such names as Snow Maiden, which "freshens the skin", Youth, which "softens the hands", Wild Strawberry, Adolescence, Red Poppy, and others. For the gentlemen, there were brightly colored neckties.

Billboard ads showed a typically bourgeois housewife tying the morning knot on her bread-winning Romeo's neck. "A necktie makes a fine gift", the slogan read. G.U.M., the huge state-run department store on Moscow's Red Square, sold 10,-000 ties a day.

In a break with the grim past, the Kremlin, ancient stronghold and symbol of Russian autocracy, was abandoned by high government officials, and during the year served largely as the setting for holiday parties and balls for children and for almost daily public functions attended by thousands of common Soviet citizens.

A growing source of entertainment was television, although the 250,000 sets in the Soviet Union compared poorly with almost 30,000,000 in the United States. Muscovites in the top income brackets, artists and bureaucrats, for example, rushed to obtain the few new sets which went on sale, paying up to $600 for small-screen models. An average day's TV program might include a travelogue about some remote Soviet region, one of the latest plays or films, and a soccer game from Moscow's Dynamo Stadium.

On Sundays thousands of families gathered at the race tracks to roar home their investment on the "doobl" (daily double), this despite track rules "categorically forbidding any shouting during the time of the running of the horses".

To the intelligentsia the new Soviet deal brought exhibits of Western art, long taboo, a production of *Hamlet*, and, in general, an atmosphere more conducive to expression of opinion. Writers experimented with new forms and musicians dared openly to talk about jazz.

Feeding the people was a colossal problem. Stalin's treadmill had created a lopsided economy. The drawing of manpower from the fields to labor-hungry factories, peasant resistance to farm collectivization, World War II, and Soviet aid to China in the Korean War all had such serious effects on food production that in 1953 Russia had no more grain per capita than in 1928. It had less livestock than before the revolution of 1917, though, since then, thanks to government encouragement of large families, the population had increased by tens of millions.

Something had to give—and many think it was Stalin. In March, 1953, Stalin suffered a stroke or, as *Times* correspondent Salisbury suggested, was possibly murdered by henchmen who feared another blood purge was impending.

The Rise of Khrushchev

Whatever the truth, peace in Korea followed abruptly after Stalin's death, and, largely under the direction of Khrushchev, Soviet agriculture was given a new lease on life.

Experts on the Soviet Union who, in years past, had conjectured about Stalin's likeliest successor, invariably had over-

POLISH WORKERS parade on May Day past Warsaw's Palace of Culture and Science. This group bears portraits of Russian bigwigs only: from left, Kaganovich, Khrushchev, Malenkov, Bulganin, Voroshilov

looked Khrushchev. But in 1954 he held Stalin's old post of First Secretary of the Russian Communist Party and ranked among the top four in the Soviet hierarchy. The three others: Premier Malenkov, army boss Marshal Zhukov, and Foreign Minister Molotov, oldest Bolshevik of them all.

Now 59, Khrushchev, a stockily built ex-miner, had by the early 1930's already become an important party official. Having gained the Order of Lenin for his work in constructing the famed Moscow subway, he was sent to the Ukraine before World War II to cope with "bourgeois nationalism" and supervise industrial and agricultural programs.

When the Nazis overran the Ukraine, Khrushchev remained to organize guerrillas (who wrought havoc upon German lines of communication) and to win glory in the Battle of Stalingrad. As the Germans retreated, he meted out merciless punishment to Ukrainians who had collaborated with them.

Khrushchev's last big job for Stalin was a failure. This was the fantastic 1950 attempt to combine the already vast collective farms into *agrogorodi* (combinations of many collectives into centralized food-producing colossi). The aim was to wipe out the last remaining differences between individualist peasants and piece-working proletarians. A slowdown strike by the peasants quickly put an end to the project.

In September, 1953, Khrushchev, by that time his own boss, revealed that he had reversed his farm policy. He blamed the low rate of farm production on the attempt to make robots out of agricultural workers. The state, he said, must "increase the material interest of the peasant".

To ease immediate shortages, the Soviet government began to buy farm products abroad. It also cancelled work on some of Stalin's grandiose projects, among them a 700-mile-long canal; the Palace of Soviets, once scheduled to be the world's tallest edifice; and the fifteen-year program to build vast forest belts from the Danube River to the Ural Mountains.

The labor of tens of thousands of convicts was thus released for the building of barns and the planting of potatoes.

Much Promised, Little Delivered

In February Khrushchev sent 20,000 engineers to the farm collectives to remedy a breakdown in mechanization which had resulted from lack of spare parts and peasant refusal to adjust to modern methods. To help with the 1954 harvest, young people, nine or older, were urged to volunteer for work in the fields. Other "volunteers", about 150,000 strong, were sent to Siberia and Central Asia to plow up some 35,000,000 acres of virgin land, an area equal to the combined size of Texas and California. In October, homes, livestock, and land grants were given to young men who would go east.

In the hope, perhaps, of reducing the number of mouths to feed, the Presidium of the U.S.S.R. issued a decree relaxing hitherto severe penalties against abortion.

Not content with these measures, Khrushchev and Malenkov toured the collectives. In one, when a party hack began his well-practiced hymn of progress and happy peasants, Malenkov cut him short. "Show me the most backward farm in your district," he ordered. Once there, Khrushchev and Malenkov insisted upon speaking directly to the wary peasants. Malenkov encouraged them by saying: "Come, come, you're not writing a report to the Kremlin now. Just tell us what goes on." Soon the peasants were outdoing one another in complaining of high-handed bosses, lack of consumer goods, taxes, and so on.

The new policy toward farmer and consumer was also under way in the satellites.

In Hungary, where 40 percent of the collective farmers had abandoned the collectives, there was talk of giving the peasants the incentives of "good income" and a "well-to-do life".

In Poland, Premier Boleslaw Bierut declared that, while industrial production during 1950-53 had increased by 118 percent, agriculture had advanced by a mere 10 percent. Vice-Premier Zenon Nowak admitted that farm collectivization had failed.

In June, the Czechs also fell in line, as Premier Viliam Široky announced that the government would direct 320,000 persons into agriculture.

Try as they might, the Red leaders behind the Iron Curtain could not overnight raise the general standard of life for the people as a whole and for peasants in particular. On April 1, for the sixth consecutive year, the Soviet government announced price cuts. But the cuts were small, especially on food items, and soon had to be rescinded.

By September there was an anvil chorus of complaints in the satellites regarding poor living standards.

"It seems," observed the newspaper *Zycie Warsawa*, in Poland, "that there is nothing else to do but put all Polish children from one to eight to bed for the winter. There are no children's pants, shirts, wool jackets, socks, sweaters, pajamas, blouses, raincoats. . . . As for grown-ups, there are simply no electric plugs, radio tubes, electric stoves, wire, or switches to be bought in Warsaw."

In Hungary, party boss István Kovacs declared: "We are producing less, worse, and dearer."

In Romania, by late December, the lack of goods made ration cards useless and the price of many basic commodities doubled.

By 1954, largely because Malenkov's foreign policies seemed less aggressive than Stalin's, there was a striking improvement in Soviet relations with many countries previously on the American side of the fence. European and Asiatic nations were tired of spending bread-and-butter money for armaments. If the Communist bloc was willing to be friends, they were eager to let bygones be bygones.

The Soviet appeal to neutralism was symbolized by touring ballerinas, art exhibits, and the crack Russian chess team. In return, numerous European and Asiatic good-will missions visited the U.S.S.R. Most notable was the British Labour Party contingent, headed by Clement Attlee, former Prime Minister, and Aneurin Bevan, leader of the left-wing Labour faction, which stopped off at Moscow on its way to Red China.

East-West Trade Growing

Effective Communist bait was the willingness of Iron Curtain countries to purchase the industrial surpluses of Western Europe. Soviet Foreign Trade Minister Ivan G. Kabanov informed a British business delegation, in Moscow, of his government's desire to buy, from Britain alone, over $1 billion worth of cargo ships, power equipment, textile and food-processing machinery, floating docks, and other goods.

Commerce was also expanded with France, Greece, Argentina, Burma, and Scandinavia. A September exhibition of consumer goods in Moscow by eighty-eight Danish firms drew 30,000 Muscovites in the first twelve hours. United States officials conceded that, during 1954, the Soviet Union had probably signed more than twenty trade agreements.

Nevertheless, for Soviet arms production it was business as usual. On June 20, Soviet Air Day, the "Flying Rhombus", a new type of jet, was unveiled. On Sept. 17 an atomic test took place, "to enable

RED WOMEN ATHLETES, best in 1952 Olympics, did better yet in '54. Left: I. Turova wins 100-meter dash in European games at Bern, Switzerland. Below: V. Roolaid tops British mark by 18 feet in javelin throw at Russian-British dual meet in London

Soviet scientists and engineers to solve problems of defense from atomic attack".

"Nothing can frighten us," said Khrushchev, "because, if they [non-Communist countries] know what a bomb means, so do we."

As always, Soviet espionage sought to worm out United States military secrets.

On this front, the U.S.S.R. did not fare so well. The arrest and execution of Soviet secret-police chief Beria, in 1953, had made many agents in the world-wide Red spy structure fearful of returning home. Coup of the year for U.S. counterespionage was the defection, in January, of Beria man Yuri A. Rastovorov, head of

the Soviet spy center in Japan. "I want to live like a decent human being," he said as he asked for asylum in the United States.

Shortly thereafter, Nikolai Khokhlov, 32-year-old captain in the Soviet secret police, arrived in Frankfurt, West Germany, on a mission of murder. Slated to die by his hand was Georgi Okolovich, head of a Russian refugee organization. The weapon of assassination was to have been a tiny apparatus, concealed in a leather-covered cigarette case, capable of silently firing poison-filled bullets.

According to Khokhlov's story, his wife had pleaded with him to give himself up in the West, lest their child have an assassin for a father. The young captain got in touch with his intended victim and told him all. Then he made contact with U.S. agents and requested asylum. On April 27 he appealed to President Eisenhower and Pope Pius to intercede to save his wife and child from Soviet vengeance.

Early in April, Vladimir Petrov, secretary of the Soviet Embassy in Canberra, Australia, placed himself in the custody of Australian security officials. In exchange for asylum he offered to give information on Communist espionage. On April 20 Petrov's wife Evdokia, while being rushed onto a plane at Sydney by Russian embassy men, managed to shout to Russian anti-Communist emigrants demonstrating at the airport.

"Save me," she cried. "I don't want to go."

Hours later, when the plane made its next and last Australian landing in Darwin, Australian police, after disarming two Soviet goons, rescued Evdokia, probably saving her from execution in Moscow.

In 1953 Jozef Swiatlo, then an official of the Polish secret police, defected. This was not made known until September, 1954, as a new chapter was added to the top spy mystery of the postwar period. The story begins in 1949.

In May of that year Noel Field, who had been a U.S. State Department expert during World War II, vanished in Czechoslovakia. He subsequently was accused of having been a Red agent. Three months later his brother Hermann, searching for

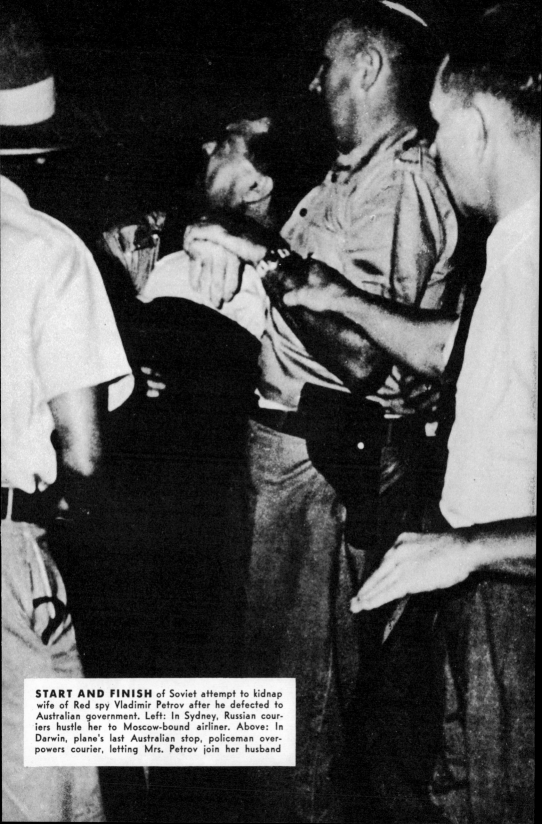

START AND FINISH of Soviet attempt to kidnap wife of Red spy Vladimir Petrov after he defected to Australian government. Left: In Sydney, Russian couriers hustle her to Moscow-bound airliner. Above: In Darwin, plane's last Australian stop, policeman overpowers courier, letting Mrs. Petrov join her husband

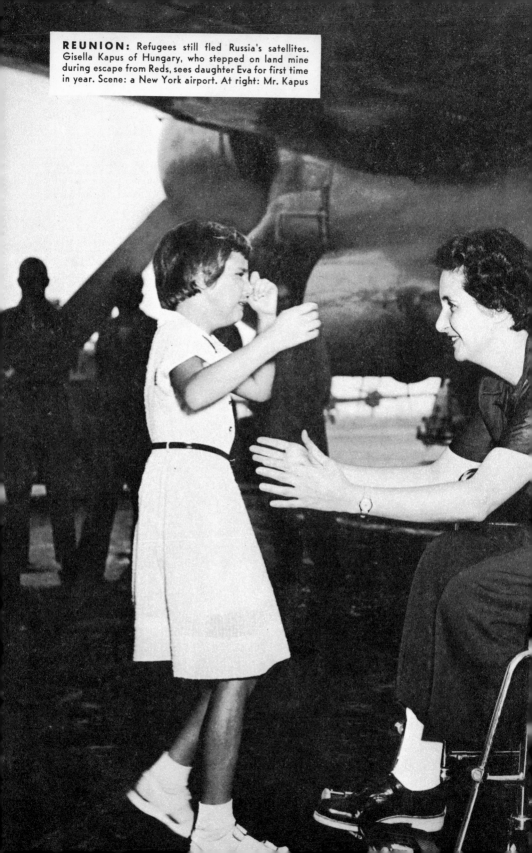

REUNION: Refugees still fled Russia's satellites. Gisella Kapus of Hungary, who stepped on land mine during escape from Reds, sees daughter Eva for first time in year. Scene: a New York airport. At right: Mr. Kapus

Noel, booked passage on a plane bound from Warsaw to Prague. He never arrived. Noel's German-born wife Herta, already in Prague trying to locate her husband, went to the airport to meet her brother-in-law. She vanished into thin air.

In the Hungarian and Czechoslovakian purge trials of 1949 and 1952, all three of the Fields, Noel, Hermann, and Herta, were named as U.S. spies.

Then suddenly on Oct. 26, 1954, the Polish government announced that Hermann Field had been released from prison, having been cleared of the charges made by American agent Swiatlo. At a press conference in Washington, however, Swiatlo denied having been an American agent. Swiatlo himself had arrested Hermann Field at the Warsaw airport in 1949, but had subsequently informed Polish officials of Field's innocence. It was his defection, Swiatlo maintained, and his knowledge of the truth in the Field matter, that had forced the prisoner's release.

When contacted by American authorities, Hermann at first appeared hesitant about leaving Poland, but in November he joined his wife in Switzerland. In a sanatorium there, he made no move to return to the United States.

On Nov. 17 the Hungarian radio announced that Noel and Herta Field also had been cleared of the charges against them. Assured of U.S. aid, Noel mysteriously replied that he was trying to cure an ulcer and would decide about his future while in a Budapest hospital. American authorities soon lost touch with both Noel and his wife.

Then, on Dec. 24, the Budapest radio announced that Noel and Herta had sought and received asylum in Hungary. Why, no one could say for sure. It was suggested, however, that the Fields feared to return to the United States lest they have to undergo questioning about Communist affiliations.

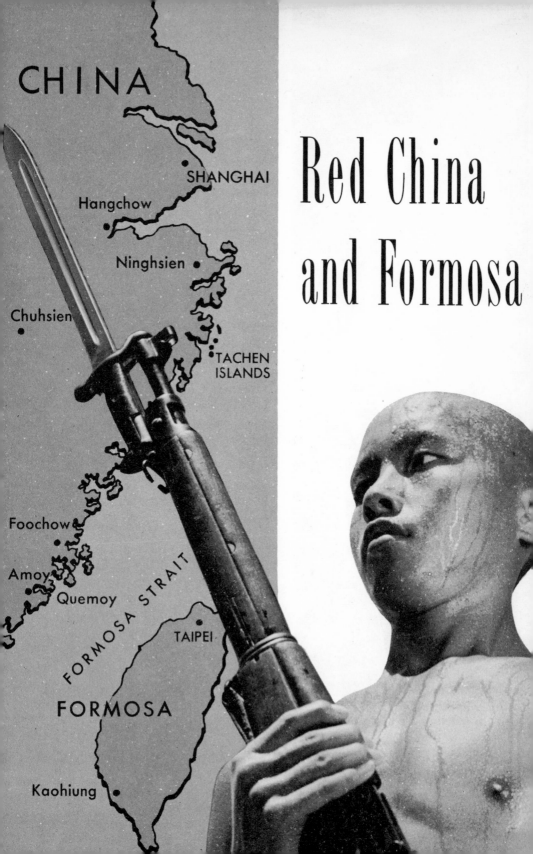

CHINA

SHANGHAI

Hangchow

Ninghsien

Chuhsien

TACHEN
ISLANDS

Foochow

Amoy

Quemoy

FORMOSA STRAIT

TAIPEI

FORMOSA

Kaohiung

Red China
and Formosa

FORMOSA'S DEFENDER, Chiang Kai-shek, poses with his two grandsons—whose mother is Russian

IN 1954 COMMUNIST CHINA BECAME A MA-
jor power. For the West, that fact was the
bitter fruit of France's lost war in Indochina, and of the Geneva conference that
ended it.

The Chinese Reds' victory was person-
alized in the deceptively boyish figure of
56-year-old Chou En-lai (pronounced *joe
en-lie*), Premier and Foreign Minister in
the Peking government. He led the 145-
member Chinese Communist delegation
at Geneva. Chou's very presence there—
technically as an invited guest, rather
than an equal sponsor—was a triumph for
the Chinese Communists.

The U.S. still did not recognize Red
China. The only Chinese government it
knew was the Nationalist regime of
Chiang Kai-shek on the island of Formosa. Chou was still considered a "bandit", as he had been during the civil war
that cost Chiang the mainland. Westerners had not seen Chou in the seven years
since the Reds launched the final round
in that war.

"Who is this Chou En-lai?" Secretary
of State Dulles asked scornfully when the
Soviets proposed inviting the Premier to
Geneva. Now the free world was to meet
Chou—as the self-confident spokesman of
a power that controlled one seventh of
the earth's area and one fourth of its population.

An olive-skinned man with striking
black brows, clad in a plain blue Chinese
tunic beneath his Western-style overcoat,
he was welcomed at the Geneva airport
by no less a Communist dignitary than
Soviet Foreign Minister Molotov. A Russian Zis limousine whisked him to his
rented villa.

His quiet, high-pitched voice with a
cultured Peking accent declared that Red
China would not "tolerate" the U.S. in
Asia. That was Chou's first speech to the
Geneva conference. It might almost have
been written for him in Moscow.

But Chou did not behave like other Soviet satellite leaders. On his way home in
June, following a preliminary talk with
French Premier Mendès-France on peace
in Indochina, he did not bother to report
in person in Moscow. Instead he stressed
his importance as an Asian by visiting India and Burma.

As a final bit of effrontery, he stopped
off in Hong Kong, the British crown colony which Red China claims as its own.
British officials were flabbergasted. The
Hong Kong airport was closed to the public. But the British governor dutifully
turned out to pay his respects.

Chou went back to Geneva for the signing of the Indochinese armistice. This
time, in triumph, he returned home by
way of Moscow. Molotov welcomed him
with a vodka-and-champagne reception
for 1000 guests. Premier Malenkov himself honored the party with his pudgy
presence.

As the number of toasts mounted toward fifty, Trade Minister Anastas I. Mikoyan grew more and more friendly with
the Chinese guest of honor—chatting
through an interpreter. They really should
learn each other's language, Mikoyan declared. "Come over to our embassy tomorrow morning at 10 o'clock, and we'll
give you your first lesson," Chou answered
—in Russian.

"Coming of Grace"

Such lordly behavior was a reminder
that Chou had long been known—and not
always flatteringly—as "the gentleman
Communist". His grandfather had been a
mandarin, one of the higher officials of
the old Chinese Empire. The family name
can be traced back some 2500 years to the
Chou Dynasty in the time of Confucius.
For generations the Chous had been
scholars and officials.

Chou En-lai (his given name of En-lai

means "Coming of Grace") was born at his family's upper-middle-class country home near Shanghai in 1898. He grew up in Manchuria, where his father held a government post under the Empire. His mother was considered a "radical" intellectual.

Chou's father lost his post with the downfall of the Empire in Sun Yat-sen's revolution of 1911. The family moved to Tientsin, where the elder Chou tried his hand as a businessman. He soon found that the "foreign devils" had a head start. He decided that his son should have a foreign-style education to match them at their own game.

The boy went to school in Japan and to Nankai University, run by American missionaries in Tientsin. There he fell in with a group of young radicals and joined a nationalist organization called the Awakening Society. He was arrested in a student riot in 1919.

Chou spent the next year in jail, where he met a plump, earnest girl named Teng Ying-ch'ao. Later, they were married. The happy ending to this Communist love story: eventually she became boss of the huge All-China Democratic Women's Federation. They had no children.

Released from prison, Chou signed up with a "work-and-study" group going to France. It turned out to be mostly work—in the coal mines of Lille and the Renault automobile factory in Paris. In China, the young man had heard little of Communism. Now he learned of it from the French workers around him. Chou was converted.

In 1921, Mao Tse-tung and his comrades founded the Chinese Communist Party in Shanghai. Chou, still in France, promptly organized branches among his countrymen in Marseille, London, and Berlin. Inevitably, he made the pilgrimage to Moscow. The Comintern bosses saw his usefulness and trained him.

Chou was—and is—no theoretician, but a shrewd, hard-driving organizer who worked best under pressure. He rose regularly at dawn. His polished manners and ready wit made him an ideal front man. He spoke French, English, German, and Russian. He never smoked, and seldom drank, but he was a graceful dancer. When it suited his purpose, he could flash a quick, warm smile. At other times his bearing, as the London *Observer* once put it, was that of "a puritan clergyman".

His wide-set eyes were frank and open, even when he was lying. But, said former Nationalist Premier K. C. Wu, who had known Chou since boyhood, they were the "eyes of a man who could kill".

Moscow sent Chou back to China in 1924. At that time, Chiang Kai-shek still was trying to work with the Communists to subdue the feudal war lords and unite the country. The heart of his movement was the Whampoa Military Academy in Canton. There Chou arrived as assistant to "General Ga-lin" (who also called himself Vasili Blücher), the Soviet military adviser to Chiang. Chou quickly worked his way into the post of political commissar with Chiang's crack First Army.

Chiang learned the hard way the impossibility of working with Communists. In 1927 he sent Chou to Shanghai to prepare it for the arrival of the Nationalists. Instead, Chou organized a workers' rebellion and seized the city for the Reds.

Chiang repaid the treachery with a blood purge of suspected Communists. Chou himself was sentenced, but escaped the firing squad by minutes—with the aid of an officer who had been one of his students at Whampoa. His ability to survive earned him the nickname of Pu Tao-weng (literally "the old man who never falls down"), the Chinese roly-poly doll that always lands upright on its round, weighted bottom.

With the Reds outlawed, Chou became

RED WELCOME of confetti and cheers greets American G.I.'s who refused repatriation after Korean War ended, later disappeared into China

VILLAGE TRIAL in northern China: judges ponder case of man who tried to sell girl relative named Spring Orchid to farmer. Above (and left, on stool beside the accused) is the girl herself

a "bandit" with a price of $80,000 on his head. He also became the chief of a secret Communist execution squad. When one Ku Hsun-chang broke from the Reds in 1932 and talked to the police, Chou and his men paid a call at Ku's home in Shanghai. Chou stood laughing on the balcony while his gang slaughtered the entire household—thirty men, women, and children.

Beaten by Chiang in 1934, the Reds retreated 6000 miles across China to the bleak caves and yellow hills of Yenan in the remote northwest. Chou arrived skeleton thin and sporting a scraggly beard. At once he began preparing for the Reds' comeback.

WOMAN WORKER digs ditch in section of Canton once occupied by Western traders. In lieu of machines, strong backs must do—and Red China has hundreds of millions of them

The Japanese invasion of China gave him his opportunity. He persuaded the Nationalist general Chang Hsueh-liang, called "The Young Marshal", that the Reds wanted only to be allowed to fight side by side with Chiang against the Japanese. Chiang, he said, wanted to fight only Communists—even at the cost of losing the country to Japan.

Convinced, the Young Marshal kidnaped Chiang and held him prisoner for two weeks at Sian in western China. Madame Chiang courageously flew to join her husband. The outside world was sure that Chiang had been—or was about to be—murdered. But Chou arranged his release. The price: collaboration between Nationalists and Communists against Japan.

The Reds kept the bargain after a fashion. They helped to fight the invader. But they also used the time thus obtained to build up their own armies until they were ready to fight their countrymen.

"Agrarian Reformers"

It was Chou and his wife—living in a carefully modest house in the Nationalist capital at Chungking—who during World War II convinced many American officials that the Chinese Communists were harmless "agrarian reformers". And it was also Chou who played a leading role in the Communist decision to resume the civil war in 1947.

At Geneva, Chou showed off his new power to the West. In August, back home

"MODERN" CHINA, despite Communist claims of progress, still depends heavily on human muscle. These Chungking laborers are lugging stone for Russian-type dormitories

again, he received a group of Westerners who seemed to be paying homage to that power. They were eight members of a British Labour Party delegation headed by dry little Clement Attlee, former Prime Minister. Among them was massive, florid Aneurin Bevan, the left-wing Welshman who wanted to replace Attlee as Socialist boss.

The party traveled to Peking by way of Moscow, where Soviet leaders went all out to plug their new line of friendliness. Premier Malenkov himself plucked a bouquet of phlox, petunias, and gladioli from the garden of his summer house for schoolmarmish Dr. Edith Summerskill, the only woman in the British group.

And Malenkov shattered precedent by dining with the visitors at the British Embassy. Nothing like that had happened there since Stalin dined with Churchill in 1942. Reportedly, Malenkov remarked: "I hope, Mr. Attlee, the purpose of this trip is not to take our Chinese allies away from us."

The Chinese seemed determined to outdo their Soviet allies' hospitality. Chou welcomed the Britons with a lavish luncheon of such Chinese delicacies as shark fins, bamboo shoots, and lotus roots. He too broke precedent by dining at the British Legation in Peking. The dinner was grimly English: melon, cold fish, and chicken.

The climax of the three-week junket was an interview with Mao. He had long been absent from the scene, amid rumors that he had suffered a heart attack. Now he appeared in his familiar plain gray tunic, glowing with health. The setting was the reception hall of the Forbidden City, with its richly lacquered ceiling and collection of ancient, priceless vases.

There the Chinese Red boss told the British Socialists his price for "world peace". It was that Britain should force the United States to (1) withdraw the Seventh Fleet from protecting Chiang and the Nationalists on Formosa, and (2) abandon Japanese and West German rearmament.

Attlee returned home to say that Formosa should eventually be handed over to the Communists. "Chiang Kai-shek and his immediate adherents, who are utterly discredited, should be retired to some safe place," he said.

Statements like that seemed to confirm the fears of many who denounced the visit to Red China as "irresponsible". Red propagandists used the visit to boost Peking's prestige to new highs throughout Asia.

On the other hand, Red China's growing prestige encouraged some to hope that, as Chou and Mao tasted more power, they would grow dissatisfied with being Soviet puppets, and might yet be encouraged to break with Moscow, as had Marshal Tito of Yugoslavia.

Cost of Obedience

Already Peking could demand—and get—a high price for continued obedience to Moscow. A Soviet mission headed by none less than Nikita S. Khrushchev, First Secretary of the Communist Central Committee, tasted Chou's hard bargaining. The results, announced on Oct. 11: Moscow gave up its half interest in joint companies to exploit metals and oil in China, to build ships, and to run the civil air lines.

Moscow agreed also to the evacuation and return to China of Port Arthur, the ice-free, landlocked naval base in southern Manchuria.

The Russian people had never forgotten that Japan took Port Arthur from them after a "Pearl Harbor" attack in 1904. (However, the port was not historically a part of Russia; it had merely been leased in 1898 from China.) They had gone wild with rejoicing when Stalin "regained" the base as part of a 1945 agreement with Britain and the United States. Now Stalin's successors were giving it away.

Moscow seemed to be trying to buy off Peking, to prevent it from invading Formosa. With Chiang's island fortress guarded by the U.S. Seventh Fleet, an invasion attempt might well bring a clash with the U.S. that would touch off World War III. Even so, the Chinese Communists in 1954 twice provoked dangerous clashes.

The first came in July when two Red Chinese fighters shot down an unarmed British-owned C-54 air liner off Hainan Island. It was bound for Hong Kong from Bangkok. Eight of the passengers and crew clambered aboard a life raft and were picked up by a U.S. Air Force rescue plane, which ventured inside Chinese territorial waters. The ten lost included an American resident in Java and his two small sons.

Two U.S. aircraft carriers, the *Hornet* and *Philippine Sea*, rushed to the area. U.S. planes searched in vain for more survivors. When Red Chinese war planes tried to stop them, navy fighters shot down two. Eventually the Reds apologized to Britain for the incident, and agreed to pay $1,027,600 in damages.

Peking's get-tough policy soon switched to Formosa. "It is imperative that the People's Republic of China liberate Formosa and liquidate the traitorous Chiang Kai-shek group," Chou blustered in August. "If any foreign aggressors dare to interfere . . . they must take upon themselves all the grave consequences."

The Communist strategy was to hit at the string of tiny Nationalist-held islands screening Formosa from the mainland. There were two dozen of them, with a total area of less than 200 square miles, stretched in a 350-mile line.

The Reds began on Sept. 3 by blasting Quemoy (pronounced *kee-moy*) Island, which blocked Amoy harbor, the Communists' best staging base for an invasion of Formosa. The Nationalists answered by sending destroyers into Amoy harbor, guns blazing. Nationalist F-84 Thunderjets and F-47 Thunderbolts bombed and strafed the mainland.

In November, the Communists shifted their attacks to the Tachen Islands, the northern anchor of the Nationalist outposts. Russian-built bombers raided the Tachens for the first time, and Red torpedo boats made their first appearance in the war, sinking the Nationalist destroyer escort *Taiping* (formerly U.S.S. *Decker*), with a loss of twenty-nine lives.

At Home

The Chinese Reds had their troubles as well as their triumphs in 1954. Their Five-Year Plan for industrialization was lagging. One list of thirty-one specific projects showed that thirty were far behind schedule.

What Peking called "the heaviest rainfall in 100 years" flooded the vast Peking-Shanghai-Hankow triangle of farmland. The loss of wheat, rice, cotton, and soyabean crops meant famine, the ancient scourge of China. "Cultivate the style of bitter struggle," the party warned the people.

Back from a trade mission to Peking, a Japanese businessman declared: "The Chinese Communists have wisely discarded those details of Communism which do not suit the Chinese character. Although large-scale production, transportation, and banking have been taken over by the state, other fields are open to the public. The regime has never tried to enforce collective farming. Former tenants who used to pay 60 percent of their crops in rent, now not only own their land, but pay a tax of only 1½ to 3 percent of its value."

Apparently, the Red bosses were settled in to stay. On Sept. 20 the rubber-stamp People's Congress in Peking formally adopted Communist China's first constitution. The proceedings also raised to new prominence General Chu Teh. A war lord, dope addict, and keeper of a harem in his youth, Chu, by his prowess in the civil war, had made himself a legend among the people. For example, many peasants believed he could fly like a bird. Now he became Vice-Chairman of the government, with the right of succession to Mao. It was a figurehead job, but it helped to move the army into political affairs. Chu was known to be a military gambler, willing to take great risks for high stakes. He was also a protégé of Chou, who had signed him up for the party in Berlin in 1921.

The partnership between the tough general and the wily politician seemed to be reflected in the Reds' December announcement that they had jailed as spies eleven American fliers and two civilian employees of the Defense Department captured during the Korean War.

On the one hand, the Communists thus risked provoking the U.S. into a blockade of the China coast, if not more drastic retaliation. On the other hand, they set the stage for a new round of profitable diplomatic maneuvering, as Secretary General Dag Hammarskjöld of the U.N., in the closing days of 1954, proposed to discuss the case with Chou in Peking.

MAN-MADE SNOW
— ticker tape — pelts
Korea's Syngman Rhee
on visit to New York

KOREA and JAPAN

THIS WAS THE SAD AFTERMATH OF THE
Korean War in 1954:

In Korea—a green truck bounced down
a road toward the neutral zone established by the 1953 armistice. Its Chinese
Communist driver wore a gauze surgical
mask. Inside the truck were the first
bodies of the 4011 United Nations dead

to be returned to the U.N. by the Reds.

"Why not just let 'em lay?" asked a
soldier assigned to the sickening job of
checking the corpses for identification.

"There are people back home," an officer reminded him. "Even if all they get
is a few bones."

In Lubbock, Texas—a young widow

REAL SNOW—winter's first—touches Japanese children with universal delight

PEACE IN KOREA brings continuing hardships. This young mother is trying to rear a child in hunger, cold, wretched living quarters. And the G.I. opposite, who helped beat back aggression, will never be whole again

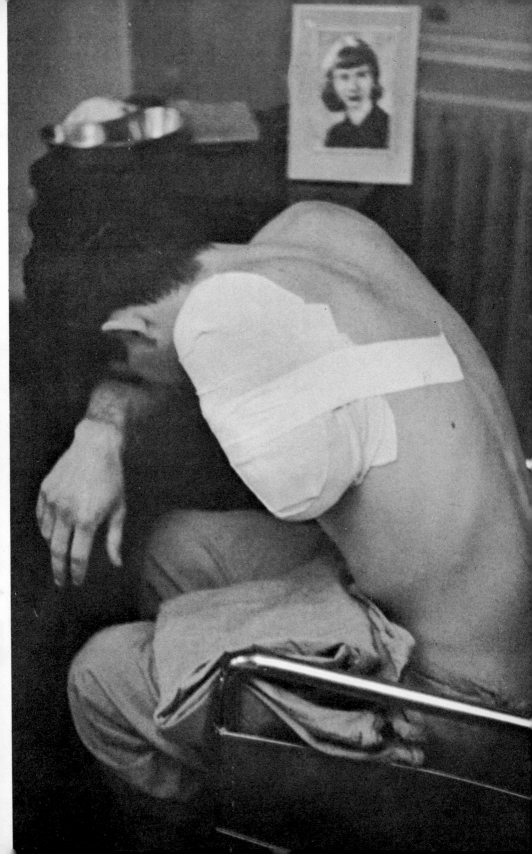

with three small children received the Medal of Honor awarded posthumously to her husband. He was Major George A. Davis. He had flown 266 missions in the Pacific war against Japan. In Korea, he had downed fourteen Reds. Then he had dived his Sabre jet into a flight of MIG's, and got two before they got him.

Mrs. Davis looked around the house her husband had bought a week before being sent to Korea. "If I could feel that he lost his life for some good reason, I could feel better about it," she said.

The Korean War had baffled and confused the American people. It was the only war in 175 years that the United States did not win. But it had tested the will of the free nations to unite against aggression, had fought Communism to a standstill in Northeast Asia, and had saved not only South Korea but in all probability Japan, Asia's No. 1 industrial power, for the free world.

The shooting had been over for nearly six months when 1954 began. The remaining problems were (1) how to negotiate a peace treaty for Korea, and (2) what to do with prisoners of war on both sides who refused to go home.

In January, 1954, the P.O.W. issue came to a head. The prisoners who refused to return home numbered 327 South Koreans, 21 Americans, and 1 Briton, all of whom wanted to stay with the Communists, and 22,500 Chinese and North Koreans who wanted to stay with the U.N. (One American, Corporal Claude Batchelor, 22, of Kermit, Texas, had changed his mind and left the Reds on New Year's Day.)

The P.O.W.'s were held in barbed-wire compounds within the neutral zone around Panmunjom, where the truce had

INCREASING Japan's trade with Red China and friendship with U.S. are aims—mutually exclusive?—of Premier Hatoyama, shown with grandchildren

been signed. A Neutral Nations Repatriation Commission was in charge of them. Its members: India, Czechoslovakia, Poland, Sweden, and Switzerland. An Indian custodial force of 5000 troops, commanded by Lieutenant General K. S. Thimayya, stood guard. They were armed with sticks and side arms only.

The Communists and the U.N. had agreed to give the Repatriation Commission authority to hold the P.O.W.'s only through Jan. 22. By then, they hoped, they would have worked out an agreement on the prisoners' fate. They failed, and as a result found themselves in a fresh dispute.

The Reds insisted that the prisoners remain in custody after Jan. 22. The U.N. commander, U.S. General John E. Hull, declared that the neutrals' authority to hold the P.O.W.'s could not be extended, and that the prisoners must be released to join whichever side they chose. He knew that the anti-Communist Chinese and North Koreans were afraid they would be killed if forced to return home.

The upshot was this: the P.O.W.'s were returned to their original captors, thus allowing the U.N. to free its anti-Communist prisoners. The Eighth Army commander, General Maxwell D. Taylor, warned that any Red attempt to interfere would be met with force and probably "start the Korean War over again". There was no interference.

Freedom Road

Early on the morning of Jan. 23, the U.N.'s prisoners started marching down the frozen, rutted road from the neutral zone. The columns kept coming until late that night. The Chinese, five abreast, carried portraits of Chiang Kai-shek and of Sun Yat-sen, the founder of the Chinese Republic. Loud-speakers blared at them: "Dear anti-Communist comrades, we have come here to welcome you." "Thanks, thanks," the P.O.W.'s shouted back.

Sousa marches played as the Chinese climbed aboard trucks waiting to carry them to Inchon. There they boarded L.S.T.'s (Landing Ships, Tank) for the voyage to Chiang's Formosa. Seven trains waited to transport the anti-Communist North Korean P.O.W.'s to Republic of Korea (R.O.K.) army camps.

At first the Reds refused to take back the P.O.W.'s who wanted to join them. When the Indian guards pulled out, these "progressives" stayed in their chill, cheerless camps. They killed time by skating on the frozen paddy ponds or running relay races that involved flogging dummy figures of Chiang, R.O.K. President Syngman Rhee, and Secretary of State Dulles.

"Solidarity Forever"

On Jan. 26, singing propaganda songs like "Solidarity Forever", the pro-Reds marched into the so-called Peace Pagoda at Panmunjom for a press conference. They waved banners with Red slogans and huge pictures of "peace doves". The Americans among them, said their spokesman, Sergeant Richard Corden of Providence, R.I., had refused to return home because there was only a "witch-hunt, McCarthyism . . . lynch law" in the U.S.

Ex-P.O.W.'s who had known them said they were "rats and stool pigeons". Thimayya, a spit-and-polish officer trained at Sandhurst, the British West Point, called them the sorriest, most shifty-eyed and groveling bunch he had ever seen.

The U.S. wasted no more time on them. Secretary of Defense Wilson ordered the twenty-one Americans dishonorably discharged from the army. Three days later, Russian-built trucks finally arrived to carry them northward—not as free men, but still as P.O.W.'s. They were briefly

BUDDHIST FESTIVAL in Saidaiji, Japan, temple finds 1500 young men scrambling for two sacred batons tossed into their midst by priests. Battered winners emerge hours later, trade "lucky" batons for cash awards — or rice. Struggle, shown in this flash photo of the darkened room, may last all afternoon. Men wear only loincloths; clothes would be torn to shreds

paraded in Communist cities in China and elsewhere. Then they disappeared, their propaganda usefulness outworn.

Even as the pro-Reds turned their backs on the U.S., thousands of American troops in Korea were preparing to go home. The 45th Infantry ("Thunderbird") Division was the first to return as a unit. It paraded up Broadway to a New York ticker-tape welcome. Then its members scattered. The Thunderbird reverted to its peacetime status as a component of the Oklahoma National Guard. Next the 40th Division was withdrawn and returned to the California National Guard.

Then the Defense Department decided to pull out four of its remaining six divisions and the bulk of its air units. America's U.N. allies in Korea also cut back or pulled out their forces. Washington promised that, if the Reds started the war again, the U.S. would honor its agreements with its allies but would fight on battlegrounds and with weapons chosen by the West, rather than by the Reds.

Outlook Unsettled

The long-delayed political conference that was to settle Korea's future finally took place in Geneva in April, but was quickly swamped with the problems created by the Indochina crisis. Korea faced the future still divided and South Korea had no new leader in sight for the day when someone must succeed President Syngman Rhee—now 79.

The leathery old patriot was limited by the R.O.K. constitution to two terms in office and was serving his second, which would expire in 1956. In December he sent to the South Korean Assembly a proposed constitutional amendment setting aside the two-term limit.

The Assembly had 203 members. The amendment needed a two-thirds majority to pass. On paper, two thirds was 135⅓

votes; in practice, it meant 136. Rhee got 135. The Speaker of the Assembly declared the amendment had failed.

"The government feeling is that the fraction must be disregarded," said a spokesman for Rhee. Obeying orders, his followers in the Assembly took a new vote declaring that 135 indeed filled the two-thirds requirement, and Rhee signed the amendment into law. He now felt free to run for a third term.

Rhee never gave up hope of reuniting his country. He repeatedly threatened to renew the war if necessary. Demanding action, he made a speaking tour of the U.S. in August. But Washington had no desire to resume hostilities, and, in spite of South Korean protests, it put the R.O.K. army on short rations of gasoline and ammunition. For front-line units, stocks were enough for no more than three to five days of operation.

To soothe Rhee's pride, the U.N. Command turned over to R.O.K. control the 2300 square miles of territory it held north of the prewar boundary between North and South Korea. This was the only ground won by U.N. forces during the three-year war.

In the U.S., the Korean War left lingering, unpleasant echoes. They came from the fact that American fighting men had been subjected to the Communist "third-degree" technique of "brainwashing". Public and military leaders alike debated what should be done with those who had cracked under it. No firm decision was reached.

In March a Marine Corps court of inquiry wound up hearings on the case of Colonel Frank H. Schwable, a 45-year-old Marine flier who had "confessed" to Red charges of waging "germ warfare". Undoubtedly, his "confession" had helped the Communists. But he had broken down only after fourteen months of solitary confinement, during which he had not been permitted to sleep at night, and by day had been forced to sit bolt upright in a wet, vermin-infested, freezing cell.

Major General William F. Dean, who had undergone a lesser degree of Red brainwashing without cracking, testified in Schwable's behalf. The court of inquiry decided against disciplinary action; there was "reasonable justification" for the Colonel's collapse. But Schwable's career as a combat officer was over. He was to be assigned to "duties of a type making minimum demands . . . upon the elements of unblemished personal example and leadership".

Among enlisted men, Corporal Edward Dickenson drew ten years for collaboration while a P.O.W.

Perhaps the most disturbing case was that of Claude Batchelor, the Texas country boy who had been the only one of the pro-Red holdouts to change his mind, but who was court-martialed all the same. Former P.O.W.'s testified that he had informed on one prisoner, recommended the shooting of another. His sentence was life imprisonment, later reduced to twenty years. To many it seemed unduly harsh—in view of the fact that Batchelor had been encouraged to return to the U.S.

Japanese Start-up

FOR JAPAN, 1954 WAS THE BEGINNING OF A new era. Just 100 years before, Commodore Matthew Perry had sailed his fleet of American ships up Tokyo Bay and opened the country to the modern world. That Japanese era had rushed on to Pearl Harbor—and had ended in surrender on the broad deck of the battleship *Missouri*.

Now, nine years later, the U.S. and Japan signed a mutual-defense agreement in Tokyo. The U.S. would help rearm Japan in spite of the provision in the Japanese constitution, dictated by General Douglas MacArthur, that "land, sea, and air forces . . . will never be maintained".

By the end of the year, Japan's new National Self-Defense Force, as it was called, comprised an army of 130,000, a 15,800-man navy, and a 6000-man air force.

The change did not come easily. Many Japanese, frightened by their islands' exposure to the Communist Chinese and Soviet mainland of Asia, felt Japan should remain neutral. Their fears of war were heightened by such incidents as the shooting down by Soviet MIG's of an American B-29, which crashed on the northern Japanese island of Hokkaido.

Other Japanese felt that their country should make friends and trade with the mainland, as it had so profitably done before World War II. The conflicting pressures brought an upheaval that, in the closing weeks of 1954, toppled Premier Shigeru Yoshida from power.

The new Premier was Ichiro Hatoyama, 71, semicrippled by a stroke, but the most popular politician in Japan. His government was pledged both to continue the alliance with the U.S., which Yoshida's Liberals had formed, and to seek trade with the Reds.

Hatoyama had founded the Liberal Party after V-J Day, and won the first postwar election. The night before he was to become Premier in May, 1946, he was suddenly "purged" from political life by General MacArthur's command. As No. 2 in the party, Yoshida took his place. When Hatoyama was "depurged" in 1951, he expected Yoshida to resign in his favor. Yoshida didn't, and Hatoyama began organizing a new party, the Democrats.

Hatoyama's ties with the West go back to his father, who was educated at Yale University. The new Premier studied law at Imperial (now Tokyo) University, and was first elected to the Diet (parliament) in 1915. He was a Cabinet minister before he was 40. In the 1930's he was often spoken of as a future Premier. But the militarists then ruling Japan considered him too Western-minded.

A Baptist who played golf until his health forced him to give it up, Hatoyama lives in a Western-style brick house on one of the highest points of ground in the Tokyo area. One of his prides is his collection of hundreds of hybrid roses. He understands English perfectly, although he prefers to talk with Westerners through an interpreter. His wife, a dignified, white-haired lady, is president of Kyoritsu Women's University, which his mother founded.

Danger Signs

The Japan that Hatoyama took over was torn by political quarrels, shaken by reports of graft among government officials, and in danger of economic collapse.

The low point politically was reached in June. Yoshida, then Premier, wanted a two-day extension of the Diet session. The Socialists determined upon a test of strength. They mobbed the Speaker of the lower house, Yasujiro Tsutsumi, in one corner of the Diet chamber. As long as he could not get to the Speaker's chair, the Diet could not come into session.

Tsutsumi, a burly judo expert, crashed through the ring surrounding him and got as far as a caucus room. There the Socialists trapped him again. He stood them off for two hours. Then a Liberal rescue party slugged its way in and swept him toward the Speaker's chair.

The battle surged back and forth across the Diet chamber. Politicians clambered on desk tops to swing at one another with chairs, inkstands, and fists. Tokyo police had to be called to restore order. The injured numbered 50—including 24 police. The Japanese public was shocked by

this display, which many claimed was proof of Japan's unreadiness for democracy.

Few, however, paid much attention to a greater danger—inflation.

The hard fact was that, during the occupation and the Korean War, Japan had known a false prosperity from G.I. spending and U.S. Army procurement orders.

Now the bubble burst. One measure of the gravity of the situation: in the fall of 1954, only six of Japan's fifty-seven shipbuilding docks were in operation.

To meet the danger, Hatoyama appointed, as Finance Minister, Hisato Ichimada, governor of the Bank of Japan and a firm believer in deflationary policies. Ichimada's task was to restore the country's dangerously low gold and dollar reserves. To do that, the 88,000,000 Japanese, whose crowded islands are not self-supporting, would have to cut their imports to the barest necessities, and boost their exports to pay for them. Only thus could Japan survive. But as one Tokyo banker remarked: "Our people have been taught to live beyond their means. We are importing far more than we need, and the tendency is upward."

Ashes of Death

A far more meaningful issue for the public was the H-bomb. The Japanese, who had been the only victims of the A-bomb, now could claim the first H-bomb victim as well. He was Aikichi Kuboyama, 39, radioman on the *Fukuryu Maru* (*Lucky Dragon*) *No. 5*.

That unfortunate fishing boat had been 80 to 90 miles off Bikini Atoll at 4 A.M. on March 1 when an American test H-bomb was exploded. Two hours later a snow-white coral ash began to shower the twenty-three crewmen. They all came down with "radiation sickness".

In September Kuboyama died. U.S.

Ambassador John M. Allison expressed his country's "extreme sorrow" and sent Kuboyama's widow a check for 1,000,000 yen ($2777). But the feeling of the Japanese against their new American allies reached dizzy heights. "Where can we take our anger?" wrote Tatsuzo Ishikawa, Japan's most popular author. "The United Nations is controlled by the U.S. . . . . We can but grind our teeth."

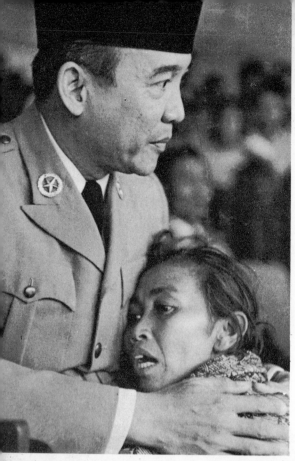

EMOTION greets Indonesia's President Soekarno on tour of western Java as he comforts a guerrilla victim (above), waves to crowd (right)

JAWAHARLAL NEHRU WAS "TIRED AND PERPLEXED", HE TOLD A meeting of his Congress Party in New Delhi on Sept. 30. The Indian Prime Minister then wrote a letter to each member of his Cabinet.

"Dear Comrade," it began. "I venture to write to you to dispel doubts and rumors." The letter went on to say he would not run for re-election as party president when his term expired in January, 1955, and that he planned not to "function as Prime Minister for at least some time".

Informed Indians thought that Nehru's threats to retire were designed mainly to prove his popular support and to silence political opponents. Nonetheless, at 64, this slim, sensitive Indian, educated at Harrow and Cambridge, bore a responsibility that would tire and perplex many a less dedicated man.

As the political heir of the late Mohandas Gandhi, Nehru was more than the leader of 357,000,000 Indians. He was the symbol of a vast, awakening South and Southeast Asia deter-

SOUTHERN ASIA

TEMPORAL LEADER: Premier Mohammed Ali of Pakistan bowls on Washington visit

SPIRITUAL LEADER: Vinoba Bhave, Indian "saint", presents appeal to Indian landlords. So far he has won voluntary gifts of land for 2½ million peasants

mined to shake off all traces of its colonial past. But although he had made India an independent republic, he remained a powerful voice in the counsels of the British Commonwealth. Above all, he was the great "neutralist"—determined to lead an Asian bloc that would counterbalance both Communist and anti-Communist worlds.

Nehru's Neutralism

In 1954, Nehru found his role as self-appointed savior of Asia harder and harder to maintain. The overwhelming fact for all of South and Southeast Asia was the victory of Communist aggression in Indochina—and thus the threat of Red Chinese expansion.

In June, Nehru invited Chou En-lai, the Premier and Foreign Minister of Red China, for a visit as Chou was returning from the first round of the Geneva conference. A cheering crowd of 2000, waving Chinese Communist and Indian flags, greeted Chou as he stepped from an Air India Constellation at Palam Airport.

Nehru beamed as his Communist visitor, clad in black silk tunic and black beret, was wreathed with flowery leis. At a state banquet, the two exchanged lengthy toasts replete with reminders of their countries' "2000 years of traditional friendship".

In October, Nehru returned the visit. "A world event in a historic sense . . . All other things are trivial," he said of his journey to Peking. He was suffering from insomnia and a bad cold. On the way, he stopped off in Hanoi in Indochina, to obtain nonaggression pledges from Ho Chi Minh, the Moscow-trained Vietminh President, who had just come into power as a result of the Geneva agreement.

Peking went all out to welcome Nehru. A crowd of 200,000, mostly blue-uniformed students, lined the 6-mile drive from Hsiyuan Airfield to the Red capital.

Within two hours of his arrival, Nehru was received by Mao Tse-tung, the Chinese Communist chief of state. There followed a merry-go-round of cocktail parties (orange juice for Nehru), banquets (shark fins and Peking duck), and speeches—translated into English and Russian as well as Chinese and Hindi.

Nehru saw through this Oriental courtesy. In his private talks with Chou in June, Indian officials let it be known, Nehru had made no secret of his dislike of Communist methods. What most concerned him, as an Indian, was the way the Chinese Reds in 1952 had swallowed up Tibet on India's Himalayan border.

In his public exchange of toasts with Chou in India, Nehru pointedly stressed the promises the Reds had given after the "liberation" of Tibet. These were first stated in a Chinese-Indian trade pact signed at Peking. The terms: "Recognition of the sovereignty and territorial integrity of each country"; "mutual noninterference with each other's internal affairs"; "equality and mutual benefit and peaceful coexistence".

What Nehru wanted in China was assurance that Peking would keep these promises. But to many who had heard Communist promises before, this seemed dangerously naive.

Diluting Nehru

Among those who mistrusted Indian neutralism were three of the four Asian Prime Ministers who met with Nehru around a satinwood table at Colombo, the capital of Ceylon, in late April. The so-called Colombo Powers were India, Pakistan, Ceylon, Burma, and Indonesia. It was the first conference ever to discuss the mutual problems of these young nations.

Nehru came armed with a key resolution denouncing "colonialism" as a "violation of fundamental human rights and a threat to the peace of the world". It made no mention of Communism. To his surprise, only Premier Ali Sastroamidjojo of Indonesia supported him. Ceylon's Sir John Kotalawala introduced a counter-resolution to put the five countries on record against "aggressive Communism".

After 100 hours of debate, the Prime Ministers adopted both resolutions. But Kotalawala's was generalized into a pledge "to resist interference in the affairs of their countries by external Communist, anti-Communist, or other agencies".

"We only wanted to dilute Nehru, not to deflate him," one Ceylonese official explained.

"Pimples on the Map"

Nehru had another set of problems. These were what he called "pimples on the map" of India—seven tiny coastal settlements belonging to France and Portugal.

Pondichéry, on the east coast, was capital of the French Settlements in India, which included also Karikal and Yanaon on the east coast, and Mahé on the west. A battered statue of Marquis Joseph François Dupleix stood as a reminder of the 300-year-old dream of French Indian Empire.

On Nov. 1 France, bowing to the pressure of Asian nationalism, lowered the Tricolor over Pondichéry and the three smaller settlements. Thereupon the 193 square miles and 318,000 population reverted to Indian control.

Portugal, however, had no intention of getting out of its three enclaves on the west coast above and below Bombay. The chief Portuguese settlement was Goa, where St. Francis Xavier, the 16th-century missionary, was buried.

When a Free Goa movement, backed by India, announced a march on Goa in August, Portugal rushed in African troops. The "liberation" fizzled. The Portuguese "pimples" remained.

Wan's Fears

WITH THE END OF THE HOT WAR IN INDO-china, the great danger to the remaining countries of southern Asia was less outright aggression than Communist infiltration.

Thailand (literally, "Land of the Free") feared it was next on the Communist timetable. Its 18,000,000 inhabitants included 3,000,000 Chinese—many of them fifth columnists. In addition, some 50,000 Vietnamese refugees had crossed the border from Indochina into Thailand, and many were Red agents in disguise.

Prince Wan Waithayakon, the Thai Foreign Minister whose daughter, Wiwan Wordwan, went to Wellesley College and spent her vacations in New York as a United Nations guide, told the U.N. of the threat of "large-scale Communist infiltrations . . . in order to subvert the government of my country".

Little Thailand would be a rich prize for the Reds. Its 2,500,000 acres of paddy fields in the central plains around Bangkok, the capital, were the greatest remaining rice bowl in the world. Its northern mountains were covered with forests of teak and other woods. Its long tail down the Malay Peninsula produced tin and rubber. Its people were the best fed in Southeast Asia.

Thailand's prosperity depended upon rice. It was more than a food. It meant jobs—growing and harvesting the crop, extracting various by-products such as fodder and fertilizer.

The profits from the government's rice-marketing monopoly took the place of taxes. Without rice Thailand could not exist.

V.I.P.'S IN INDIA: Premier Nehru (above) surprises guests with his skill at ancient stick game, *kalaripayattu*. Right: En route from Geneva, China's Chou En-lai doffs shoes on entering Indian memorial

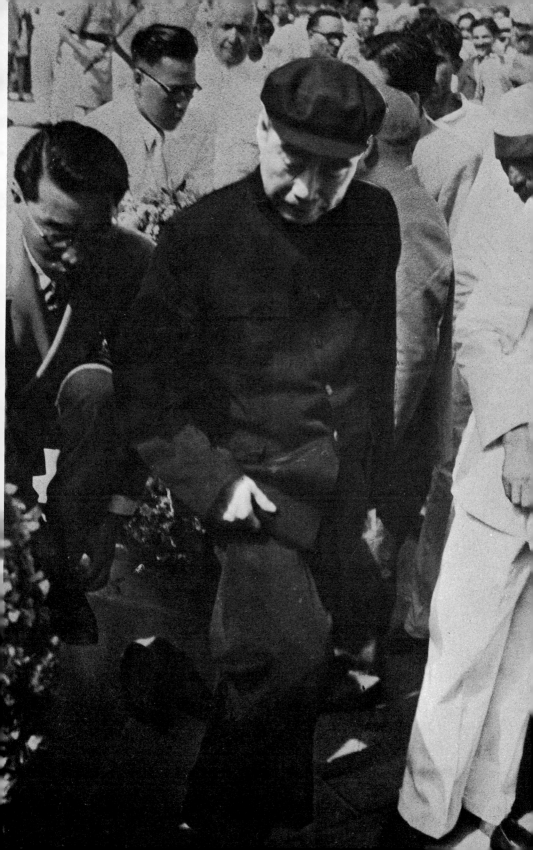

Unfortunately, in the years of shortage after World War II the government had gone too far in exploiting its seller's market in neighboring countries. Customers in India and Indonesia had been antagonized. As their own crops improved, they stopped buying from Thailand. By 1954, Thai granaries were filled with unsold rice, some of it two years old and spoiling. The Communists counted on the situation getting worse, creating poverty they could exploit.

Communist plans for Thailand centered on a former Premier and Regent named Pridi Phanomyong. A wartime Socialist underground leader, Pridi had been ousted in a coup following the 1946 murder of King Ananda Mahidol.

Since Pridi had discovered the King's body, shot through the head, and had tried to pass off the death as an accident, many Thai believed he was the murderer. Their suspicions persisted even after the conviction in October of a former royal secretary and two former royal pages.

By that time, Pridi was established under Communist auspices in nearby Yunnan Province of China. He headed a Red front called the Free Thai Autonomous Government. The Peking radio relayed his rallying cry to his countrymen to "wage a struggle against [their] rulers —American imperialism and its puppets".

But the cheerful, easygoing Thai cherished their freedom, and the government of Premier Luang Pibul Songgram seemed determined to defend it. The driving force behind the scenes was General Phao Hriyanonp, pink cheeked, gray haired, still in his 50's, and chief of all Thai police.

"At first he looks like a cross between a camp counselor and a clergyman. Actually he is a combination tiger and wild ox," said one of his aides. One of Phao's typical exploits: infiltrating the Bangkok Communist organization with loyal Chinese who gathered enough evidence to jail dozens of Reds.

The government also was alert to the danger of outside aggression. With the aid of an American mission headed by Major General William J. ("Wild Bill") Donovan, who served as U.S. Ambassador to Bangkok, Thailand built up its armed forces to 134,000 fighting men. Plans called for doubling the army by 1956, and providing it with U.S. heavy equipment.

U Nu's Firmness

NO COUNTRY IN SOUTHERN ASIA HAD MORE experience in fighting Communists than Burma. In fact, since Burma became an independent republic outside the British Commonwealth in 1948, it had been plagued by rebellions of no fewer than three varieties of rival Communists—one group loyal to Moscow; another loyal to the memory of Joseph Stalin's defeated enemy, Leon Trotsky; the third, a home grown group interested primarily in banditry. In addition, the government had to fight rebellious Karen tribesmen and marauding Chinese Nationalist soldiers who fled into Burma at the end of the Chinese civil war.

Dealing with these assorted dangers was the job of 47-year-old Premier U Nu. His given name, Nu, means "soft" or "gentle". U is simply a courtesy title of respect (Burmese do not use family names). A rowdy street urchin who was a habitual drunkard at twelve, he reformed in his teens when, he says, "something deep down inside suddenly changed". He went on to become a philosophy student, schoolteacher, playwright, and statesman.

After six years, his government's army of 60,000 had the home-grown rebels well in hand. In his dealings with huge Red China also, the gentle Nu could be firm

For example, when Chou stopped off in Rangoon the day after his June meeting with Nehru, Nu met him at the airport. But Nu stood unmoving, and waited for Chou to approach. By contrast, Nu had walked half way to meet Richard M. Nixon when the U.S. Vice-President visited Rangoon late in 1953. It was a snub that Chou could not have missed.

For resisting Communism by infiltration, Burma's best bet was the land-reform program begun in June with the distribution of 21,000 acres to 4500 landless peasants. The plan called for the distribution of 10,000,000 acres to 2,000,000 peasants in nine years. Landlords would be compensated for their lost acres with one year's rent. And the new farm owners would have a new stake in their country's future.

Magsaysay's Victory

IN THE PHILIPPINES, PRESIDENT RAMÓN Magsaysay, a national hero at 46 as a result of his successful fight against the Communist-led Hukbalahap rebels, scored his biggest victory in May.

After months of secret negotiations, the chief Huk leader, Luis Taruc, surrendered to a young *Manila Times* reporter. The scene was a tiny village at the foot of a volcano; the time, shortly after dawn. As the reporter, Benigno Aquino, walked along the highway, a thin man in gray peasant shirt and brown trousers stepped out.

"Do you accept the President's terms?" asked Aquino. "I accept," Taruc replied.

The terms were unconditional surrender. Taruc must stand trial for his crimes without any promise of a "deal" with the government. He pleaded guilty to twenty-three counts of murder, arson, kidnaping, and robbery. The government asked life imprisonment, but in September a Manila court sentenced Taruc to only

twelve years and a $10,000 fine. The Huk leader, who read a dog-eared copy of *The Reader's Digest* in court, beamed. His relatives crowded around to congratulate and kiss him.

"I am shocked," said Magsaysay. "Such a light sentence is a mockery of justice." He ordered Taruc re-tried on a new charge—the 1949 ambush-murder of former President Manuel Quezon's widow.

Indonesia

ONE OF THE SHAKIEST SPOTS IN ASIA WAS the island republic of Indonesia. For 350 years the Indonesians had been ruled by the Netherlands. They had won their independence in December, 1949, after a bloody revolution. Ill-trained for a sudden plunge into self-government, and still nursing the memories of colonial hatreds, the Indonesians turned increasingly away from the West. In 1954 they cut one of their last remaining ties by dissolving their five-year-old loose partnership with the mother country.

They also demanded that the Netherlands give them West New Guinea, the last remnant of the Dutch Empire, a 150,-000-square-mile jungle wasteland. Its 1,000,000 inhabitants have no racial ties with the Indonesians, but until it was surrendered, Indonesian Foreign Minister Soenarjo blustered, "peace in Asia, Australia, and the West Pacific will remain threatened".

The Reds worked hard to cash in on Indonesia's state of mind. Premier Sastroamidjojo's Nationalist government was the only one in all of free Asia to depend upon the open support of Communists in Parliament. And Moscow sent Dmitri A. Zhukov as the first Soviet Ambassador to Jakarta, the Indonesian capital.

The 45-year-old veteran troublemaker, once expelled from Chile for his activities, set up headquarters with his staff in

Jakarta's rambling Des Indes Hotel, formerly a symbol of Dutch wealth and prestige.

Ali's Troubles

THE WEST'S BEST FRIEND IN SOUTH ASIA was Pakistan. Newly allied to Turkey, it formed the eastern anchor of the free world's Middle East defense arc. It outlawed the Communist Party. But Prime Minister Mohammed Ali's country—the largest Moslem nation in the world—was divided into two parts separated by 1000 miles of hostile, Hindu India. Worse still, the two parts were antagonistic.

West Pakistan was an arid land. Its people were the tall warriors who once formed the backbone of the old British Empire's Indian Army. Their language was Urdu, their biggest city, Karachi, the capital of the entire country.

East Pakistan was a wet, steamy, over-crowded land. Its people were short, slow-to-anger Bengalis. Their per capita income was only one third that of the West Pakistanis. Ali himself is a Bengali from East Pakistan, but that did not keep people from grumbling that the Karachi government treated them "like some sort of colony".

The first sign of trouble came in the East Pakistan provincial election in March. Ali's Moslem League, which had ruled since the British withdrew in 1947, was nearly wiped out; it lost all but 10 of the 309 seats in the provincial legislature.

The winner was a five-party United Front that included Reds and other leftists. At their head was the "Lion of Bengal", 81-year-old Abdul Kasan Fazlul Huq. He ruled as East Pakistan's chief minister. His campaign slogan had been: "I love you all, and if you love me, you will vote for me." He called for independence from West Pakistan.

Trouble broke out at a jute mill in Narayanganj where Bengali laborers were bitter about the better wages and housing they felt were given to workers recruited from West Pakistan. In the village bazaar, a fireman from West Pakistan warned the keeper of a tea stall that his fire was too high. An argument followed. The West Pakistani was stabbed. Suddenly a full-scale riot was on—with guns, swords, pickaxes, and knives. In two months a series of such clashes left at least 600 dead.

Thereupon Ali cracked down. "Disruptive forces and enemy agents are actively at work, setting Moslem against Moslem, class against class, province against center," he said. He ordered Huq deposed for "treasonable activities".

But Ali's troubles were not over. In October he visited the United States seeking economic aid. In his absence, the Governor General of Pakistan, Ghulam Mohammed, declared a nationwide state of emergency, dissolved the Constituent Assembly, and ordered Ali to reorganize his Cabinet pending new elections. Ali flew home to face the crisis, carrying with him a pledge of $105 million in United States aid. He found that the Governor General was ruling the roost.

Meanwhile Pakistan continued to quarrel with India. In July, Nehru opened the first link in a 4500-mile, $237 million canal system to divert the waters of the Sutlej River to India's East Punjab. Pakistani engineers claimed that this would dry up their irrigation canals, and their nation's 5,000,000-acre granary in West Punjab and Bahawalpur would become a "dust bowl". Both sides agreed to talk it over, with the International Bank for Reconstruction and Development as the mediator.

FOREIGN FRIEND: Comedian Danny Kaye, making round-the-world tour for U.N., pauses near Delhi, India, to meet a wee villager

THE SUDAN AND EGYPT now are partners, to judge from handclasp of their respective Premiers, El Azhari (left) and Nasser. They were wildly acclaimed by these Cairo demonstrators

The MIDDLE EAST

DURING THE SUMMER OF 1954, TWO BIG breaths of diplomatic fresh air cooled off the superheated deserts of the Moslem Middle East. Egypt won Britain's agreement to evacuate its $1 billion military base in the Suez Canal Zone. Iran won Britain's agreement to give up its $1 billion oil concession centering on the great refinery at Abadan.

These two settlements were won by Moslem dictators. But they were applauded also by the Western democracies. By ending the West's worst diplomatic feuds with the Moslem world, they partly offset its military disaster in Indochina.

Egypt and Suez

ON THE NIGHT OF JULY 27, 1954, IN CAIRO's marble-walled Cabinet room, Premier Gamal Abdel Nasser (pronounced *nah'-ser*), a strapping Egyptian of 36, reached

TOP EGYPTIANS signal "unity" to quell public demonstrations. From left: Cabinet member Salah Salem, titular President Naguib, Premier Nasser. Harmony did not last. Nasser soon forced Naguib out

into a pocket of his lieutenant colonel's uniform. Wearing a toothy grin beneath his bristling mustache, he disdained the fountain pens outstretched by a dozen of his hangers-on and took out his own.

With it he initialed a two-page document. The British Secretary of State for War, Anthony Head, also initialed it. With no pun intended, the document was called the "Heads of Agreement". Thus Britain agreed to transfer the Suez base

from London's to Cairo's control. And thereupon Nasser's henchmen smothered their hero with kisses.

"Nasser howwa el nasser" ("Nasser is the victor"), Cairo crowds shouted—*with* a pun intended. They celebrated with iced mango and tamarind sirups passed out free by Cairo cafés. Nasser dashed off a lemonade, in accord with the Koran's nonalcoholic teachings. Then he proclaimed to the people over the Cairo

radio: "Fate has stored this day for glory."

"O Free and Glorious," the radio effused to Egypt's downtrodden peasants, "we have cast away the last fetter on glorious independence." It was seventy-two years since British troops had first landed in Egypt.

Now the British agreed that within twenty months they would remove their 80,000 troops from the Canal Zone's 5000 sun-drenched square miles, and leave the sprawling storehouses there to be maintained by civilian technicians. They transferred their Middle Eastern headquarters to the big Mediterranean island of Cyprus—which was promptly torn by anti-British riots incited by Greece's claim to the island because its population is 80 percent Greek. The British shipped the bulk of their Suez manpower home to give their ill-protected motherland, for the first time in recent years, a sizable strategic reserve.

In return, the Egyptians agreed to let the British come back to Suez at any time within seven years if Turkey or any of the Arab League's eight members (Egypt, Libya, Lebanon, Syria, Iraq, Jordan, Saudi Arabia, and Yemen) were attacked. The potential aggressor, presumably, was the Soviet Union.

Only nine years earlier, Sir Winston Churchill had branded a proposal to withdraw from the Suez zone as "great shame and folly". Now he revealed that the hydrogen bomb had made his past strategic thinking "utterly obsolete" and the withdrawal "absolutely necessary".

Foreign Secretary Eden chimed in: "What we need now is a working base and not a beleaguered garrison. We shall be creating a new pattern of friendship throughout these Middle Eastern regions."

"We can start at once to build a new basis of relationship with Britain and the West," Nasser rejoiced.

The United States showed its approval of the Suez settlement by removing its ban on economic aid to Egypt. Truly Nasser was the "victor".

Yet only five months earlier, Egypt's kinky-haired, hawk-faced leader had seemed to be vanquished in the frenetic feuding within Cairo's Revolution Command Council (R.C.C.), the ruling army junta which had packed King Faruk off into Italian exile on July 26, 1952.

Brilliant but shy, Nasser was the selfless soul of the R.C.C. junta. He worked twenty hours a day, asking nothing for himself. With his wife and four children he lived in a somewhat shabby bungalow and kept his desk in his bedroom. He abstained from liquor and never let himself be photographed smoking a cigar, lest the peasants be reminded of the licentious living of the Faruk era. Often he lunched at his office on *fool*, an Egyptian variety of chili con carne.

Although the real creator of the revolution, Colonel Nasser had tried to stay in the background as Deputy Premier. His R.C.C. clique had set up Major General Mohammed Naguib as front man, serving as the Egyptian Republic's Premier and first President.

Egypt's No. 1 military hero, "Papa" Naguib at 53 lent a fatherly sense of maturity to the youthful R.C.C. Whether pipe smoking or baby kissing, he looked both venerable and amiable. But Naguib was not content to front for his juniors, none of whom was even 40. He craved power as well as prestige.

Naguib and Nasser ceased to be on speaking terms. The General often pretended to be sick or threatened to quit in order to win his own way. The Colonel faced his bust of the President toward the wall.

At 7 A.M. on Feb. 25, President Naguib tuned in to the Cairo radio. He heard that the army junta had rejected his bid for "absolute individual power", accepted his resignation as both President and Premier, and named Nasser to be Premier.

Down from Naguib's modest stuccoed villa came a banner reading "Allah Save Naguib". His house was ringed by soldiers. His telephone was cut off.

However, Colonel Nasser, for the moment, had overreached himself. The Naguib symbolism was not so easily destroyed. A cabal of cavalry officers led by the pro-Communist, 33-year-old Major Khaled Mohieddin, himself a junta member, clanked out in tanks to insist on Naguib's restoration. Cairo crowds, rallied by Moslem extremists and Red agitators, shouted: "No revolution without Naguib!" Civil war loomed.

Colonel Nasser sounded a temporary retreat. A Nasser aide found Naguib in his pajamas, and asked him to return to power. The General agreed, saying: "These things happen in all revolutions. Just a family quarrel." On Feb. 27 the "Allah Save Naguib" banner was again flying over the President's villa. To a Cairo crowd he said: "I owe you my life."

But Nasser was not vanquished. He got Major Mohieddin dropped from the army junta. His followers rallied Cairo crowds to chorus "Long live Nasser!" and "We will kill Naguib!" One R.C.C. member, Wing Commander Gamal Salem, told the President he would assassinate him. More moderately, Nasser told Naguib that the whole junta would quit if the people wanted it to.

At that, the people in the streets, rallied by Nasser, shouted: "We want the revolution!" Strikes swept Egypt, army officers refused to command, police refused to maintain order, the navy sailed out to sea—all in support of Colonel Nasser.

"Bowing to the people's will," an R.C.C. officer announced, the junta would stay in power. The scheduled return to democracy—which by Egyptian traditional

tion would have meant blatant demagoguery and rank corruption—was called off. Naguib was made a mere figurehead. He remained temporarily as titular President. But Nasser in mid-April took over again as strongman Premier.

The Suez settlement won Nasser mass popularity, but not as much as did eight bullets fired at him on Oct. 26 by a would-be assassin in Alexandria. Resounding in the middle of a Nasser radio oration, the shots were heard by all Egypt.

"I am ready to die for you," the Premier shouted out, as an entire nation listened in anxiety. "If I die, you will carry on with the struggle. I brought you freedom and human dignity. If Gamal Abdel Nasser dies, every one of you is a Gamal Abdel Nasser." Actually the shots missed their mark. But they served Nasser well.

The gunman, a Cairo plumber, confessed he had been hired by the fanatically anti-Western Moslem Brotherhood. The confession gave Premier Nasser a long-awaited excuse to crush the terrorist Brotherhood, the biggest threat to his rule. Its headquarters were burned by Cairo mobs. Hundreds of its leaders were arrested. Six, including the would-be assassin, were hanged.

When Brotherhood leaders testified that President Naguib knew in advance of the assassination plot, he was summarily ousted and placed under house arrest. Premier Nasser, taking over the presidential duties, now ruled supreme.

Iran and Oil

BY THE BEGINNING OF 1954, IRAN HAD BEEN brought to the brink of bankruptcy and Communism as the result of ex-Premier Mohammed Mossadegh's 1951 nationalization of the concession of the Anglo-Iranian Oil Company.

But now "Old Mossy", ousted by an uprising of conservatives in 1953, was in sol-

BEAUTIFUL Queen Soraya of Iran visits U.S. Note her matching diamond necklace and earrings

alienated the Moslem world from the West.

On Aug. 5, in the Elahyeh Palace's garden near Teheran, the Zahedi government initialed a pact under which Iranian oil would be brought back into the world's markets by an international consortium of eight giant British, American, French and Dutch companies. By August, Premier Zahedi admitted, Iran was so broke that "there is hardly anything for anyone to steal".

The man who brought the Iranians and British together was Herbert Hoover Jr. a 50-year-old American engineer and geophysicist, serving as $11,000-a-year special adviser to Secretary of State Dulles. Hoover had a passion for anonymity. His father, the ex-President, liked to say: "It's wonderful to have a son who is making a great success of life, and is doing it by himself."

Tirelessly the younger Hoover commuted among Teheran, London, and Washington. His philosophy: "Everything is possible where there's good will." His secret of success: listening attentively, through his hearing aid, which he never sought to conceal.

So successful was he in performing his first important public service that in September President Eisenhower drafted him to succeed General Walter Bedell Smith as Under Secretary of State.

The oil pact, as worked out by Hoover, gave something to everybody, by:

(1) Recognizing Iran's title to its nationalized oil industry and giving Iran the 50-50 split in net profits that had become the norm in Middle Eastern oil countries. Iran expected thereby to receive $200 million annually.

(2) Allowing the Anglo-Iranian Oil Company to retain a 40 percent interest in Iranian oil, and compensating it with $70 million from Iran and $600 million from its new partners.

itary confinement for three years for treason. He trotted out all his trickery as he appealed his sentence. He refused to appear in court until after the chief prosecutor offered to kiss his big toe. He vowed to "fast unto death"—until he was caught eating cookies and vitamin pills.

With him out of the way, Premier Fazlollah Zahedi, a soldier-strongman, broke the three-year-old deadlock with Britain that, together with the Suez issue, had

(3) Giving five American oil companies—Jersey Standard, Socony, Texaco, Gulf, and California Standard—a share (40 percent) for the first time in Iran's fabulously rich oil fields.

Premier Zahedi, rounding up a far-flung assassination and espionage ring of 600 Communist officers in the army, air force, and police, now urged his people to abandon the "absolute blunder" of trying to steer a neutral course between Communism and freedom. Iran, he said, must do its part in "support of the free world".

Middle East and Defense

DURING THE YEAR, AMERICAN STRATEGY IN the Middle East relied, not on the defenseless deserts of the eight Arab League nations far south of the Soviet frontier, but on the "northern tier" embracing the tougher non-Arab nations—Turkey, Iran, and Pakistan—adjoining the Soviet border. In Karachi on April 2, Turkey, the strongest Moslem nation, and Pakistan, the most populous, agreed on a policy of "friendly collaboration".

Thereupon Washington, already allied to Turkey in N.A.T.O., announced it would re-equip Pakistan's sturdy soldiers with modern matériel. Turkey and Pakistan agreed to "widen the scope" of their mutual-defense treaty—for example, by adding Iran, the missing link between their frontiers, or Iraq, the oil-booming British ally adjoining Iran and Turkey.

Iraq was the only Arab nation to make a real contribution during 1954 to the West's defense strategy. It broke with the generally neutralistic policy of the Arab League by agreeing to accept military aid from the U.S. At 66, for the twelfth time, the pro-British Nuri es-Said took over as Prime Minister.

He was a mere boy compared to Hashem el Atassi in neighboring Syria.

ATHLETIC Shah Pahlavi of Iran, touring America with his Queen, enjoys water skiing in Florida

בנ̇ת א̇ג̇ד̇ אש̇ר
ליום אילת
לחלוצי הנגב

UNSAFE HIGHWAY in Israel was traveled by this bus, which was attacked in the Negeb desert. Authorities said 11 men, women, and children were killed. Jordan was blamed

There a comic-opera coup d'état brought El Atassi, at 89, back to the presidency for the third time. It sent the pint-sized dictator Brigadier General Adib Shishekly, anti-Western and anti-Israeli, off in Adolf Hitler's old Mercedes, headed for Saudi Arabian exile as he prayed: "Allah save Syria."

Israel and Arabs

IN THE HOLY LAND, DURING 1954, ABOUT the only four-day stretch without a single shooting occurred during the rare coincidence of the Christian Easter, Jewish Passover, and Moslem Evening of Creation. Otherwise a rash of border incidents, caused by Israelis and Arabs alike, pockmarked Palestine during the year.

Moshe Sharett, Israel's new Prime Minister, warned that the armaments which the Arab nations were promised by the U.S. and Britain, supposedly for defense against Soviet attack, might be used to wipe out his Jewish island in a Moslem sea.

The United Nations Mixed Armistice Commission for the Israel-Jordan frontier was powerless. Its machinery broke down after an Israeli bus was ambushed by Arab tommy gunners in Scorpion Pass near the Jordanian border. Eleven Israelis were killed. Only four survived. A waitress named Miriam Lesser later said: "I played dead. One of the Arabs dragged me up by the hair to see if I was alive, then shot at my head but missed."

Israel insisted: "The Jordanian government bears full responsibility." But the U.N. commission, headed by Commander Elmo H. Hutchison, U.S. Navy, publicly refused to censure Jordan and privately blamed the outrage on Bedouin tribesmen living inside Israel. Thereafter Israel boycotted the commission as "impotent".

In Israel's absence the commission blamed it "in the strongest possible" terms for a midnight raid in March (nine Jordanians were killed), for a border violation in May (a U.N. inspection team was peppered by a mortar barrage), and for a battalion-sized raid in September (two Arab Legionnaires were killed and three abducted). But toward the end of 1954, Commander Hutchison was called home and replaced, Israel ended its boycott of the U.N. commission, and its borders quieted down—at least temporarily.

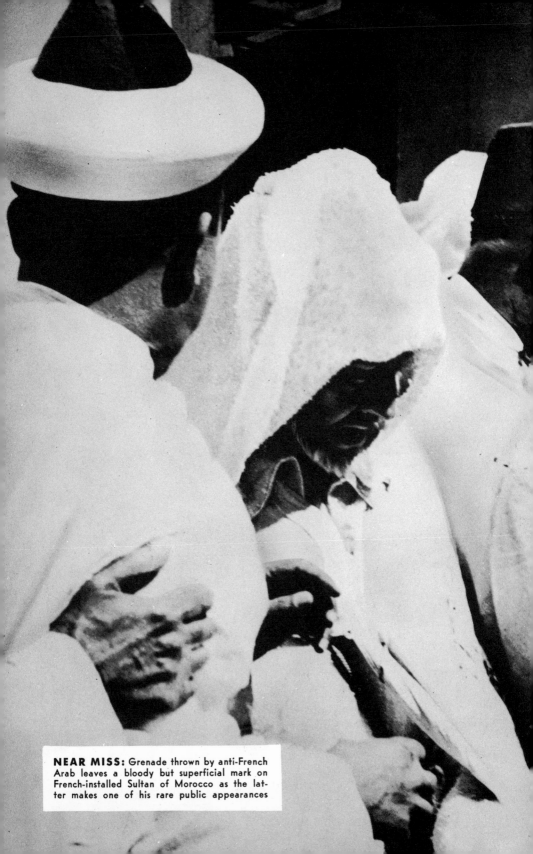

NEAR MISS: Grenade thrown by anti-French Arab leaves a bloody but superficial mark on French-installed Sultan of Morocco as the latter makes one of his rare public appearances

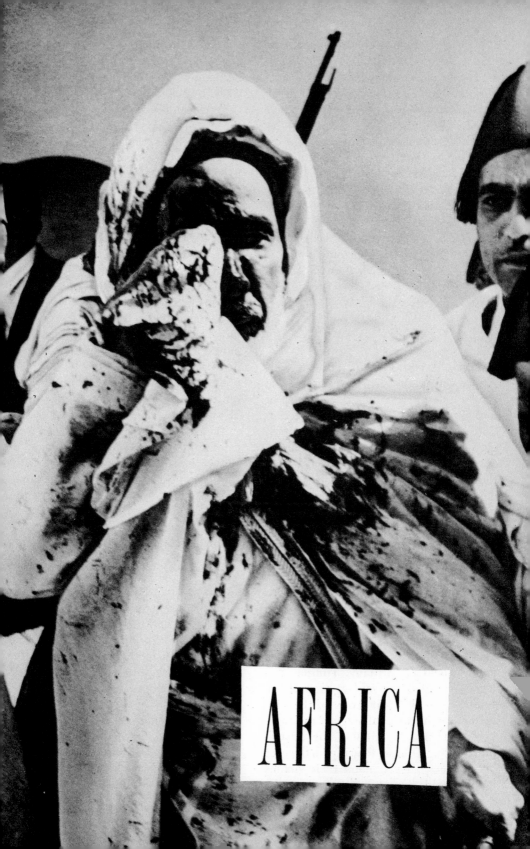

AFRICA

FRANCE HAD TROUBLES IN NORTH AFRICA IN 1954 as well as in Indochina. By summer its twin protectorates of Tunisia and Morocco seemed to be going the way of its empire in Southeast Asia. But French Premier Mendès-France had learned the lesson of Dienbienphu. He was bent on avoiding another "too little, too late" policy that would lose France's rich North African territories. For "without North Africa," he said, "there will be no history of France in the 21st century." His problem was to satisfy nationalists' demands for more freedom while keeping both Tunisia and Morocco under French control. He decided to deal first with Tunisia, under French rule since 1881.

Tunisia

MAKING A FLYING VISIT IN JULY, MENDÈS-France called on the 72-year-old *Bey* (Ruler), Sidi Mohammed el Amin, at this French puppet's fabulous palace in Carthage. There Mendès-France proclaimed "without reserve the internal autonomy of the state of Tunisia" within the French Union. But he was not just handing over to the Arab nationalists the deserts that France had made bloom. He insisted on the right of French colonists to live and work there. He threatened "pitiless measures" if the Arab-vs.-colonist violence did not end.

By the summer of 1954, 300 persons had been slain in Tunisia in three years. The French had exiled the ascetic Habib Bourguiba, leader of the outlawed New Constitution (Nationalist) Party, to a lonely island off Brittany. Tunisian *fellagha* (pronounced *fel-leg'-a*) outlaws, calling themselves the Army of the Liberation, plundered, sabotaged, and murdered. Hoping to frighten the French into quitting Tunisia, they raped, they cut out tongues, they blinded their victims with lighted cigarettes.

They were inflamed from Franco Spain by Radio Tetuán, from the Arab world by Radio Cairo, and from the Communist world by Radio Budapest.

Terrorism bred counterterrorism. Near the French naval depot at Ferryville Arabs machine-gunned a café terrace and a bus, killing eight persons. In retaliation French colonists in speeding cars machine-gunned the terraces of Arab cafés.

Mendès-France, who had once served as legal counsel to a North Africa terrorist, sought to end this violence. He created the French Cabinet's first Ministry for Tunisian and Moroccan Affairs. He legalized the New Constitution Party. He put in a pro-French landowner, Tahar Ben Amar, as Tunisian Premier, with a largely New Constitution Cabinet. He moved Habib Bourguiba from island exile to a French villa.

Bourguiba observed: "Mendès-France represents the last chance for Franco-Tunisian friendship."

To appease those colonists who were calling him "Judas Iscariot", Mendès-France installed as Resident General of Tunisia tough Lieutenant General Boyer de la Tour du Moulin. The Premier also weakened France's defenses on the European continent by massing 30,000 French troops in Tunisia to hunt down the fellagha outlaws.

In adjacent Algeria, when a terrorist "Army of Allah" killed seven persons one November night, Mendès-France struck back with 20,000 more troops. Since Algeria was not a protectorate but politically a part of metropolitan France, the French government regarded members of the Army of Allah as traitors. Rather than negotiate with them, it warned: "The only negotiation is war."

To end the fighting in Tunisia, the Mendès-France regime took a daring gamble. It promised to let the outlaws go free, without punishment, if they surrendered with their weapons by Dec. 9. The gamble paid off; 2713 outlaws surrendered.

Morocco

BECAUSE MOROCCO WAS MORE PRIMITIVE than Tunisia, the French policy there was to crush the terrorism before experimenting with home rule. Morocco had been ruled by the French only since 1912. Its native population was split between the anti-French Arabs and the pro-French Berbers.

In one year 100 persons had been murdered. The fun-loving Sultan, Sidi Mohammed ben Youssef, had become the hero of the Arabs' underground Nationalist Party. Accordingly the French had exiled him to far-off Madagascar. However, they had permitted him to take his favorite concubines.

Moroccan terrorists boasted: "Casablanca will be another Dienbienphu." One of them tossed two hand grenades into a prayer meeting in a Marrakech mosque and inflicted head wounds on Sidi Mohammed ben Moulay Arafa, the aged puppet Sultan who had replaced Ben Youssef. El Glaoui, the octogenarian Pasha of Marrakech, pulled a pistol from under his sheetlike robes and put four bullets through the terrorist's head.

At Casablanca, one Arab stuck a butcher's knife, 15 inches long, into a European. At Port Lyautey, a Frenchwoman was stabbed and her daughter was choked to death, and two French soldiers were castrated. At Petitjean, six Jewish shopkeepers were murdered and their bodies put to the torch. At Fez, Arab nationalists stoned the police, shouting "Long live Ben Youssef!" The police opened fire and killed five.

Even Communists took to calling for Ben Youssef's return.

Would the use of pitiless measures to crush this terrorism work or backfire? Correspondent Frank White, in *Time* magazine, described the "raking-in" which the French conducted in the *medina* (native quarter) of Port Lyautey after the murder of seven Europeans:

"The legionnaires, working systematically, began breaking down the doors of every house. Once a door smashed, in went the *goumiers* and drove out every male, except small boys. Women cried out in terror, and were beaten back with clubs or gun butts.

"On top of a low hill in Port Lyautey's *medina* is a dusty sheep market. Legionnaires drove the Arab men there and herded them under the muzzle of a Patton tank. A dozen policemen formed a gantlet, six on either side. One by one, the Arabs were thrust forward, each with his hands on his head. . . .

"Said a reserve police colonel: 'The session is about to begin.' He smiled broadly, then hit a middle-aged Arab with his right fist, below the belt. As the Arab went down, the colonel kneed him in the groin. The Arab tried to get up; another cop caught him across the jaw with a club. Down went the Arab and the next cop kicked him, twice. . . .

"Altogether, more than 20,000 Arabs were routed out of their homes to run the gantlet that day. Slugging, clubbing, and beating that many men is an exhausting job, so the police spelled one another. They invited civilians to lend a hand, and one brute of a youngster accepted and enjoyed himself. . . .

"Before the day was done, 6,000 men, including most of those between 17 and 25, had been . . . loaded into cement trucks and hauled off to jail. As they went, their womenfolk came pushing out of the houses, screaming and crying 'Allah'. The police fired into the air . . . The cops were not too careful about keeping their fire high. . . .

"That evening, as the troops and tanks rumbled back to their barracks . . . French men and women poured out from their sidewalk cafés, lined the streets, and cheered the military. The office of the French Resident General announced tersely that 20 Arabs died."

No Kid Gloves in Kenya

"YOU CAN'T CONDUCT WAR AGAINST MUR-derers with kid gloves," said an old-time British administrator in Kenya. Like French colonists in North Africa, British settlers in this East African colony balked at any conciliation to end the bloody terrorism begun in 1952 by a black-magic society known as the Mau Mau.

A psychologist's report, too obscene to be released publicly in Britain, explained how the Mau Mau ceremonies turned docile natives into savage terrorists: "The ceremonies were devised to break every tribal taboo . . . The effect on the mind of primitive people is overwhelming . . . After taking three or more oaths, the personality of the oath taker has changed . . . These people do not hesitate or think any more. They just kill on being instructed to kill—their own mother, their own baby. They admit themselves they are no good to anybody any more . . . Death for them means the only deliverance."

In spite of what the white settlers warned, the British High Command tried using kid gloves at the beginning of 1954. It captured Waruhiu Itote, 32, a blood-thirsty ex-corporal in the King's African Rifles, who had been shot in the throat. Using the alias "General China", he had been the Mau Mau's second-ranking chief under Dedan Kimathi, the scar-faced boss who was called "Field Marshal Russia".

General China was sentenced to death by hanging. Rather than carry out this

MAU MAU ROUNDUP (I): In disturbed Kenya, native home guards chase a suspected terrorist into the open to be taken captive

MAU MAU ROUNDUP (2): Captured tribesmen squat five abreast, guarded by soldiers and native police. British took these suspects in Nairobi, Kenya's capital

sentence, the British spared his life in return for his cooperation against the Mau Mau. They chiseled the ball and chain from his legs, and let him out of jail.

Into the hollow trees used as Mau Mau mailboxes, General China delivered a series of appeals: "The white elders and the elders of the forest must now meet to end the war . . . Those who fight on now are criminal fanatics."

General China's entreaties led several guerrilla commanders to give up, but just when Operation China seemed on the verge of success, it fell flat on its face. Under cover of a temporary cease-fire, hundreds of Mau Maus marched up to surrender.

But by error they trespassed a few hundred yards beyond the appointed area. At that, Brigadier John Reginald Orr ordered his King's African Rifles to fire, slaughtering 25 Mau Maus and putting the rest to flight. The Brigadier felt "nothing but satisfaction". Now the terror was resumed in full fury.

A Royal Air Force officer's 4-year-old son was virtually decapitated as he was riding his tricycle. Arsonists burned the picturesque Treetops Hotel, high up in a wild fig tree, from which Queen Elizabeth II had watched jungle animals parade the night before the death of her father, King George VI. One Mau Mau, wounded and captured, announced "I am General Kago"—only to have a loyal African guard ask "Are you?" and shoot him dead.

Gradually Britain's 13,000 troops got the upper hand. By the time the Mau Mau uprising was two years old in October, 6741 Mau Maus had been killed and 12,000 captured, at the cost in killed and wounded of 900 soldiers, 27 white civilians, and 2000 loyal natives. Although 6000 Mau Maus were still at large, the end seemed to be in sight.

In the hope of preventing the perennial Black-vs.-White struggle from developing into new Kenyas, the British during 1954 made several concessions to the natives in their other African colonies.

In Uganda, in East Africa, the exiled 30-year-old *Kabaka* (King), a Cambridge-schooled Grenadier Guardsman known to the British as "Freddie" and to the natives as "Best and Strongest of All Men", was restored to his throne.

In the Gold Coast, in West Africa, Prime Minister Kwame Nkrumah's Convention People's Party captured two thirds of the seats in the first all-African Legislative Assembly and thus won the largely illiterate voters' approval of the Nkrumah goal—"complete independence within the Commonwealth".

No Compromise in South Africa

IN THE UNION OF SOUTH AFRICA, "THE white man must remain boss" was the motto of zealot Johannes Gerhardus Strijdom (pronounced *stray'-dom*). A ramrod-backed Boer, he spoke only Afrikaans in public. His ambition was to pull his gold-mining nation out of the British Commonwealth and turn it into an Afrikaans-speaking republic. Once an ostrich farmer, he liked to be known as "The Lion of the Transvaal".

His racial policy for his overwhelmingly Negro nation was uncompromising white supremacy. Like the rest of the anti-British Nationalist Party, he was devoted to *apartheid* (racial segregation). But he was an extremist even among extremists. He frankly admired Hitler's racism. He derided "the detestable British-Jewish and liberal democratic system" as meaning "equal rights for everybody irrespective of color or smell".

Even the rabidly Nationalist Prime Minister, Daniel F. Malan, was too easygoing and moderate to suit Strijdom. The Lion roared what he thought of the Prime

Minister: "The old man is holding us up."

In November, at the age of 80, Prime Minister Malan retired. Although Malan sought to have a moderate Nationalist succeed him, Strijdom swept a party caucus and thus moved into the Prime Ministry. Malan admitted: "I have miscalculated." The outlook was for a new wave of racial trouble in the richest corner of Africa.

DEMONSTRATION (1): Communist-led students in Bogotá, Colombia, are fired on by troops as, in defiance of the soldiers' orders, they try to march down city street to demonstrate before the Palace of the President

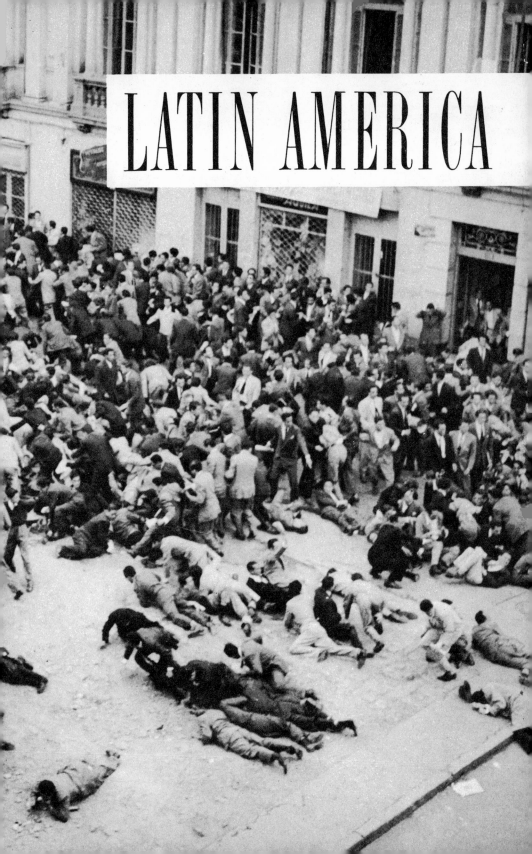

LATIN AMERICA

DEMONSTRATION (2): Rifles ready, troops (right) wait after firing on Bogotá students. Toll: 15 killed, 20 wounded. Students had just decorated grave of student killed in similar incident 25 years before

TO U.S. TOURISTS, EXOTIC, GREEN GUATE-mala is a dream vacationland. In its central highlands, where the climate is springlike, there are fragrant coffee plantations, lovely lakes, symmetrical volcanoes, picturesque Indians, and modern hotels. To east and west are tropic forests, ancient Mayan ruins, and banana plantations.

But early in 1954, few tourists visited the Central American republic. Night clubs were deserted, marimba bands unemployed. The reason: Guatemala was lush territory for the Reds.

The Communists had pushed into the brand-new democracy that followed the overthrow of long-time dictator Ubico in 1944. Under the leadership of a few intellectuals, they organized Guatemala's first labor unions. Then they moved on to take over the official press and radio.

With nearly two thirds of the 3,000,-000 Guatemalans downtrodden illiterates, with half of the land owned by 22 feudal families, and with the United Fruit Company of Boston, which operated huge banana plantations, being charged with "imperialist exploitation", the Reds made propaganda capital.

By 1953 they dominated the social-security offices and ran the new agrarian-reform program which gave to the peasants some of the land owned by United Fruit and other big owners. The Communists had only four seats in the 56-member Congress, but they pulled strings on their colleagues and pretty much got their way.

The U.S. State Department was well aware of this Red menace to the Panama Canal, only 850 air miles from Guatemala. Late in 1953 it sent John ("Smiling Jack") Peurifoy down as U.S. Ambassador with one objective: Get rid of the Reds.

Everyone told him President Jacobo Arbenz Guzmán was no Communist. The handsome young President was a regular army colonel who had helped to throw out Ubico. Arbenz pooh-poohed talk of Reds running his government. He could turn them out any time, he said.

Trouble-shooter Peurifoy, who knew the Communists well from his days in postwar Greece, wasn't so sure. A long conversation convinced him that, although Arbenz didn't consider himself a Communist, he certainly talked like one.

Peurifoy sent an urgent report to the State Department. But Washington was reluctant to act lest Latin Americans scream "intervention". In March, Secretary of State Dulles took the problem to the Tenth Inter-American Conference in Caracas, Venezuela.

At this town meeting of the Americas, held every five years, Dulles struggled to awaken his neighbors to the menace of Communism in Guatemala. He offered a resolution calling for the Americas to join forces and act if Reds gained control of any republic in the hemisphere.

Uncle Sam Attacked

Opposing him was the charming, gregarious young Guatemalan Foreign Minister, Guillermo Toriello. A virtuoso on the guitar, handsome Toriello was the social lion of the conference. He hotly defended Guatemala as the most truly democratic country in the hemisphere and violently attacked Uncle Sam. And he got a lot of support from fellow Latins.

When the final vote came on Dulles' resolution, sixteen Latin nations stood up beside the United States. Mexico and Argentina abstained. Guatemala alone voted "no". Dulles considered it a victory, but many of the votes were cast half-heartedly.

Then in May the United States spotlighted a direct link between Guatemala and Communist Eastern Europe.

The Swedish freighter *Alfhem,* after following a devious course from the Iron Curtain port of Stettin, Poland, finally docked at Puerto Barrios, Guatemala. Its cargo was listed as optical glass and laboratory instruments. But the ship was met by the Guatemalan Defense Minister and soldiers sealed off the pier. Some 2000 tons of Communist small arms—about $10 million worth of rifles, machine guns, burp guns, and so on—were loaded onto railroad cars and sent to the capital.

President Eisenhower found the shipment "disturbing". Smooth-talking Toriello said the purchase was "perfectly normal", that the alarm raised by Washington was "malicious and unjustified". The U.S. had refused to sell arms to Guatemala. "If a bartender won't sell you a drink," said Toriello, "you go to another bar, no?"

Many Latins agreed. But Guatemala's small southern neighbors were worried; why did Arbenz need such a powerful army? Nine Latin nations joined the U.S. in requesting the Organization of American States to call an emergency meeting to deal with this threat to peace.

To a modest yellow house in Tegucigalpa, Honduras, the headquarters of Colonel Carlos Castillo Armas, the arrival of the *Alfhem* came almost as a signal. The slight, wiry little colonel with the toothbrush mustache was the leader of anti-Communist Guatemalan exiles.

Since he escaped from Arbenz' jail in 1951 Castillo had been quietly collecting arms, money, and men. Now he began recruiting an army for invasion. Clandestine radio stations bombarded Guatemala with anti-Red exhortations. Finally Castillo radioed his countrymen: "Have faith and confidence. I shall be with you very shortly."

In Guatemala City, the tension grew. Soldiers with submachine guns slung over their shoulders trudged the deserted streets. Arbenz swept away all constitutional guarantees and started a virtual reign of terror. Secret police swooped down on anti-Communists, carried them off to jail, torture, and sometimes death. Luckier ones found refuge in foreign embassies.

D Day

June 18 was D day for the rebels. Colonel Castillo strapped a string of hand grenades around his waist, clapped a steel helmet on his head, and flew to join his "Liberation Army" on the Honduran-Guatemalan border.

A tall young coffee planter described the "invasion" later: "Early in the morning we started walking into Guatemala. The radio was saying a huge army was invading—there were 178 of us. We were most of the army. The radio said we had tanks, big guns, and flame throwers. All we had was our feet and rifles and bazookas."

A tiny Cessna plane, carrying hand grenades and a light machine gun, blew up vital gas tanks at the Pacific port of San José. A couple of other rebel planes buzzed the capital. Arbenz' small air force was unavailable: his top airmen had joined the rebels.

Foreign Minister Toriello immediately demanded an emergency meeting of the United Nations Security Council to deal with the "invasion". At a special Sunday session in New York on June 20, Guatemala accused Honduras and Nicaragua of open aggression and attacked the U.S. and United Fruit. Colombia and Brazil suggested taking the case to the Organization of American States (O.A.S.). Russia, backing Guatemala, vetoed that idea. At a tense moment, U.S. delegate Henry Cabot Lodge Jr. flared out: "I say to the representative of the Soviet Union: Stay out of this hemisphere! Don't try to start

your plans and conspiracies over here." The crowded galleries cheered.

The U.S. issued a cease-fire request. On its own, the O.A.S. sent a peace commission to Central America. But there was hardly any fighting. Arbenz held his army back, not sure of its loyalty. Castillo fought radio battles, gathered volunteers, began training them. His tiny air force dropped a few bombs.

Foreign Minister Toriello broke first. He called Jack Peurifoy from a Sunday golf game and offered to resign. Then army chief of staff Colonel Carlos Enrique Díaz talked to Peurifoy. At 4 P.M. Díaz and two other officers informed President Arbenz the jig was up. That evening Arbenz told Guatemalans he was resigning "with bitter grief . . . because of overwhelming means at the disposal of my enemies".

Colonel Díaz was the new President. Rebel leader Castillo was not impressed. "Díaz is only a mask for the Communist Party," he broadcast from Liberation headquarters. As a punctuation mark, Castillo's planes bombed the chief Guatemala City fort.

Peurifoy wasn't impressed with Díaz either, especially as he made no effort to hold the top Reds. The Ambassador got in touch with an anti-Communist army officer, Colonel Elfego Monzón.

Early Tuesday morning Díaz told Peurifoy he was resigning because he couldn't make a deal with Castillo. Suddenly Colonel Monzón strode in. Peurifoy leaned back and crossed his arms over his chest, a hand near his shoulder holster. A Marine guard stepped closer.

Monzón announced he was taking over, and Díaz, as Arbenz had done, sought sanctuary in the Mexican Em-

NEW "STRONG MAN" in Guatemala, Colonel Carlos Castillo Armas, eyes straw-hatted volunteers (right) who helped oust Red-backed Arbenz regime

bassy across the street from the National Palace. A few hours later a cease-fire was announced. Immediately Monzón launched a roundup of Reds. More than 2000 were jailed.

The next day Monzón, wearing a new business suit and white shirt, flew to El Salvador to confer with liberator Castillo, who arrived tousled and hatless, dressed in field khaki. The rivals haggled for hours. Peurifoy again took a hand. Finally at dawn on July 2 the two colonels, with tears in their eyes, embraced in typical Latin American style. The civil war was over.

Under their agreement, Monzón would be temporary head of a five-man junta, with Castillo No. 2 man. "My men aren't satisfied," Castillo told reporters. It was obvious he wasn't either.

On July 3 Castillo entered the capital in triumph. Crowds, in fiesta mood, shouted praise of their liberator.

The governing junta soon recognized popular Castillo as head man, later made him sole ruler. His first months were not easy. Soft-spoken Castillo kept his .45-caliber automatic, "Chabelita" (Betty), with him always. "We are inseparable," he said. "Wherever I go, Chabelita goes."

The Reds had been deeply entrenched. He struggled to pry them out and find other leaders to take their places. The national treasury was nearly empty. Castillo charged that Arbenz and his gang had stolen thousands of dollars.

Nearly a thousand Reds and fellow travelers had scuttled to safety in foreign embassies. At first Castillo refused to give them safe conduct out of the country, insisting they were murderers and thieves. Finally he let them fly to exile, after expropriating most of their assets. Mexican officials tried to slip Arbenz quietly out of the country at midnight. But word got out and crowds gathered at the airport, screaming "Assassin! Death to Arbenz!"

as the former President, pale and tense, took off for Mexico City.

Castillo ruled by decree, suspending the constitution, but he called an election for delegates to write a new one. On Oct. 10 Guatemalans voted for delegates on a single list presented by the National Anti-Communist Front. Voters also had to stand up and answer "*sí*" or "*no*" to the question: Do you approve of Castillo? It was not surprising, under the circumstances, that the President got 99 percent approval.

The constituent assembly thus elected voted a six-year term for Castillo, and swore him in as President in November. The popular little colonel sat firmly in the saddle, but he had to keep his balance between the non-Communist leftists, on one side, and the reactionaries on the other.

Nagging Neighbors

PRESIDENTS JOSÉ ("DON PEPE") FIGUERES of Costa Rica and General Anastasio ("Tacho") Somoza of Nicaragua have nothing in common except an uneasy frontier. Slight, hawk-faced Don Pepe is an intense, crusading liberal. He governs one of the few truly democratic nations in Latin America, and has no love for dictator Somoza.

Tacho is well fed, relaxed, gregarious. For seventeen years he has practically owned Nicaragua, body, soul, and real estate. Says he of neighbor Don Pepe: "He has inferiority complexes. But why should he worry about my being here?"

Each President shelters his neighbor's enemies. In April, 1954, a band of Nicaraguans, based in Costa Rica, crossed the border and tried to kill Somoza and his two sons. Tacho squashed the attempt without too much trouble. (Officially the death toll was 25, unofficially, 150.) But his feelings were hurt. He didn't mind an

BEAUTY DAZZLES LATINS: Italian film star Gina Lollobrigida, visiting Argentina, meets a school mascot near Buenos Aires. Her escort: President Juan Perón

honest revolution, he complained. He could handle that. Murder was something else again. He accused Figueres of harboring and arming the conspirators. Don Pepe denied any responsibility.

In July the situation blew up again. Anti-Figueristas, with little attempt at secrecy, were trying to pin the label of Communist on democratic Don Pepe and pull a Guatemala-style revolt on him. Insurgents tried a flash-in-the-pan revolution, and the Costa Rican Civil Guard chased them across the San Juan River into Nicaragua.

Costa Ricans and Nicaraguans skirmished along the river border, and Somoza ordered a mile-long convoy of armored cars and trucks rushed to the frontier, but Washington told him to take it easy. It wanted no Central American war.

In November Costa Ricans were alarmed by rumors of an impending invasion from Nicaragua.

Washington suddenly ordered jet fighters to the Panama Canal Zone, where no jets had been based for six years. "Routine transfer", the State Department called it. "Wonderful!" said Don Pepe. "I don't think any action will be needed." Later he reported "absolute calm reigns", but the threat of invasion was keeping tension high.

Argentina

IN SEPTEMBER PRESIDENT JUAN D. PERÓN of Argentina declared war on the Roman Catholic Church.

His vitriolic press launched the assault. Peronista newspapers called Argentine Catholics everything from "agents of discord" to Communists and perverts. Peronista labor leaders chimed in. Soon Juan D. himself jumped into the fight.

Once Perón had courted the clergy—after all, Argentina is 90 percent Catholic. He had actively supported the Church, and most priests had supported him. But relations cooled when the dictator's late wife, the glamorous Evita, tried to make a religion out of Peronism: "Perón is like a god to the Argentines. . . . I cannot conceive of heaven without General Perón."

Church leaders bitterly protested a law granting legal rights to illegitimate children, which Peronistas shoved through the Chamber of Deputies in September, 1954. Catholics doubled their efforts to fight the legalization of divorce and prostitution.

In the city of Córdoba, Catholics formed a Christian Democratic Party similar to those in Europe. It was a small beginning, but someday might attract the votes of many anti-Peronistas. Catholics also became active in the labor movement, and there came another rub. Perón refused to share with anyone his role as sole champion of the workers.

The newspaper *La Epoca* warned the Church: "Eschew temporal power and stick to souls."

On Nov. 10 Perón lashed out against the clergy in a broadcast. He violently denounced three bishops for "fostering agitation" against him and named twenty-one priests as plotters. He carefully pointed out that his quarrel was not with the Church but with a "handful of priests". El Presidente proclaimed: "I have never had any trouble with Christ."

The President appointed an interventor to "clean up" one province. A number of priests named in his speech were arrested; two got five-day sentences for "disturbances and disorders". When a Buenos Aires priest compared the situation in Argentina to conditions in Nazi Germany he was jailed.

And on Dec. 14, at three in the morning, while Argentine congressmen were wearily plowing through an omnibus bill "for the protection of the family", a Peronista suddenly rose to offer an amendment which was immediately passed. It did not mention divorce, which is still a bad word in most Latin nations, but to the horror of Argentine Catholics it made legal divorce possible.

In a pastoral letter Luis Cardinal Copello and all of Argentina's bishops urged the people to be good citizens but reminded them that their first obligation is "the sacred interests of the Church". They made it clear they would continue to influence the nation's moral and social, as well as spiritual, affairs.

Two nights later, more than 25,000 Peronistas met in Luna Park stadium to protest against clerical "meddling" in politics and labor. Party leaders burned priests in effigy.

Perón was more conciliatory. He told the emotional crowd to go home quietly and stop thinking about the problem. "No force in the world can control our government."

The following Sunday churches were packed. After services hundreds of worshipers gathered to demonstrate their

FUN IN PANAMA: A Guaymie Indian leaps high to dodge pole flung full-force at his legs. If pole misses, he gets to throw. To enliven game, contestants bet their wives (background)

support of Cardinal Copello. Instead of the government slogan "Our Lives for Perón", they chanted "Our Lives for Christ".

It looked as if Perón had taken on the toughest opponent he had ever faced.

Brazil

IN THE STREETS OF BEAUTIFUL RIO DE JA-neiro, Brazilian crowds chanted "Vargas out! Vargas out!" Popular President Getulio Vargas heard the cries with surprise, not alarm. In his eighteen years of power the wily old politico from the Gaucho country had come out on top of many a crisis.

His people adored him—in 1950 they had swept their former dictator back into the presidency. Now the tough, stocky chief told his critics: "I will not resign. I was elected by my people to serve five years . . . I will leave this place before that only when I am dead."

But pressure increased, and the specter of civil war haunted Brazil. Military leaders and government officials came and went at Catete Palace, Vargas' residence. At an all-night Cabinet meeting the President's best friends urged him to step down. Finally, at dawn, he agreed to take a three-month leave of absence. Then, rising slowly from his straight-backed chair, the 71-year-old man bowed and said "Goodnight, gentlemen."

He talked things over with his family: his wife Darcy, his doctor son Lutero, his attractive, politically wise daughter Al-zira, his playboy brother Benjamín. As he left them Alzira rushed up to her father, hugged him tight, and murmured: "Papá, what happens now?" Getulio patted her head gently and assured her: "Everything will be all right, my dear. Now I am going to get some rest."

He retired, but not to rest. He changed into brown and white striped pajamas.

Three hours later he pressed the barrel of a gun firmly to his breast and pulled the trigger.

At the sound of the shot his family rushed to his unlocked room. Lutero felt his father's pulse. With tears streaming down his cheeks, he whispered: "Papá is dead." Darcy Vargas cried: "Getulio, Getulio, why did you do this?"

A crusading editor, restive military officers, and a murder—all these things drove Vargas from power to suicide.

The crisis began early in August, when three gunmen ambushed editor Carlos Lacerda on his way home from a political meeting. The thugs merely shot Lacerda in the foot, but his companion, an air force major, was killed. In blazing editorials, Lacerda accused Getulio Vargas of instigating the crime.

Air force officers took over the investigation of the shooting. They hunted down the thugs, who turned out to be allied with Vargas' personal bodyguard. Their confessions led to the offices of "Lieutenant" Gregorio Fortunato, chief of the bodyguard, in Catete Palace. "The more we look into Gregorio's documents the more it seems like we're delving into Borgia's cellars," an investigator commented. The dirt convinced the generals that Vargas would have to resign.

Just before his death, Vargas scribbled a note: "To the hatred of my enemies I leave the legacy of my death." In the old man's pocket his son found an extraordinary farewell letter, neatly typed three days earlier. Vargas blamed Brazil's troubles on a subterranean campaign of both international and national groups. "I have fought against the looting of my people," he said. "I have fought bare breasted . . . I gave you my life. Now I offer my death."

As news of his suicide broke, Brazil erupted in a wave of emotion. Grief-stricken crowds gathered in the streets

Shouting "We want the head of Carlos Lacerda!", a mob massed at his newspaper offices. Others ripped down anti-Vargas campaign posters, attacked opposition offices and the Air Ministry.

Communists went into action within minutes. They turned Vargas' vague charge against "international groups" into a specific blast at the United States. Reds led an attack on the glass-walled U.S. Embassy, but police opened up with machine guns and routed the mob.

Soldiers finally enforced order in Rio's streets. But in Porto Alegre, capital of Vargas' home State, mobs set fire to the U.S. Consulate and the offices of two American firms.

On the night of Vargas' death, humble people queued up in a 2-mile line to shuffle past his bier. His family declined a state funeral, but thousands marched behind the coffin to the airport, weeping, chanting "Getulio, Getulio", and singing the national anthem. They broke through police lines as the family boarded a plane for São Borja, Vargas' home town. There Gauchos carried the old man to his grave in the municipal cemetery.

Café Takes Over

Former Vice-President João Café Filho, whose name in English would be John Coffee Jr., was sworn in as chief of state to complete Vargas' term.

Café inherited a country in sad straits. Vargas had been the voice of Brazilian nationalism. Inflation had run wild as the old man wooed the workers with wage raises. The U.S. had stopped buying coffee because the price was fixed too high, and Brazil starved for foreign exchange. Vargas was hostile to foreign investments, hence industry lagged. And, though ostensibly anti-Communist, he apparently had some sort of deal with the Reds. Brazil's C.P. had been outlawed in

1947 but continued to be the biggest and brashest in the hemisphere.

Quiet, bespectacled Café was no Vargas man. He was a Roosevelt-type progressive, a good friend of the U.S. In his days as a fighting journalist in the north, Café was kicked out of several towns and exiled by dictator Vargas for his liberal ways. He had won the vice-presidency on a coalition ticket.

Café, a modest family man of 55, preferred not to live in Catete Palace, Brazil's White House. He continued to occupy his unpretentious apartment two blocks from the Atlantic Ocean. There he liked to take an early-morning swim with his 10-year-old son Eduardo.

Almost overnight, Café changed the whole character of the government. First he went after the Reds: he jailed 100 or more who had sparked the anti-U.S. rioting. He squashed a leftist strike for higher wages in São Paulo. He declared war on inflation, pledged austerity, began putting Brazil's badly kept house in order. And he held out a hand to foreign investors.

His first test came with the October congressional elections, when Brazilians had a chance to choose between the old way of Vargas and Café's new deal. Neither name was on the ballot, and twelve different parties listed candidates. Vargas' Labor Party, supported by the Reds, used Getulio's death notes as campaign songs. The opposition parties hammered away at corruption, bad administration, and skyrocketing living costs under Vargas.

Election results proved the Vargas legend had lost its magic. Middle-of-the-road parties which supported Café won a majority. Café and his Cabinet of nonpolitical experts were free to go ahead. For Brazil, the fabulous Land of Tomorrow where tomorrow never seems to come, the future looked bright.

CANADA

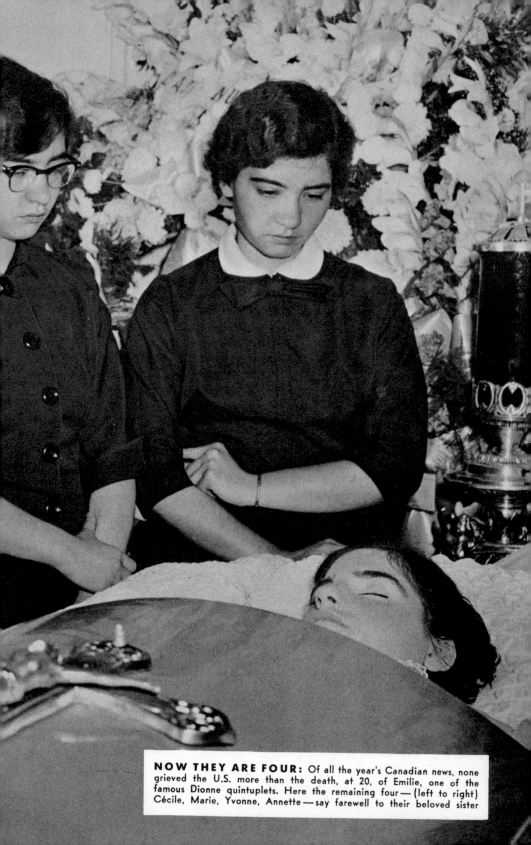

NOW THEY ARE FOUR: Of all the year's Canadian news, none grieved the U.S. more than the death, at 20, of Emilie, one of the famous Dionne quintuplets. Here the remaining four — (left to right) Cécile, Marie, Yvonne, Annette — say farewell to their beloved sister

IN 1954 THE WORD "CANADIAN" HAD A magic sound to American investors. The news had gotten around that Canada was a treasure chest of strategic minerals and hydroelectric power. Stockbrokers found they could sell almost any Canadian security. "Canadian oil" and "Canadian uranium" were especially hot. Would-be Rockefellers bought almost as many Canadian stocks in June, July, and August as they had in the peak period in 1952 when Alberta oil-fever was running high.

As the get-rich-quick urge mounted, so did the number of slick securities peddlers. When the Ontario Securities Commission cracked down on phony brokers, they moved to Quebec. In October New York State's Attorney General charged that four Montreal companies "took the American public for over $5,000,000 . . . by fraudulently portraying a gushing picture of oil prospects in the Gaspé region".

Royal Visitor

During the summer, Philip, Duke of Edinburgh, flew over to have a look at the now-celebrated Canadian economic boom. When he visited Canada in 1951 with Queen (then Princess) Elizabeth, their social engagements and public appearances gave them little chance to see the nation. Now Philip came to see the sources of Canada's wealth.

On July 29, Prime Minister Louis S. St. Laurent formally welcomed Philip in steaming Ottawa. An hour later, Philip dove into the country-club swimming pool to cool off. The next day he toured the Chalk River atomic-energy plant where Canada produces radioactive isotopes for medical and industrial use. Unlike the U.S., Canada makes no atomic bombs. Then Philip flew west to see one of the industrial wonders of the world at Kitimat, British Columbia.

Three years ago Kitimat was just a quiet Indian village on the rugged coast about 400 miles north of Vancouver. Now it was a bustling industrial town.

In the mountains behind Kitimat, the Aluminum Company of Canada (Alcan) had found unlimited sources of the cheap electric power needed to cook bauxite into aluminum. High in the western wilderness Alcan workers had dammed a river to make it flow west instead of east, hurled its waters into a chain of glacial lakes, tunneled through 10 miles of rock to the coast, and forced the water through great pipes. Out of living granite tough construction men carved a powerhouse big enough to hold the liner *Queen Mary* and a six-story office building. There the water pressure generated the electricity to feed Kitimat's new aluminum smelter.

On Aug. 2, Prince Philip saw the first aluminum ingot poured. The alumina (refined bauxite) came all the way from the island of Jamaica to be processed by Alcan's massive amount of power.

The Kitimat project employed some 10,000 men and machines, and cost $275 million. Only two months after Philip watched production begin, Alcan announced a $45 million expansion program to raise Kitimat's production from 91,500 tons of aluminum a year to 151,500.

After a visit to Vancouver to see the British Empire Games, the Duke of Edinburgh flew to the far north for a look at some of Canada's arctic defenses, at Eskimos, the Klondike, and gold, uranium, and base-metal mining centers. Back in the east, he inspected the fabulous Ungava iron-ore development on the Quebec-Labrador border.

In this wilderness of lake and muskeg, which was once called "the land God gave to Cain", were huge fields of rich iron ore. Four years ago Canadian mining companies joined the M. A. Hanna Company of Cleveland, a vast coal and

TRUE FANS: Ottawa mother and children wait in rain with Mountie to hail a royal visitor. Duke of Edinburgh toured national-resource and industrial areas that are revolutionizing Canada

iron-ore firm, and five U.S. steelmakers to form Inco, the Iron Ore Company of Canada. Inco financed the project of getting out the ore. Biggest chore was the construction of a 365-mile railroad to connect the fields with the tiny fishing port of Seven Islands on the bleak north shore of the St. Lawrence River.

Chief money raiser and driving force behind the Ungava project was energetic George M. Humphrey, former president of M. A. Hanna, now U.S. Secretary of the Treasury. Before entering Eisenhower's Cabinet he had often visited the men who were carving the railroad through rock and bogs. "There's no fertilizer like the footprints of the boss," he believed.

A seventeen-plane airlift flying as many as ninety-six flights a day had lugged men and freight into the wilderness to lay out town sites, build power plants, and dig ore pits. Bulldozers had scraped a network of roads out of the rugged ground.

Humphrey's slogan "Iron Ore by '54" was realized in August. The job cost more than $250 million. By 1956 production will be up to 11 million tons a year. Eventually it may reach 20 million.

St. Lawrence Seaway Project

Late in August, in an oat field on the banks of the St. Lawrence River near Massena, N.Y., Governor Thomas E. Dewey pushed a button, a charge of dynamite exploded, and a fifty-year dream began to come true. Work started on the St. Lawrence power project "for the benefit of the people of two nations". The ceremonies were repeated later at Cornwall, Ont., on the Canadian side.

The joint project will cost more than

PLUCKY WINNER: Marilyn Bell, 16, of Toronto is helped into lifeboat after becoming first human to swim across Lake Ontario — 32 miles in 21 hours. At left, she flashes a victory smile

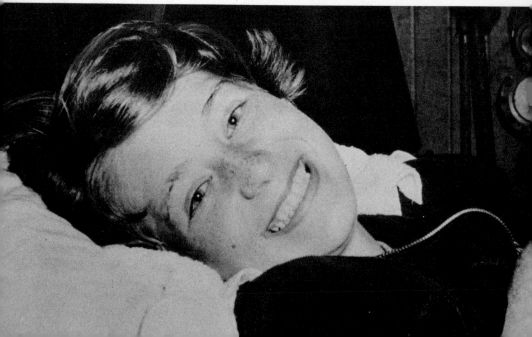

$600 million, split between New York State and the province of Ontario. When it is finished, in five years' time, each side will get more than 6 billion kilowatt-hours of power a year.

Canadians approved of the joint power project as an economic necessity. But they unhappily watched the breath-taking prospect of an all-Canadian St. Lawrence Seaway slip from their grasp.

For more than twenty years Canada had tried to sell the seaway idea to the United States. It was too big a job for Canada to do alone. Time after time Congress had turned it down. Finally in 1951 Canada had threatened to go ahead on its own. The threat succeeded: in

May, 1954, Congress belatedly voted to join in the development of the Seaway.

But the bluff had also worked on Canadians. They had become sold on the idea of an all-Canadian seaway and resented their government's sharing the project with the U.S. "We could be denied the freedom of our own ports if the U.S. controls the canal," one Torontonian complained. However, officials of both countries sat down and settled their differences at the conference table. And Prime Minister St. Laurent told Canadians that an all-Canadian seaway would have been "childish stubbornness and inexcusable wastage".

The congressional act called for the

dredging of a 27-foot channel to permit ocean-going ships to pass from the St. Lawrence River into the Great Lakes. The U.S. will put up $105 million to dredge and build locks in the International Rapids section; Canada will spend $200 million on the rest of the seaway down river to Montreal. Excavations near Montreal were started in November. Engineers figured it would take five or six years to complete the channel from the mouth of the St. Lawrence to Lake Erie.

Youthfully conscious of their nationhood, Canadians were proud of their economic sturdiness. But they had contributed comparatively little to international sports—only ice skater Barbara Ann Scott was a world champion.

In September, 1954, however, a small (5'2", 119 lbs.), 16-year-old Toronto high-school girl hit the headlines of every sports page in the Western Hemisphere. In just under 21 hours, freckle-faced, blond-haired Marilyn Bell swam the 32 miles across cold, choppy, unconquered Lake Ontario from Youngstown, N.Y., to Toronto. Moreover, she beat the world-famous American swimmer, Florence Chadwick, who gave up after 15 miles.

The Canadian National Exhibition (C.N.E.) had offered Miss Chadwick $10,000 to swim to its lakeside fairgrounds. Marilyn, sponsored by the Toronto Star, followed her into the water, "because I thought it was time someone did something for Canada".

Marilyn swam right into Canada's heart and imagination. When it was learned she was the only swimmer left in the lake, Toronto whipped itself into a frenzy of excitement. Radio stations broadcast half-hour bulletins on her progress; newsboys inaccurately shouted "Marilyn only two hours away." Thousands of people began gathering on the chilly lake front.

Miles out in the lake, Marilyn had stopped swimming. For the fourth time she wanted to quit. "My arms were tired, my legs ached, my stomach hurt in one big awful pain and I couldn't get my breath," she said later.

Her coach, Gus Ryder, kept urging her on with messages written on a blackboard: "If you quit, I quit." Once her best girl friend jumped into the water to wake her up and swim alongside for a while. During the last hour before she touched the Toronto breakwater, her swimming seemed automatic and trance-like.

When she made it, Canadians indulged in an orgy of national pride and adoration. Marilyn had a hectic fortnight. She appeared before 100,000 people at the C.N.E. to accept the $10,000 promised only to Miss Chadwick, had a ticker-tape parade through Toronto which drew the biggest crowd since the visit of the Queen, kicked off ineptly at three football games, was interviewed twice on television and four times on radio, had a civic reception in Hamilton, Ont., and flew to New York City to appear on Ed Sullivan's "Toast of the Town" TV show.

When she finally had time to look at all her gifts in a Toronto warehouse, she found she had acquired enough to furnish a house, keep it warm and clean, fill the kitchen cupboards, the clothes closets, the garage, and overload the basement. "Oh my gosh," she commented.

Hollywood and Broadway offered screen tests and contracts. Old pro Barbara Ann Scott sent some advice: "All I wanted was to finish a home-economics course at school—and I wasn't able to . . ." Every Canadian had an opinion. "They're going to ruin that kid if they shoot her into pictures and appearances right now. Give her a rest, a break," one cab driver said.

Two weeks later, Marilyn returned to the twelfth grade at Loretto College School.

NERVE CENTER of booming Canada, Ottawa Parliament buildings appear framed in the logs and overhead workings of a basic Dominion industry

BUSINESS

BUSINESS

BY THE MIDDLE OF 1954, IT WAS SAID, THE United States would be in "a rapidly mounting emergency". "Drastic measures" would have to be taken to avert a depression. Only if Congress enacted a $20 billion tax cut would the country turn the corner.

That was the prediction in November, 1953, of Colin Clark, world-famous Australian economist and Oxford University professor. In previous predictions, he had called the turns with uncanny accuracy. Now, employing the same statistical methods, he was counting Uncle Sam down and out.

But no "drastic measures" were taken, Congress cut taxes by only $4.5 billion, and there was no depression. Instead, the American economy had the second most prosperous year in history. Employment dipped but recovered. Production remained high. So did personal incomes

HARDFISTED — aggressive financier Robert R Young makes sign to show he now bosses New Yor Central Railroad. Right: A pneumatic-drill oper ator's gloves stiffly await his return from lunch

and both spending and savings. Industrial common stocks reached averages not attained within twenty-five years.

What went wrong with experts' gloomy forecasts?

These prophets judged the future by figures and charts of the past. When curves coincided with those at the beginnings of previous hard times, they looked for stormy weather. What they couldn't chart and graph was people and their behavior. Americans continued to buy what they needed, they kept on building new houses, and they weren't afraid of starting new businesses or expanding old ones.

It was widely realized, however, that there cannot be too many "second best" years. A prosperous American economy requires expansion. And a growing population means there will be more people of working age. The question unresolved in 1954 was whether business expansion would keep pace.

Pick's Lucky Pick

BIGGEST BONANZA-LUCK STORY TO COME out of 1954 was that of 50-year-old Vernon Pick. He was a Wisconsin farm boy who got as far as high school. By the mid-1920's he was working at Flin Flon mine in northern Manitoba, Canada. Returning to Wisconsin, he married and sank his $40,000 savings in an electric-motor repair business in the little town of Royalton. In 1951, his shop burned down. Insurance amounted to $13,500. "Let's drive down to Mexico and see the country," he said to his wife. "This is the last vacation we can take for a long time."

In truck and trailer, the Picks got as far as Grand Junction, Colo., where folks were feverishly prospecting for uranium. Pick got the fever, too. He questioned a mining engineer in the local office of the Atomic Energy Commission as to the

most likely place to hunt uranium. The A.E.C. man went to a big wall map and swept a hand over southeastern Utah. "If I was looking for the stuff," he said, "I'd work the Henry Mountains country."

Pick collected camping equipment, bought a rock pick and a scintillometer, which is a sort of extra-special Geiger counter, and set out. For nine months he floundered around in one of the most God-forsaken wildernesses in the United States. Not once did the scintillometer needle show any activity.

Sand worked into the soles of his feet and made blisters. "I'd pick sand out of my blisters at night," the prospector said, "and when I started out in the morning it was like walking on red-hot marbles. After the first half hour my feet got numb; then it was all right."

In June, 1952, Pick was down to his last $300. For days he had eaten nothing but oatmeal cooked with dried milk, and he was poison-sick from drinking arsenic-tainted water. He sat down to rest on a rock, wondering whether he had strength enough for the four-day trek back to town. Glancing down at his scintillometer, he noticed the needle acting wildly. "Batteries must be going dead," he decided.

But when he moved the scintillometer away from the rock, the needle came to rest. When he moved it back, the needle jiggled again. With his pick he chipped at the rock and laid bare bright orange-yellow uranium ore. After locating the site of the main ore deposit, Pick staked out a claim and hobbled back to civilization.

He raised some money by selling his trailer, truck, and camera. He rented a bulldozer and jackhammer and hired a few men. By September, he was shipping out ore. The deeper he mined, the more high-grade the stuff turned out to be. For two years he continued mining, grossing as much as $50,000 a month. He had struck a deposit of more than 300,000 tons of uranium ore, one of the richest finds of the atomic age.

In September, 1954, Pick went to New York to sell his mine. He found a customer in Floyd Odlum of Atlas Corporation. A Colorado University alumnus, Odlum had been snapping up promising uranium claims all along the Colorado River plateau. "Uranium," he said, "is the oil of tomorrow, and tomorrow isn't very far off."

Vernon Pick didn't wait for tomorrow. After dickering a few days, he sold out for $9 million to Odlum's Atlas, which moved to put the property into large-scale production. Pick stayed on as chief executive officer of the mine.

Price Fixing

FEDERAL ANTITRUST LAWS ARE VIOLATED when combinations within an industry agree to fix prices. But in all States except Missouri, Texas, and Vermont and in the District of Columbia, it is also against the law for storekeepers to undersell the retail price which a manufacturer has fixed upon his advertised brand product.

In 1954, country-wide defiance or evasion of these "fair trade" laws came to a head while their legality awaited a Supreme Court test.

Many retailers complying with the fair-trade laws feared that they would be forced to the wall by cut-rate establishments which did a $5 billion business during the year. These discount houses mushroomed in almost every large U.S. city. By year's end, they numbered more than 10,000.

The bulk of the discount-house trade is in "hard and white goods": refrigerators, washing machines, air conditioners, TV sets, electric toasters, small radios, cameras, watches, and sporting goods. Discounts ranged from 15 to 45 percent off list or "fair trade" prices.

In 1954, about 95 percent of all electrical appliances sold in New York City went at cut-rate prices. In Los Angeles, nearly 70 percent of the sales of electric refrigerators, ranges, and washing machines were made at below-list prices. In Boston, the cluster of cut-rate electrical-appliance dealers near North Station was known as "Burglars' Row".

The typical discount house operates on low rent, few personnel, a large volume of sales, and a small markup and percentage of profit. It has no repair or delivery service. Thus does it cut corners.

Frequently it costs more to distribute articles than to make them. In 1939, The Twentieth Century Fund, a research foundation, found that on manufactured goods 59¢ of the retail-sales dollar went for distribution—wholesale and retail markups, transportation, advertising, installment fees, and the like. Although that average cost may have fallen since 1939, there is still a wide margin between the maker's price and the figures on a retail store's price tag. This margin leaves the discount house room to operate.

Big rubber companies turn out automobile tires for Sears, Roebuck, which undersells their own name brands. R. H. Macy & Co., Inc., in New York has long challenged fair-trade merchandise prices by offering similar goods under its own label at less than brand-name prices. What is new is the number of discount houses, their ingenious ways of circumventing fair-trade laws, and their threat to normal retail trade both big and small.

Many cut-raters issue "membership" and "identification" cards, mailed out by the bale to labor unions, church groups, clubs, and fraternal organizations. Some even require "references". These dodges enable the discounters to claim that they do not sell to the general public and

therefore are not violating fair-trade laws.

Some of the biggest houses operate by direct mail. One Chicago giant sells only to members of the armed forces, reservists, and national guardsmen. It does a $26 million yearly business in 6000 items, including new cars at nearly one fifth off authorized dealer prices.

There are many other ways of evading State fair-trade laws. For example, a discounter with a large block of orders for a certain make of washing machine may go to an authorized dealer for them. The dealer sells to him at slightly above the wholesale price but delivers the machines to the customers, just as if the transactions were his own. Thus everybody gets a break. The authorized dealer and the discounter make profits, and the customer gets a cut price.

In other instances, an authorized dealer may be overstocked and have to sell to discounters at distress prices. Or the dealer may get a low price from a manufacturer by buying in large lots, take part of the goods for his own sales operations, then sell the rest to a discount house, preferably in another city.

Another dodge is for the discounter in one city to become an authorized distributor in another city and thus get at wholesale supplies for his cut-rate store.

Finally, a few manufacturers who paw the air indignantly over violations of their "suggested" or "fair trade" retail prices are not above selling directly to discounters. "All this talk about manufacturers not wishing to sell to us is hooey," says a mid-West cut-rate operator.

It costs money for a manufacturer to police retailers handling his goods. In the electrical-appliance field, Westinghouse and Sunbeam crack down on "fair trade" violators. General Electric spent a half

AMBITIOUS Louis Wolfson considers strategy of his campaign to take over Montgomery Ward

UNCOOPERATIVE Sewell Avery, Montgomery Ward chairman, is tough nut for any challenger. Back in 1944 he resisted government wartime "seizure" of firm until soldiers carried him out (above)

million a year investigating retailers, and in 1954, in New York City alone, got 100 injunctions against price cutting on its "fair trade" products. But in the latter part of the year, in recognition of the widespread sale of its appliances at discount prices, G.E. abandoned the policy of "suggesting" retail prices on its major items.

Few manufacturers either can or will go to the lengths taken by W. A. Sheaffer Pen Company. Not only did Sheaffer drop 200 retailers from its maker-to-dealer distribution system in 1954, but it spent over a half million in buying back pens and pencils found on cut-rate counters.

During 1954, an increasing number of retailers quit fighting the cut-raters and cut rates themselves. Detroit's biggest department store, J. L. Hudson Company, advertised reduced prices on more than 150 price-fixed items ranging from electric roasters to movie cameras and watch bands. Other stores followed suit.

In Washington, D.C., where there are no fair-trade laws, Hecht's slashed appliance prices as much as 40 percent. In Newark, N.J., Bamberger's held "warehouse sales" which offered whopping discounts to customers willing to lug away refrigerators and TV sets.

In some fields, notably groceries, undersellers were being undersold. Roadside stands added canned and packaged foods to their lines of perishable fruits and vegetables. Low rents, if any, minimum service, and next to no overhead enabled many a roadsider to sell at below the prices of supermarkets, which themselves had become successful by underselling. As the big cash-and-carry places added new lines to their displays, so did the roadsiders.

By the end of 1954, cut-rate operators were encountering heavier operating expenses and unexpected competition. Some suffered from the curse of big-

ness. When they took on more employees, the unions got after them with demands for bigger pay and shorter hours. Moreover, customers were no longer satisfied with cash-down sales but demanded installment arrangements and repair services, features which would increase overhead. Also, department stores were paring their costs. The gap between established retail practices and discount-house techniques was still wide, but it was narrowing.

Food

IN 1954, THE SCRAMBLE TO DO MORE OF the housewife's kitchen work intensified among food processors, restaurant proprietors, and electrical-appliance people.

More than 6.5 million home freezers were in use, forty times the number eight years before. While nine out of ten electrically wired homes had electric refrigerators, only three out of twenty had deep freezers. Even so, 1954 sales of home freezers fell off nearly a quarter. "Purely temporary," chirped the manufacturers.

During the year, competition in cooking devices also affected the kitchen. Having driven out the old-fashioned coal-burning range, gas and electric stoves faced replacement by lightweight portable equipment. Hottest item was electric skillets—the market couldn't get enough of them. Easy to carry, useful wherever there are electric outlets, these skillets bake, braise, chafe, fry, or stew. Supplementing them were electric French friers, small roasters, and automatic table ovens. "In another five years," said one enthusiastic supplier, "nobody will need a kitchen stove."

Ready-prepared foods were also chalking up bigger sales. Emulating frozen fish sticks, Hormel introduced ham sticks, cut and prepared on the same principle, and ready for the table after being heated for a few minutes. The frozen-food item which showed the fastest rise in popularity was chicken pie—150 million were sold. Just put a pie in the oven for a half hour to brown the crust and warm the precooked filling, and it's ready to eat.

These pies helped to raise poultry consumption 75 percent over the figure for prewar days. There has been a revolution in processing and dressing chickens, turkeys, ducks, and geese. In 1940, about 80 percent were sold either alive or, if dead, merely bled and with feathers removed. In 1954, 85 percent of the birds had innards out and were ready for the stove. One processor introduced pre-stuffed frozen poultry in plastic bags. All the lady of the house had to do was turn on the oven and slide the bird in, bag and all.

Another cause for increased poultry consumption was the sale of chicken by the part. A few years earlier, raw, disassembled chicken was mainly a specialty of big cities, in which turnover was so rapid that only normal refrigeration was needed. In 1954, thanks to the quick-freezing process, consumption of chicken by the part was six times greater.

Buying chickens by the part solves the housewife's traditional problem—how to satisfy several diners, each demanding a drumstick from a two-legged chicken. Chicago folk go big for drumsticks but won't buy necks and backs, which Louisiana people like. In New York City, frozen chicken livers are always in short supply, but gizzards can't be given away. They too go South.

Despite all recent short cuts in home cookery, the number of people who ate out was about the same in 1954 as in previous years, but their checks weren't quite so big. They ordered stews and spareribs more often than steaks and roast beef, and "blue-plate specials" more often than full meals with soup and dessert.

In some localities restaurant trade fell off because people remained home and ate from trays in front of their TV sets. One proprietor of a Tacoma eatery put up special TV box suppers. "Everybody's staying home to watch television," he said, "so I put up and sell 'em full course meals in individual boxes instead of the French fries and hamburgers they used to rush in to buy between programs."

Another answer to TV competition was furnished by a chain of Pacific coast cafeterias which advertised dinners starting at 4:30 so that patrons might eat out and still be home in time for their favorite shows.

Do-It-Yourself

IN 1954 AN OUT-OF-THE-ORDINARY, RAPIDLY growing industry reached the $6 billion-a-year status, grossing more than the year's returns from the mining of coal and metals. Its revenue approached that from the annual sales of automobiles. This multibillion-dollar industry caters to the do-it-yourself trade.

Despite present-day mass-production assembly lines, the American people are rivaling and perhaps excelling their ancestors as handymen and jacks of all trades. Seventy percent of all wallpaper bought in 1954 was hung by novices. Three quarters of all paint used was slapped or rolled on walls, ceilings, and window sashes by amateur painters. Painters' unions attacked this trend with ineffectual resolutions and threatened vague reprisals against paint manufacturers encouraging home-scab labor. Many a painting contractor lost jobs to schoolteachers and others who hired out as painters on weekends.

Eleven million amateur carpenters of varying skills used up 180 square miles of plywood in 1954. Their 25 million power tools consumed electricity enough to sup-

COMMERCIAL "CONCERT" is directed by Paris designer Christian Dior (center, hand raised) as models display new creations

ply the 200,000 inhabitants of Worcester, Mass., throughout the year. Half the women of the United States made their own clothes. They gave themselves, or each other, 32 million home permanents.

All these hobbies and nonprofessional crafts not only occupied spare time and saved money but upped the nation's accident rate. According to the American Mutual Liability Insurance Company, nearly 640,000 persons "annually suffer everything from broken fingernails to broken legs" on do-it-yourself jobs.

Hobbyists include $100,000-a-year business executives and dollar-an-hour clerks. Former Secretary of State Dean Acheson makes furniture in a home workshop. Edgar Bergen and Fibber McGee build shelves and kitchen cabinets. Desi Arnaz and Perry Como build boats and furniture. Just under the White House roof is a studio for Sunday artist Dwight D. Eisenhower.

Hobbyists Build Everything

U.S. industry put out millions of do-it-yourself kits during 1954. These ranged from prefab houses to knockdown cabin cruisers. Build-it-yourself boats are ordered from some of the supposedly least nautical sections of the country. Newest localities are lakes made by irrigation and electric-power dams.

Surprisingly, among the year's popular items were roofed-in cruisers complete with sleeping and cooking facilities but powered by outboard motors hung over the stern. Contrasted with none in 1950, thirty different models were shown at the 1954 Chicago National Motorboat Show. Knockdown craft sold for 60 percent of the cost of completed boats. Assembly of an 18-foot cruiser takes about 250 hours, roughly 15· weekends, and 2500 screws are used in the process.

A Cohasset, Mass., company makes and sells knockdown reproductions of colonial furniture. Among its designs are a bed copied from one in New York's Metropolitan Museum of Art, a replica of a 1725 tuck-away table in the Boston Museum of Fine Arts, and a blanket chest from an original in Old Sturbridge Village. Customers live as far away as the Pacific coast. They get knockdown kits of pre-shaped maple or pine, together with powdered glue, stain, and furniture wax for finishing—everything but the required elbow grease.

Another 1954 do-it-yourself novelty was packaged asphalt in 100-pound bags —just rake and roll, and there's a finished hot-top pavement in a few minutes. Besides such back-yard furnishings as barbecue grills, there were knockdown swimming pools 25 by 13 feet long, from 3 to 6 feet deep, holding 100,000 gallons of water, and accommodating 25 people.

In Los Angeles, a do-it-yourself exposition with 300 exhibitors drew 100,000 visitors in five days. They paid $1.10 admission and bought $1 million worth of stuff. In Seattle, McVickar hardware clears its counters on Friday nights for a do-it-yourself clinic. Customers sip coffee and listen to manufacturers' agents hold forth on new interior-decorating and gardening ideas and gimmicks. Georgia Institute of Technology has a twice-a-week course for housewives and husbands in carpentering, painting, and paper hanging.

Although a floor-covering dealer lures hobbyists with the slogan "We guarantee your work," not all amateurs are successful. Some even make more work for the professionals whose services they attempt to bypass. An official of the carpenters' union in Cleveland says his members are frequently summoned to straighten out "wood butchery" by home busybodies.

"Usually," he adds, "the work has gone so far in the wrong direction that we have to rip it out and begin all over." The lord and master of a house in St. Louis started to do a little electric-wiring job. He gummed things up so thoroughly that he had to pay a contractor $1700 to rewire the whole place.

The do-it-yourself trend stems from a number of causes. The forty-hour, five-day week, longer vacations, and more holidays have added to American leisure.

Another cause is high wages in the tightly organized building trades. A $1.25-an-hour office worker cannot afford a $3.50-an-hour carpenter. Still another cause is the mass movement from city to suburbs. After World War II, some 7 million more Americans got houses of their own. Many new homes were only partly finished, many old houses needed modernizing, and the owners promptly got busy to paint and paper and to finish kitchens the way they wanted them.

The Stock Wars

NOT SINCE THE "FRENZIED FINANCE" OF FIFty and more years ago had any stock war approached the 1954 battle for control of the New York Central Railroad. Next to the Pennsylvania, the century-old Central is the country's biggest railway system. Its 100,000 employees operate along more than 10,000 miles of track in eleven States and two Canadian provinces, and in the district around New York's Grand Central Terminal it owns some of the world's most valuable real estate. Nevertheless, it has been on the brink of insolvency, a number of times since the Great Depression. Its popularity as a passenger line has been costly, for most railroads today lose money hauling humans.

One Sunday afternoon in February, 1954, William White, New York Central's president, answered a long-distance call at his Scarsdale, N.Y., home from Harold S. Vanderbilt in Palm Beach. Vanderbilt was a New York Central director. His great-grandfather, the Commodore, won control of the Central in a stock raid. Grandfather William H. extended the road's lines but went down in history as author of the phrase "the public be damned."

Harold Vanderbilt informed White that his Palm Beach neighbor, Bob Young, said he was buying New York Central stock with intent to become chairman of the board and the road's chief executive officer. "Looks like a proxy fight at next May's annual meeting," White and Vanderbilt agreed.

Robert R. Young of Palm Beach, Newport, and the Waldorf Astoria is regarded by Wall Street as a financial maverick, and by old-time railroaders with near-apoplexy. Five feet six, white haired, 57, and with a flair for the spectacular, he fancies the label "Smallest Texan in the World".

At Culver Military Academy, he declined election as valedictorian of his graduating class because he was too shy, a deficiency he overcame after starting as a powder monkey with Du Pont. That start propelled him toward the post of assistant treasurer of General Motors. Later he joined a Wall Street stock-exchange firm which specialized in buying seemingly worthless securities, then restoring earning power of the down-and-out concerns by reorganization and efficient management.

Gradually, Young got control of Alleghany Corporation, which in turn controlled the Van Sweringen brothers' almost worthless railroad empire. The most valuable asset of that empire was the coal-running Chesapeake & Ohio. Becoming C. & O.'s chairman, Young fancied himself an expert on sick railroads. He sought to entice passengers with free newspapers and below-cost meals in diners and club cars decorated with bowls

FEMALE FEROCITY: Women pickets at strike-bound Detroit electrical plant boo nonstriking workers going home by cab under police protection

of goldfish, which soon expired of train sickness.

Shortly after World War II, Young dreamed of a transcontinental system of which he believed New York Central should be the keystone. To lay groundwork for this coast-to-coast vision, he launched an arresting newspaper advertising campaign: "A Hog Can Cross the Country Without Changing Cars—But You Can't." He also took advertising space to berate old-line railway management: "Nine Out of Every Ten Sleeping Cars Belong in Museums."

After his talk with Vanderbilt in Palm Beach, Young flew to New York and a luncheon with White. He described his plans for New York Central—roller-bearing freight cars and "Train X", a high-speed, low-slung coupling of two-wheeled cars constructed along airplane lines. If White would step down in favor of Young, he could be chief operating officer. White refused.

White had a contract with Central under which he would get $120,000 a year until he retired eight years later at 65. Then until reaching 70 he would get $75,000 a year as consultant, and thereafter an annual pension of $40,000 for life. This contract was binding no matter what happened to New York Central control, but White said he would abrogate it if Young entered the picture. He was ready, he said, for a "bare-fisted" battle for control of the road.

Thus lines were drawn for the most bitter and spectacular proxy fight in railroad history. Before the days of strict federal regulation, the old "robber barons" used to get control of railroads by big stock-market raids and squeezes. The new technique is to woo stockholders, big and little, into signing proxies with which the operator can vote himself into control at the annual meeting.

Both Young and New York Central management hired professional proxy solicitors. For White's group, a hundred fanned out across the country to call upon Central's 41,000 stockholders by phone or in person. In addition, several hundred New York Central employees volunteered for proxy persuasion. Young's forces included fifty professional solicitors and some 600 volunteers, a few of whom were New York Central men.

The White group engaged the public-relations firm of Robinson-Hannagan Associates. New York Central's advertising department suspended its $1,250,000-a-year activities and concentrated on the proxy battle. Young took full-page advertisements in big-city newspapers to attack New York Central management: "A Dismal Dividend Record" and "Last Minute Tricks to Whitewash Central's White."

White and New York Central fired back with big black type: "What Manner of Man is Robert R. Young Who Asks You to Give Him Power Over Your Money in New York Central?" and "How Does Mr. Young Make This Inside Deal Jibe with Morals and Methods?"

There were sheaves of news releases from both headquarters, press conferences, much wining and dining of newsmen and posing in front of newsreel cameras. Both Young and White made TV appearances. Young was the more practiced performer. White, a railroader since sixteen, obviously did not enjoy the ordeal.

"A Woman's Touch"

Young was also more adroit in making the headlines. His top public-relations adviser was urbane, quick-thinking Tom Deegan, a former press agent who had helped to raise Sonja Henie to fame. Hearing that White frowned upon the idea of a woman on Central's board of directors, Young hastened to add to his slate of proposed directors Mrs. Lila Acheson Wallace, coeditor with her husband of *The Reader's Digest.* "We need a woman's touch on the railroads," he said.

"I agree," said Mrs. Wallace. "I think everything needs a woman's touch."

All this whoop-de-do cost both sides millions. New York Central spent $340,-000 in newspaper advertising alone, and $50,000 more to mail copies of its ads to stockholders. Add to that fees to public-relations men, retainers to proxy-soliciting firms, and travel and other expenses of more than 1500 professional and volunteer proxy hunters.

New York Central's stockholders' meeting was held on May 26 in the drill shed of the Washington Avenue Armory in Albany. Both White and Young left New York early that morning on one of the two sections of the Shareholders' Special which the Central runs to its annual meetings. The rivals went up and down the aisles doing last-minute politicking.

The armory session was a king-size Mad Hatter's Tea Party. The 2000 stockholders present were called to some semblance of order at noon. A reading of the opposing slates for election as directors was punctuated with war whoops and rebel yells. All over the floor stockholders arose and, without waiting for recognition from the platform, made gesticulating speeches which appeared to interest few others.

When White attempted to read his annual report, the public-address system went haywire and screamed like a Gehenna of lost souls. A box lunch of fried chicken stilled the tumult temporarily. Meanwhile groups of stockholders who had not mailed proxies or who wished to change their votes ambled up to the ballot box. Shortly before five, the last ballot had been cast and White adjourned the meeting.

Counting the ballots was a complex, tedious task. Some stockholders had switched their proxies as many as a dozen times, then voted in person in the armory. It took days for three college professors to straighten out the mess. Results were announced June 14. White had an almost two-to-one margin in number of shareholders voting, but Young had a majority of 1,067,273 of Central's 6,447,410 outstanding shares. A new hand was at the throttle of old Commodore Vanderbilt's New York Central.

Young Man in a Hurry

While no other proxy fight of 1954 approached that of New York Central, another big battle for corporation control shaped up for 1955. The stake was Montgomery Ward & Co., the country's oldest mail-order house, topped in size only by Sears, Roebuck and Co. During recent years, its annual business had remained about $1 billion. During the same period, Sears leaped from $1 billion annually to almost $3 billion.

Rivals for control of Montgomery Ward were as different one from the other as day and night. For twenty-three years Sewell Lee Avery, 80, had been Montgomery Ward's crusty board chairman. He was put there by the J. P. Morgan banking house when the firm was losing $9 million a year. In three years, he converted Monty Ward's loss into a $9 million profit. Then he forced the Morgan interests out of the company.

"I banana-peeled into this place," he said, "then couldn't get out." But he got others out. Four presidents and forty vice-presidents either resigned or were fired in differences over Avery's policies. "I'll be here," said the old man, "until I'm 6 feet under ground."

Since World War II Avery has seen depression just around the corner. While

Sears expanded operations, confident of prosperous years, Avery sat tight and built up cash reserves against his long-predicted business crisis. At each annual meeting, minority groups sought to force him out. Only once did he have to quit.

During World War II, when he defied a War Labor Board decision, the federal government moved to take temporary control of the company. A military detail arrived at his Chicago offices. When Avery resisted, two soldiers grabbed him by arms and legs, lugged him out, and deposited him on the sidewalk. Pictures of this extraordinary heave-ho were printed all over the country.

Challenging Avery in 1954 was a man about half his age, one of the fastest-moving corporation jugglers of this decade. Louis Elwood Wolfson, 42, was a junk dealer's son who had borrowed $10,000 some twenty-two years earlier and parlayed it into a $200 million industrial empire. Until a Yale tackle jarred loose his shoulder bones, Wolfson's ambition was to be the greatest end in the University of Georgia's football history. Studies being secondary with him—as a junior he was still taking freshman English—he left school for his father's scrap yard in Jacksonville.

Business was poor, so he borrowed $5000 on insurance and another $5000 from a friend and formed the Florida Pipe and Supply Company. For $275 he bought a lot of pipe and building materials which he sold, piece by piece, for $100,000. Rejected by army medics for military service, he did a $4.5 million business with the government, then engaged in some split-second buying of war surplus.

After the war, he really hit his stride. He specialized in ferreting out companies whose dividends were meager but whose book values were far above market prices of their common stocks. Then he sought the cause. It might be high-salaried management uninterested in paying dividends; it might be overcautious stashing away of reserve cash; it might be internal dissension. Satisfied as to cause and cure, Wolfson would buy up stock control, then move in with his own management.

In this manner, he acquired and in rapid succession revived a number of firms that had been long in the red. In four years he raised the net of Merritt-Chapman & Scott, a ninety-year-old heavy-construction and marine-salvage concern, from $775,000 to $3,500,000. In two years he changed New York Shipbuilding's deficit to a profit of nearly $2 a share and a 50 percent extra dividend.

His biggest windfall was Washington (D.C.) Capital Transit Company. It had a $5 million surplus yet its stock was selling at $18.50. By paying $20 a share for 109,000 shares, Wolfson bought control, then paid out $30 a share in dividends and nearly trebled his money.

In addition, this young man in a hurry controlled the two-century-old paint firm of Devoe & Raynolds Company, Newport Steel, Somerville Iron Works, light-metals producer Nesco, and a string of Negro movie theaters in the South.

In 1954, he took a look-see at Montgomery Ward, whose $700 million assets included $293 million in cash and government bonds Avery had piled up against the hard times he still believed were coming. Quietly, Wolfson began buying Monty Ward stock at prices ranging from $54 to $77. By the end of August he had put up some $37 million and controlled one sixth of the stock. Then he declared his intention of conducting a proxy fight to oust Avery, whose policies he pronounced "a glaring and notorious example of private enterprise in reverse gear".

In Chicago, Sewell Avery sniffed: "Wolfson? Never heard of him till the other day."

Look, Ma, No Hands!

In a Ford Motor Company plant at Brookpark Village, just outside Cleveland, an electronic brain packed with 27 miles of wiring masterminds operations which machine automobile-engine blocks without the aid of human hands. Colored push buttons—green, red, yellow—control an almost countless number of manufacturing steps. When a tool somewhere along this line of robots is wearing out, warning lights flash on control boards.

In Ford's Detroit engine-block plant, conventional machining methods require 117 men. At Brookpark Village, the same output is achieved by 40 men, half of whom merely watch signal lights to replace worn-out tools.

Close by is a 20-acre foundry which takes in molding sand, scrap, and pig iron at one end and drops out engine castings at the other.

The $70 million Brookpark Village plants are leading examples of a new trend toward push-button, automatic production. The trend has prevailed for a number of years in the chemical, public-utility, and oil-refining industries; 1954 saw it more widely applied in the manufacture of durable goods.

Early in the year, at Columbus, Ohio, Westinghouse opened a $45 million plant expected to turn out 4000 refrigerators and freezers a day. Twenty-seven miles of conveyors take them through automatic enameling and assembly and even robot boxing for shipment. Outside Louisville, a 100-acre plant with 42 miles of conveyors was started for General Electric. And a big slice of General Motors' billion-dollar expansion fund would go for automatic production.

The push-button trend is not limited to the giants. Raytheon Manufacturing Company started an automatic-assembly line capable of producing 1000 radios a day. Under previous production methods that would have needed 200 workers. Automatic assembly was done with 2.

A Michigan maker of aluminum cups paid $60,000 for a machine which automatically transforms aluminum strips into 2000 cups an hour. For this operation, instead of 55 workers, he needs but 1 part-time operator. His daily labor saving is $640, which in a year would amount to more than twice the cost of the machine.

Although machine-tool makers say there isn't a product which cannot be turned out automatically, push-button production is economical only in mass volume. Wherever it can be applied, possibilities are dramatic—lower costs for manufacturers, better goods and lower prices for consumers, greater safety for labor, together with less worker fatigue and higher wages. In many instances, greater automatic production has increased employment. Despite its new labor-saving equipment, General Motors has hired 200,000 more workers during the last two years.

Almost equally dramatic is a changing attitude on the part of labor. Some unions still preserve the traditional hostility to the machine and are fearful of push-button production and technological unemployment. Many labor contracts in the steel industry provide that a man displaced by a machine shall be shifted to another job. Automobile labor leadership, however, is qualifiedly friendly.

"So long as it doesn't lower the purchasing power of our people," says one United Auto Workers regional director, "we're not against technological improvement." Another says: "We'd like to see it result in lower prices." With these opinions go drives for higher wages. At the Ford push-button plant at Brookpark Village, machine operators get 12 percent more pay than in older plants.

Arts, Sciences, and Entertainment

YEAR'S RARE TWINS included
Volkje and Tjitske de Vries (above) of
Holland, who survived cutting of their
joint abdominal membrane, and Daniel
and Donald Hartley (X ray) of Indiana,
who shared one body from the waist
down, could not be severed, and died

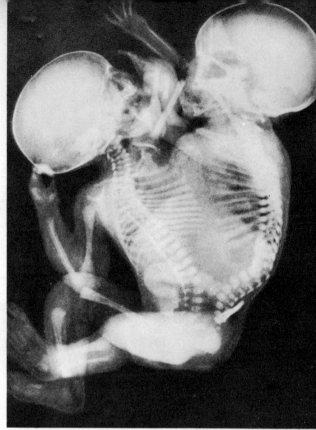

SCIENCE

1954 WILL BE REMEMBERED AS YEAR 1 IN the Solar Energy Era.

For nearly a century man has lived in fear of running out of the fuels that turn the wheels of his mechanical civilization. In 1954, that fear was diminished by the invention of a device for turning the energy of sunlight into electricity. The device was the solar battery and it came from

CHIN UP, FEET UP in defiance of heavy leg braces, 5-year-old polio victim Mary Kosloski of Collierville, Tenn., enjoys swing in New York park. Mary was chosen 1955 March of Dimes "poster girl"

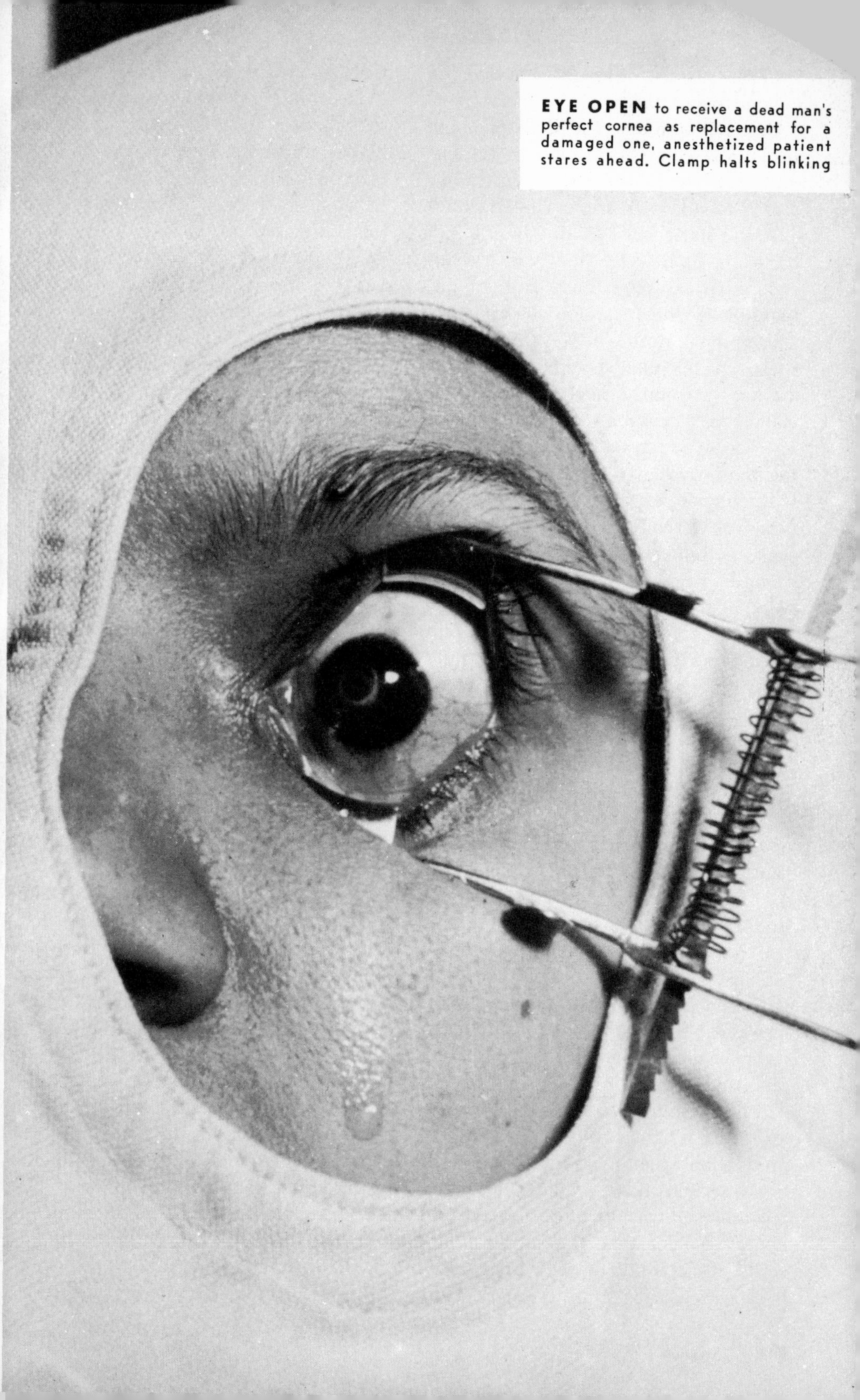

EYE OPEN to receive a dead man's perfect cornea as replacement for a damaged one, anesthetized patient stares ahead. Clamp halts blinking

"Ma Bell's House of Magic", the Bell Telephone Laboratories.

Bell Laboratories, the Bell telephone system's research arm, is among the biggest and best of the 3000 industrial-research laboratories in the United States.

It was started in 1925 in a building on the Manhattan water front which it still occupies. It occupies also two other buildings in New York, a huge center and three smaller laboratories in New Jersey, and space in telephone-company buildings around the country. There are nearly 10,-000 people (including 3000 scientists and engineers) on the staff and the cost to the telephone system is $100 million a year.

Its mission, says soft-spoken Missouri-born Dr. Mervin J. Kelly, Bell Labs president, is better telephone service. For example, when the telephone system decided to connect Havana to Key West by underwater telephone cable, Bell Labs researchers invented vacuum tubes guaranteed to work night and day for twenty years at the bottom of the sea.

Telephone research at Bell Labs is defined broadly. Twenty-nine years ago Dr. Herbert E. Ives was encouraged to experiment with television. When TV burst upon the country in 1946, the phone company was ready with "video pair" wires to bring sports and public events to TV studios, and with coaxial cables to carry network programs around the country.

Thus, Bell scientists, before World War II, began probing into the properties of materials like silicon, a constituent of common sand, although these researches promised nothing for the telephone.

A first result was a vital "crystal detector" for wartime radar, rushed into production when it was found that sometimes vacuum tubes would not work. A second result was the transistor, a revolutionary gadget that is bringing a new world of electronic devices, from matchbook-size hearing aids to supercalcula-tors. A third result was the solar battery.

Deceptively simple in appearance, the solar battery looks like a series of razor blades connected by fine wires and cemented to a board. The "razor blades" are of specially treated silicon. When sunlight strikes them an electric current is generated. In bright sunlight, a square yard of the "razor blades" delivers 50 watts of electric power—more than enough to operate a standard light bulb, a telephone, or a table radio.

The Bell system expects to have the solar battery at work on an experimental rural telephone line in Georgia in the summer of 1955. Other uses will be slower in coming because of the difficulty of storing solar electricity for use at night. But, declare the experts, the harnessing of the vast power of the sun is on its way.

Weather by Machine

Late in 1954, trucks backed up to the U.S. Weather Bureau building in Washington. A dozen crackle-gray metal cabinets were unloaded. Installation men followed. The Weather Bureau was going to predict weather by machine. The cabinets housed the "gray cells" of a giant electronic calculator.

The machine was expected to break a bottleneck that has prevented better forecasts and caused the Weather Bureau to miss storms like several of 1954's tornadoes. For better forecasts, weathermen have needed to study more weather observations from more places. More observers, amateur and professional, could easily be obtained. However, the forecaster could not add their reports to his calculations and still get his prediction worked out in time to be of use.

The obvious solution was an electronic "brain" that could figure faster than a human weatherman. But when the Weather Bureau first became interested n machine forecasting, neither the right machine nor a method of using a machine for weather predicting existed. They had to be created.

The job was done at the highest-powered (human) brain center in the U.S. A youthful weather expert, Dr. Jule G. Charney, of the Institute for Advanced Study at Princeton, N.J., worked out a method of "numerical forecasting" fit for a high-speed calculating machine.

It was "proved out" on the Institute's machine by the Institute's mathematician extraordinary, Dr. John von Neumann, who has received fees as high as $1000 a day for his advice to industry on calculating machines and mathematical problems.

Weathermen were uncertain what their machine would do for much-desired 5- and 30-day forecasts. But they were certain it would increase the over-all accuracy of 24- and 48-hour predictions. Most important, they were sure it would end the recurrent nightmare of "unpredicted" storms that move too fast for human forecasters to keep up with them.

Digging Up the Past

In 1954 two exciting discoveries were made concerning man's past.

The first came in May. One day, workmen cutting a road around the Great Pyramid of Giza uncovered a crude stone wall. Beneath it, an alert supervisor for the Egyptian government's Antiquities Department, a 34-year-old architect named Kamal el Malakh, noticed a row of stone blocks. It took two stonecutters three days to chisel a small hole through one of the blocks. El Malakh peered through.

When his eyes adjusted to the darkness, he found himself looking forty-seven centuries into the past. He made out the shape of a ship, a "solar ship" for the after-death journeys of a Pharaoh across the heavens with the sun god Ra. It had been built by Khufu (or Cheops, as the Greeks called him), the builder of the Giza pyramid.

Solar ships (including three others built by Khufu) had been found before. But all had long since been stripped by grave robbers. El Malakh's ship—a six-decked bark about 100 feet long—was intact. Coils of rope and fragments of cloth could still be made out on the top deck.

The chamber had been sealed so tightly that El Malakh could still smell incense. Archeologists expected to find the ship a treasure-trove of royal objects that would fill in the picture of Khufu's time. One of the first discoveries was that the ship's beams were held together by copper nails —the first known use of metal nails in a ship.

The sensational discovery embroiled El Malakh in a bitter controversy with a comic-opera ending. Jealous senior members of the Antiquities Department procured an order forbidding him to write about his discovery and handing further work on the ship over to a five-man committee, of which El Malakh was the lowest-ranking member.

One of the men involved in these maneuvers was the senior inspector of antiquities, Dr. Mohammed Zakaria Ghoneim. Dr. Ghoneim meanwhile was himself making a find that was expected to take attention away from El Malakh's ship. At a site only 15 miles from the Giza pyramid, Dr. Ghoneim found an unfinished pyramid even older than the pyramid of Khufu. Within it, he discovered an apparently unrobbed sarcophagus. Dr. Ghoneim was confident it contained a royal mummy of the Third Dynasty. Newsmen and high officials were summoned for the opening. Dr. Ghoneim had a fizzle instead of a triumph. The sarcophagus was empty.

The other great archeological discovery of the year was made in a laboratory halfway around the world—at the Smithsonian Institution in Washington, D.C. During 1953, a pipeline welder, Keith Glasscock, had found some ice-age stone points on a ranch near Midland, Texas. Further digging by University of New Mexico experts, called by Glasscock, brought to light pieces of human cranium and jaw, teeth, finger bones, and part of a rib.

After a year of chemical tests and reconstruction work, Dr. T. D. Stewart of the Smithsonian announced that the fragments of Midland Man were at least 20,-000 years old. Thus man had been a resident of North America for at least twice as long as anyone had thought.

Polio Vaccine Trial

The year 1954 witnessed one of the largest medical undertakings in history— the mass trial of the polio vaccine developed by Dr. Jonas E. Salk of the University of Pittsburgh, himself the father of polio-age boys. This huge experiment may make the 1955 polio season the last.

In the three months before the 1954 season, 425,000 children in 217 areas of 44 States and in 3 sections of Canada received one or more injections of the Salk vaccine. For purposes of comparison, another 210,000 youngsters received injections of salt water, which has no preventive value.

The object of this enterprise was to measure the vaccine's worth. A promising preliminary test in 1953 on 600 children in the Pittsburgh area had encouraged the National Foundation for Infantile Paralysis to invest $7.5 million in the 44-State field trial. The question was: Is the Salk vaccine good enough to halt the mounting polio menace?

To find out, the polio record of the in-

"GIANT INSECTS" prepare to fix machinery in Richland, Wash., plutonium plant. They actually are technicians in flexible, airtight suits that guard them against radioactive dust

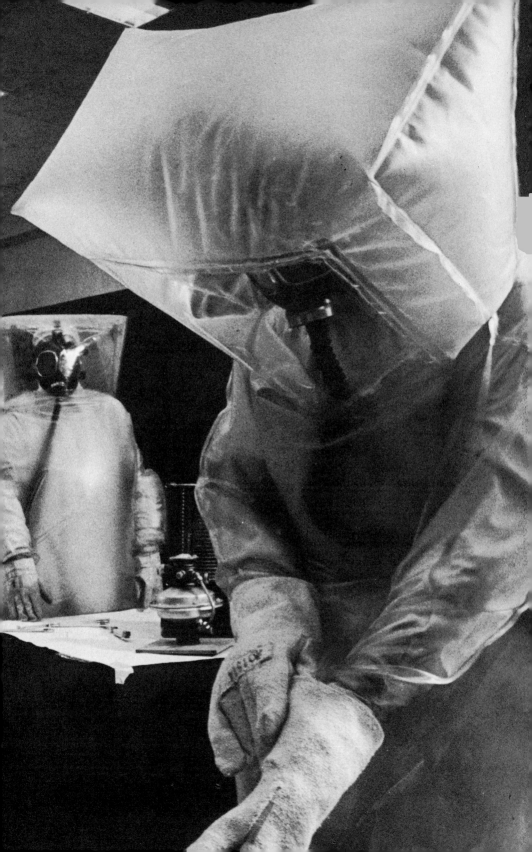

oculated children was being compared with the record of the children who received salt solution, and with the record of others who received no shots at all. At year's end, an army of field workers, twenty-seven laboratories, and a team of experts headed by Dr. Thomas Francis Jr.—Salk's former teacher—were still busy with the comparison.

The polio foundation expected the vaccine to show up well. Late in October, it announced that it was buying $9 million worth of the vaccine—enough to inoculate 9 million children.

Cancer Cure on Way

The year 1954 brought the first solid evidence that a cure for cancer would be found. Probably it will come from the same place that has yielded most of the wonder drugs that have transformed medicine—the chemical laboratory.

A decade and a half ago, a tall young chemist named George H. Hitchings got an idea while working for his doctor's degree at Harvard. To cure cancer, he reasoned, a difference must be found between cancerous and normal cells. An obvious difference is that cancerous cells multiply, whereas normal ones seldom do. Cancer might be cured, then, by a drug that blocks the formation of substances concerned in cell multiplication.

When he started searching for a drug that might do the trick, he searched all but alone. But in 1954 he headed a laboratory with a staff of seventy-five chemists at a pharmaceutical plant in Tuckahoe, N.Y. Many other laboratories in the U.S. and abroad were also following this line of research.

By arrangement with the U.S. Public Health Service and the American Cancer Society, anticancer drugs all go for testing to the laboratory at the Sloan-Kettering Institute, the research unit of New York's famous Memorial Cancer Center. In June, 1954, Sloan-Kettering issued a progress report: no fewer than ten drugs had been found that cure one or more types of animal cancer.

One drug cured 100 percent of one variety of animal tumor. Two others together cured 98 percent of one type of leukemia in mice. Among the ten successful cancer-killers were two drugs discovered by Dr. Hitchings personally and several others stemming from the line of attack he had initiated.

So far, the report emphasized, drugs have not cured a single case of human cancer. "But," commented Dr. C. Chester Stock, director of the testing laboratory "the lives of many cancer sufferers are already being prolonged by treatment with drugs ranging from hormones to chemical synthetics."

Moreover, the success of drugs in animals indicates that effective anticancer drugs exist. It is only a question of finding the right ones.

Turning TB Tide

The year 1954 brought plainly into view a great moment in the history of medicine. Near at hand was conquest of the White Plague, one of man's stubbornest and wiliest disease foes, which only ninety years ago caused nearly as many deaths as all other diseases combined.

On Dec. 1, the Trudeau Sanatorium at Saranac Lake, N.Y., founded in 1884 by Dr. Edward Livingston Trudeau and the world's best-known institution for treating tuberculosis, closed its doors. The reason: lack of patients. Only a chest-disease research laboratory would remain.

From California, Illinois, Massachusetts, and elsewhere in New York came similar reports. In Los Angeles, for the first time in the city's history, there were more TB beds than patients. And in New

York the new Nathan B. Van Etten Tuberculosis Hospital, which had never admitted a TB patient, was being used as a general hospital.

In 1954, tuberculosis claimed the lives of 15,000 Americans. Another 400,000 still had active tuberculous disease. Nevertheless, the tide had turned.

When streptomycin, isoniazid, and other new antitubercular drugs were introduced, physicians kept their fingers crossed. Like earlier methods of treatment, the new drugs only arrest tuberculosis and do not cure it. Patients may relapse at any time. Moreover, tuberculosis germs rapidly become resistant to drugs.

Even if the new drugs worked well, they could have boosted the need for TB beds suddenly and greatly (by saving patients who would have died quickly). In short, they might have postponed the TB problem rather than helped lick it.

The empty beds and closed sanatoria showed that the new drugs were licking it. Hospital stays were shorter. Tuberculosis was often being treated successfully at home or in the doctor's office. And death rates were sliding downward—over 40 percent in the past two years.

Wonder Drugs of 1954

The young woman certainly seemed headed for a mental hospital. Whenever anyone approached, she rushed to the window shrieking that her family was scheming to help a neighbor rape her. Her doctor, a psychiatrist, decided to try a drug with which he had been experimenting.

After it was administered, she remained unapproachable and unmanageable for two or three hours. Then she became quiet, indeed almost immobile, though she wasn't asleep. She answered promptly and freely when she was spoken to.

She remained calm, and even cheerful.

Psychiatrists in 1954 were excited about not one but hundreds of cases like this. Two remarkable drugs promised to make a dent at last in one of the greatest problems of our time—mental illness. The drugs were chlorpromazine or Thorazine (the drug given the young woman) and reserpine or Serpasil.

They were not panaceas. The young woman, for instance, still had her delusion about her family's and her neighbor's designs upon her. She would need lengthy treatment to overcome it. But she did not seem to mind her delusion. She could lead a near-normal life during treatment.

In some mysterious way, the new drugs eased anxieties and calmed excitement and agitation. They quieted tense or excited patients without knocking them out or impairing intelligence. Said Dr. N. William Winkelman Jr. of Philadelphia: "These drugs could be the biggest thing in decades in psychiatry. For tension and agitation are symptoms of well over half of all mental disorders."

Reserpine is extracted from the Indian snakeroot, a herbal remedy used in India for 3000 years. Chlorpromazine is a chemical synthetic discovered in France.

Twenty years ago, Indian scientists extracted reserpine from the snakeroot and found it valuable not only in mental disorder, but in one of the other major ailments of the modern world, high blood pressure. No one paid much attention until a Western-trained Indian physician got a report published in a British medical journal. In 1954, reserpine was being hailed as a "wonder drug".

Chlorpromazine came from a French drug firm's decision to make a virtue of necessity. Everyone who has taken antihistamine drugs to relieve allergy, such as hay fever, or in the treatment of colds is aware that they make people drowsy. Drug manufacturers have spent a fortune

in efforts to overcome this effect. The French firm, Rhône-Poulenc Specia, decided to look instead for an antihistamine that could be used to put people to sleep.

What the drug firm's chemists came up with was useless as a sleeping tablet, for huge doses are required to bring sleep. But it was able to do innumerable things done by few or no other drugs.

In addition to its remarkable effects in cases of mental illness, chlorpromazine was found the most effective drug ever discovered for stopping vomiting. In combination with the antialcohol drug Antabuse, it proved a superspeedy soberer-upper. It also stopped hiccups. It relieved patients' fears before surgery and kept them worry-free afterward. It quieted women during labor. To cap it all, it seemed suicide-proof.

Dr. Winkelman told of a woman suffering from involutional melancholia, an illness of women in their 50's. Sufferers are greatly upset by feelings of being worthless. To calm them, barbiturate sedatives have often had to be prescribed, though these patients may attempt suicide.

Dr. Winkelman's patient, bent on suicide, swallowed forty-four chlorpromazine tablets. She merely went to sleep for twenty-four hours, was awakened and brought to Dr. Winkelman's office for a checkup, went back to sleep, and finally on the fourth day got up—without having had any special treatment and none the worse for wear.

No one understood precisely how either chlorpromazine or reserpine does what it does. But physicians were busy finding out what else the two drugs would do.

LEAPING ON DRUM, real gone band leader Lionel Hampton (extra cool in Bermuda shorts) climaxes his composition, *Flying Home,* in a New York night club

Music and The Dance

THERE WAS AN EXPECTANT HUSH AS THE 92-piece orchestra, with its gleaming brasses and its mellowed strings, appeared on the huge stage in New York's Carnegie Hall. The playing, from a Berlioz overture to a Wagner prelude, was meticulous. Not a cue was mislaid.

In some respects, the concert was like many another distinguished music event in 1954. There was one important difference, however; there was no conductor on the podium!

The orchestra was the world-famed N.B.C. Symphony, the members of which had been hand-picked by the greatest maestro of them all, Arturo Toscanini. In April, volatile, wiry, 87-year-old Toscanini, who, more than any other individual, had put America on the world musical map, retired as the Symphony's conductor. In its seventeen distinguished years under Toscanini, the orchestra had been heard by 10 million radio listeners each time it broadcast. Record sales grossed $35 million. Suddenly, it was all over.

But the conductorless orchestra refused to die. In one of the most dramatic and touching stories in American music an-nals, the musicians reorganized themselves as a nonprofit corporation, renamed themselves the Symphony of the Air. The valiant orchestra decided not to invite a permanent conductor during the maestro's lifetime. All ninety-two men knew Toscanini's methods well. Rehearsals were democratically conducted; points of interpretation were decided by consensus. It was a unique musical experiment.

After the Carnegie Hall concert, which was hailed by the critics as "wizardry" and a "modern phenomenon", financial aid began pouring in. At year's end, it

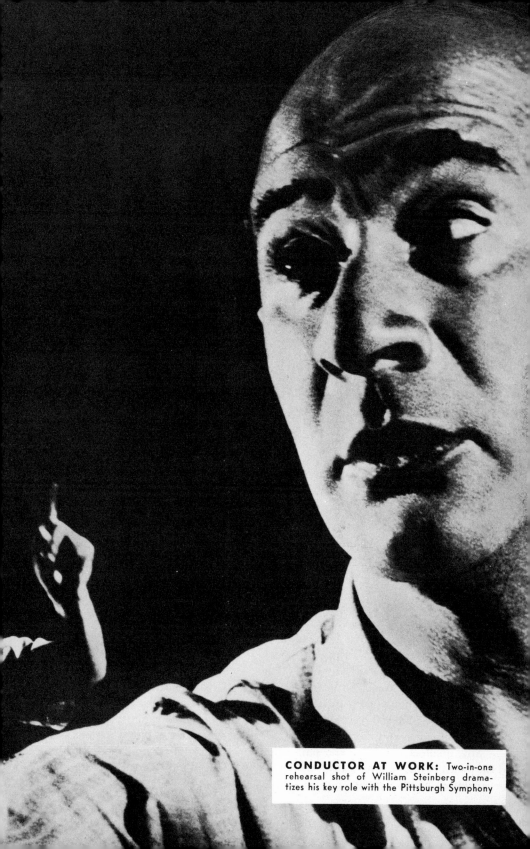

CONDUCTOR AT WORK: Two-in-one rehearsal shot of William Steinberg drama-tizes his key role with the Pittsburgh Symphony

looked as though the $10 million endowment the orchestra sought might become a reality.

In retirement in his beloved Italy, Parma-born, leonine-headed, sharp-eyed Toscanini noted with approval his orchestra's fight for survival. Mr. Music could also look back with enormous satisfaction on his career in America, where he had created a musical standard without equal.

Tales of his incredible musicianship were legion. During the year, a double-bassoon player reported that his instrument was faulty and would not hit E-flat. Toscanini blandly replied: "That's all right, there are no E-flats in any of the pieces we are rehearsing this afternoon."

Love, Love, Love

In 1954 the youngsters of the nation were in a teen-age tizzy. Two of their idols, 26-year-old crooner Eddie Fisher and 22-year-old movie star Debbie Reynolds, announced their engagement at a party given for them by Eddie Cantor in Hollywood. It was the entertainment world's most refreshing romance.

Bachelor Fisher, the nation's No. 1 popular singer, came up the hard way, getting off to a singing start by warbling in the Philadelphia streets about the merits of his father's fresh vegetables. Eddie Cantor discovered him singing in small clubs in New York's Catskill mountain resorts, took him on a cross-country tour in 1949. In the five years since he made his first record, Eddie has had nineteen smash hits and sales of 15 million discs. Three of his recordings ("Anytime", "I'm Walking Behind You", "O Mein Papa") sold over a million apiece. In 1954 Eddie grossed over $400,000, via records, radio, TV, night clubs, and theater dates.

Shy, unaffected Eddie, who sang from the heart without any tricked-up style, worshiped another great song salesman:

"Al Jolson was my idol. I saw the movie of his life ten times."

Bubbly, pert Debbie Reynolds, daughter of a railroad carpenter, confided that the nation's top crooner was really named Edwin. "We'll have six children," she said.

TV's Liberace

The Liberace craze showed no signs of abating in 1954. In June, Liberace packed New York's Madison Square Garden with his followers, having outgrown Carnegie Hall. Some 15,000 persons, mostly women over 21, filled the cavernous Garden at prices up to $6 a seat. It was the first piano concert held in Madison Square Garden since Paderewski played there in 1932.

With a wink, a smile, and his ever-present candelabra, Liberace offered his fans everything from Chopin to the "Beer Barrel Polka". Afterward, the darling of the nation's mothers exclaimed: "It was overwhelming, and I got all tingly." It was the triumphal end to a thirty-day tour that had grossed more than $300,000, causing Liberace to shout: "God bless TV!" To sour critics who disapproved of his Madison Square Garden concert, he sent the following message: "So sorry you did not like my music. I cried all the way to the bank."

It was the female television viewers of America who had made the 34-year-old pianist the hottest property in show business. His dimples were displayed on 217 TV stations in the nation, and on every single station in Canada. He was the first authentic matinee idol created by TV.

When he was 10, Milwaukee-born Wladziu Valentino Liberace was playing background music for silent films at 50¢ a session. Later came tours as a boy wonder at the piano, grueling sessions as a dance-band member, and moderately successful night-club solos. Then came TV—and the pot of gold. Liberace bought a mansion in San Fernando Valley, Calif., where he lived with his mother, his poodle, and a staff of servants. His swimming pool shaped like a piano became a national joke or dream, according to the point of view.

The delicate-mannered, sweet-voiced, doll-faced star analyzed his success thus: "I guess you could say I have an intimate type of breathy voice. And I try to dress with a little more flash [samples: 22-carat gold silk brocaded smoking jacket, gold cummerbund, diamond ring, matching cuff links, formal white trousers, white shoes]. Only certain types respond to me, and I am where I am because of them. I'm too earthy and unsophisticated for some people."

Grandma Wows Las Vegas

Marlene Dietrich, barely wrapped in 35 yards of flimsy white chiffon, still the world's glamour queen at 50, packed the customers into flashy, wide-open Las Vegas' Hotel Sahara—for a $35,000 weekly salary. Outlined provocatively by a breeze from a giant fan, she was the only grandmother in the world who could knock down five-figure money by offering an off-key voice inside a remarkable body. For in 1954 Marlene Dietrich became a night-club singer—with a vengeance.

As the year began, she appeared at Las Vegas' Sahara in a $6000 dress made of rhinestones-and-nothing. She broke all records. She then flew to London, again broke all records at the swank Café de Paris. In October, she made a triumphal return to Las Vegas in that transparent chiffon. Glamorous Dietrich, with a grandchild's first baby bottle dangling from her dressing-room mirror, was doing all right.

Born Maria Magdalene Dietrich in Berlin, she became famous overnight by her sizzling performance as a seductive and raucous cabaret trouper in a 1930 German film, *The Blue Angel.* La Dietrich then made more than twenty-five films in the U.S., and her sculptured face, her lovely legs, and her smoky-eyed allure became the hallmark of glamour in Hollywood.

In her New York apartment, the fabulous grandmother displayed not only the U.S. Medal of Freedom and the French Legion of Honor (for entertaining troops during World War II) but a unique bedroom in which the lights, going from dim to bright by degrees, could be operated by buttons built into the bed.

Among her onetime romantic companions she could count novelist Erich Maria Remarque, actors Jean Gabin, Douglas Fairbanks Jr., the late John Gilbert. And she could count as a good friend her husband Rudolph Sieber, with whom she did not live but whom she had never divorced.

She was also a devoted mother to her daughter, TV and Broadway actress Maria Riva, and companion to her two grandsons. She often pooh-poohed false, Hollywood glamour. Said *Hausfrau* Dietrich: "Beauty comes from within, and though it sounds horrible, it's quite true." France's Maurice Chevalier, who knew a beauty when he saw one, added: "Dietrich is something that has never existed before, and may never exist again. There's a woman—a real, ripe woman."

Marian at the Met

A moving story of 1954 music concerned statuesque, gentle, dusky contralto Marian Anderson. Thirty years earlier, the Negro singer had tried to buy a ticket to the Metropolitan Opera in New York, clutching the first money she had saved. She recalled: "When they told me the price of the ticket, I thought they meant the price for a season. I didn't have nearly enough for one performance."

JAZZ BALLET, Richard Rodgers' *Slaughter on Tenth Avenue,* originally danced by Tamara Geva and Ray Bolger, is performed by Vera Zorina, who did it in 1954 revival of its 1936 source, *On Your Toes*

In October of 1954, she signed a contract to sing at the same opera house—the first Negro to join the Met's roster in its seventy-year history. Sometime in 1955, she was to sing Ulrica in Verdi's *A Masked Ball*.

Interviewed at her 105-acre farm near Danbury, Conn., she remembered all the many friends who had helped her along the way. She scrupulously avoided the pronoun "I", and explained her odd manner of speech thus: "When you realize that whatever you do in life is not something you do absolutely alone, you do not like to be saying . . . I, I, I."

The 46-year-old contralto told the press: "Ever since one was in high school, one wanted to sing in opera, if that could be." The first singer to break the color line at the august Met then called her aged mother in Philadelphia, and that devout woman answered: "We thank the Lord."

But many Americans asked why the Metropolitan Opera had waited so long, waited until the great singer was past her

FRIGHTENING FORM is assumed by French dancer Yvette Chauviré in *Metamorphosis*, based on the Franz Kafka story about a man who was transformed into a giant cockroach

SATCHMO SWINGS ON: After thirty years of success — as trumpeter, singer, composer, band leader — Louis Armstrong in 1954 published book

prime. "A voice that comes only once in a hundred years" was Arturo Toscanini's opinion, expressed long before.

Miss Anderson refused to make anything sensational of her forthcoming Met debut. She stated in her dignified manner: "Music is my way. Some are born to do one thing better than another. Some of us are, by nature, militant—I am not. There's a spiritual called 'Stay in the Field'. I think that it might be a good motto for Negro musicians. If they will, they will be recognized in time according to their worth."

The contralto was born in the slums of South Philadelphia. Her widowed mother took in washing to support her. The local Baptist Church passed the hat, managed to get her a singing coach. Of her church-choir singing, Miss Anderson recalled: "I sang soprano, alto, tenor, and bass. When one of the choir members was absent, I sang that particular part."

Her first concert tours in the United States were not a success. So she went to Europe in 1932, became an immediate sensation in Paris, Berlin, Moscow, Helsingfors. Astute American impresario Sol Hurok heard her in Europe, brought her back to the United States in 1935. She was soon one of the most successful concert singers in music history, earning $2500 for each concert. These recitals alone brought her $200,000 a year, not counting radio, TV, or recording sessions. In 1954, the woman who was once barred from singing at Washington's Constitution Hall because of her color was a very rich lady.

Jazz on the Upswing

America enjoyed a renaissance in 1954 —a renaissance of jazz, hot and cold, New Orleans and bop. To those who had predicted the demise of the ailing jazz world, 1954 provided surprises.

The person most responsible was a supercharged, fast-talking, 36-year-old *aficionado* named Norman Granz, who sent out jazz-concert tours, labeled "Jazz at the Philharmonic", to a good part of the Western world and who operated a fabulously successful record company.

Los Angeles-born Mr. Jazz became the first person to mass-produce jazz successfully. Total worth of these enterprises was estimated in 1954 at $5 million. Half of the jazz records produced during the year came from the Granz factories. At salaries ranging to $6000 a week for singer Ella Fitzgerald, Granz during the year sent troupes of jazz missionaries to concerts in more than a hundred European and American cities.

The big jazz event of 1954 was not a Granz operation, however. In July cats from all over the nation converged on lucre-laden, social Newport, R.I., for a monster two-day Jazz Festival, which its sponsors hoped would become to jazz what the Berkshire Music Festival (Lenox, Mass.) was to classical music.

Newport was an unlikely setting for the clambake, with such jazz greats as Eddie Condon, Dizzy Gillespie, Pee Wee Russell, and Wild Bill Davison blasting the weathering old mansions of America's richest men with gone music.

Chief sponsor was young tobacco heir and jazz devotee Louis Lorillard. Manager was George Wein, entrepreneur of two Boston night clubs (Storyville, named for the bygone New Orleans red-light district, and Mahogany Hall, named for a famed house in that district).

Both men were jubilant. For 12,000 cheering fans filled the venerable, open-air Casino. The original financing, $20,-000, was cleared the first night. America's first Jazz Festival was certain to become an annual event. And extravagant jazzbos from the cities would continue to mix with some of society's most elegant dowagers—to dig America's unique contribution to world music.

The Russians Dance

In 1954 the biggest news event in the world of dance happened—or rather did not happen—in Paris. A full-sized Soviet ballet company, whose fabulous art had long been praised by diplomats stationed in Moscow, was to make its initial appearance in the Western world. Prima ballerina was fabled Galina Ulanova, whom many consider the world's greatest living dancer. Critics and dance-followers from the United States, Canada, and every Western nation converged on Paris to see the publicized Russian performers. Tickets sold for more than $100 apiece on the black market.

But on May 7, the eve of the gala première, Dienbienphu in Indochina fell. Premier Laniel announced that the three-week ballet season was called off, for fear of angry demonstrations by the pride-pricked French people. The dancers left Paris in a huff.

They soon turned up in East Berlin, however, and gave twelve performances at a 3000-seat music hall. Intrepid Western observers who journeyed there reported that Soviet choreography and settings were uninspired and hopelessly old-fashioned. However, they did confirm reports that Galina Ulanova was a truly great ballerina.

Ulanova, a frail, 44-year-old woman, was Russia's top dancer, decorated four times by the Soviet government. She was completely a product of the Soviet regime; her government boasted that she kept her youth and beauty by reading Marx and following world communism. Cynics argued that make-up helped, too.

America's top choreographer, George Balanchine, was also a Russian, had studied in the Soviet ballet schools in the first days of the Revolution. But he chose to leave his country shortly afterward and seek freedom to dance and do choreography as he pleased in the West. In 1954, he was primarily responsible for the phenomenal box-office success of ballet in America.

His company, the New York City Ballet, had the Standing Room Only sign up when it appeared in Los Angeles and San Francisco as well as New York. His full-length, evening-long version of the venerable *Nutcracker* ballet, with Tchaikovsky music, was the year's biggest hit.

The elaborate $90,000 fantasy, with sugarplum fairies, a huge Christmas tree, and an enormous cast including thirty-five children, was a smash hit during the early part of the year. In an unprecedented move at year's end, the ballet was repeated in New York nightly for seven weeks. It was a complete sellout.

The 50-year-old choreographer had been imported to America by ballet-lover Lincoln Kirstein (who had given untold thousands of his Boston department-store fortune to dance projects). Balanchine busied himself in many fields, including films and Broadway musicals. In 1954 two Broadway hits, *On Your Toes* and *House of Flowers*, featured choreography by the master. But he preferred working for no salary (royalties from his ballets brought him an average of $200 a week, however) at the New York City Ballet Company.

He had another interest, too—in pretty girls and matrimony. All five of his wives, Tamara Geva, Alexandra Danilova, Vera Zorina, Maria Tallchief, and the latest, 25-year-old Tanaquil LeClercq, were ballerinas.

Wife No. 4, raven-haired, delicately bronzed, 29-year-old Maria Tallchief, was America's top dancer in 1954. She was the first native ballerina the U.S. had produced who could successfully compete

HEROIC BUST of composer Ludwig van Beethoven, sculptured by Dr. Emil Seletz, broods over Seletz' grandson as he listens to a performance of Beethoven's *Moonlight Sonata*

with Britain's Margot Fonteyn, France's Yvette Chauvire, Russia's Galina Ulanova.

American Princess on Her Toes

On Oct. 1, waves of applause rolled across the footlights of Baltimore's Lyric Theater—applause for a star, Maria Tallchief. Beginning on that auspicious evening, she was the prima ballerina of the reorganized Ballet Russe de Monte Carlo, and would tour 102 cities in the United States. Her salary was a reputed $2000 a week, more than any other American ballerina received.

Lovely Maria Tallchief, equally adept as the tempestuous Firebird or the coldly classic Swan Queen, was born on an Osage reservation in Oklahoma. Her father was a full-blooded Indian, her mother Scottish. The Osage Tribal Council named her Princess Wa-Xthe-Thonba. Her great-grandfather was Chief Big Heart.

She recalled of her youth: "The era of the Indian oil millionaires was over, but we lived comfortably, in a house, not a teepee." She studied the dance in California with Bronislava Nijinska, sister of the fabled Nijinsky. At 17 she joined a touring ballet company, later married Balanchine, and rose to prominence.

Miss Tallchief is a new kind of prima ballerina, a typically American product. She likes difficult dance feats: "You do as much as you choose to do. If you have a challenge, you do more." She is friendly and unaffected, more likely to be found dining at the local corner drugstore than at a de luxe restaurant. In the plush, lush days of ballet, caviar was the traditional food of top-ranking ballerinas. Maria Tallchief prefers Fig Newtons.

MOBILE FACE of conductor Arturo Toscanini is captured for posterity. He retired in 1954 at 87

LOST TO JOURNALISM in 1954 was photographer Robert Capa, killed by land mine in Indochina. Last picture of him (above) was taken in Malaya. Right: One of his notable wartime shots shows French townsfolk, newly liberated in 1944, jeering shaved-headed, pro-Nazi collaborationist

SHRIEKS OF LAUGHTER ROCKED A NEW YORK courtroom one day in 1954 as fierce-tempered Westbrook Pegler, chronically indignant Hearst columnist, stated on the witness stand: "I don't hate anyone."

Peg had landed in court as defendant in a $500,000 libel suit brought by Quentin Reynolds, author-correspondent. The seeds of the trial were sown in the early '30's in suburban Connecticut where the pair, along with the late Heywood Broun, columnist and founder of the American Newspaper Guild, were poker-playing neighbors. Pegler, far right of center, began to snipe at the liberal tendencies of "Old Bleeding Heart" Broun, who replied by calling Pegler the "light-heavyweight champion of the upperdog". As Pegler's attacks became increasingly savage, Reynolds lined up in Broun's corner.

Later, reviewing a Broun biography, Reynolds made comments that Pegler interpreted as accusations that his attacks had hastened Broun's death. Pegler shot back unsentimentally:

"Like Broun, Reynolds was sloppy and ran to fat, but the fact was not to be established until we got the war which he had been howling for that his protuberant belly was filled with something else than guts . . . Reynolds was largely an absentee war correspondent. . . . Although he was a giant and a bachelor he let several million kids about 18 years old do the fighting."

Pegler also accused Reynolds of "nuding along the public road" in Connecticut with "his wench . . . absolutely raw" and of proposing marriage to widow Connie Broun while riding with her to Heywood's grave.

But in court Pegler had trouble making his insults stick. Reynolds' courage as a war reporter was vouched for by a parade of witnesses including John Gunther, Edward R. Murrow, and Eisenhower's wartime aide Captain Harry Butcher. Mrs.

Broun herself denied the proposal yarn. The nudism charge was countered with a statement that Reynolds is allergic to sunshine. At one point, Pegler enlivened proceedings by labeling as "pro-Communist propaganda" an unidentified statement from one of his own 1937 columns.

Finally, the jury agreed that in the Reynolds column Pegler had gone too far. Reynolds was awarded a record $175,000 in punitive damages, with $1 added to compensate for the damage done to his reputation. However, Pegler would not pay up personally; his contract provided that Hearst settle any damages for libel.

Dollars and Cents

In 1954 one of journalism's most hardy fighters in the right-wing camp, Colonel Robert R. McCormick, publisher of the Chicago *Tribune*, surprised everyone by giving up a major battle. Six years before, the prosperous *Tribune* had bought the Washington (D.C.) *Times-Herald* from heirs of the Colonel's cousin, Eleanor ("Cissy") Patterson. The Colonel said his aim was to "bring the United States to Washington".

Following the *Tribune*'s isolationist, Old Guard line, the *Times-Herald* often collided with the internationalist, anti-McCarthy Washington *Post*, owned by 78-year-old Eugene Meyer. The morning *Post*, a *Tribune* editorial once said, was "chalking up a telling record for defending Reds and pinks, slavish devotion to the Truman Administration, and violent attacks on pro-American members of Congress".

But business is business. After amiable and secret negotiations, the Colonel in March suddenly sold the *Times-Herald* to Meyer for $8.5 million. His stated reason: "The doctors told me that I would have to do less work." Another possible reason: The *Times-Herald*, slipping in circulation and advertising, was losing $1 million a year against the competition of the *Post* and two evening papers.

The Colonel was by no means softening up. Toward the year's end a short, sharp editorial in the *Tribune* indicated that he was conceding nothing: "President Eisenhower should be nominated for President in 1956—by the Democrats. If he is so nominated, he will get most of the Democratic votes, all of the Demi-Rep votes, and if Sen. Watkins is their leader, all of the Mormon votes, unless Jimmie Roosevelt runs. Americans will have to look elsewhere for their candidate."

The continuing economic squeeze that had affected the Washington *Times-Herald* also had cut the number of U.S. dailies from 2042 in 1920 to 1760 as the year began. During 1954 newspaper circulations and revenues hit new highs, but production costs—rising faster—were pushing profits down to record lows.

Some hope of a long-range solution began to appear as revolutionary mechanical improvements came into use. One promised simpler, faster, cheaper newspaper production by eliminating the use of lead type. This was the first important change in newspaper-production methods since the linotype was introduced in 1886.

In the process, called phototypesetting, machines put the letter characters directly on film, which then can be used to make an engraving plate for printing. In 1954, the St. Petersburg *Times*, the Milwaukee *Journal*, and the Quincy (Mass.) *Patriot Ledger* were pioneering in phototypesetting operations, which involve also a new high-speed engraving process that puts a picture onto a magnesium plate in a fraction of the time required by older methods.

It will be many years before big newspapers can be printed entirely without lead type. But these new, fast, cheaper methods foreshadow the day when newspaper plants will have lighter equipment and look less like steel mills, when men will not have to be millionaires to start new dailies, and when there will be fewer one-paper-monopoly towns.

End of Assignment

"Outlined against a blue-gray October sky, the Four Horsemen rode again. In dramatic lore they are known as Famine, Pestilence, Destruction, and Death . . . Their real names are Stuhldreher, Miller, Crowley, and Layden."

The sports writer who composed that lead died during the year at 73. It was Grantland Rice; he had been describing the 1924 Notre Dame backfield as it rode through Army. Kindly "Granny Rice", respected and beloved, had been a sports writer for fifty-three years.

Cut off also in 1954, at the peak of his career, was Robert Capa, 41, conceded by colleagues to be the best of the combat photographers. He stepped on a land mine and was killed during the war in Indochina.

Capa hated war, which he found "like an aging mistress; more and more dangerous and less and less photogenic". But always he had been in the thick of it—sweating out the Spanish civil war in which his photographer wife was crushed to death by a tank; jumping into Germany with the paratroopers in World War II; landing at Anzio with assault troops; hitting Omaha Beach on D day.

His art is best described in his own comment on some shots he got in Sicily: "They were simple pictures and showed how dreary and unspectacular fighting actually is. Scoops depend on luck and quick transmission and most of them don't mean anything the day after they are published. But the soldier who looks at the shots of Troina 10 years from now

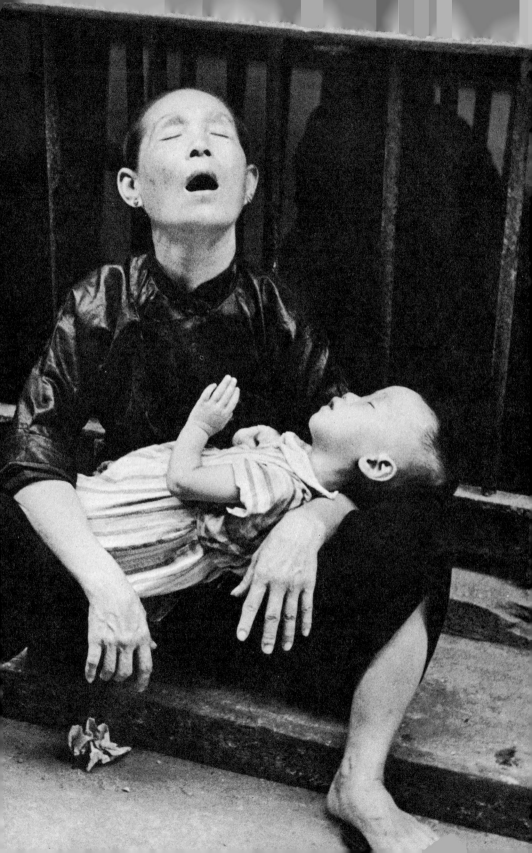

in his home in Ohio will be able to say, 'That's how it was.'"

Capa invented himself. He was born Andrei Friedmann in Hungary. As an unknown photographer in Paris, he found he could sell pictures by posing as the assistant to a "rich, talented American photographer named Capa". Eventually, he became Capa—and an American citizen. He was a short, stocky man, a good drinking companion, always seen with the prettiest girls, familiar with half a dozen languages.

Easygoing, cocky, in and out of jobs, he founded his own agency, Magnum Photos, with four other crack lensmen after World War II. He deliberately skipped the Korean War, saying he was happy to be an unemployed war photographer. But when *Life* magazine asked him to cover Indochina, he went promptly. "I am a gambler," he had written in his candid autobiography, *Slightly Out of Focus*. His last, losing gamble made him the eleventh U.S. correspondent killed on war assignments since 1945.

By strange coincidence, a few days before Capa's death a Magnum partner and close friend, Werner Bischof, was killed when his truck plunged off a 1500-foot cliff in the Peruvian Andes. Bischof was a commercial photographer who became a photo-journalist after World War II. A researcher and careful technician, he shared with Capa the qualities of imagination and human sympathy, as well as a gift for catching the great moment in his pictures.

Scoops, Headlines, and Headliners

The biggest news beat of the year, the story that Dr. J. Robert Oppenheimer had been suspended from atomic-research work by the Atomic Energy Commission, was shared by columnists Joseph and Stewart Alsop of the New York *Herald* *Tribune* and James ("Scotty") Reston, Washington bureau chief of *The New York Times*. From January until April they sat on the story—the Alsops because their friend Oppenheimer did not want publicity; Reston because *The Times* wanted to get more information on the story before breaking it. Then one April weekend it became evident that Senator McCarthy intended to publish the news before long. Also, security hearings on Oppenheimer were about to begin. Simultaneously, but separately, the Alsops and Reston persuaded Oppenheimer and his lawyers, with A.E.C. approval, to let them tell what had happened.

The No. 1 news story of the year was the Army vs. McCarthy affair. The hearings in Washington generated a flow of 16,000 words a day for 36 days on Associated Press wires. But surely the most fun-to-handle news was that swirling around curvesome Marilyn Monroe.

Her marriage in January to Joe DiMaggio, baseball's former "Yankee Clipper", got the full words-and-pictures treatment. Even the San Francisco judge who performed the ceremony made copy with his desolate confession: "I forgot to kiss her." The honeymoon trip with Joe to Tokyo had the Japanese press reeling. "How long have you been walking like that?" one Oriental reporter asked Marilyn. "I started when I was six years old," replied the witty wiggler. And in the fall nearly every paper found some reason to run the publicity shots showing her on movie location with her skirts blown up, as the script required.

Her separation from Joe in October gave headline writers an opening into which they plunged: "Joe Must Go" . . . "Nights Were Dull at Joe and Marilyn's" . . . "Marilyn and Joe—Out at Home" . . . "It Begins to Look Like Joe Said 'Go'". And so on until the divorce, when, as millions of red-blooded American males scratched their heads incredulously, Marilyn testified that the home-run slugger was "cold" and "indifferent".

Sports, Ads, and Red Ink

In the magazine field the big 1954 news was the birth of an important new weekly and a significant policy change for a giant publication.

Sports Illustrated was introduced in August by Henry Luce's Time, Incorporated. Harassed staffers nicknamed it "Muscles" and "Sweat: The Magazine of Blood and Tears". Some $2 million had been spent in preparation for it. The final product was a slick, smoothly edited, lavishly illustrated, and definitely upper-class mixture of news, features, and comment on everything from baseball to bubble gum.

Many critics thought S.I. had too little detailed sports dope to please shirt-sleeve fans and too much to hold the moneyed leisure lovers, the obvious advertising market. But the magazine quickly built up a circulation of more than 500,-000. The trade did agree that the Luce organization had the money and talent to put it over if anyone could.

There was little doubt that the mighty *Reader's Digest* would make good in its new venture. For the first time in its 33-year history *The Digest* offered its 10 million circulation to advertisers. The reason why shy DeWitt Wallace and his vivacious wife, Lila Acheson Wallace, co-owners and coeditors, broke the no-advertising tradition on which they had founded their phenomenally successful reprint magazine was simple: *The Digest* needed the money. Although the firm was making good profits on its twenty-nine international editions (total circulation: 7½ million), which had carried ads since 1940, and on its books division, the domestic *Digest* faced a deficit operation.

Since the magazine was begun in 1922 its price had stayed at 25¢ a copy, but its contents had tripled while editorial and production costs soared. It was a choice of raising the price to readers or accepting ads. A secret survey indicated that *The Digest*'s loyal following preferred advertisements in their magazine to a higher price.

However, the ads will be as carefully selected as are *The Digest*'s "Articles of Lasting Interest". Only thirty-two pages of advertising will be accepted for each issue, and there will be no reduction in editorial content. Ads for liquor, tobacco, and medical remedies will be barred. Wallace himself will pass on the copy. The rate, up to $31,000 for a four-color page, is the highest in the business—for the world's greatest circulation.

In a matter of hours after the new policy was announced, *The Digest* was flooded with more advertising orders than it could handle for a year.

Another kind of battle against real, not potential, red ink was being fought at the venerable Crowell-Collier Publishing Company by the new president, 45-year-old Paul Smith, the ex-boy wonder West Coast newsman. During the year Smith assumed the active editorship of the house's three magazines—*Collier's, The Woman's Home Companion,* and *The American Magazine*—and began borrowing money to pep up editorial and advertising efforts. *Collier's*, the big money-loser, was getting the most attention. Smith wanted it heavy on serious, fact-filled articles and light on sensational, Sunday-supplement stuff—"scope, not scoop".

Smith is a onetime Marine, a former editor of the San Francisco *Chronicle*, a protégé and close friend of Herbert Hoover, and a man of fabled persuasiveness. Under his direction, *Collier's* circulation increased and its ads looked bet-

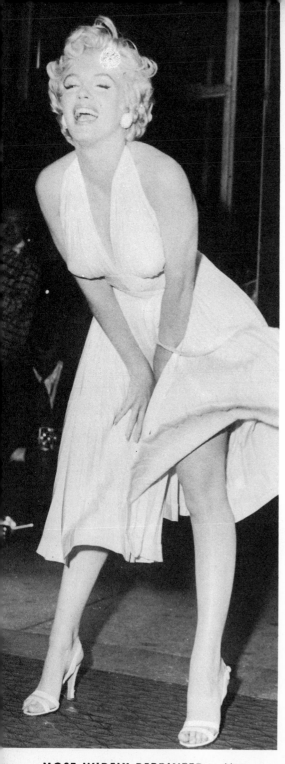
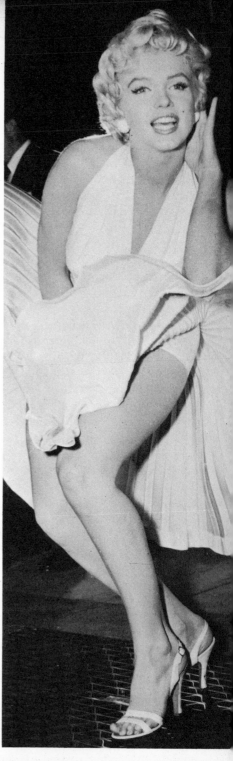

MOST WIDELY REPRINTED publicity pictures of the year were these shots of Marilyn Monroe making a movie scene "on location"—i.e., over a sidewalk grating with a blower beneath—in New York. Sequence, from *The Seven Year Itch,* was made in early morning but hundreds of fans turned up nevertheless

ter, partly because of his own top-level sales efforts. If he could put the magazine back in the black again, it would be one of the industry's great personal triumphs.

Reading for the Children

1954 was the year when the comics began to get funnier and cleaner. In the newspapers, the swing was toward the laugh-making strips and away from the outer-space, supercrime fantastic serials so popular a decade ago. Editors reported growing interest in wholesome comics like *Dennis the Menace, Pogo, Beetle Bailey,* and *Peanuts*.

Beetle's creator, Mort Walker, won the annual Billy De Beck Award—the cartoonists' Oscar—for his bemused G.I. character. Walt Kelly, the man behind Pogo, was invited to present a series of original drawings to the Folklore Section of the Library of Congress—the first time a cartoonist had been so honored. Wise, witty Kelly's *Pogo* strip deals with a philosophical possum and his astonishingly human-type animal friends in the Okefinokee Swamp. On the market only five years, it appears in some 415 papers and has a growing army of devoted fans.

Comic books, especially the so-called horror comic books, enjoyed no such success as did comic strips in 1954. Protests against them from church, school, and parent groups brought action. Actually, the gruesome ones represented only about 15 percent of the 78 million comic books sold on newsstands every month, but they were bad enough to give the trade a whopping black eye.

During April a Senate committee investigating juvenile delinquency took a long look at the problem. The self-styled originator of the horror books, William Gaines of the Entertaining Comics Group, testified that the only limitation on his publications was "good taste".

"Is this good taste?" asked Senator Estes Kefauver, holding up a Gaines comic cover that showed a man with a bloody ax in one hand and a woman's head in the other.

"Yes—for the cover of a horror comic," Gaines answered. "I think it would be bad taste if he were holding the head a little higher so the neck would show with the blood dripping from it."

That sort of thing did it. With city after city enforcing long-neglected ordinances to ban the sale of indecent literature, the comic-book industry in desperation formed a self-policing association, drew up a code of publishing ethics, and appointed a czar, Judge Charles F. Murphy of New York City. (One firm that did not join the association was Dell Publishing Company, which accounts for nearly one third of all comic books sold and, having its own strict standards, does not issue crime or horror books. In 1954 the top publication in nationwide newsstand sales—about 2⅕ million a month—was Donald Duck, a Dell comic book about the adventures of Walt Disney's querulous drake.)

At the year's end comic-book czar Murphy reported results: in 440 comic books set for publication in 1955 he had ordered revisions of 5656 drawings and rejected 126 stories. More than 25 percent of the changes involved "reduction of feminine curves to more natural dimensions and extending the line of clothing to cover a respectable amount of the female body". His office called it "giving ladies the Dior look".

In England, children were being offered a different kind of reading fare to lure them away from horror comics. Three leading London dailies, the *Mirror,* the *Express,* and the *Sketch,* began putting out weekly "junior" editions. The *Junior Sketch* was included free in the regular Wednesday edition; the other

Juniors sold separately for tuppence (2⅓¢) each. They were full of news and features about animals, planes, sports, science, and the doings of youngsters. There were lots of puzzles, pictures, competitions. The market: England's 5 million boys and girls aged 8 to 15. So far the response was encouraging. The *Junior Express*, for example, got 2000 letters a day from enthusiastic young readers.

Hoax and Joke

As usual the press in 1954 carried some stories that belonged more in the realm of folk tales than news.

Early in the year an old favorite turned up again. A headline in the Los Angeles *Mirror* screamed: 'WOLF BOY' REARED BY ANIMALS BOLTS RAW MEAT, SNARLS, BITES. Many other papers throughout the country picked up wire-service stories out of New Delhi, India, telling of the discovery in a railroad car of a strange, speechless lad, about 9 years old, with a double set of incisors (fine for tearing meat) and deformed hands and knees (as though he often ran about on all fours).

Local medical opinion held that the boy "was raised by animals of some sort". There was semiscientific speculation that, like Romulus and Remus of ancient days, he had been adopted by she-wolves, "known to have strong maternal instincts".

But the wolf boy was a product of vivid —and in this case, cruel—exaggeration. Actually, he was a sick, mentally deficient, partially paralyzed child, apparently abandoned to public care.

In a happier, but equally phony, vein was one of the most widely published short stories of the year. The A.P. put it out from Rhode Island: A motorist had stalled with a dead battery on a highway and flagged down a passing woman driver to give him a push. He explained that his car had an automatic transmission so she would have to give him a good push— at least 35 miles an hour—to get his car started. The obliging lady nodded, drove back up the road, turned around, and pulled in behind him—going at a good 35 miles an hour. The crash cost $300 in damages.

When delighted A.P. clients called for more details a checkup was started. Apparently the story had sprung up at several points in New England within a few days—but no one ever found a trace of such an accident. The A.P. account actually had carried a "red flag" warning that, although the story was unconfirmed, "a newspaper would have to be pretty selfish not to pass it along". Most editors, who seemed to share the popular conception of woman drivers, thought so too.

STARTLING were stories of Stalin's death by Harrison E. Salisbury, crack foreign correspondent

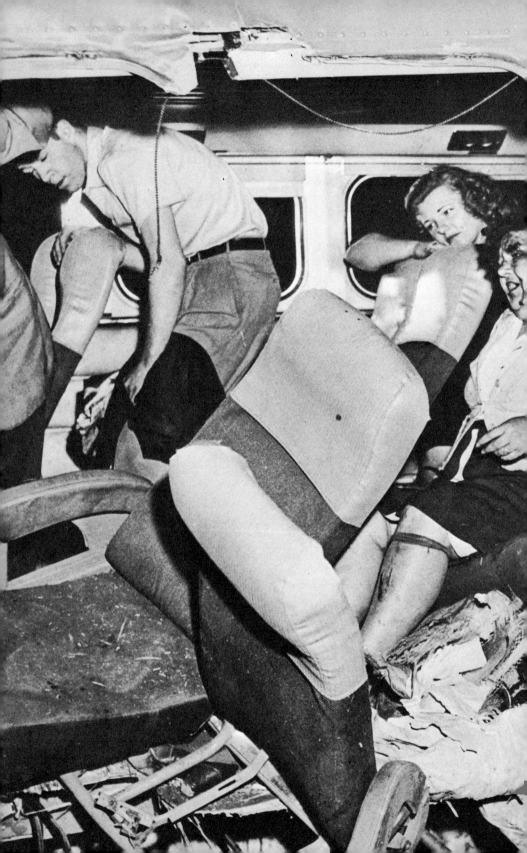

QUICK WORK by Frank Rutherford of the Los Angeles *Herald and Express* produced this eye-stopping photo of a Greyhound bus and some of its twenty-seven injured passengers—minutes after the bus crashed against a bridge pillar

THEATER

WATER-SPRITE role in *Ondine* gave full play to Audrey Hepburn's elfin charm, made her the darling of Broadway early in 1954

DREAMY TEEN-AGER portrayed by Eartha Kitt in late-fall hit, *Mrs. Patterson*, launched her Broadway acting career. Above: Eartha in more sophisticated mood

THE TWO TOP THEATER PERSONALITIES OF 1954 never appeared on stage. They were 67-year-old George Abbott and 45-year-old Joshua Logan, and the stage had made millionaires of both.

These two fabled men, whom the public never saw, were regarded by Broadway solons as the most brilliant directors in the American theater. At all events, they brought in the big money. In 1954, two of the smash-hit musicals, *Pajama Game* and *Fanny*, grossing $52,000 weekly apiece, were respectively the work of miracle-men Abbott and Logan.

Tall, lean, bald George Abbott had the Midas touch. Productions of which he had been playwright, director, or producer (or all three) had grossed more than $100 million. From the theater, movies, television, real estate, and three oil wells in Oklahoma, he had earned more than $20 million.

Known in show business as The Great Stone Face, Abbott was reserved and cold to a degree unique in the extrovert, tinsel world of Broadway. And his parsimony was legend. Characteristically, he once remarked of his father: "He was a gregarious man, prone to lend money to strangers, a habit which I did not inherit."

Born in Forestville, N.Y., Abbott was an electrician's helper, cable splicer's assistant, and a crane man in a Buffalo steel mill before he essayed the theater in the 1910's. Encouragement came from Harvard professors when he briefly attended that university. After Broadway brought him millions, he lived in New York's swank Hampshire House, summered in a 22-room whitewashed-brick mansion in Port Washington, Long Island.

Since World War I, he had directed more than seventy shows, including such hits as *Pal Joey, Call Me Madam,* and *Wonderful Town.*

The Abbott Method

The Abbott method had been successful in many emergency operations. *Brother Rat* was rejected by thirty-one producers. Abbott grabbed it, polished it. The farce grossed more than a million. *Room Service* closed on the road before it hit Broadway. Under Abbott's wise doctoring, it was revived, ran two years in New York, and Hollywood finally bought it for $225,000.

The great director was the playwrights' terror: he slashed their scripts without mercy. One author lamented: "George could be doing Eugene O'Neill, and if the third act was slow, out it'd go."

His formula for making flops into hits was deceptively simple: sex, speed, and happy endings. He advised actors: "You've got to believe what you do and have a good time; if you do, the audience will, too."

Perhaps more important was his keen eye for talent. He employed many small-salaried unknowns in his shows. Abbott graduates include Gene Kelly, Van Johnson, Shirley Booth, Betty Field, June Allyson, Desi Arnaz, Eddie Albert, Joan Caulfield, Richard Widmark.

Like Abbott, tireless, round-faced Joshua Logan, sporting a gray mustache which he constantly fingered, was a self-made Broadway millionaire. Unlike Abbott, the 6-foot director was a volcanic, flamboyant man who talked with anybody and everybody.

His success was phenomenal. Since World War II, Logan had staged *Annie Get Your Gun* (three-year run on Broadway), *Mister Roberts* (four years), and *South Pacific* (five years). In 1954, *Fanny*, a musical which he coauthored, produced, and directed, was a smash hit with a long run clearly indicated.

Logan grew up in Mansfield, La., in a rambling house covered with wisteria and bordered by cotton fields. From his gentle mother he acquired a love for poetry and flowers. For the benefit of his stepfather, a staff officer at Culver Military Academy, he determined to be as manly as possible. He became a crack football tackle and boxer. He once recalled: "There has always been in me a fight between the tough guy and the soft guy."

At Princeton, he distinguished himself in theatricals. With a group of classmates, including movie actor James Stewart, he organized the University Players, a summer-theater group which performed in a small showcase on Cape Cod, Mass. The five seasons of this playhouse inaugurated the careers of Henry Fonda, Margaret Sullavan, Stewart, and Logan himself.

After a long, grueling spell in minor jobs on Broadway and in Hollywood, Logan in 1938 directed a Broadway hit, *On Borrowed Time.* Sometime thereafter, he had a nervous breakdown. He often disappeared for weeks, turned up in cities hundreds of miles away. He could not sleep. He suffered intensely from an over-abundance of energy. Finally he had himself committed to a mental hospital in Philadelphia.

There, for three months, he painted, studied music, read, sculptured. In 1942 he was back at work in the theater, and his *By Jupiter* was an enormous hit. From then on, it was a straight course to the top and a fabulous fortune. In 1954, he averaged $10,000 a week.

Logan's expensive apartment in New York, staffed by a cook, butler-chauffeur, two secretaries, and a secretaries' secretary, and his rambling mansion in Connecticut were filled with mementos of his travels all over the world. An inveterate tourist and collector, he once sent his wife, actress Nedda Harrigan, a post card from India with a picture of the Taj Mahal on it. He wrote: "Just bought this."

His one worry was health. Ever since he had followed the Charles Atlas muscle-building courses as a boy, he had practically lived in gymnasiums and on health farms. He cut out drinking and smoking. His constant ambition was "to see my stomach muscles".

Cinderella Story

Logan's hit musical, *Fanny*, which starred Ezio Pinza and Walter Slezak, also starred a 20-year-old, country-fresh blonde named Florence Henderson. In a hectic paper-moon world where beauty was a commodity on the market, she was the year's Cinderella story.

Born in Rockport, Ind., and reared in Owensboro, Ky., Miss Henderson planted, weeded, picked tobacco on her father's small farm along with her nine brothers and sisters. Her father advised her early in life: "We don't have much, but we do have character. No one can take it from you, unless you lose it yourself. If you do, you lose everything."

Florence had always loved to sing. As a child, she won ice-cream cones at the village grocery by singing. Neighbors admired her lovely voice, pooled enough money to send her to New York for music and drama lessons. A timid country girl with an ill-fitting bathing suit, she auditioned for the chorus line of *Wish You Were Here*. Each girl had to state her name, birthplace, and experience. She announced: "I'm Florence Henderson of Rockport, Indiana, and I haven't done a thing."

Astute Joshua Logan, who knew a fresh, lovely girl when he saw one, hired her on the spot for a bit part. After that, she toured in a road company of *Oklahoma!* Now, in her third Broadway show, the former choir singer had the title role in *Fanny*.

Of her future, the religion-minded star announced: "I do my best and never expect any rainbows. I've learned that everything is in His hands. If it happens, fine. But if it doesn't, He wants it that way."

1954's Box-Office Boom

In 1954 the theater was in a healthy state, nationally as well as on Broadway. Everywhere, from Boston to Dallas, box-office cash registers tinkled merrily. Professional mourners who had wailed about the theater's coming death were in hiding; such prosperity had not been known in eight years. Broadway grosses in 1954 were reported at more than $23 million. Both musicals (*Kismet, Can-Can, Peter Pan*) and straight plays (*The Seven Year Itch, The Teahouse of the August Moon, Dear Charles, Tea and Sympathy*) played to standees.

Not all of the important stage news was made on Broadway. The box-office bonanza was felt in the nation's mushrooming summer theaters, also. From June to September, 5 million people visited 550 barns, old mills, town halls, and tents to

NIMBLE FEET helped several 1954 shows. Carol Haney's (top) twinkled in *The Pajama Game*; Dee Dee Wood's (below) were an adjunct to *Can-Can*

DANCER Sally Forrest (above), who can act as well as dance, took over female lead in *The Seven Year Itch*. Dorene Kilmer (right) appeared in *On Your Toes*

view dramas and musicals. Estimated gross for the flourishing summer-theater industry: $7 million.

Just a few years earlier, summer theater had spelled amateur talent, hard seats, stifling heat. In 1954, many theaters were air-conditioned, the seats cushioned, and the talent—top-rank stars emoting for perhaps $5000 a week plus a percentage of the gross. Celebrities like Tallulah Bankhead, Wally Cox, and Farley Granger filled the cashboxes.

Two of the most publicized theater debuts of the year occurred not on Broadway but in the unpretentious Pocono Playhouse in Mountainhome, Pa.

Customers overflowed the tiny summer theater to view 30-year-old concert singer Margaret Truman, who used to live in the White House. She made her drama debut in *The Autumn Crocus*, in which she portrayed a drab Indianapolis schoolteacher who finds love while vacationing in the Tyrolean Alps.

Whether or not Miss Truman would attempt Broadway was anybody's guess. She announced that "theater work is both stimulating and slimming", and all agreed she had made a promising start.

Another famous 30-year-old, Gloria Vanderbilt Stokowski, emerged as a dramatic actress at the Pocono Playhouse. A striking brunette, she had once been the center of a sensational court case. Charging that she was a neglected child, her maternal aunt, Mrs. Harry Payne Whitney, won custody of the "poor little rich girl" from her mother, Mrs. Reginald Vanderbilt.

Since then, the young lady had been publicity-shy. She lived quietly with her husband, famed 67-year-old orchestra conductor Leopold Stokowski, and their two small sons, Christopher and Stanley.

In 1954, she emerged from her self-enforced privacy. Critics applauded her appearance in *The Swan* at the Pocono

Playhouse. She made a single television appearance in Noel Coward's *Tonight at 8:30*. Salary: $5000. At year's end, she was up to her swanlike neck in Hollywood screen tests.

In New York, the theater was booming not only on but off Broadway. Playhouses were springing up all over the city—in former night clubs, cellars, church basements, movie houses, lofts, stores. Experienced actors and actresses like Montgomery Clift, Judith Evelyn, Robert Ryan, and Hurd Hatfield were appearing in these makeshift theaters for nominal salaries ranging from $24 to $100 weekly.

What accounted for the off-Broadway boom? For one thing, people were fed up with the Broadway hit psychology. If a show was not a smash hit, designed to please everybody, it had little chance. With the rising costs of materials and labor and rentals, a Broadway production represented an investment of between $75,000 and $200,000. Off Broadway, you could produce on a shoestring and do plays that would not stand a chance in the so-called "commercial theater". Many actors and not a few customers found this kind of theater exciting. And, quite often, so did the critics. One, for example, averred that a production of Shakespeare's *Twelfth Night*, presented in a small church basement, was far superior to any Broadway version he had ever witnessed.

Oscar Winners Go East

Two Academy Award winners from Hollywood were Broadway stars in 1954: charming, hoydenish Audrey Hepburn and dark-haired, intense Jennifer Jones.

Miss Hepburn, at 25, became one of the best-known actresses in the world when, early in the year, she won a Hollywood Oscar for her first film performance in *Roman Holiday*. In New York, she captivated critics and public alike as a puckish mermaid in *Ondine*. Her short hair bob was carefully copied by young ladies all over the nation.

Daughter of an Irish father and a Dutch mother, Brussels-born Audrey Hepburn suffered privation during the five years Holland was occupied by the Nazis. She hid in cellars to avoid slaving for the Germans in their military kitchens. After World War II she went to London to study ballet, and financed her lessons by bit parts in British musicals and films.

Later, the unknown beauty was walking through a hotel lobby in Monte Carlo. France's late, great novelist, Colette, spied her, suggested her to friends for theater roles. The rest was history.

At 25, she said: "I have lived a lifetime of bad things, now everything is looking up." The good things included marriage in the summer of 1954 to Mel Ferrer, the 37-year-old film and stage actor who was her leading man in *Ondine*.

Another Hollywood glamour girl, Jennifer Jones, deserted her swank Malibu Beach house to star in an adaptation of Henry James' novel, *Portrait of a Lady*. It was Broadway's first look at the star of Hollywood's four-handkerchief films, the most recent of which was *Indiscretions of an American Wife*.

Born Phyllis Isley in Tulsa, Okla., 34 years ago, she had come up the hard way. Her parents operated a traveling tent show, starring in such oldies as *The Old Homestead* and *East Lynne*. Between acts, her father would recite perennials like "The Face on the Barroom Floor" and "The Shooting of Dan McGrew".

As she grew up, Phyllis (now Jennifer) toured the Midwest in various tent shows. Finally, she saved enough money to study at New York's American Academy of Dramatic Arts. In New York she met and married the late actor Robert Walker. They found it difficult to support their two children with their meager earnings. Finally, in desperation, Miss Jones burst hysterically into film tycoon David Selznick's office in New York, announcing with great passion that she "could play 'Claudia' better than anybody". Selznick himself happened to be at the New York office at the time and was impressed by the young girl's fiery manner. He hired her, not for his film version of *Claudia*, but for the lead in his religious epic, *Song of Bernadette*. For that film, Jennifer Jones in 1943 won the coveted Oscar. Though she always referred to *Song of Bernadette* as her first film, she had actually appeared previously as a gun-toting cowgirl in a number of inferior Westerns. Her screen name then was Phyllis Isley.

In 1945 she divorced Robert Walker, who had also enjoyed success in films, and four years later married producer Selznick, the man who had discovered her.

Of her New York theater debut in *Portrait of a Lady*, which flopped with a resounding thud, the 5'5" slim brunette gamely commented: "I cried because some of the critics did not like me. Ethel Barrymore once said that in this profession you should have the hide of an elephant. When I started out, I was timid. Now I think I can take it."

Playboy Makes It Pay

The wealthiest of the tunesmiths, Cole Porter, always manages to do a show a year. In 1954, he just made it. His musical, *Silk Stockings*, opened in Philadelphia with Hollywood's Don Ameche and Hildegarde Neff as its stars. A musical remake of the Greta Garbo film, *Ninotchka*, Porter's twenty-seventh musical was reported a hit before it ever reached Broadway.

This surprised, least of all, small, sleek, 61-year-old Cole Porter, whose songs

SOVIET WOMAN commissar who falls drolly in love with an American is played in Broadway musical *Silk Stockings* by Hildegarde Neff (above). Role was created by Garbo (right) in movie *Ninotchka*

(samples: "Night and Day", "Begin the Beguine", "You're the Top", "What Is This Thing Called Love") are all-time American favorites. His musical, *Can-Can* (a holdover on Broadway from 1953), grossed $4 million in 1954.

Playboy Porter, who was born in Peru, Ind., was one Broadway professional who did not come up the hard way. He started out with almost $2 million left him by his grandfather, coal and lumber tycoon J. O. Cole. Yale-graduate Porter was determined to spend his life and his grandfather's money having fun. At first his songs were really written to amuse his international-set friends in New York and Paris and Venice. But not for long.

Ever since he had written the words and music for a hit musical, *Hitchy-Koo*,

in 1919, he had been minting millions from his astonishing dexterity with words. His sophisticated songs have earned him more than $6 million. For the film biography of his life, *Night and Day*, Porter had been paid $300,000—just for allowing it.

The carefree Indianian, who lived like a king (or better) in his suite in New York's Waldorf-Astoria Towers, in country homes in Massachusetts and California, once said that to live on $150,000 a year would be poverty.

His life had not been all champagne and caviar, however. In 1937 he was thrown from a horse, suffered compound fractures of both legs, required thirty-one operations. But he walked again—painfully—with the aid of a cane. In 1953 his

beloved mother died (she left her son a half million). And his wife, Linda, died in 1954.

But the dapper leprechaun's music was as blithe as ever. He confided to his friend, international party-giver Elsa Maxwell, that the only thing he ever feared was boredom.

The theatergoers who packed his shows were never bored. Who else but Cole Porter would rhyme the Tower of Pisa with the *Mona Lisa*, and an O'Neill drama with Whistler's mama?

"C'est Si Bon"

A dusky, glamorous singer, with a silky, suggestive voice, who had made a fortune singing "C'est Si Bon" in night clubs and on records, became a dramatic actress in 1954. She was Eartha Kitt, a piquant,

small Negro who moved like a luxurious cat.

The 26-year-old singer portrayed a sensitive, 15-year-old Southerner in *Mrs. Patterson*, and proved she could act as well as sing. Her own life story was more dramatic than any play.

The girl whom Orson Welles once called "the most exciting woman in the world" was born in a poverty-stricken family that farmed the land near Columbia, S.C. She remembered it thus: "I was brought up in a world of superstition and race hatred. When crops were good, we ate well; other times, we lived off the forest by hunting."

At 8, she went to live in New York's Harlem with an aunt. She recalled that her aunt thought she was quite fat when she arrived on the train from the South. Her family had put her entire wardrobe on her: she wore five pairs of stockings, three dresses, four petticoats, two thin coats.

"I spent my first days in wonder," she remembered. "I saw my first electric light, my first bathroom, my first telephone. I played with such gadgets for weeks."

At 15 she quit school, went to work in a factory making army uniforms. A friend took her to meet Katherine Dunham, a noted Negro dancer and singer. Miss Dunham signed her for a company she was taking on a European tour. Miss Kitt left the company in Paris, landed a singing job in a chi-chi club called Carroll's. Her haunting, sexy voice made her a hit in Paris, and eventually in other European cities. When she returned to America, she scored in *New Faces of 1952*, in both stage and screen versions.

Known for her tantrums and her hypersensitivity, actress Kitt said in 1954: "I used to be more intolerant, intolerant of both Negroes and Whites. I think I'm calming down a bit now. Travel has broadened my viewpoint."

She announced she was buying an elegant four-story town house in New York's fashionable East 80's. The mansion had been the home of one of New York's wealthiest families. Asked about it by reporters, the girl who had once lived in a Carolina shack replied tartly: "Why not? A girl needs a roof over her head."

She Flies Through the Air

In 1954, one of Broadway's most beloved stars, Texas' Mary Martin, spent a large part of her time flying gaily through the air. Miss Martin had the title role in *Peter Pan*, and such flying on stage had never been seen outside the Ringling Brothers-Barnum and Bailey Circus.

She first flew in Los Angeles and San Francisco, to capacity audiences, then on Broadway in the fall. Assisted by invis-

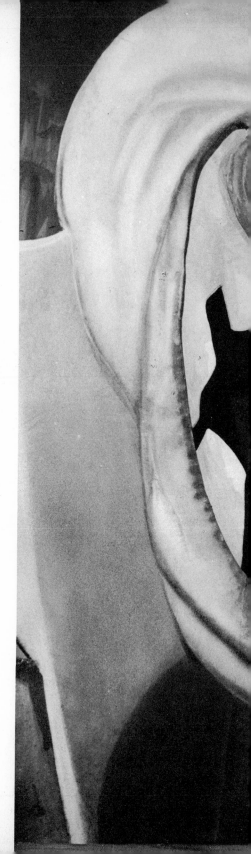

BOARDWALK BOUNCE: Shirley Booth, back in musical comedy, enjoys a Coney Island fun house with a friend in *By the Beautiful Sea*

ible wires, Miss Martin was the most ingratiating and reckless flyer ever to appear in the theater. The 41-year-old star reckoned that, if *Peter Pan* ran a year, she would have more than 200 flying hours to her credit.

Miss Martin had been Broadway's darling ever since she sang Cole Porter's "My Heart Belongs to Daddy" in *Leave It to Me* back in 1938. Her greatest triumph came as navy nurse Nellie Forbush in *South Pacific*, and she washed that guy right outta her hair for two years on Broadway and a year in London.

The musical version of *Peter Pan* was largely a family affair. Mary Martin's husband, Richard Halliday, was one of its producers. And her charming, 12-year-old daughter Heller made her debut in the production as the maid Eliza.

The flying songbird said she first saw *Peter Pan* in her home town of Weatherford, Texas—the silent-film version with Betty Bronson. Declared Mary: "I wanted to be Peter the first time I saw him—before I ever thought of being an actress."

New Playhouse

The nation got a new theater in 1954, its first new legitimate theater in twenty-seven years. The 43-year-old A. & P. grocery scion, Huntington Hartford, erected the million-dollar playhouse in Hollywood. Some said it was built as a showcase for his actress wife, former nightclub cigarette girl Marjorie Steele. For its opening, Hartford engaged the first lady of the stage, Helen Hayes, to appear in *What Every Woman Knows*, a play she had done on Broadway twenty-eight years before.

Every star in Hollywood from Marlene Dietrich to Ethel Barrymore, turned up in diamonds and furs for the gala opening. Miss Hayes announced that it was "the most beautiful theater she had ever played", and the 52-year-old veteran had appeared in all of them.

The new showcase, topping anything on Broadway, was faced with white Vermont marble, and the sidewalk was black terrazzo. The 1050-seat auditorium was handsomely decorated in gray with black trim. There was one radical innovation. Mr. Hartford had installed a bar on the mezzanine, where theatergoers could get a drink at intermission, in the style of European theaters. Price: $1 per drink.

Shakespeare in Canada

A sleepy little Canadian town, Stratford, was very much alive in July and August, when the second annual Shakespeare Festival was held in a 1988-seat tent in Queen's Park. Visitors poured in not only from all over vast Canada but from the United States, too. The enticements were Shakespeare's *Taming of the Shrew* and *Measure for Measure*, plus Sophocles' *Œdipus Rex*.

Star of the proceedings was the 45-year-old actor James Mason. As the town's six hotels and two motels began to bulge with visitors, one long-time resident succinctly summed up Stratford's feelings: "That fellow Shakespeare has really put this town on the map." Summer box-office total: $392,000.

At year's end, it looked as if the United States might soon have its own Shakespeare Festival. The cornerstone was laid in Stratford, Conn., for a replica of London's Globe Theatre, where most of Shakespeare's works were presented during his lifetime. A group of determined, affluent Americans, headed by the Theatre Guild's Lawrence Langner, hoped to outrival the phenomenally successful presentations in Stratford, Canada.

HIGH JINKS in Broadway hit *The Boy Friend*, British export lampooning musicals of the 1920's

SCREEN SENSATIONS, such as the success of newcomer Sheree North (with Jerry Lewis, above) in *Living It Up*, continued to provide subject matter for gossip columnists like Hedda Hopper (right) in 1954

MOVIES

WITH MOVIE STOCKS SKYROCKETING, 1954 in Hollywood was a year of Glamour and Gold.

Greatest furor of the year was caused by Twentieth Century-Fox's gilt-edged personality, Marilyn Monroe, who, it is said, in one short week became better known to more people in more places than even Eleanor Roosevelt.

That eventful week occurred in September, when Miss Monroe was flown to New York to make a four-minute scene for *The Seven Year Itch*. When she arrived at Idlewild Airport, blue eyed, moist mouthed, and smiling, police reserves had to be called out to rescue her 118 pounds from too-eager worshipers.

To a reporter who helped shield her, Marilyn murmured: "I'm just a pretty girl who will soon be forgotten."

Later, some 5000 persons jammed into a Manhattan street to watch Miss Monroe, attired in diaphanous slip and slippers, lean bosomly out of a window, shake her golden locks, aim her baby-stare at the cameras, and speak six words: "Hi! I just washed my hair." ("Maybe," said Marilyn later, "it was only five words. Is 'hi' a word?")

Perspiring police, afoot and ahorse, strained to hold back the crowd, and the street was closed to traffic for four hours.

TOP MALE STAR of the year—Marlon Brando—so ranked for his work in On the Waterfront, is pictured at home (left) and in Bandol, France, his fiancée's native village

This scene, as well as photos of another sequence in which she stood over a subway grating while the wind from a passing underground train blew her skirts over her head, landed on Page 1 in hundreds of U.S. newspapers.

Then, within a week after she and her husband, ex-Yankee baseball player Joe DiMaggio, had returned to Hollywood, Miss Monroe landed on the front pages again—this time to announce her impending divorce after less than nine months of marriage. Two months later it was granted.

Movies' No. 1 Glamour Gal

Who was this blond beauty whose career frequently paced and certainly paralleled Hollywood's record-breaking 1954?

Marilyn was born in a Los Angeles charity ward, and raised in an orphan asylum and eleven foster homes. She married a sailor at 16, hit the model-and-nude-calendar trade at 18, and became a movie bit player at 20. At 22 she was a "starlet", and at 26, the brightest star in the whole glamour-gal galaxy.

Marilyn had come a long way since the time when, at the age of 9, she got 5¢ a month for helping in the pantry of the Los Angeles Orphan Home. In 1954 her estimated income was in six figures.

Miss Monroe has wit as well as beauty. As the subject of the most popular portrait *au naturel* since *September Morn* shocked the art world forty years ago, Marilyn is not the least bit ashamed of the photograph that has meant millions to her in publicity. She says quite frankly: "I was hungry and out of a job. And they paid me $50."

Asked by a reporter whether she had anything on when it was taken, she answered: "I had the radio on."

Marilyn dislikes the sun and sun-tan-

ning. "I like to feel blond all over," she says. And as to what she wears to bed (a routine peep-hole-reporter query), her answer: "Chanel No. 5."

Realizing that she had become the biggest female box-office draw in Hollywood, Marilyn began to take herself and her career more seriously. She seemed intent upon trying to improve her personal and professional status. Accordingly, in 1954 she signed up at the University of the City of Los Angeles for a course in literature—with excursions into psychology, metaphysics, and proper speech.

As to whether she would also learn to act, the feeling in Hollywood was: Who cares?

"After all," as one popeyed producer put it, "anybody can *act!*"

Glamour Is for Guys, Too

In 1954, the chief of the glamour males was Marlon Brando, one of Hollywood's most controversial personalities. Big, brawny, aggressively masculine in manner and movement, Brando at 30 has been (extravagantly) called both "a harlequin who hasn't been housebroken" and "the greatest romantic actor since Booth".

Although he was the most publicized actor of the year, Brando bitterly disliked the usual movie type of personal publicity. Said he: "I certainly don't want to be promoted as a matinee idol—which I'm not—or as some kind of drooling romantic goon."

With no more than seven pictures behind him (including four prize winners), Brando, by year's end, shaped up as the movies' top actor. Three of his pictures were showing simultaneously: *The Wild One*, about youthful motorcycle-riding delinquents (Brando is a motorcycle addict himself); *On the Waterfront*, about New York harbor's union racketeers Brando, in sweat shirt and sneakers, is

ON SCREEN OR OFF, Italy's Gina Lollobrigida cuts a pretty figure. She appears (left) in *Bread, Love and Dreams,* (above) tries on an evening gown

FILM BRUTALITY is offered whole-sale in *Riot in Cell Block 11*. Convicts were used in crowd scenes. Jail breaks provided story matter for Hollywood in 1954

an old habitué of the Hoboken dock area); and *Désirée*, about Napoleon and one of his youthful loves (history, as well as psychiatry and esoteric primitive music, is a Brando hobby).

The young actor began the year with a Hollywood explosion when he walked off the set of *The Egyptian*, disappeared, and then turned up in his New York apartment after wiring Twentieth Century-Fox that—on the advice of his psychiatrist—he would not return to the studio to complete the picture. He had been undergoing analysis for at least seven years to help him "mature as a person".

After threatening him with a $2 million lawsuit, the studio relented and allowed him to make *Désirée* instead.

As soon as it was completed, he sailed for France. There he announced he would marry a fisherman's 19-year-old daughter, Josane Mariani-Berenger, who had recently won a beauty contest and planned to become an actress. He went on to tour Europe while she went to New York to await him.

The New Brando

For years Brando's favorite costume, informal and formal, had been T shirt, blue jeans, sweat shirt or dark sweater, and sneakers. However, when he returned from abroad to greet his fiancée, he astonished friends, fiancée, and newspapermen alike. Smoothly shaven, with a neat haircut, he looked like a young banker in smartly pressed business suit, immaculate white shirt, and solid-toned four-in-hand tie. His jauntily angled Tyrolean hat might have been twin brother to a diplomat's Homburg.

Was this The New Brando? Or just Brando having fun?

Brando has always had a juicy sense of humor. His earliest antics dealt with inkwells, girls, and teachers—and got him

kicked out of elementary school. Othe youthful exuberances got him expelle from military school too.

As a boy in Nebraska, Marlon gathere garter snakes, white mice, turtles, bats and stray animals of various kinds whic he distributed about the house. As a ma he shared his midtown New York bach elor apartment with Joe, the Cat, an Russell, the Raccoon. (Russ was late sent home to Brando's folks for trying t deprive Joe of at least one of his nin lives.)

Marlon loves animals ("except," h says, "the two-footed kind") and owns cattle farm which his father runs, an which he calls Penny Poke Farms, sinc his surplus pennies and dollars created i

During his early years in New York h supported himself with odd jobs rangin from elevator operator to substitut drummer in a Greenwich Village nigh club.

Then, following in the footsteps of hi sister Jocelyn, who was already doin well on Broadway, he took up acting mainly because, as Humphrey Bogart pu it, "It's the easiest way I know of to mak a buck."

After a few small parts in summer stoc and on Broadway, Brando was hired fo the role of Stanley Kowalski in *A Street car Named Desire*. After that, he was in

His first movie was *The Men*, a stor of war-made paraplegics. To learn to pla his role convincingly he spent a month i a wheel chair in the Birmingham Veter ans Administration Hospital—an indica tion of the earnestness and devotion t character he brings to every acting as signment.

Instinctively, moviegoers seem to rec ognize these qualities.

Despite the fact that the movies hav been very good to him, Brando still take mischievous pleasure in biting the han that feeds him. "If I have any persona reticences," he says, "they have been inspired by the irritations and fraudulent standards of the films."

However, in 1954, aside from the furor he kicked up over *The Egyptian*, Brando was behaving himself.

"And why shouldn't he," demanded one executive, "at $150,000 a picture!"

Movies in the News

Various items in the newspapers amused or otherwise entertained movie-minded readers.

In England, where movie production was booming, actors were told to lose their Oxford accents and speak plainer English, "so that our American as well as our Dominion cousins may understand us better".

Most outstanding publicity job, aside from Marilyn Monroe's, was that which attended the month-long visit to American shores of the voluptuous-looking young Italian movie actress, Gina Lollobrigida.

Gina (after whom a Parisian brassière maker was inspired to name his latest creation "Les Lollos") came to New York to promote Italian pictures in general and her newly released *Bread, Love and Dreams* in particular. At a welcoming press cocktail party held in a hotel suite normally accommodating 75 persons, 800 gate-crashed. Millions watched and heard her in televised shows from coast to coast; millions more read about her in newspapers and saw her picture on the covers of the country's largest magazines. The pattern continued in South America, next on Gina's itinerary.

At the star-studded New York opening of *The Egyptian*, an embarrassing setback was given the growing trend toward big-movie "world premières". Among the hundreds of invited distinguished guests was a bejeweled, turbaned, Oriental-looking gentleman introduced to television, radio, and newsreel audiences as "the famous Maharajah of Barata".

He was effusively greeted, interviewed, and photographed. Next morning, however, the bubble burst. He was exposed as a fake by an enterprising bilingual newspaperman who pointed out that "barata" in Portuguese means cockroach.

Most outstanding movie make-up job of the year was reported from Hollywood when ten huge Indian elephants—each weighing 7000 pounds and having roughly 200 feet of skin surface—were painted red, green, yellow, blue, and cerise for M.G.M.'s spectacular Technicolor musical, *Jupiter's Darling*.

In Italy the film makers' tendency to dub pictures for U.S. export in "the American language" sometimes led to strange sight-and-sound combinations.

In the Italian film *Anna*, in which Sylvana Mangano starred, an anonymous off-screen soprano sang Mangano's songs. In the American-language version another anonymous actress spoke Mangano's lines as well. Thus, no U.S. moviegoer yet had heard the Mangano voice, although millions believed they had.

Sinatra and Crosby as Thespians

In 1954 there were two astonishing reversals of Hollywood "type-casting".

Frank Sinatra, famed for his crooning and his wife Ava Gardner (at year's end teetering on the edge of divorce), decided to show the world he had become a dramatic actor.

Two years before, in Universal's *Meet Danny Wilson*, Sinatra had made a small beginning, as a tough little crooner with a fast fist and a glass jaw. Early in 1954, for his role in Columbia's *From Here to Eternity*, he walked off with Hollywood's Oscar for the best performance by a supporting actor.

MANY "MARILYNS" were ballyhooed in 1954. Among the beauties said to resemble Miss Monroe were England's sultry Mara Lane (opposite page) and Joan Collins (left), New Jersey's lovely Elaine Stewart (below)

Later, as a full-fledged star in United Artists' *Suddenly*—a melodrama about a psychopathic gunman who plans to assassinate the President—Sinatra made all aware that he was indeed an actor of power, depth, and intelligence.

His cinema colleague and fellow crooner, Bing Crosby, also accepted a dramatic role, that of "the cunning drunk" in Paramount's film version of Clifford Odets' Broadway hit, *The Country Girl*, which is about an alcoholic actor, his decline and eventual regeneration.

Late in the year the picture and Bing's performance both won critical and popular acclaim. It looked as though Crosby was certain to win an Academy Award nomination.

Censorship in the News

Even those who administer movie censorship in good conscience and with the best will in the world often pose baffling problems and face paradoxical perplexities.

Quebec, for example, which barred *Martin Luther* "except in churches"—and permitted its showing there only when tickets were stamped "Catholics Not Admitted"—was chided by Chicago newspaper editorial writers, who gleefully pointed out that although Quebec children may marry at 14 they may not attend movies until they are 16.

The Quebeckers promptly retorted that in Chicago girls become women by law at 18 but cannot go to an "adult" movie until they are 21.

In Memphis, Lloyd Binford, the 88-year-old, one-man censor board, barred all pictures "with or by Charlie Chaplin". Further, he threatened to close any hall, "including churches", that might ignore his ban. Several Memphis clergymen promptly showed old Chaplin comedies in their churches and dared the octoge-

narian to make good his threat. Censor Binford backed down.

The subject of birth, which many consider sacred and certainly not obscene, came up twice in connection with movie censorship. In New York the censors cut a birth scene of humans in the sex-hygiene drama, *Mom and Dad*. But they allowed the birth of a buffalo to remain in Walt Disney's prize-winning nature film, *The Vanishing Prairie*.

By general consensus the quality of U.S. pictures had so improved in comparison with much-touted "foreign" films that one of the neatest lines of the year (in *The Barefoot Contessa*) seemed almost to have lost its satirical point.

In a scene on the French Riviera among the international "snob set", a royal pretender, asked by a lorgnetted countess whether he ever went to the movies, replied superciliously: "Oh, yes, my dear—but only to those fine foreign films, the British and the American."

Hollywood's concentration upon fewer pictures had enabled it to make those few better.

However, shrewd Hollywood producers still thought it wise to cushion their big-screen, big-budget picture investments by re-releasing several of their most popular films of past years.

Thus moviegoers in 1954 saw such memorable hits as the 1939 four-hours-long *Gone With the Wind* (which had earned $65 million by the end of the year), the 1946 three-hours-long *The Best Years of Our Lives* ($16 million), and the 1933 giant-ape thriller *King Kong* ($5 million).

Hollywood struck another gold vein when it decided to remake old hits, bigger, better, or with songs and dances added for big-screen presentation.

Most notable was the three-hour musical version of the 1937 dramatic prize winner, *A Star Is Born*, with Judy Gar-

GAY DECEIVER: In a dress designed for *The Barefoot Contessa* by Zoe Fontana of Rome, Ava Gardner beams after "modeling" incognito in a Fontana show, fooling Fontana clients

BROTHERS ALOFT: Gene (right) and Fred Kelly hit a dancing high in musical, *Deep in My Heart*

OOPS: Playing spinster tourist intent on taking movies in Venice, Italy, Katharine Hepburn walks backward, accidentally plunks stern-first into Grand Canal. Sequence is from the movie, *Summertime*

land making a spectacular comeback after her poor showing in *Summer Stock* four years before.

Other important remakes included *Mogambo*, with Clark Gable and Ava Gardner, which Gable first made in 1932 with Jean Harlow under the title *Red Dust*, and *The Student Prince*.

But biggest remake of 1954 or any other year (although it was not scheduled to be released until Christmas, 1955) was Cecil B. DeMille's second version of his classic 1923 silent-film epic, *The Ten Commandments*. Filmed in Egypt and Israel at a cost of $8 million, this, 74-year-old DeMille's 71st picture, was the most expensive motion picture ever made.

The flood of gold that poured into Hollywood in 1954 came from the vast audience (65 million) that crowded into theaters to see bigger-budget pictures spread across big-size screens. More than 90 pictures out of about 400 cost $2 million or more—twice as many as in 1953.

The Census Bureau announced that in 1954 the total seating capacity of all U.S.

theaters, including drive-ins, was 25 percent greater than that in 1948.

Other surveys showed that millions who in the early excitement of owning TV sets had stayed away from movies had begun to return.

International Give-and-Take

This was a year in which many movie stars went abroad—and many foreign actors came here—sometimes for the same reasons. Reduction of Hollywood studios' overhead, coupled with substantial income-tax cuts on earnings abroad over an extended period (since sharply reduced by new Internal Revenue Service rulings), spurred many U.S. actors to seek greener-moneyed pastures far from home.

In a sort of professional reciprocity, as well as an international search for new faces, foreign producers welcomed American actors and Hollywood studios opened their doors to many highly touted overseas stars. From Italy, Spain, France, Germany, England, Ireland, Sweden, Mexico, and Japan they came—and found opportunity waiting on U.S. screens.

For Hollywood actors wishing to go "on tour" it was only a step from the movie capital to the night clubs in Las Vegas, Nev., where many broke in new acts in personal-appearance tryouts. Thence they could go on to Miami, New York, and across the oceans to Europe, Africa, Asia, and places in between.

From every continent came news of picturemaking, with faces more familiar on Sunset Boulevard than in foreign lands:

Katharine Hepburn was being tossed into Venice's Grand Canal, for *Summertime*. Kirk Douglas was making movie love in Paris and playing *Ulysses* in Rome. Gregory Peck was harpooning whales in the North Atlantic and Alan Ladd was hunting them in the antarctic.

Humphrey Bogart had just returned from North Africa, Clark Gable from the Congo, and Charlton Heston as Moses was leading the Israelites out of Egypt for *The Ten Commandments*.

Joan Fontaine had finished Boccaccio's *Decameron Nights* in Spain, and Elizabeth Taylor was riding an elephant in Ceylon. (A little later she was dancing barefoot in a Paris fountain for *The Last Time I Saw Paris*.)

Van Johnson flew in from Paris, caught his breath in Hollywood for a picture, went on to the South Pacific for another, and then flew to London for *The End of the Affair*.

Richard Widmark made a picture in Germany, Anthony Dexter hunted movie treasure in El Salvador, Cary Grant chased thieves in France, and Gary Cooper and Burt Lancaster pursued gold, adventure, and Sarita Montiel in Mexico. Jane Russell was busy in Paris exuding "la sex appeal" in *Gentlemen Marry Brunettes*, while an ocean away John Agar pursued pirates in the Caribbean.

Hollywood frequently looked like No Man's Land.

The news at home and abroad, for all this frenetic around-the-world movie making, seemed to spell out one thing: More than ever the emphasis in 1954's movies was upon pure escapist entertainment. Upon comedy, music, romance, adventure, personal drama, spectacle—with wide detours around any serious theme that might in the least smack of "a message".

As one movie mogul summed it up: "Let Hollywood make entertainment—and let Western Union carry the messages!"

STAR AT EASE: Audrey Hepburn is snapped in a moment between "takes". Award-collector Hepburn was married during year to actor Mel Ferrer

RADIO - TV

TELEVISION IN 1954 HAD ELEMENTS OF irony. In the fall, the industry got hit by its own boomerang when it cut loose with $25 million worth of color shows—color that only a few could see because color sets were not available.

MASS APPEAL on television was proved in 1954 by low-comedy, high-salaried Jackie Gleason (left) and pianist Liberace, candle-lit idol of the tiny screen

The National Broadcasting Company splurged on ninety-minute color shows that cost more than $300,000 each. They were called "spectaculars". The Columbia Broadcasting System rounded up the brightest stars obtainable, gave each a piece of Fort Knox, and put on a series of sixty-minute color shows. The "Battle of the Behemoths" was hot and furious.

Betty Hutton, a blond, hip-wiggling H-bomb, opened the color era over N.B.C. in a show titled "Satins and Spurs". It laid an egg. Critics soon began to pan the "spectaculars" as being overambitious, but, as time wore on, the presentations showed some improvement. N.B.C. felt certain that eventually they would pay off. Said Sylvester L. Weaver Jr., N.B.C. president: "It's hard to get word to the public about a one-shot show. The great American masses have lots of other things on their minds."

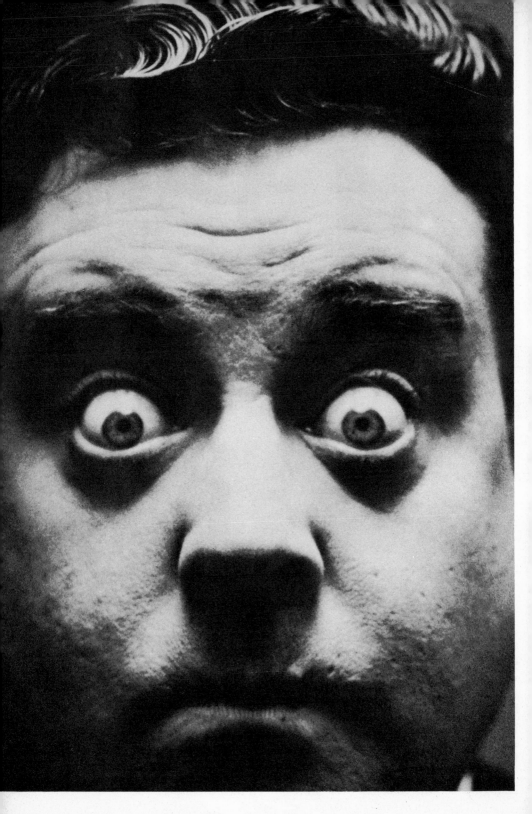

WIDE EYES of Jackie Gleason (left) reflect popular reaction to shapely girls on his show. These are some of hundreds he auditioned

Just how many people were watching the "spectaculars"—in black and white, of course—depended on which rating service you believed. Nielsen, Trendex, and American Research Bureau all came up with different figures. N.B.C. strung along with Nielsen, whose ratings on the "spectaculars" were highest.

Salaries paid to stars of the color shows were stratospheric. Betty Hutton reportedly got $50,000 for her golden egg. For "Tonight at 8:30", Ginger Rogers got $40,000, plus $10,000 for her wardrobe.

But the juiciest deal of all was made by the temperamental tenor, Mario Lanza. He collected $40,000 from C.B.S. for just mouthing the words to a few songs, the actual sound being furnished by his old recordings. Suspicious viewers caught on. Two days after the show C.B.S. admitted Lanza's singing had come from records. Seems he had dieted furiously to lose 40 pounds and had been too weak to sing.

The people who staged the color shows had a real problem. Their colors had to be pretty enough for both the handful of viewers who saw the programs in color and the vast majority who saw them in black and white. Only a few thousand color sets had yet reached the market; the manufacturing industry was bogged down in confusion over technical details. A Long Island housewife summed up the early days of the color TV era by saying: "I can't get color on my set, so why should I waste time watching a show when the best thing about it is its color?"

Television Commercials

What do viewers think of television commercials? According to a survey by Edward L. Bernays, New York public-relations counsel, many think they contain "too much yak-yak about nothing".

Bernays first polled educators, sociologists, church leaders, and businessmen.

When most said nothing nice about commercials, the television industry yelled "foul". It claimed the survey was filled with "loaded questions" designed to bring just the answers Bernays had wanted. It also charged that he had polled only eggheads and longhairs—not representative viewers.

Determined to justify his findings, Bernays put the questions to barkeepers, barbers, beauticians, and butchers. They too said they were "fed up" with commercials.

"Many critics in both groups," said Bernays, "use precisely the same words in giving their views on commercials. The main difference between the two is that barbers, barkeepers, butchers, and beauticians have a more colorful literary style than our previous respondents."

The "colorful literary style" included the following clear-cut phrases:

"Nerve-racking, bigmouthed and low, cheap, noisy, unutterably silly, air of limburger, boring, lying, unscrupulous, too much borax and bunk."

Tide magazine, a trade publication covering the advertising field, asked 2200 advertising executives which television commercials they considered most objectionable. More than 100 different commercials were singled out, but among the eight listed as most irritating were plugs for cigarettes. Typical comments were:

Philip Morris: " 'Vintage tobacco' both unbelievable and unconvincing; too brassy; wild and reckless claims; always detestable."

Lucky Strike: "They exaggerate, they lie, they insult my intelligence; too smug, too negative."

Camels: "Phony and without foundation; exaggerated claims; lack believability."

Old Gold: "An oily attempt to be ethical; 'treat instead of a treatment' is an out-of-date pitch; just bunk."

The television industry was not frightened, however. Whatever the gripes of viewers, apparently TV commercials sold merchandise.

Giveaways

"Strike It Rich", a radio and television program that featured human misery, ran into some legal misery of its own. New York City's Welfare Department ruled that the giveaway program needed a license as a welfare agency because it solicited public contributions for the persons it aided. The department demanded that the program stop luring to the city people who later went on relief because they had no money to return home.

Henry L. McCarthy, Commissioner of Welfare, cited fifty-five families who had come to New York from all over the country in quest of "easy money" on "Strike It Rich" only to wind up on relief. Said the Commissioner: "Programs like this are a national disgrace. They create the impression that destitute people in the United States have no place to go. Every time these poor souls have to expose their souls in public we are playing into the hands of the Communists. It is a return to the tin cup begging idea of charity."

The Travelers Aid Society called "Strike It Rich" a "headache". It said it received appeals every day from stranded persons whose tales of woe lacked sufficiently dramatic misery to get them on the show. "These people, in almost all cases, are without funds, physically ill, sometimes crippled, and often frightened and confused by the bigness of New York."

Walter Framer, producer of "Strike It Rich", said he was surprised that "we are being subjected to an attack for helping people who deserve help". He denied that the program solicited funds and said that contributions by listeners and viewers were purely voluntary.

But a question arose as to just how thoroughly "Strike It Rich" checked the stories of contestants before putting them on the air. An ex-convict was arrested in Spring Valley, N.Y., after winning $165 for his hard-luck story. When the program was shown in Austin, Texas, he had been recognized as a fugitive from an indictment for embezzlement and theft.

Real Life on Radio

The Columbia Broadcasting System's radio network put on a new kind of cops-and-robbers show. "Night Watch" came straight from real life, recorded right on the spot as cops shot at robbers and were shot at in return.

The program's originator was Donn Reed, a radio actor, who spent his nights riding police cars in Culver City, Calif., to make recordings of police investigations, arrests, and interrogations. He carried a 14-pound recorder that would handle anything from the sound of footsteps to a shotgun blast. In covering such diverse situations as the arrest of dope peddlers and the thwarting of suicides, Reed had been beaten with handcuffs, slugged, and shot at. Said he: "It's important to know when to duck."

Reed himself is the narrator on the show. If the events seem sordid, it's because that's the way they actually are. Once Reed accompanied the police to an apartment where a woman with a bloody face lay on a divan and explained that her husband had hit her. Defending himself, the husband was heard to say that she had hit him first, with a flowerpot. They told police they loved each other.

Another woman, who had burned her house down, said she did it because her husband had been "clottin' me around". She said he drank heavily, that her par-

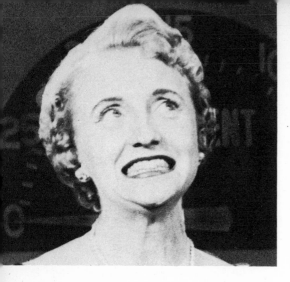

ents drank when she was a child, and that her father used to beat her.

Each half-hour episode of "Night Watch" usually covered two cases. Reed commented: "For example, we'll have a razor fight, fast and bloody—a major case. Then there'll be one about a little boy who steals newspapers, a quiet thing. This show could run forever, because no two police cases are ever alike. Even two drunks differ so much that each makes fascinating listening."

Reporter Reed doesn't get a story every night he goes prowling, but some nights he gets enough material for three shows. Getting the material on tape, however, is only part of the battle. It has to be edited and boiled down. Said Reed: "All extraneous matter must be eliminated. Also profanity. We have found, incidentally, that drunken women are the worst offenders here."

Ike on TV

The problem of looking one's best in front of a merciless television camera is as well known to President Eisenhower as to any actor. Ike used to get all kinds of free advice, but TV directors confused rather than aided him. Ike just didn't

come through as warmly on TV as he did in person.

The White House decided that a new kind of adviser was needed—one to tell the President how to "act" on television. Robert Montgomery, a former Hollywood actor, was engaged. He began shuttling between his office in the White House and Radio City in New York, where he produced his own television program.

To size up his protégé, Montgomery spent three months just watching Ike's habitual behavior away from a camera.

"If you watch how a man does things," said Montgomery, "at the office, at home, and in public, you learn his methods for conveying what he wants to say. Extending these methods into television requires no magic."

Montgomery got results. Ike became a new TV personality—looking at ease, for the first time, and smiling frequently. The President, getting out from behind his desk and throwing away a prepared script, would move around, fold and unfold his arms, lounge against the desk front, and deliver his talk ad lib. For one half-hour chat he had only forty words

REMARKABLY MOBILE face of Margaret Truman registers varied reactions (left) on TV show, "What's My Line?". Below, panelist Steve Allen enjoys her climactic emotion: frank surprise

of notes printed on big cue cards off-camera.

Montgomery made some technical changes, too. One was a lower camera angle that eliminated Ike's bald spot from view. The presidential squint was relieved by changing the location and intensity of television lights.

Ike also switched from heavy, horn-rimmed glasses to lighter rims that flattered his face. The heavy rims reportedly had been recommended by Winston Churchill. Montgomery commented wryly: "There's nothing I'd argue with Mr. Churchill about—except his technical knowledge of how best to present the President of the United States on television."

Murrow on the Screen

No other commentator on the air made as much news during the year as Edward R. Murrow of C.B.S. But neither did any other commentator weigh as many controversial public issues as did Murrow on his "See It Now" television program.

Murrow likes nothing better than diving into a hot topical issue and coming up with lucid and enlightened commentary. His basic technique is to trot out the pros and cons of an issue, progress subtly to his editorial viewpoint, and leave his audience to carry on its own thinking.

Murrow became a center of controversy when he created a televised profile of Senator Joseph R. McCarthy. It was done mostly with film clips of the Senator's speeches, but there was never any doubt as to how Murrow felt about McCarthy's methods of conducting investigations. Response to the program by telephone, telegram, and letter overwhelmingly favored Murrow.

The commentator turned over his program one week to Senator McCarthy to permit him to reply. But instead of appearing in person, McCarthy made a filmed reply which cost $6336.99 to produce. He sent the bill to Murrow's sponsor, the Aluminum Company of America, which refused to pay on the ground that its contract was with C.B.S. Murrow also declined to pay the bill out of his own pocket. After six weeks, C.B.S. finally paid it.

Murrow received many awards during the year. He was cited by the George Foster Peabody radio and television awards committee as being "fair-minded, courageous and a fighter for justice" in his news reporting and commentary. The Overseas Press Club also honored him for "the best television presentation of for-

TV VENUS Roxanne beautified "Beat the Clock" (C.B.S.), here outsparkles jewels worth $3,350,000

eign affairs". Other awards came from Freedom House, The Sidney Hillman Foundation, and The Newspaper Guild of New York.

The Fortunes of Jackie Gleason

Comedian Jackie Gleason has fame and fortune but not all of his luck is good. He has taken many a pratfall for the amusement of his fans, but one night he made an unscheduled flying exit from his television show and wound up in the hospital with a fractured leg.

Gleason was playing "Peck's Bad Boy" in a satirical sketch when the accident occurred in the closing minutes of his C.B.S. show. Not even Gleason himself expected such a sock finish. He was about to spray flour over the stage with an electric fan when he stepped on a slippery spot left by dry ice and catapulted into the wings.

Thousands of telephone calls immediately flooded the C.B.S. switchboard, and the accident produced one of the most celebrated fractured legs in show-business history. Gleason was off the program for several weeks.

Jackie also encountered marital difficulties, but finally reached an agreement with his wife on a financial settlement resulting from her uncontested separation suit. His wife was to receive 14½ percent of his income, which she estimated at $336,000 in 1953.

Late in the year the Buick division of the General Motors Corporation announced plans to trade in its old comedian for a new one. In dropping Milton Berle, Buick agreed to pay $6,142,500 to Jackie Gleason for seventy-eight half-hour television films to be shown over a period of two years. Buick also took a third-year option on him, which, if exercised, would mean an additional $3,412,500 for Gleason. How much the comedian would retain for himself remained to be seen, since he was to foot all costs, including film production.

But blue chips kept falling on Jackie during the year. Not only did his production company make a deal with C.B.S. to produce other television shows in which Gleason would not appear, but C.B.S. signed a fifteen-year personal contract with Gleason which guaranteed him $100,000 annually whether he worked or not.

Other TV Personalities

Comedian Wally Cox got married twice in 1954.

The first time was in his television role of "Mr. Peepers", the awkward but heart-warming science teacher. As millions looked on, Mr. Peepers plunged into matrimony with the school nurse, Nancy Remington (played by Patricia Benoit). The show's writers at first considered an elopement, but finally ruled against it. Robinson Peepers, they decided, just wouldn't do a thing like that.

But a few weeks later the off-stage Wally Cox did. He eloped with an actress named Marilyn Gennaro and got married in Maryland.

Another family matter, dictated by real life, popped up in the "Mr. Peepers" program toward the end of the year. Patricia Benoit, who in private life is the wife of a magazine executive, revealed that she was expecting a baby. The show's writers got the idea immediately. They put Mrs. Peepers to dreaming of a visit from the long-billed bird, too.

Another stork incident—this one not in the script—turned out to be anything but funny for comic Milton Berle. Ruth Gilbert, who played the part of Uncle Miltie's man-crazy secretary, Max, was fired from the show because of what Berle's lawyers called physical disfigurement occasioned by her pregnancy. In private life

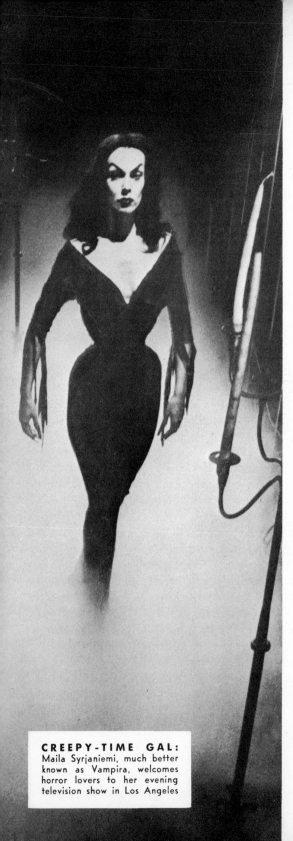

she is the wife of a business executive.

"I don't feel disfigured," said Miss Gilbert, protesting her firing. "Anyway," she added, "on my last show they changed my character to a married woman by announcing that I was pregnant. They're the ones who make it impossible for me to return in the character I was signed to play."

Miss Gilbert argued that the Berle organization knew she was going to have a baby when she signed her contract for the season. Irving Gray, Berle's manager, replied that she signed her contract on April 29 and that no one could have known then that she would have a baby in February.

Even so, Miss Gilbert charged that there was no reason why she should have been dropped from the show as early as she was. She retorted: "Milton's stomach is bigger than mine."

TV in England

Britons who look down their noses at commercial television soon won't have far to look. England's sacrosanct air waves, heretofore free of advertising plugs, are going to echo with claims about the crispy, crunchy goodness of various edibles.

A bill authorizing commercial television squeezed through Parliament by a scant majority. The issue had aroused great controversy and, when the measure finally passed, some charged that it combined the worst features of government and commercial television. Exclaimed the London *Daily Mirror*: "It is all snaffle, bit and blinkers, but no horse."

Commercial TV in England will be operated quite differently from the British Broadcasting Corporation's subsidized programs, but will not ape American television. The noncommercial B.B.C. programs will continue, but in addition the

THE OLD MASTER: Jack Benny, radio mainstay now established on TV, gives his long-time side-kick "Rochester" the benefit of a Benny specialty: a slow "double take"

newly created Independent Television Authority (I.T.A.) will operate commercial channels.

The I.T.A. will have its own transmitters and sell air time to program contractors, who, in turn, will peddle the time to advertisers. But Britannia and not the advertiser will still rule the air waves. Commercials will be limited to the beginning and ending of programs or "natural" breaks, and advertisers will have no say as to what programs their plugs adjoin. The advertiser cannot sponsor a program as such. He will merely buy air time for his message.

Sir Kenneth Clark, chairman of the I.T.A., did not believe his network would borrow any ideas from television in the U.S. He said: "What I saw there was pretty hair-raising. People do say they have very good things in the United States. Perhaps I struck it unlucky."

Sir Thomas Beecham, however, took four columns in the London *Sunday Times* to laud American television. The world-famed symphony conductor voted wrestling his favorite TV fare.

"I know of little more virile and exciting," he wrote, "than the sight of one gentleman weighing about 17 stone [238 pounds] picking up another of similar avoirdupois and throwing him over his head with as much facility and address as if he were handling bales of cotton or sacks of coal."

Apparently Sir Thomas was unaware that most American wrestling is as well rehearsed as his symphonic concerts.

Although some Britons say proudly that B.B.C. television is quite different from TV in the United States, actually the B.B.C. is using more and more programs from America. Its recent imports include that great American institution, "Amos 'n' Andy", and "The Range Rider", a shoot-'em-up. Said one B.B.C. television officer: "We feel that they are good program material. They will inject new blood into our programming." Viewers in England had divided opinions about "Amos 'n' Andy", and the program did not catch on there as it had in the U.S.

Other Uses for TV

Television is fast becoming a Peeping Tom and an electronic watchdog. Many people who watch it in their homes for entertainment are unaware that it is being used in new ways almost daily.

Private eyes have found it helpful. A detective, hired by a husband to spy on an unfaithful wife, installed a camera behind a one-way mirror in a hotel room and watched the proceedings from another room. He snapped a few photos of what he saw on the television screen and got enough evidence to effect an out-of-court settlement for his client.

The television eye never sleeps. In jails in Houston, Texas, and Redlands, Calif., TV cameras scan corridors, cells, exercise yards, and the bunks of prisoners. The legalized gambling houses in Nevada also have experimented with television to catch cheating customers or croupiers who steal from the boss.

In Hawaii a television camera checks the speed of sugar cane moving along a conveyor belt and tips off workmen when a jam occurs. The armed forces use video to get a close look from a safe distance at automatic shell-loading operations. Scientists at the Argonne National Laboratory in Chicago handle radioactive material with "slave hands" by means of a three-dimensional TV camera.

Television has also gone under water. A camera went down 285 feet to the rocky bottom of the English Channel to locate and identify the lost submarine *Affray*. And cameras were lowered off the coast of Elba to seek out a Comet jet airliner that had crashed into the sea.

HARLEQUIN HUG: Groucho Marx and Betty Hutton embrace at a movie première. Groucho was hilarious TV fixture in 1954, but Betty's first television "spectacular" was panned

1954 WAS THE YEAR OF THE HISTORIC MILE. Roger Gilbert Bannister of Great Britain was the first man in the world to run a measured mile in less than four minutes.

On May 6, a slim crowd of 1500 turned out to watch a dual meet between the British Amateur Athletic Association and Oxford University. A stiff, 15-mile-an-hour cross wind swept the rain-soaked four-lap Iffley Road track at Oxford. Lowering clouds darkened the sky.

Although few in the stands knew it,

Bannister, running for the British A.A.A., had planned his race carefully. His teammates, Chris Brasher and Chris Chataway, would act as pacemakers, running as fast as possible as long as possible. When they lagged, Bannister would go it alone for the record. Just before the race, Bannister remarked: "Conditions are stupid, but . . . you have to accept the weather. . . . Today is the day."

As the race began, Brasher jumped into the lead. Chataway was second. Close on their heels, Bannister followed with his effortless, loping stride. They covered the first quarter in 57.5, the second in 60.7. Brasher faded at the half-mile mark. Chataway took over to continue the torrid pace.

"We reached the three quarters in just a shade over three minutes," said Bannister. "So I had to take over then to do the last lap in about 59 seconds."

Bannister lengthened his stride. Chataway struggled to stay with him, but was soon outdistanced. Some 300 yards from the finish, Bannister charged down the track with his famous finishing kick. His head was rolled back, his mouth agape sucking in air. In a final burst of speed he hit the tape, stumbled, and collapsed into the arms of his trainer.

An excited buzz passed through the stands. Then the carefully articulated, undramatic voice of the announcer silenced everyone: ". . . a time which is a new meeting and track record, and which, subject to ratification, will be a new English native, a British national, a British all comers, European, British Empire and world record. The time was three . . ."

A mighty roar drowned out the rest of the announcement: ". . . three minutes, fifty-nine and four tenths seconds."

Two Amazing Men

One month later, a new world record was set. On a lightning-fast track at Turku Stadium in Finland, John Landy of Australia became the second man in the world to run the mile in under four minutes. His time: 3:58.

In 1952, few experts would have chosen either Bannister or Landy to run a mile in under four minutes. In the Olympics of that year, Landy couldn't even qualify for the finals of the 1500-meter run (the Olympic mile), and Bannister finished fourth.

Neither looked the part of a great runner. The 24-year-old Landy was thin, slightly under 6 feet. Bannister, a year older than Landy, was taller and walked stooped over in a gangling, loose-jointed way.

Bannister's manner was scholarly. A New York reporter called him the most articulate and intelligent athlete he had ever met. A brilliant medical student, he received his degree at London's St. Mary's Hospital shortly after his historic run.

Landy was an amateur entomologist and spent hours racing across the Australian countryside adding to his collection of insects. He planned a teaching career in agricultural science and was in his final year at Melbourne University.

Neither man received any formal coaching. Yet both, on opposite sides of the world, arrived at the same conclusion —that to reach the peak of athletic endurance the body must be pushed to the limits of its physical capacity and then pushed again and again.

Every day, the year around, both ran themselves to the point of collapse. Incessantly, they practiced for speed and endurance, and gradually their bodies adjusted to the punishment.

They developed into two amazing human beings—men whose hearts had massive power and whose bodies utilized oxygen with fantastic ease. When he was 17, Bannister's pulse rate had been a normal 65. It dropped to 45. Landy's was 50. Bannister's heart, under the X ray, measured 25 percent over normal in relation to his size.

The Mile of the Century

After setting their records, these two great runners met at Vancouver, Canada, in the "Mile of the Century". Thirty-five thousand fans jammed into Empire Stadium while 40 million watched the race on TV and 20 million more listened to radio descriptions.

Landy, wearing the green emblem of Australia, took his position at the pole. Bannister, with the red-barred colors of England across his chest, stepped into lane five. Six other Empire milers toed the mark, but the crowd had no eyes for them.

The gun banged, and they were off. After a lap, Landy moved into the lead. Bannister moved up with him. Landy, running with precision, started pulling away. The crowd roared and the roar mounted as Landy increased his lead by 5, then 10, then 15 yards. Bannister let him move ahead.

"It was a frightening thing to do," said Bannister later, "but I believed he was running too fast. I had to save for my final burst and hope to catch him in time."

The other runners had fallen far behind. At the turn of the half mile, Bannister began moving up. Almost imperceptibly, the gap was closed. The full-throated roar of the crowd rolled across the field.

As they moved into the final quarter, Bannister was within striking distance. Landy put on more speed. Bannister stayed with him. One hundred yards from the finish, Landy glanced briefly over his left shoulder. In that split second, Bannister, on the outside, burst past him on his winning drive to the tape.

"I had hoped that the pace would be so fast that he would crack," said Landy. "When you get a man in that sort of situation and he doesn't crack, you do."

For the third and fourth times, four minutes had been broken. Bannister's time was 3:58.8. Five yards back, Landy was clocked in 3:59.6.

Four months later, Dr. Bannister, working an eighteen-hour day as an intern, spoke to a group of English sports writers.

He recalled the grind of training, of running through the winter rain and mud. He told them of the companionship of his pacemakers, Brasher and Chataway. And then he announced his retirement from international competition.

"I shall not have sufficient time to put up a first-class performance," Bannister said. "There would be little satisfaction for me in a second-rate performance, and it would be wrong to give one when representing my country."

On that same day, as though by some curious affinity, John Landy also announced that his racing days were over.

The New Power

While other nations were absorbed by individual performances, the Russians prepared for athletic domination of the world. The Soviet Union viewed its athletic program so seriously that it gave Cabinet status to the head of the Committee on Sports. Its goal was to win the 1956 Olympics in Melbourne, Australia.

Throughout the year, the Russians displayed their prowess. In late summer, Russian track-and-field men dominated the European games in Switzerland. The Russian hockey team drubbed Canada at its own national game. A Russian rowing crew won at historic Henley in England. Russian teams won international victories in speed skating, skiing, weight lifting, soccer, and basketball. Russian chess teams were unbeatable.

Since the Olympics were revived in 1896, no American track-and-field team has ever been defeated. But in 1954 experts, awed by Russian performances in Europe, said the Soviets had already taken over track leadership of the world.

"If Americans think they will win the next Olympics," said British athletics official Jack Crump, "they are in for an unpleasant surprise."

The Blockbuster

On a Friday night in June, 1954, the glare of the ring lights in New York's Yankee Stadium focused on heavyweight champion Rocky Marciano and former titleholder Ezzard Charles.

Charles, a ring tactician and fine boxer, was overimaginative and tended to be cautious. Marciano, crude and even clumsy, was a chunky ball of a man with enormous strength and stamina.

For five rounds Charles gave the awkward Marciano a boxing lesson. He slashed the champion with sharp jabs, uppercuts, hooks, and crosses. He opened a 1½-inch cut over Marciano's left eye.

FINISHING POWER: Britain's Roger Bannister surges past Australia's John Landy in last 100 yards of "Mile of the Century" at Vancouver, B. C., to win in 3 minutes, 58.8 seconds.

To the crowd of 47,000 fans, an upset seemed in the making. But Marciano kept boring in, his face and body smeared with his own blood.

Slowly the tide turned. Charles lost his sharpness and Marciano began to deal out punishment. By round twelve, Charles was operating on courage alone. Again and again, until the final bell, Marciano pounded the challenger with a two-fisted attack. Again and again Charles refused to go down.

When the fight ended, Charles had gained more stature in defeat than he had known as champion. And he had earned the right to a rematch.

In his dressing room, Charles, his face misshapen, said: "I wasn't thinking of the pain. Pain's part of this business."

In the return bout three months later, after eight rounds of hit, run, and clutch, Charles sprawled to the canvas and was counted out. Marciano was still champion.

Sports writers probed the minds of these men who fight for a living. Why do they fight? For money certainly, but money is not the whole explanation.

Marciano, a quiet and pleasant man outside the ring, recalled a morning years before he was champion. He was jogging along a road in the better section of his home town, Brockton, Mass., shadowboxing as he trotted. Two well-dressed old ladies looked at him. As he passed, one said: "There's that fighter from the other side of the tracks. He certainly doesn't impress me."

Right then and there, Rocky made up his mind. "I'll impress people," he decided.

The Hurricane

One of 1954's big storms, Hurricane Carol, caused more damage but stirred up hardly more conversation than a fighter nicknamed "Hurricane" Tommy Jackson. Hurricane Jackson, a 22-year-old with an astonishing lack of style, roared into the headlines when he kayoed Rex Layne and then battered ranking heavyweight Dan Bucceroni half senseless.

Arms flailing, head bobbing, feet dancing strange jigs, Jackson did everything wrong. He didn't know how to get leverage into a punch. He had no jab. He invented a spectacular but harmless two-handed uppercut. His chief weapon

was condition. He didn't really knock opponents out. He exhausted them and they dropped by themselves.

"If you put him in with the devil," said an observer, "he'd wear the devil down."

Jackson was the first man in the gym in the morning and had to be chased out at night. He ran 20 miles every day.

"I ain't never stopped running since I started," he boasted. "I run rain, shine. I don't even care if it snows."

Next-to-the-youngest child in a family of seven, Tommy lived with his mother.

"He never did like to go to school," she said. "He always wanted to be a fighter. I tried to stop him, but when I saw how set he was I tried to help him. I see he gets to bed early and gets good food."

Like most Hurricanes, Tommy did not last long. Jimmy Slade, a clever, veteran light-heavyweight, outpointed him. And then Cuban heavyweight Nino Valdes knocked him out in one round and the Hurricane was over.

Basketball

The basketball story of the year was the retirement of "Mr. Basketball" George Mikan, the fabulous giant (6 ft 10 in.) of the professional Minneapolis Lakers, walked into the office of his general manager and said he was quitting to practice law.

"I always dreaded that day," said Laker coach John Kundla.

Mikan had made De Paul University of Chicago a national basketball power and continued to dominate the game as a pro. In his seven years with the Lakers, the team won six championships.

Nearsighted, Mikan wore extra-thick lensed glasses taped to his head. Despite poor vision, he totaled an amazing 11,37_ points in his career, 5000 more than his nearest rival. He drew huge crowds wherever he played, and he was a key factor in popularizing professional basketball.

College basketball was dominated by smart, fast, All-American Tom Gola from La Salle, a Christian Brothers institution in Philadelphia. Led by Gola, La Salle moved into the finals of the National Collegiate basketball tournament at Kansas City to swamp Bradley, 92 to 76.

Some experts called Gola "the greatest college basketball player in history" but, with all his ability, he was primarily a team man. He had never been top scorer in the nation, but only because he would pass the ball to teammates instead of shooting himself.

On the court and off, Gola was an affable giant. He played with dispassionate precision.

"If Gola ever gets angry on a court," said his coach, "he'll score a hundred points."

Gola was born within walking distance of the college. When he finished high school, he received sixty-two offers of college scholarships, but he preferred to stay close to home.

In Philadelphia, hero-worshiping high-school kids imitated Gola's gliding run, his phlegmatic manner, even his soft speech. And they tried to imitate his skill on a basketball court.

The King Is Dead

Ben Hogan has been called the automaton, the mechanical man, and the greatest of all golfers. But in 1954, Hogan failed to win a tournament.

In the Masters Golf Championship at Augusta, Ga., one of the prestige events of the year, Hogan lost in a play-off to his old rival, Sammy Snead. In the National Open, Hogan finished fifth.

Said Snead: "The sun don't shine on the same dog all the time."

A host of new golfers stole the headlines. Ed Furgol, a 37-year-old teaching pro from Clayton, Mo., won his first U.S. Open championship. Hogan was never a serious contender and Sammy Snead, in his fourteenth try for the only major U.S. tourney he had never won, finished seventh.

Furgol, the victim of a playground accident that shattered his left elbow, had held to his boyhood dream of being a golfer and a pro.

"It never set right, even after two operations," he said. "So I exercised to strengthen my hands. I used my shoulder muscles because there's no strength in my left hand."

In 1953, Furgol, broke and sick of the constant travel and tension of big-time golf, decided to give up the tournament trail for a steady job as a teaching pro. His attractive wife, Helen, helped him.

"I was never so happy," said Furgol.

As a teaching pro, Furgol could take time off to play in a few big tournaments. The biggest, of course, was the National Open.

The Beginning and the End

The most electrifying baseball player of the year was a 24-year-old farm boy from Fairfield, Ala. Willie Mays, center fielder of the New York Giants, ran like a rabbit, made spectacular catches, threw the ball accurately for amazing distances, and was powerful at the plate. Winner of the batting championship, he was voted baseball's "Most Valuable Player" award by the baseball writers.

Bubbling, exuberant Willie was the butt of a hundred practical jokes, and the Giants' clubhouse was a happy place.

Without Mays in 1953, the Giants had finished thirty-five games behind Brooklyn. With Mays in 1954, the Giants finished first in the National League.

After a hot afternoon at the Polo Grounds, Willie usually scooted home to

play stickball (baseball played on the street with a sawed-off broomstick and a soft rubber ball) with the neighborhood kids. For Willie, playing ball was fun.

In the American League, 1954 was the year the Cleveland Indians won a record 111 games to stop Casey Stengel's Yankees in their drive for six straight pennants.

The jubilation of Cleveland fans was short-lived. In the World Series, the Giants, sparked by Mays and aided by the home-run pinch hitting of Jim ("Dusty") Rhodes, thrashed the Indians in four straight games.

1954 also marked the end of an era. The Philadelphia Athletics, founded fifty-four years ago by Connie Mack, were sold to a vending-machine tycoon, Arnold Johnson, for a reported $3,350,000, and the franchise was shifted to Kansas City. Philadelphia had been incapable of supporting two big-league baseball clubs.

A onetime catcher, the 91-year-old Mr. Mack had witnessed the growth of baseball from a sand-lot pastime into a big-business enterprise. Manager of his own club until recent years, he led the A's to their first pennant in 1902.

For more than fifty years, with his high, old-fashioned collar and his straw hat, Mack had been a familiar figure. Fans remembered him sitting in the blue, shadowed dugout directing his team by a wave of his scoreboard.

Hard pressed for cash in the early '30's, Mack broke up one of the greatest teams in baseball, and the A's never recovered. Debt-ridden, perennially in the second division, in 1954 they lost an incredible 103 games of the 154-game schedule.

Mack finally yielded to pressure from friends and associates. He made one last

ON HANDS AND KNEES, ex-heavyweight champ Ezzard Charles is counted out in eighth round of second comeback try against Rocky Marciano (left)

'WAY UP: A fearless climber high in the Swiss Alps edges to the tip of a "needle-point"

'WAY DOWN: Skin diver Wally Potts of San Diego, Calif., after firing arrow from spear gun, wrestles with 401-pound black sea bass he finally landed after three-hour fight

futile plea to the assembled club owners to keep the team in Philadelphia. When they refused, he retired to his home, old and broken in spirit.

Kansas City, delighted to have a big-league team, bought more than $2 million worth of tickets for 1955. City Manager L. P. Cookingham summed up the situation accurately: "We have opened our heart and home to someone who appeared in need of shelter."

Emotion

The year in sports had started off spectacularly. The most sensational single football play took place when Rice met Alabama in the Dallas Cotton Bowl on Jan. 1 before 75,504 screaming partisans.

With a slim 7-6 lead in the second quarter, Rice's Dick Moegle broke loose from his own 5-yard line. Racing down the side lines, he was headed for a touchdown. On the bench, big, bruising Alabama fullback Tommy Lewis watched Moegle come closer and closer, then, amazingly, leaped on the field to tackle him.

"I kept telling myself I didn't do it, I didn't do it, but I know I did," contrite Tommy said.

Rice, given the automatic touchdown, went on to win 28-6.

A Legend

In the Sport of Kings, Alfred Gwynne Vanderbilt announced the retirement of his big, gray, 4-year-old colt Native Dancer because of a leg injury.

Fourth-highest money-winner of all time, the colt had earned over three quarters of a million dollars in three years.

"No one will ever know how good he really was," said trainer Bill Winfrey. "He's lazy. He runs only as fast as he has to."

But the Dancer was a legend in his own time. Hundreds of people sent him letters and greeting cards. Young girls organized fan clubs in his name. Betters put up $2 on him to win 5¢. He was an idol of a vast TV audience, many of whose members had never been to a race track. His trademark was a breathless, thundering finish.

Eric Guerin, his jockey, tried to express his feelings about the Dancer: "You can't tell someone how good it is, how strong he feels, and what it's like to ride him. You can only try to tell them. A guy's got to ride him to know."

A dark-gray horse as a 3-year-old, he had begun to lighten around the flanks as most gray horses do. If he lives long enough, Native Dancer will turn snow white.

Winner of twenty-one starts (his only loss was to Dark Star in 1953's Kentucky Derby), the Dancer ran his last race on a sloppy track at Saratoga, N.Y., in a non-betting feature. Toting 137 pounds, he ate up the track with his long strides. The crowd cheered as though it had bet millions on him—a stirring tribute to one of the greatest horses since Man o' War.

The Smell of Oil

Driving another kind of horse power, Bill Vukovich of Fresno, Calif., joined speedway immortals by winning his second successive Indianapolis Speedway 500-mile race before a huge crowd of 175,000. Only two other drivers had won two straight: Wilbur Shaw in 1939-40, and Mauri Rose in 1947-48.

Vukovich, gunning his gray fuel-injector special to a record 130.840 miles an hour, took just 3 hours, 49 minutes, and 12.27 seconds to complete the grind.

Short, olive skinned, untalkative, Vukovich had no intention of retiring to his 40-acre grape farm. "First," he said, "I want two or three more wins."

GOOD TRY: Mrs. Stanley Emmerson of Dayton, Ohio, applies body English on 5-foot putt in Women's Western Open Tourney. Sad to say, it didn't drop

POSES A LA PICASSO: These portraits, four of thirteen done in six months of 1954, represent the "Sylvette period" of aging, Spanish-born Pablo Picasso — shown (right) with his newest subject, a 19-year-old Paris blonde named Sylvette David

Art and Architecture

BRITON Augustus E. John, still active at 75, had a historic one-man show in London — fifty years of his painting, plus works in sculpture, his new medium

TOP ART SHOW OF 1954 WAS ALSO THE year's biggest disappearing act.

In June, the world's collectors, critics, and just plain art lovers converged on Paris for a rare showing of pre-World War I paintings by modern art's kingpin, Pablo Picasso.

Owned by the Soviet Union, the costly canvases (many of Picasso's works have sold for as much as $50,000 apiece) had been loaned to Paris' Maison de la Pensée Française in an unexpected gesture of good will. These early oils, painted between 1900 and 1914, had not been seen outside Russia since the Revolution. Paris was jubilant, for this was an art event of the first magnitude.

But shortly after opening to capacity crowds on June 9, the exhibition (scheduled to run through September) was abruptly ended. In one of the oddest happenings in the eccentric annals of modern art, the oils were literally snatched from the gallery walls.

Most of the forty-nine canvases had once belonged to a discriminating czarist industrialist, Serge Stchoukine. They had been confiscated by the Soviets at the time of the Revolution. The late magnate's daughter, Irene, lived as a refugee in Paris. When the paintings arrived there, she started legal proceedings to regain what she considered her rightful inheritance—a tidy fortune in Picassos.

The Iron Curtain came down with a bang. A black truck sped to the gallery, loaded the disputed oils aboard, and whisked them off to the Soviet Embassy. There the paintings were technically on Soviet soil, where heiress Stchoukine had small chance of ever retrieving them.

Leathery, tanned Picasso, a millionaire through the sale of his oils, was off to a bullfight the day his paintings disappeared. "I am sorry," he commented. "I would have liked to see them again." An avowed Communist, he loyally added that he did not think Stchoukine's daughter had any right to the oils—"What if the Comte de Paris took it in his head to lay claim to Versailles?"

Picasso's own career was equally an Alice-in-wonderland adventure. He was vocal in his love for Communism. Yet his own cubist distortions were anathema in the Soviet Union, where Western modern art had been labeled "bourgeois decadence". His ultramodern paintings had not been publicly exhibited in Russia for many years. To a bewildered and inquisitive American tourist who queried him about his politics and art, he angrily retorted: "Don't ask questions of the man at the helm."

Death of Matisse

All was not farce in 1954 art, however. The year's greatest art loss was the passing of 84-year-old French painter Henri Matisse, who, with Picasso (aged 73) and Braque (72), was one of modern art's Big Three.

Four years earlier, plump, bearded, pink-faced Matisse had calmly announced: "My bags are packed, and I am waiting for the last train." That train stopped for him in November at his Riviera apartment in Nice. To the end, he painted prodigiously, usually from his wheel chair, where he sat racked with pain from intestinal cancer. He often worked while resting in bed, drawing designs on the wall with a piece of charcoal attached to a long pole.

The onetime law student did not find his individual art style until 1905, after years of experiment and study. At that time, he suddenly stopped imitating nature and created a highly original, sun-drenched world. An orgy of color burst on a startled public—purple trees, tangerine rivers, a blue girl with green hair.

At first he was ridiculed. Even friends

called his canvases "monstrous" and "fit for a child's bedroom". An American art critic in Chicago tabbed him a "foreign fourflusher". He wrote anxiously to America: "Please tell the U.S.A. that I am a devoted husband and father, with a comfortable home and a fine garden, just like other people." That was, however, a half century ago. In 1954, his flat mosaics of brilliant color were reproduced on countless living-room walls. His 40″ by 50″ paintings sold for more than $20,000 apiece. The rebel had long since become a millionaire.

The old man called a small Catholic chapel in the French village of Vence his "masterwork". During World War II, a Dominican nun nursed the ailing painter. In gratitude, Matisse painted the entire Dominican Chapel of the Rosary, consecrated in 1951. By 1954, visitors from all over the world had visited Vence to view the chapel, its walls, windows, and altarpiece alive with bold, modern color and abstract design.

Just before his death, Matisse counseled the next generation of artists: "The most important thing is to keep the naïveté of childhood. You study, you learn, but you guard the original naïveté. It has to be within you, as desire for drink is within the drunkard, or love is within the lover."

Death of Marsh

Americans were saddened in 1954 by the death, at 56, of painter Reginald Marsh. He died July 3, without warning, of a heart ailment, at his summer home in Vermont. Auburn-haired, moon-faced, blue-eyed Marsh was America's foremost painter of slum kids, sidewalk shills, burlesque queens, subway straphangers, bleary-eyed bums, pretty and curvaceous trollops. And he painted them with sympathy, with respect, and never with condescension.

Artist Marsh was a regional painter. He did not paint, however, the corn fields or the prairies or the Grand Canyon. His province was New York—its subways and elevateds, Coney Island, the gangster-ridden docks, the Bowery. He was not at all concerned with the plush, glamorized aspects of the city. He saw the drama of the seamy side, and painted it with the brush of a true artist.

Of the city, he once remarked: "I love New York. It stinks and is earthy and real. It is a mass of color. The suburbs are just places where nothing goes on. When I go out to the country and look at the green leaves, I am bored."

No other artist has ever caught the quintessence of tawdry Coney Island, with its swarming thousands of Sunday bathers, as vividly as Marsh. He painted the bathers with a Rabelaisian relish for humanity. His figures bulge and burst with vitality. Coney Island was to him "like the great compositions of Michelangelo and Rubens".

For the lifeless abstractions of the ultramodern painters, he had only scorn. "It is phony subprimitivism," he would argue. "Critics may not know what's wrong with Picasso, but any layman can tell you. The question is, what does it mean?"

The man who had a gusto for painting the bottom crust himself came from the higher social echelons. His parents were of conservative New England stock, and he was educated with rich men's sons at Lawrenceville (a private school) and Yale. His first job was drawing vaudeville sketches for New York's racy tabloid, the *Daily News.*

Before long, he won recognition as a superb draftsman. Today his paintings of New York hang in every important museum in the nation. Just a few weeks before his death, Marsh was awarded the Gold Medal of the National Institute of

FRENCHMAN Henri Matisse, 84, died during the year, ending an era in French painting. Here, bedridden, he entertains a visitor in his apartment (above), works on a figurine (right)

Arts and Letters. Painters and public alike would long mourn one of America's great artists.

A Sculptor's Holes

Sculptor of the year was England's short, tweedy, pink-faced Henry Moore. His controversial works won raves from the critics when they were exhibited at London's Leicester Galleries early in 1954 and at New York's Curt Valentin Gallery in November. Moore was the sculptor of holes, huge holes scooped out of his figures, holes in the heads and bodies of Madonnas, family groups, reclining nudes. The 56-year-old son of a coal miner explained his style: "Holes have a mysterious fascination for me, the fascination of caves in hillsides and cliffs. A hole can

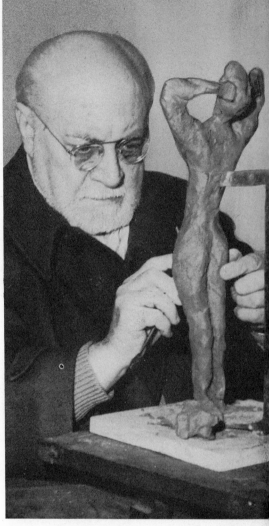

have as much meaning as a solid mass."

Not everybody liked his holes, however. Percy Uris, president of a company which owned a spanking-new skyscraper in New York, admired Moore's larger-than-life "King and Queen", purchased it on a trial basis for the lobby of his office building. Reluctantly, he returned it to the sculptor with this lament: "About 80 percent of the tenants disliked it. What really distressed me were the wisecracks. Some of the secretaries said the two figures were hit by an ax."

But sculptor Moore did not fret. His strange creatures were selling at figures between $2000 and $10,000, and he could not make enough to meet the demand.

Another sculptor, who had once outraged the public quite as much as Moore did in 1954, was becoming respectable. Jacob Epstein, whose art G. K. Chesterton once called "an insult" and the London *Times* dubbed "repellent", was on the New Year's Honors List. Queen Elizabeth II made him a Knight Commander of the British Empire. From now on, Epstein,

PLENTY OF NOTHING sustains this "Seated Figure", on view during a London show of sculpture. Work is by Emilio Greco

born 73 years before in New York's slums and a British subject since World War I, would be addressed as Sir Jacob.

A Birthday and a Face Lifting

Two top American showcases celebrated in 1954—New York's Metropolitan Museum and Museum of Modern Art.

The glass, steel, and marble Museum of Modern Art, which had successfully sold Picasso & Co. to a resisting public, had a twenty-fifth birthday. The acknowledged national headquarters of modern art in the U.S. recalled bitter struggles and sweeping victories.

The museum had been born on a camel in Egypt, or rather on two camels. The camel riders who conspired to present, or con, according to one's point of view, the American public with the New Art were two of New York's most respected and wealthy ladies—the late Abby Aldrich Rockefeller and Lillie Bliss. They met on a camel cavalcade while on a leisurely holiday, pondered together the education of Americans to the new ideas in art. In 1929, with the aid of other wealthy friends, they opened the Museum of Modern Art.

The chosen path for these missionaries was thorny, however. On many occasions,

RECLINING FIGURE is admired by its British creator, Henry Moore, one of world's best-known sculptors. Great holes in his sculptured figures aroused controversy

the stubborn Customs officials would not allow sculpture headed for the Museum of Modern Art to enter the country duty-free, a normal arrangement for works of art. The officials contended that the modern stuff was just a collection of wood, bronze, and marble and not art at all.

A rash of angry editorialists attacked the museum as a model of chi-chi decadence when it displayed a fur-lined tea-cup by a now forgotten artist, Meret Oppenheim. A wooden cage containing some lumps of sugar and a thermometer, entitled "Why Not Sneeze", did not help mat-

SURREALISM — NOW AND THEN: Ultramodern Salvador Dali (left) poses with his "Visage of War". "The Market Gardener" (above) by Italy's Giuseppe Arcimboldo, born in 1530 and lately "taken up" by Paris art lovers, raises the question: How modern is modern?

ters much, and eyebrows went up considerably when the museum displayed a bootblack's shoeshine stand, decorated with buttons, bottle caps, and other gaudy insignia, as a local masterpiece.

But the battle for the new-fangled art was eventually won. In 1954, there was nothing left to revolt *against*. The only revolt possible might be a return to old-fashioned realism. For all its excesses, the museum had led the public to tolerance of art in all its guises.

In 1954 New York's Metropolitan Museum, an 83-year-old matriarch with the most valuable art cache in the nation, had a $9 million face lifting. Overhauling included a new $1.5 million auditorium, a Dorothy Draper-decorated restaurant built around a pool, gallery rooms done in pastel shades and brocades, indirect lighting, windowed nooks for the convenience of smokers. Met Director Francis Henry Taylor (who resigned at year's end to return to the peace and quiet of the Worcester, Mass., Art Museum) explained the modernization succinctly: "The public has had a bellyful of prestige and pink Tennessee marble."

Critics of its New Look still regarded the Metropolitan as a relic, an uncomfortable, neoclassic pile. The face lifting was all for the better, they argued, but why not spend the $9 million on a new building rather than mere patchwork?

The Metropolitan was still America's top museum. Its million objects had come from the nation's richest men. The late financier Jules S. Bache had left the Met a stunning $12.5 million collection; newspaper publisher Frank A. Munsey had given $10 million worth of valuables. Million-dollar bequests were common. And the public came in droves. In 1954, a record-breaking 2 million persons filed past the Metropolitan's uniformed guards.

Collector—Baconian

One of the nation's most colorful art collectors died in 1954. He was Walter C. Arensberg, 75, of Hollywood. He was born in Pittsburgh, son of steel and banking leader Conrad Christian Arensberg. He wrote slender and intense volumes of poems until 1920, when he deserted rhyme to prove that Sir Francis Bacon really wrote the masterworks of Shakespeare. His Hollywood mansion had been the international headquarters for all those unorthodox scholars who held this view of the Bard's writings.

Arensberg's servantless home in the film capital was filled from floor to ceiling with modern art—Picassos, Dalis, Cézannes. The paintings spilled out onto porches, even into the kitchen and bathrooms. Every museum in the nation coveted his $2 million collection. A couple of years before his death, he awarded most of it to the Philadelphia Museum of Art.

To the end, Arensberg doggedly pursued the Bacon-Shakespeare controversy. Shortly before he died, he proclaimed: "There is no more doubt that Bacon wrote Shakespeare than there is about the worth of my modern art collection." Americans could well appreciate the value of his immense art treasure, but they remained skeptical about the first premise.

Spiv Primitive

London in 1954 came up with a young man hailed as "England's first 20th-century primitive, a Grandma Moses in embryo". He was 25-year-old Jack Taylor, who a few months earlier had pushed a wheelbarrow on construction jobs. Grandma Moses and he were both self-taught painters, but there the similarity ended.

In contrast with Grandma Moses' literal landscapes, Taylor painted a dream world far removed from the drabness and squalor of the London slums in which he lived. His shimmering landscapes were bright with unlikely color, his happy figures dressed in rich and regal costumes, his neoclassic buildings festooned with cupolas and arches.

Taylor had never been outside his native London. He was the son of an odd-job Cockney. One of eleven children, he left school at 14 to earn a living. He recalled: "I was always fightin' and boozin' and gettin' in scrapes with the police. I was a spiv all right." But he always painted, hiding his canvases from his disapproving family.

On a dare from cronies who kidded him about being an artist, Jack Taylor walked into London's fashionable Redfern Gallery. To his astonishment, the directors gave him £10 ($28) for one of his oils, urged him to return with more. In June, the gallery displayed forty-four of his paintings, sold all of them in a few days at prices up to £35.

Spiv Taylor, rejoicing in his slum lodging over the spiraling prices for his canvases, remembered the taunts of his mates: "They think anybody who wants to paint is queer. Why, I get more out of paintin' one little picture than some of those bums pick up in a year."

The Mexicans Build a School

Big architectural news of the year came from Mexico City. After four years of construction, the most modern college in the world was complete. Just north of Mexico City on a vast bed of lava rock spewed from the Ajusco volcano 2000 years ago, it was a 1500-acre "city" housing the 400-year-old National University of Mexico. The world's fanciest campus was Mexico's biggest construction job since the Halls of Montezuma (about 1500 A.D.). Its twenty-two buildings would accommodate no fewer than 30,000 students.

Under the direction of brilliant, 29-year-old architect Carlos Lazo Jr., Mexico's best designers, engineers, and muralists completed the privately owned school. The campus was as modern as the day after tomorrow, and as variegated as a Mexican market scene. Set in wide open spaces, the buildings formed a remarkable grouping of cylinders, rectangles, and pyramids. One rectangle sat on thin steel stilts. Another edifice, the huge Olympic Stadium (seating capacity: 110,000), was shaped to resemble a volcano's crater.

The engineering school made dramatic use of sixteen glass cupolas to harness solar illumination for its laboratories. Concrete walls surrounding the game courts suggested the truncated pyramids of the ancient Indians. And everything, even the pavements and the exteriors of the buildings, was dabbed with riotous color, a profusion of color that had not been equaled in modern times.

Star of the stunning new campus was the poolside library, a rectangle sitting upright on a long slab. The color-drenched building was splattered with bright, intricate mosaics of Aztec design. It was the work of Juan O'Gorman, the most-discussed architect in Mexico.

For O'Gorman, the 49-year-old son of an Irish mining engineer and a Mexican-Irish mother, 1954 was a busy year. In addition to the National University library, he also completed the strikingly designed Communications and Public Works Building in Mexico City, a ten-story, glass-and-steel structure covered with brilliant red, yellow, and green mosaics depicting national heroes, revolutionists, emperors, and Indian deities.

The shy, hard-working artist was as brilliant a muralist as he was an architect. And he preached a message of realism to other Mexican artists: "Realism is easier to look at and live with. In general, good as ultramodern art can be, you get tired of it after a while. Art should be like making love or eating. It is a pleasure, not something you have to learn to like."

Tireless Juan O'Gorman had traveled hundreds of miles—sometimes on donkey—to find naturally colored stones which would keep their hues through decades of punishment by sun and rain. He wanted native stones for his huge mosaics. A geologist friend warned him that some of the rocks were too soft—they might not last more than 500 years. "Fine," replied O'Gorman. "That's long enough for me."

SAMARITAN, a high priest of the dissident sect rejected 2500 years ago by the Jews, prays with a heavy scroll containing the laws of Moses. Samaritans now number but a few hundred and live near Israel, in Jordan

RELIGION

ONE DAY A PLUMP, BESPECTACLED PREACH-
er by the name of Norman Vincent Peale
walked into a bookstore to check up on
the progress of his best seller, *The Power
of Positive Thinking* (more than 850,000
copies sold since its publication in 1952).

Dr. Peale asked the girl behind the
counter how the sales of his book compared with those of another very popular
volume by Dr. Alfred Kinsey, *Sexual Behavior in the Human Female.*

"You know," the girl told him, "religion
is more popular than sex this year."

The year she was talking about was
1954. And, though college presidents,
ministers, politicians, and writers tried,
nobody put the religious temper of the
times into better words than that name-
less salesgirl. For in 1954 human beings,
not only in the United States, but all
around the globe, were displaying an
amazing interest in religious matters.

Machine Gun of God

Throughout Europe and America, for
example, masses of people exposed themselves to the fire of the polished young
evangelist Billy Graham, who became
known as "the machine gun of God". In a
three-month campaign in England, rapid-
talking Graham preached to 1,761,000
people, and persuaded 34,586 to come
forward to give their names as newly
awakened Christians.

In Germany, he talked to crowds of 80,-
000 in Berlin's vast Olympic Stadium.
With the aid of an interpreter who
pounded the Bible when Billy pounded it
and pointed to heaven when Billy
pointed, he even surmounted the language barrier. In France, he drew a select
crowd of 2500 French, Belgian, and Swiss
pastors.

The figures, however, tell only part of
the Graham story. More important than
the quantity was the quality of the Graham mission. Nearly everywhere his arrival was greeted with scorn and derision
by sophisticated members of the press.
The London *Daily Mirror's* widely read
columnist "Cassandra" (William Con-
nor), who pontificates on everything from
religion to politics, warned readers to be
on the lookout for a "Hollywood version
of John the Baptist".

But the handsome, 36-year-old Graham, who is given to conservative blue
suits and a fundamentalist interpretation
of the Bible, generally turned the scoffers
into something close to men of prayer.

During his tour of England, Graham
showed himself to be equally at home
drinking lemonade in a London pub or
tea with Dr. Geoffrey Fisher, the Arch-
bishop of Canterbury. Before Graham
left England, a chastened "Cassandra"
wrote: "I think that he [Graham] is a
good man. I think that he is also a simple
man. And goodness and simplicity are a

OUTSIZE "YO-YOS", hurled down the road as brothers go for long walks, are rare relaxation for usually meditative Carmelite monks of Caprarola, Italy. Their motto: Serve God with Joy

couple of tough customers . . . In this country, battered and squeezed as no victorious nation has ever been before and disillusioned almost beyond endurance, he has been welcomed with an exuberance that almost makes us blush behind our precious Anglo-Saxon reserve. I never thought that friendliness had such a sharp cutting edge. I never thought that simplicity could cudgel us so damned hard. We live and learn."

The feverish pace of his European crusade cost Billy Graham 12 pounds. It also aggravated a condition which put him to bed with several painful kidney-stone attacks. But he lost none of his enthusiasm. At year's end, he was back stumping the U.S. with his gospel message.

In Nashville, Tenn., he cried: "You know why God blessed the meetings in London. It wasn't great organization. It certainly wasn't great preaching. It was because millions of people around the

world banded themselves to pray. And when I stood up to preach, I was lifted up . . . on the power of prayer. Prayer! Prayer! Prayer!"

Billy Graham has refined his preaching technique since he started delivering gospel talks in Florida trailer camps eighteen years ago. The most distinctive feature of his preaching is the speed with which he delivers his sermons. He paces the platform (often covering more than a mile during a sermon) and stabs with his fingers, but he does not indulge in the extravagant theatrical effects favored by some evangelists. To keep up his energy, the 180-pound Graham often eats five meals a day. He doesn't smoke or drink. He seeks relaxation on the golf course.

Like a business executive, Graham draws a flat salary of $15,000 yearly; the rest of the money he takes in goes into the Billy Graham Evangelistic Association, Inc., which pays the "team" (including assistant evangelists, musicians, publicity men) and hires radio and TV time on an annual budget of $2 million. Graham never visits a town without being asked to do so by local Protestant ministers, never leaves without turning over to local churches the names of converts.

Faith Healers Abroad

But even Billy Graham's ringing call for a personal faith in Jesus Christ was not reassuring enough for many troubled people in 1954. Among them were the people who, in England, deluged a mild, white-haired spirit healer named Harry Edwards with mail (he got twenty times as many letters as Prime Minister Churchill) or flocked to his estate, "The Sanctuary", 30 miles from London, hoping to find relief from their often incurable ailments. There Edwards and his two assistants—George Burton, an ex-butcher, and Burton's wife, Olive—dispensed their peculiar

form of treatment, consisting of meditation and massage.

At a typical session, a woman complained to Edwards: "I seem to have lost power in my arms and legs."

Dressed in medical white, Edwards began rubbing the limbs gently. After a few minutes, he inquired: "You feel better now, don't you?"

"Yes," said the woman uncertainly, "much better."

Then Olive Burton placed her hands on the woman's forehead while George stood behind the patient with a firm grip on her shoulders. Edwards took her hands. All three closed their eyes. This part of the treatment is what Edwards calls "attunement".

Said Edwards: "We get in tune with the spirit people. They receive information that we can give them, and they direct the healing."

The woman was only one of some two dozen people Edwards saw that afternoon. Though he charged no fees, there was a plate at the door of "The Sanctuary" for contributions.

In France, many people believed in an even more incredible faith healer, a man who called himself Christ. His story began on Christmas Day, 1953, when Georges Roux, a hunchbacked, balding man of 51, walked off his job as a postal sorter at the railway station in Avignon. Proclaiming himself "master of the earth", he said: "I started the movement on Christmas because it was my birthday during my first stay on earth."

Within six months, Roux had built up a following of more than 4000 people in France, Germany, Italy, and Switzerland. They called their movement "Witnesses of Christ", and renamed Roux "Georges-Christ". Sect members had to give up alcohol, tobacco, and canned food, and were forbidden to seek medical advice. Result: In a few months, four children died of uncomplicated childhood diseases despite a pious "laying on of hands" by the faithful.

Blandly, Roux remarked: "If a patient dies, that is no tragedy for the healer. On the contrary, it is a great achievement, for the patient passes into a better world."

At one point, Roux wrote to the Vatican, offering to cure Pope Pius XII, who throughout the year suffered increasingly from attacks of hiccups and gastritis. When his services were declined, Roux wrote angrily to the Pope: "You were never Christ's vicar on earth. You should recognize me as such."

Despite the deaths, Roux' faith-healing movement continued to grow. Alarmed French officials could not prosecute him for practicing medicine illegally, because he did not charge for "healing". But postal authorities estimated that his disciples sent him some $1400 monthly in money orders.

Witnesses of Christ met in bars, theaters, and other public gathering places in the towns of southern France. Frequently, they had to contend with hostile mobs. On one occasion, Roux' son-in-law, René Van Gerdinge, was tossed into a village fountain. A former 400-meter champion, Van Gerdinge had to sprint 1.2 miles for police protection.

Piety in Practical Life

Meanwhile, in the United States, a very different kind of witnessing was taking place. "I can remember the day when they used to say there were two things an American wouldn't talk about—politics and religion," reported a prominent Protestant leader. "I'm not so sure about politics, but I know that was certainly true of religion. Now the picture has changed."

In Washington, President Eisenhower and Cabinet members like Secretary of Agriculture Ezra T. Benson regularly opened staff meetings with prayer. Senators, congressmen, supreme court justices led devotional services at religious breakfast meetings.

In business, men like Lem T. Jones, head of a nationwide, $10 million candy firm (Russell Stover) with headquarters in Kansas City, Mo., mixed prayer with work. Frequently, Jones would finger a palm-sized silver cross in his pocket, switch on the plant public-address system, and ask his employees to stop work. "I tell them that the firm is faced with some decisive action and ask them to join me for a couple of minutes of silent prayer for divine guidance," he explained. "It makes them feel a part of the team. The prayers make solution of the most difficult situations easy."

Even in Hollywood, a town not noted for piety, girls who were previously engaged in plugging their ideal measurements were out selling the Word in 1954. Most famous of these were "The Four Girls", a religious quartet that came into being almost by accident.

Connie Haines (Presbyterian), Jane Russell (nondenominational), Beryl Davis (Episcopalian), and Della Russell (Catholic) agreed to entertain at a charity performance at the Hollywood Episcopal Church.

But they had nothing prepared when they arrived. "Why don't we all go on stage together and try harmonizing a spiritual?" Connie suggested.

Their jump version of *Do Lord* got so much word-of-mouth publicity that recording executives came flying out from New York. The quartet recorded its first spiritual in February. Within a month, 200,000 copies had been sold.

By year's end "The Four Girls" (with Rhonda Fleming replacing Della Russell) were still going strong on records and in personal appearances. The money they earned went to their churches.

The fact is that there was no corner of American life untouched by this new interest in religion. Alvin Dark, shortstop of the New York Giants, made front-page news when he told a Baptist Sunday School class that he planned to give one tenth of his winner's share in the World Series ($1114) to the church.

And, in a very different way, Nathan Marsh Pusey, new president of Harvard University—center of an American intellectual tradition which has not been notably religious—made news when he devoted his first efforts to strengthening the Divinity School.

Said Dr. Pusey: "It is leadership in re-

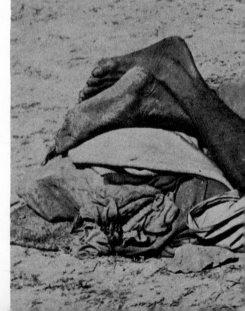

ligious knowledge, and even more, in religious experience . . . of which we now have a most gaping need."

Behind the Iron Curtain

While religion seemed to flower in the atmosphere of the free world as never before, the world's prevailing westerly winds carried some seed behind the Iron Curtain. Best evidence that it was taking root there in 1954 was a stepped-up effort in Communist countries to stamp out religious seedlings wherever they arose.

In Moscow, headquarters of the Communist movement which has been militantly atheistic since its inception, a new publication was planned expressly to spread antireligious propaganda. Called *Religion and Life*, it is the first such periodical since the weekly *Godless* was abandoned in 1941.

In addition, some thirty antireligious "museums" were being reopened. Such activity was strong testimony to the growing strength of the Russian Orthodox Church during the eleven years that its

existence had again been tolerated by the Communist regime.

In Prague, Czechoslovakia, police were at their wits' end trying to track down a youth organization which scrawled such messages as "Christ will save us all" on walls with indelible ink.

Midway between East and West, in Yugoslavia, a census showed that 84 percent of the people still believed in God despite nine years of Communist rule.

But believers behind the Iron Curtain were still strongly curbed by government. Nowhere was this more clearly demonstrated than at Mecca, in Saudi Arabia, when twenty-one Soviet Moslems arrived for the 1954 *al-îd al-kabîr*, the Great Festival. Unfortunately for the Red representatives, two former Russians, Hamid Raschid and Rusi Nasar, who had been living in Brooklyn for three years, also made the *hadj*, or sacred pilgrimage.

Raschid and Nasar were determined to see that the Soviet delegation did not foist any Red propaganda off on the 500,-000 hadjis at Mecca. So they managed to arrive in Jidda, the port of Mecca, on the

FERVOR OF HINDU FAITH is indicated by 4-year-old (left) and holy man (below) with head in sand at month-long ceremonies in Allahabad, India. Both have "renounced the world". Both seek alms

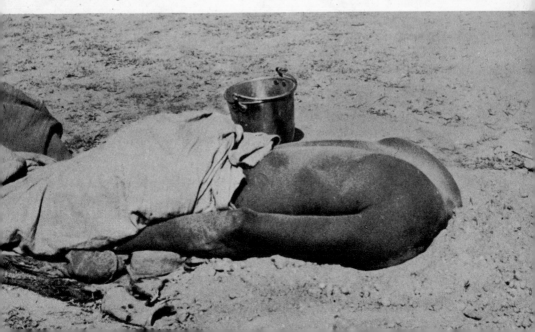

BRAHMA THE CREATOR in the form of a sculptured bull, 2000 years old, dwarfs this Hindu holy man meditating on a hilltop in Mysore, India

morning of the day the Russians were due. When the twenty-one Soviet hadjis showed up, they were pelted with ripe tomatoes and Arabic shrieks of "Communist propagandists!"

Later, at Mecca, Raschid put some sharp questions to the Russians. "How many religious books have been printed since the U.S.S.R. 'liberated' the churches to help the war effort?" he inquired.

After a long silence, one old man replied: "The Koran is coming out soon."

"Why did only twenty-one hadjis come this year although there are 35 million Moslems in the Soviet Union? Under the Czars, more than 35,000 pilgrims used to go to Mecca every year," Raschid persisted.

There was no answer. In fact, by the time Raschid and Nasar were through with them, the Soviet hadjis were jeered and booed wherever they went.

Other Religious Events

While 1954 was a year for unusual religious eruptions around the globe, it was also a year for historic events in the great established religious traditions.

At Evanston, Ill., Protestant leaders representing some 168 million Christians gathered for one of the greatest attempts in 400 years to achieve Christian unity— the Second Assembly of the World Council of Churches. More than 120,000 people met in Chicago's Soldier Field for a giant "Festival of Faith". Statisticians estimated it would take 6½ tons of paper to publish the reports, speeches, and documents relating to the assembly's theme, "Christ—the Hope of the World".

Halfway around the world from Evanston, where the Protestant Christians were gathering, thousands of saffron-robed, shaved-headed monks assembled in the Great Cave, 7 miles outside of Rangoon, Burma, for the sixth Great Council of the Buddhist world. The purpose: to codify changes in the Buddhist scriptures. Only five other such meetings have been held in the 2480-odd years since Buddha attained Nirvana.

Pope Pius XII, despite his recurring illness, continued to follow a heavy schedule throughout the Roman Catholic Church's Marian Year, celebrating the 100th anniversary of the declaration of the dogma of the Immaculate Conception. In an important, 4000-word encyclical, the Pope wrote: "The Son of God reflects on His . . . Mother the glory, the majesty, the power of Regality which springs from being associated with [Him] . . . Hence the Church . . . acclaims her . . . Queen of Heaven."

And for American Jews, 1954 was a special year. The 300th anniversary of the founding of the first Jewish community in North America by twenty-three Sephardic Jews was also an occasion for taking note of a strengthening of faith in America's Jewish congregations, similar to that in the Christian churches.

Reform congregations, for example, were continuing, but in greater number, to restore long-discarded rituals and ceremonies, such as the *bar mizvah* when 13-year-old boys assume the religious duties of adults. Statistics indicated that almost 3½ million of the 5 million Jews in the U.S. were affiliated with synagogues or Reform temples.

But despite the many evidences of piety in 1954, many spiritual leaders—in the U.S., at least—were not sure that religion was making much progress toward producing a better world. Said Dr. Henry P. Van Dusen of Union Theological Seminary in New York: "Religion is gaining ground—morality is losing ground. This is one of the most surprising and overlooked facts in America today . . . Either there will be a moral renewal or [religion's gains] will fritter out into futility."

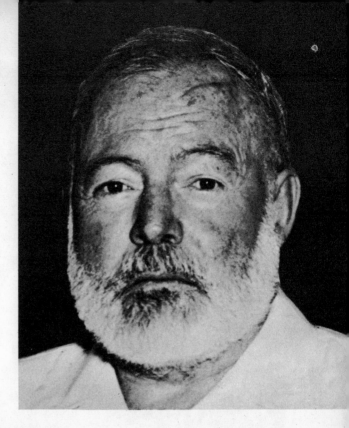

BOOKS

HUMORIST MARK TWAIN ONCE JESTED THAT a report of his death had been greatly exaggerated. Late in January, 1954, novelist Ernest Hemingway found himself in the same fix. He woke up one morning in Africa—where he had gone on an assignment for *Look* magazine—to learn that newspapers all over the world were mourning his sudden demise.

Five months before, the author and his wife had junketed by truck into the jungle country, occasionally flying out in a four-place Cessna operated by a pilot named Roy Marsh. It had been twenty years since Hemingway had bushwhacked through Africa, the scene of some of his best stories and of one of his books (*The Green Hills of Africa*). Then one day he was confronted by a situation that he might have plotted himself.

He and his wife hired Marsh to fly them to Africa's east coast to fish. On the way they planned to circle spectacular Murchison Falls of the Victoria Nile. Coming close, they swerved to avoid a flock of birds and impaled themselves on a tree. Hemingway and party climbed down, unhurt, spent the night on the riverbank shooing away curious elephants. Next day they hitched a ride to Butiaba, on Lake Albert, in a passing launch.

But a B.O.A.C. passenger plane, diverted from its course to look for the missing Cessna, saw the wreckage and no sign of life. Word went out that Hemingway probably had been killed.

In the fierce competition for what looked like the biggest literary story of the year, the newspapers killed Hemingway off without much compunction or any verification. Ironically, he almost complied with the premature reports.

On the take-off from Butiaba, the plane in which he and his wife were riding crashed and burned. The Hemingway luck held, but only by a thread. Ernest's spine was broken in two places, his right kidney ruptured. Butting his way through the emergency hatch, he fractured his skull. When the door opened, flames were sucked in and his hair was burned off.

Full of chagrin, the newspapers eventually restored the Hemingways to life. Author Ernest thereupon did what every great writer would like to do: he sat down and read his own obituaries.

For Hemingway, 1954 ended as dramatically as it had begun. Late in the fall, the Nobel Prize Committee in Stockholm announced that he was being awarded the prize for literature—the fourth American ever to be so honored. The others: Eugene O'Neill, Pearl Buck, William Faulkner.

The man whom the Nobel Prize Committee had so honored was born in Oak Park, Ill., 55 years ago. The son of a suburban doctor, he went to Europe during World War I as an ambulance driver and (later) a war correspondent, joined the Gertrude Stein-Sherwood Anderson circle in Paris, and was world famous (with *The Sun Also Rises*) before he was 30.

Hemingway has lived a violent, reckless life. He typified the "lost generation" that came into vogue following World

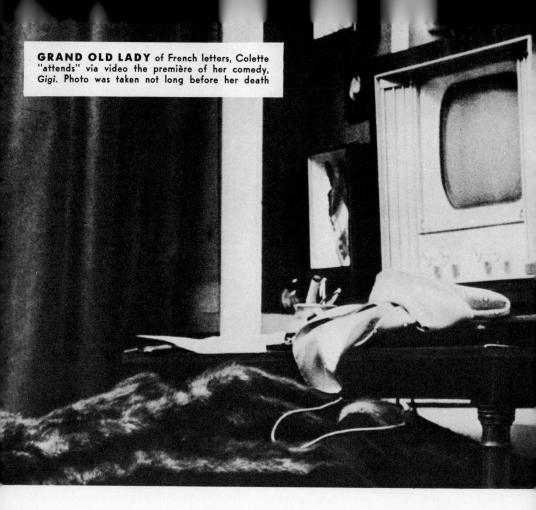

War I, and his novels provided his generation with a set of attitudes based on physical hazards voluntarily assumed—bullfighting, big-game hunting, deep-sea fishing, war. As a stylist, he is simple, sensuous, and direct. No other writer of his time has had so much influence on his contemporaries.

By coincidence, perhaps, Hemingway's interest in Africa in 1954 marked a trend. For nonfiction tends to run in cycles. Three years earlier it had been the sea, two years earlier the mountains. In 1954 Africa came in for the lion's share of attention.

There was a steady stream of books explaining South Africa's politico-social problems (the best: *Tell Freedom*, by Peter Abrahams). There were almost as many more on the equally impenetrable jungle country. Such books as *Madami; My Eight Years of Adventure with the Congo Pigmies* entertained thousands of readers who were tired of climbing Mt. Everest in an armchair or spearfishing with an aqualung on the front porch.

'54's Book Fare Was Varied

In 1954 the book buyer—and borrower—although confronted with fewer than usual volumes of genuine literary merit, had a wide choice of subjects from among the 11,000 new titles copyrighted.

He read autobiographies by such diverse figures as Louis ("Satchmo") Armstrong, the trumpet player, and Clement Attlee, the ex-Prime Minister of Great Britain. He read the life story of Bob Hope, told by himself, and that of Groucho Marx, told by his son Arthur. He read military memoirs by generals who got there lastest but not necessarily with the leastest (example: *General Dean's Story*, by Major General William F. Dean). He read life stories written by two condemned murderers, one of whom (kidnaper Caryl Chessman) was granted a stay of execution after publication of his book; for the other (Nazi Foreign Minister Joachim von Ribbentrop), who had been executed after sentencing by the International Military Tribunal at Nuremberg, it was eight years too late.

If he wanted to "do it himself", the reader had his choice of new books on such subjects as growing pecan trees, building outdoor fireplaces, and hand painting on china. In the publishing business, the "how to do it" rage, which had been building up for years, reached a climax in 1954, with some trade houses putting out books on practically nothing else.

Judged by the popularity of this type of book, the average American wanted most of all to (a) reduce, (b) refurnish an antique Chippendale highboy, or (c) get religion. There were 100 "How To" magazines on the market. The New York Public Library's collection of "How To" books numbered 3500 and dozens of new ones were being added every month.

The most written about of the year's novels was William Faulkner's *A Fable*. The diminutive, graying Nobel Prize winner spent ten years writing this long, turgid, and obscure, but powerful, allegory on the crucifixion of a modern Christ. Primarily, it is a protest against the senselessness of war. (Faulkner himself flew with the Canadian air force in World War I.) But critics were far from unanimous in liking it. The best account of the Christian fight against evil, many thought, is still to be found in the Bible.

A surprising number of people bought *A Fable* (it rose as high as fourth on *The New York Times Book Review*'s bestseller list). But a great many more bought an outsize (1000-page) chronicle of a man who was determined to be a doctor —*Not as a Stranger*, by Morton Thompson.

Despite its bulk, its repetitiousness, its sometimes crude writing, this book was a clear winner in the fiction sweepstakes. There was, moreover, a touch of irony in its success. Thompson's doctor-hero saves many lives. But Thompson himself, at 45, died of a heart attack before publication of his book. Grief-stricken, his wife (and former literary agent) committed suicide soon afterward.

The two deaths created a problem for Thompson's executors. Divorced and the father of two minor children by his previous marriage, the author left the children nothing in his will. Everything had been bequeathed to his second wife. With her death, the royalties—estimated to be in excess of $150,000—would pass to her relatives. Thompson's own children sued to recover them. As the money piled up, no one (by the end of the year) had established a final claim.

Book Condensation

The success of this thousand-page book pointed up a curious paradox in publishing. For the trend was toward condensations. Although the public seemingly preferred authors to write lengthy (or at least conventional-sized) books, most people chose to read them in highly abridged versions.

The most spectacular example of this

development was the mushrooming growth of the Reader's Digest Book Club, which in 1954 boasted 1,600,000 members. Each of its volumes, which are published four times a year, contains abridgments of four or five current best sellers. At $2, the volume is a bargain for the reader, who may get the equivalent of $15 worth of books. And with payments of $60,000 to $100,000 for condensation rights, authors, too, had hit pay dirt.

The editor behind this newest trend in streamlining books was DeWitt Wallace, a tall, lithe, shy man of 65. Perhaps no other American editor has had so much influence on magazine journalism. In 1921, with his wife, Lila Acheson Wallace, he conceived the idea of selecting the best articles published each month in American magazines and reprinting them, in shortened form. His capital, at the time, was a ream of copy paper, a ping-pong table (his desk), and the garage of a friend in Pleasantville, N.Y. From that tenuous start, *The Reader's Digest* has grown to be the most successful magazine ever published. Its circulation in 1954 exceeded 17 million. It was printed in twelve languages, including Finnish and Portuguese.

Midway in the *Digest*'s career, Wallace got the notion of doing with books what he had so successfully done with articles. Publishers, reluctant at first, soon discovered that condensation in the *Digest* meant extra sales.

The condensation idea spread like a prairie fire. In 1954 the Book-of-the-Month Club, granddaddy of all book clubs, stepped into the field with an offshoot called Books Abridged. Doubleday's Best-in-Books varied the formula by presenting two full-length works and excerpts from four or five others, all in one volume.

Magazines, too, vied for condensation rights to established hits. *Not as a Stran-*

ger, for example, ran the complete gamut. It began as a full-fledged selection of The Literary Guild, was condensed (to 250 pages) by the Reader's Digest Book Club, and ended up as a 20,000-word abridgment in *The Woman's Home Companion*.

War Babies Begin to Read

The book business was better in 1954 than it had been the previous year, partly because the mammoth crop of war babies was getting old enough to read. There were 41 percent more children under 14 than there had been in 1940. In many cases, young people's books were ringing more sales on the cash register than any other kind. Ten percent of all new books published annually in the U.S. were for children, and there was hardly a major publisher who did not issue from fifteen to thirty new juvenile titles a year.

Such fabulous success stories as Simon & Schuster's Little Golden Books (so fabulous that sales figures are unavailable from the publisher) reflect the potentiality of this new market. And Random House's Landmark Books dealing with American and world history have opened a vast field for young people's nonfiction.

Landmark was started when publisher Bennett Cerf, on vacation, tried to buy a book about the founding fathers for his young son. Since there were practically none to be had, he contracted to have some written. Landmark Books were a hit from the start, and are now widely imitated.

Children, like adults, have their favorite authors. Among the youngest, she was Miss Frances (Ding Dong School) Horwich. Some years before, this 44-year-old Chicago schoolteacher, the wife of a navy officer, had started a television program for preschool children. Her object was to apply tested educational methods in en-

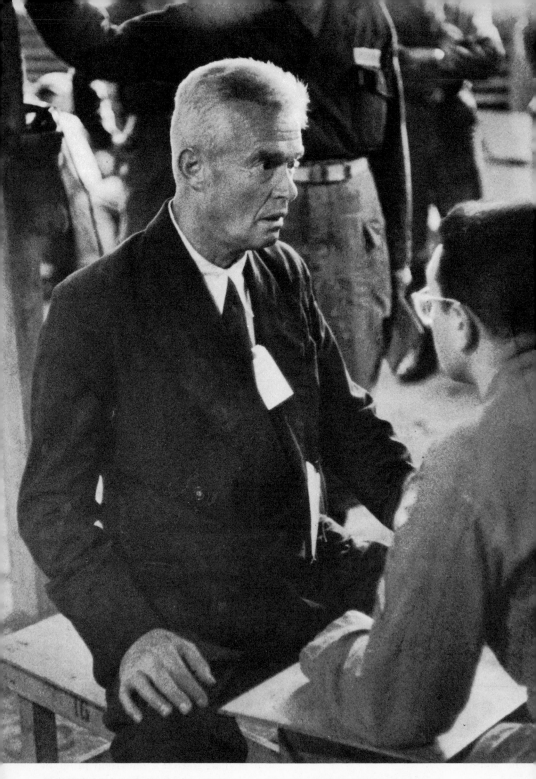

TAGGED on chest as Red prisoner in Korea, General William Dean is shown being interviewed on his release in 1953. In 1954 his book, *General Dean's Story*, was published

FACE CONCEALED, Paris author "Dominique" meets the press after publishing his latest book. Reason for the secrecy: his police novels often quote real documents

tertaining the young. Basically, Miss Frances combined storytelling, visual aids, and demonstrations to excite the child's interest. In a short time the "Ding Dong School" rivaled the strictly commercial "kiddie shows" in popularity.

At this point, a Chicago publishing house, Rand McNally, stepped in. Why not tap Miss Frances' popularity for the book world? The "Ding Dong School" went between the covers of a series of inexpensive (25¢ to $1) books, and 2 million copies were sold in less than two years. The success of these books apparently answered a vital question in publishing—would TV wean youngsters away from reading? To date, the answer is: if anything, TV has whetted their interest.

Reprint Slump

But the general prosperity of hardcover publishing in 1954 was accompanied by a critical slump in the reprint industry. The slump posed a paradoxical question: Why are more people willing to pay $3.50 to $5 instead of 25¢ to 50¢ for a book? The paperbacks were hit hard. An industry accustomed to talking in terms of 300 million books a year found its 1954 total nearer 200 million. Some firms went under. Others retrenched or combined. One top executive estimated that the industry as a whole took a "$10 million licking" in terms of unsold books, unearned advances, and liquidated inventories.

What happened? Far more competitive than hard-cover publishing, the reprint field had become grossly oversupplied. There were more titles than dealers could handle. Books began backing up in the supply lines. Some dealers paid for one shipment of books by giving the wholesaler an unopened bundle from another firm. Money that had been paid to authors in advance, based on the expected sales of their books, was not earned back.

By the end of the year, literally millions of books had been destroyed to make way for new titles. Many were ground into pulp as waste paper; others were simply burned.

The shakedown, costly as it was, helped put the industry on a more normal footing, and by any standards, with receipts running close to $50 million, the paperbound reprint was still big business.

One author—Erle Stanley Gardner—could boast that reprints had accounted for the vast majority of the 75 million books sold under his name since 1939. Such a sure thing is "Perry Mason", the author's lawyer-hero, on the reprint racks that Gardner's trade publisher, William Morrow, signed a contract guaranteeing him $500,000 over a five-year period.

In 1954 another top mystery writer, Ellery Queen, celebrated the twenty-fifth anniversary of perhaps the most unusual collaboration in American letters. For Queen, as most mystery fans know, is two men: Frederic Dannay and Manfred B. Lee. *The Glass Slipper,* published in August, is their twenty-eighth novel.

What is remarkable about their venture is that they live, and work, in different States—Lee in Connecticut, Dannay in New York. Most of their collaboration is done on the telephone, with one doing the plotting, the other the actual writing. When the first draft of a book is finished, they frequently switch roles.

The partnership was born during the depression when Dannay and Lee, who are cousins, entered a mystery-novel contest conducted by *McClure's* magazine. The first prize was $7500, which they won —though *McClure's* promptly went bankrupt and "Ellery Queen", the pseudonym under which the story was entered, never got paid. When the manuscript was accepted by a book publisher, Queen was an immediate hit.

Besides writing books, Dannay and Lee edit *Ellery Queen's Mystery Magazine* and many short-story anthologies.

Title-wise, the best sellers of 1954 continued to defy prediction. For the second year in a row, Norman Vincent Peale's *The Power of Positive Thinking* headed the nonfiction list. Sales by the end of 1954 had exceeded 850,000 copies, all in hard covers. In fact, the book sold better in 1954 than in 1953.

Peale is one of the most prolific of authors. Besides a page of advice to the troubled (in *Look* magazine), he writes a syndicated newspaper column. His weekly sermons go to almost 200,000 persons by mail. In 1954 he wrote *The Power of Positive Thinking for Young People*, which went into two printings, totaling 75,000, in three weeks.

Writing is just one of his activities. He is pastor of the oldest Protestant church in America, Marble Collegiate Church in New York City. He lectures widely and appears regularly, with his wife, on television. He is also the founder of a religious-psychiatric clinic, operated in conjunction with his church.

If there is a "secret formula" in Peale's success, it is the marriage of psychiatry and religion. His books reflect this approach. He believes that the findings of modern psychiatry are most practically applied when they are used to restore man's faith in God.

Executioner at Bay

The book that did the most for its author in 1954 was *Cell 2455, Death Row*, by Caryl Chessman. What it did was get him a stay of execution. Scheduled to die in San Quentin's gas chamber on May 14 (under California's "Little Lindbergh" law), he found himself suddenly transformed from an obscure criminal into a national case history.

Actually, Chessman had held the executioner at bay for six years; it was while sweating out what he thought were the last few months of his life that he wrote his autobiography.

The story is not a pretty one. Chessman's exploits are admittedly violent (although he denies the crime for which he is sentenced to die); he frankly labels himself a criminal psychopath. But the book is a genuine piece of underworld confession, with remarkable insight into the social conditions which helped make the author what he is. It is also a moving declaration of repentance.

In this, it served its purpose. Chessman received a sympathetic hearing by the public and another reprieve by the governor of California.

Cell 2455, Death Row was scheduled to be made into a movie by Columbia Pictures. From the sale to Hollywood and from book royalties, Chessman at the close of 1954 had earned about $25,000. Under his will, the money will go to the two minor children of his fiancée, who was formerly his father's housekeeper.

Whatever else might have been wrong with American publishers in 1954, it was not lack of selling ingenuity. Book buyers could still walk off with bargains by joining almost any of the 100 book clubs in the country (which were serving an estimated 11 million members). . . . Trenton, N.J.'s Food Fair stores gave a different best seller each month to anyone who ponied up 99¢ and bought $3 worth of groceries. . . . Putnam's inaugurated a money-back guarantee—if you don't like the book, bring it back and get a rebate. . . . And Doubleday went one better with one of its titles: pay for the book only after you read—and like—it.

1954 was not a year of great literary achievements, but the industry proved that it could stay alive and prosper without them.

PEOPLE MAKE NEWS: Here are four who made it in 1954. Above: U.S. Ambassador Clare Boothe Luce and husband, publisher Henry Luce (*Time, Life*), arrive at formal party in Rome. Right: Actress Zsa Zsa Gabor and much-married Dominican Porfirio Rubirosa alight at Nice, France, from his private plane

PEOPLE

IN 1954, AS USUAL, HUMAN BEINGS, GREAT and small, well known and unknown, continued to act like human beings. Here is a sampling of the things they did. Some got much attention in newscasts and news columns, others got little. But they all contributed to the year's pattern of human behavior.

January In Mount Palomar, Calif., thieves entered the cabin of whodunit writer Erle Stanley Gardner, creator of sharp-eyed detective Perry Mason, and took his silver, clothes, and typewriter. No clues.

★ In Ironton, Ohio, 6-year-old Johnny Earhart upset his parents by complaining that he could hardly see the blackboard at school. A hastily consulted optometrist found nothing wrong, asked Johnny: "Why can't you see the blackboard?" "Because," said Johnny, "there's a great big boy right in front of me."

★ In Detroit, Mich., John Vlaikov, 64, arrested for drunkenness, declared he rarely drank but admitted he had a few drinks when his 70-year-old wife Theresa came home and told him she had just bought forty dresses and thirty-five hats.

★ In New York City, two well-publicized girls traded husbands for cash. Barbara Sears ("Bobo") Rockefeller, a Lithuanian miner's daughter, agreed to a $5.5 million settlement in an uncontested divorce from multimillionaire Winthrop Rockefeller. Former swimming star Eleanor Holm was divorced from diminutive showman Billy Rose. Alimony: $600 a week, plus $20,000 a year for ten years.

★ In Washington, D.C., to restore "prestige" to officers, new navy regulations specified that ceremonial swords must be worn on official or social occasions. Officers must pay the $50 cost of the sword themselves.

★ In New York City, returning to the U.S. from her native Scotland for a lecture tour, onetime operatic soprano Mary Garden, 76, laughed off proposals for a Hollywood screen version of her colorful career. Said she: "None of those dumb blondes can play me."

★ In New York City, Charles A. Lindbergh, 52, sold the movie rights to his best-selling *The Spirit of St. Louis*, the book about his 1927 Atlantic solo flight, for $1 million.

DEATHS: ALFRED DUFF COOPER, VISCOUNT NORWICH, 63. A British statesman and writer of biographies, he held several Cabinet posts in Conservative governments, resigning one in 1938 to protest the Munich agreements with Hitler.

WALTER EDWARD ("DEATH VALLEY SCOTTY") SCOTT, 78. A California prospector, he lived in self-publicized splendor in the Nevada desert. In 1941 he confessed that the gold mine on which his legendary wealth was based did not exist; he had been subsidized, as a gag, by a wealthy Chicago insurance man, the late Albert Johnson.

COUNTESS DOROTHY (TAYLOR) DI FRASSO, 66. An American-born international hostess, she used part of her $12 million fortune, inherited from her leather-manufacturer father, to entertain Hollywood and gangland celebrities.

SYDNEY GREENSTREET, 74. An English-born stage comedian, he went to Hollywood and played the sinister fat man in many pictures, notably *The Maltese Falcon* and *The Hucksters*.

EDWIN HOWARD ARMSTRONG, 63. A professor of electrical engineering at Columbia University, he made a fortune on patent royalties. His radio inventions are basic to the vacuum-tube system and the AM and FM circuits.

February In Chicago, the National Safety Council announced that 95,000 U.S. residents had been killed in highway, home, and job accidents in 1953. Auto accidents accounted for 38,000.

★ In Gadsden, Ala., farmer Miles Johnson told the court he did not send his two children, aged 9 and 11, to school because they both took snuff and in the classroom there was no place to spit.

★ In Oklahoma City, George V. Fried, launching a campaign for the U.S. Senate, came up with a simple platform: "If it's right, I'm for it."

DEATHS: FREDERICK LEWIS ALLEN, 63. Author, historian, editor (of *Harper's* magazine from 1941 to 1953), he was best known for his nostalgic, discerning accounts of the recent past in books like *Only Yesterday.*

THOMAS WILLIAM PIERREPOINT, 83. Before he retired in 1945 after thirty-five years as Britain's official hangman, he had executed more than 300 criminals.

THE VERY REVEREND WILLIAM RALPH INGE, 93. The "Gloomy Dean" of St. Paul's Cathedral in London, a religious mystic, outspoken, pessimistic, he once said the church was "only a secular institution in which the half-educated speak to the half-converted".

March In Boston, the Massachusetts House of Representatives passed a bill reversing the conviction of six Salem women hanged for witchcraft in 1692. The State Senate rejected it. One solon said it would be "a blow to the tourist business".

★ In Baltimore, Siegfried Weisberger closed up his famed Peabody Bookshop with the sorrowing comment: "The age of the boob is upon us."

★ In Washington, a Civil Aeronautics Board examiner lifted the private-pilot license of Arthur Godfrey for six months. The radio-TV star was charged with deliberately buzzing the control tower at the Teterboro Airport in New Jersey.

★ In Trenton, N.J., Mrs. Patricia Schau-

er, seeking a divorce, charged that her husband beat her whenever the Yankees lost a ball game.

★ In Stillwater, Okla., college officials at Oklahoma A. & M. surveyed the members of the freshman class to see what their chief worry was. It was finding parking space for their cars.

DEATHS: WILL H. HAYS, 74. One-time G.O.P. National Chairman and Harding's first Postmaster General, from 1922 to 1945 he was the $100,000-a-year czar of the movie industry. He enforced production and advertising codes, heading off public demands for government censorship.

WALTER C. HOWEY, 72. Veteran Hearst editor of the slam-bang Chicago school, he was the model for the hard-boiled, conniving managing editor in the rollicking, profane newspaper play, *The Front Page,* written by ex-newsmen Ben Hecht and Charles MacArthur.

DR. JOHN FREDERIC ERDMANN, 90. A Manhattan surgeon, he performed more than 20,000 operations, including secret chest surgery on tenor Enrico Caruso and a jaw-cancer job on President Grover Cleveland.

April In Washington, the head of the U.S. Internal Revenue Service, T. Coleman Andrews, was so busy working on federal income-tax returns that he forgot to file his own State return. He paid a $25 fine to Virginia tax authorities.

★ In Jenner, Calif., while wading in the ocean hunting mollusks, James Antone, a husky bulldozer operator, was attacked by a 40-pound octopus with 8-foot tentacles. "Big Jim" seized the monster in his arms, killed it by bashing its head against a rock.

★ In New York City, J. Fred Muggs, star chimpanzee of the Dave Garroway TV show, got temperamental, nipped costar Martha Raye on the elbow, bit

BRUMM GUM: Clarence Brumm of Colton, Calif., blowing big economy-size bubble, snaps to second in National Little League championship game with Schenectady, N. Y., team. Colton lost

"LOOK, MA, NO PAWS!"
Sepp — a 3½-year-old Alsatian, of
Munich, Germany — makes light of
balancing coffee service for four

Vicki Carlson, Miss Raye's stand-in, over the eyebrow.

★ In Eugene, Ore., Mrs. Ida Lewis was driving with her bright lights on when an oncoming truck stopped in front of her. The driver got out, smashed both her headlights with an iron bar, drove on.

DEATHS: JACQUIN ("JACK") LAIT, 71. Veteran Chicago newsman and since 1936 editor of Hearst's tabloid New York *Daily Mirror*, he wrote, with night-club columnist Lee Mortimer, a series of books exposing crime and vice in U.S. cities — *Washington: Confidential, Chicago: Confidential,* etc.

GENERAL HOYT S. VANDENBERG, 55. Air Force Chief of Staff from 1948 until he retired in 1953, he was largely responsible for the adoption of the strategic-air concept making long-range bombers the key U.S. weapon.

DONALD RAY DANIEL KAYE HARTLEY, 4 months. A two-headed baby born in Petersburg, Ind., it had two hearts which stopped beating 35 minutes apart.

FRITZI SCHEFF, 72. A Viennese soprano and Metropolitan Opera star, she became an overnight success on Broadway in 1905, singing "Kiss Me Again" in Victor Herbert's *Mlle. Modiste.*

PIERRE SAMUEL DU PONT, 84. Head of the giant E. I. du Pont de Nemours chemical company from 1915 to 1940, he invested in General Motors in the early '20's, saving it from bankruptcy. He put Du Pont's munitions profits into development of products like cellophane, nylon, and synthetic rubber.

May In New York City, when Mrs. Ivy Baker Priest had trouble getting a check cashed by a cautious hotel clerk, she asked him to compare her signature with one on a dollar bill. Her signature had appeared on all currency since January, 1953, when she became Treasurer of the United States.

AWA-A-AY WE GO: In Calvisson, France, a *royale de vaches*—in which men show courage by knocking cockades off heads of fighting cows— ends with cow prodding contestant out of arena

WALKING ON AIR as borrowed skis drop off during Berlin amateur contest, jumper Heinz Mannstedt provides one of 1954's most risible pictures

★ In Hollywood, mystery-film director Alfred Hitchcock revealed that he had slimmed himself down from 300 pounds to 187, added: "It's been murder . . . one meal a day—a lamb chop and a few beans. And not a drop to drink."

★ In Camden, N.J., Mrs. Marie A. Walsh was sentenced by a federal court to sixty days in prison and fined $5000 for failing to report her 1945-51 income properly. It had included a $10,293 check from the government for informing on her former employers as tax delinquents.

★ On Long Island, Mrs. Mona Williams, 57, long-time "best-dressed" woman and widow of utilities tycoon Harrison Williams, who left her some $100 million, opened a flower-and-fruit stand on her 60-acre estate.

DEATHS: DR. EARNEST ALBERT HOOTON, 66. A Harvard anthropologist and author (*Apes, Men, and Morons*), he was an outspoken and witty advocate of birth control, euthanasia, and sterilization of defectives.

MARIA ISABELLA PATIÑO GOLDSMITH, 18. Daughter of Antenor Patiño, who was an heir to a $200 million Bolivian tin fortune, she ran off with James Goldsmith, son of a British hotel director, eluded her father's detectives, was married. She died suddenly of cerebral hemorrhage as doctors delivered a 5-pound baby girl by Caesarean section.

June In Berkeley, Calif., life-insurance agent Howard C. Martin encountered sales resistance from prospect Paul B. McCracken, at whose home he was calling. Then a bullet fired by a neighbor attempting suicide crashed through a window, ricocheted around the room, dropped at McCracken's feet. McCracken bought a policy.

★ In New Brunswick, Canada, 80-year-old naturalist-author Thornton Burgess promised that as long as he writes his continuing bedtime story—he has written it for forty-four years—Rèddy Fox will never catch Peter Rabbit.

★ In Hanover, N.H., Alfred Lunt and Lynn Fontanne, husband-wife acting team, received Dartmouth's first double-barreled honorary degree, Doctor of Humane Letters. Said President John Sloan Dickey: "What the Lunts have joined together, Dartmouth will not set asunder."

★ In Philadelphia, the police department sent back twenty-one new snub-nosed .38-caliber revolvers ordered for its policewomen. The lady cops couldn't pull the stiff triggers.

★ In Minneapolis, Carlton J. West stopped his car on a bridge, pulled a drowning woman out of the Mississippi River, restored her with artificial respiration, returned to his car, found a ticket for illegal parking.

DEATHS: MAURY MAVERICK, 58. Democratic Representative from Texas (1935-39), he was a strong New Dealer but hated governmental red tape. He coined the word "gobbledygook" to describe official language.

CHARLES FRANCIS ADAMS, 87. Banker, noted yachtsman, and Secretary of the Navy under Hoover, he was a direct descendant of Presidents John Adams and John Quincy Adams.

DR. KARL TAYLOR COMPTON, 66. Physicist and top government adviser on the atomic bomb, he was president of the Massachusetts Institute of Technology from 1930 to 1948.

July In Copenhagen, at an industrial fair, Henry Ford II examined some Russian automobiles, declared: "As far as I can see, these cars are not very good."

★ In Glasgow, Dr. A. H. Douthwaite told a medical group that snoring may be based on race memory, and that, atavistically, the male made the noise at

ZOO SUICIDE: Czech refugee Joseph Hajek, 21, lies dead after climbing into lions' den in Nuremberg, West Germany. An A-1 scholar, he apparently had been despondent over ranking second in high-school class

night to keep marauders from the den. Therefore, he pointed out, a wife might assume that the louder the snore the greater the affection.

★ In Long Beach, Calif., Miss Miriam Stevenson, a freckled, blue-eyed, blond senior at Lander College, at Greenwood, S.C., nosed out seventy-eight U.S. and foreign beauties to become "Miss Universe". Statistics: 5 feet, 6 inches; 120 pounds; top-to-bottom, 36, 24, 36.

★ In Los Angeles, 16-year-old Arthur MacArthur, son of General of the Army Douglas MacArthur, told newsmen he wasn't sure whether he would go to West Point because "It's sort of losing its appeal. Even Daddy is not so keen about it now. Maybe he's had enough of the army."

DEATHS: F(OREST) E. BOONE, 61. A tobacco auctioneer, his "Sold American" chant became a familiar radio commercial.

GABRIEL PASCAL, 60. British film producer and director, he persuaded George Bernard Shaw to let him make movies of some of his plays, such as *Pygmalion* and *Major Barbara*.

GEORGE R. ("MACHINE GUN") KELLY, 59. An Oklahoma bootlegger who formed a gang of hoodlums, he kidnapped oilman Charles F. Urschel, collected $200,000 ransom, was caught by the F.B.I., sent to Leavenworth where he died. Reportedly, he could write his name on a wall with a machine gun.

RUTH BRYAN OWEN ROHDE, 68. Daughter of the late William Jennings Bryan, she became the first U.S. woman envoy to a foreign power on her appointment as Minister to Denmark (1933-36). She was a Representative from Florida from 1929 to 1933.

August In Jersey City, Mrs. Carolyn Reidy admitted she had not worked a day as clerk in the school system since 1950 although she had collected $12,000 in pay since that time. She explained: "I would have come to work if anyone had asked me to."

★ In Newark, N.J., at Minsky's burlesque house, Mrs. Tommy Manville, 31, estranged ninth wife of the asbestos heir, opened a one-week engagement to supplement her $1000 a week allowance from her husband. Manville said he would not go to see the routine: "I haven't been to a burlesque for forty-six years—and I won't start again with her stinky show."

★ In Ripley, Tenn., Judge J. R. Lewis opened the trial of three boys charged with stealing watermelons by saying: "Anyone here who has never stolen a watermelon when he was a boy, let him raise his hand." Not one lawyer, court official, or visitor moved a muscle. "Case dismissed," said the judge.

★ In Hollywood, Ditra Flame, known as the "woman in black" who appeared annually at Rudolph Valentino's crypt in Hollywood Cemetery on the anniversary of his death, made her twenty-eighth appearance, dressed in white. She said it would be her last.

★ In Switzerland, at a divorce hearing, socialite Joanne Connelly Sweeny Patiño, 23, told the judge that her husband, Bolivian tin heir Jaime Ortiz Patiño, was "a real sadist". She added, dead-pan: "On our honeymoon he beat me so much I had a miscarriage."

★ In Sacramento, the Sutter Sales Company advertised its sale of air-conditioning units with the line "Come in and steal 'em." Burglars stole four.

DEATHS: DR. HUGO ECKENER, 86. German dirigible pioneer, he guided the ZR-3 across the Atlantic in 1924 and took the *Graf Zeppelin* around the world in twelve days in 1929. His dream of a lighter-than-air transport system went up in smoke when the hydrogen-filled *Hin-*

denburg exploded at Lakehurst, N.J., in 1937 and the U.S. refused to export fire-proof helium to Germany.

September In Lewisburg, Ohio, John F. Lock got his mailbox moved 1056 feet nearer to his home after a 52-year battle. He claimed that in that time he had walked 6250 miles to pick up his mail.
★ In Norwalk, Calif., an immigrant dairyman, Gerben Van Dyke, hooked up twenty-four of his cows to a milking machine, watched horrified as a short circuit knocked them down, killing thirteen. He complained: "Nothing like this ever happened in the old country."
★ In Hollywood, to play the brief role of a Governor of Texas in a new film, *Lucy Gallant*, Paramount signed Allan Shivers, Governor of Texas.
DEATHS: EUGENE PALLETTE, 65. A heavy-set, gruff-voiced character actor, he appeared in more than 1000 films before his retirement in 1946.
BERT ACOSTA, 59. Pilot of the first multi-engined flight across the Atlantic (in 1927) with Admiral Richard Byrd and Bernt Balchen, he was a fearless speed and endurance flier. He died in a tuberculosis sanatorium where he was taken after collapsing, ill and broke, on a New York street two years before.
HARRY C. ("BUD") FISHER, 69. One of the earliest comic-strip artists, he started *Mutt and Jeff* in 1907. In 1954 it was being drawn by his assistant, Al Smith.
GLENN S. ("POP") WARNER, 83. Coach of the Carlisle Indians (when Jim Thorpe played) and later at Pittsburgh, Stanford, and Temple, he developed the double-wing back formation, bringing new speed and deception to football.

October In Oklahoma City, at a military ceremony, A. B. Rowland, a World War I private, fulfilled a long-time urge —to boo a general. He booed 300 of them, plus Secretary of the Army Robert Stevens. Police took him away.
★ In Mexico City, Walter Gieseking, German pianist, interrupted his performance of a Beethoven sonata, went to the footlights, bawled out a youth with a camera, seized the camera, resumed playing the sonata.
★ In Danbury, Conn., Edward Schlemmer, a $64-a-week machinist expecting his fourteenth child, was presented with triplets by his 41-year-old wife.
★ In Chicago, Gus Scopos, a restaurant owner, who was charged with pouring hot grease over a customer, was freed when he told the judge: "He ordered one hamburger—mind you, just one—then poured a whole bottle of catsup over it."
★ In Washington, D.C., Rear Admiral Lewis L. Strauss, Chairman of the Atomic Energy Commission, touched off a domestic H-bomb by saying that spinach isn't good for children because experiments with radioactive isotopes indicate that it "removes calcium from the body".
★ In Kingston, Canada, British inventor Sir Robert Watson-Watt, a developer of radar, was fined $12.50 for speeding. Police had clocked his car by radar.
DEATHS: PATRICK ANTHONY McCARRAN, 78. Democratic Senator from Nevada since 1932, he was a powerful right-winger, a self-styled "lone wolf", a skilled politician.
EDWARD HALL CRUMP, 80. A Mississippi backwoodsman, he was the undisputed political boss of Memphis, Tenn., from 1909 and of the State from 1930, until Democratic Senator Estes Kefauver challenged him successfully in 1948.
CHARLES P. SKOURAS, 65. Son of a Greek farmer, he came to the U.S. at 19 and became head of a chain of 650 theaters. He brought over his brothers Spyros, who became president of Twentieth Century-Fox, and George, who became

president of United Artists Theater Circuit.

GEORGE MCMANUS, 70. Creator of the comic strip *Bringing Up Father*, he made a million out of the marital squabbles of Jiggs and Maggie, followed by readers of 750 newspapers printed in twenty-seven languages.

November In Hasland, England, Stanley Wright, a 35-year-old, $22-a-week laborer, won $168,000 in a football pool. In January, 1952, he had won $210,000 in the same pool. He said he'd go on working because "I like it."
★ In Omaha, Mrs. John Schrank was told she is allergic to paper money.
★ In Washington, D.C., Senator Homer Capehart, Indiana Republican, absent-mindedly following the senatorial custom of referring to members by complimentary titles, twice in one speech referred to himself as "the able Senator from Indiana".
★ In Roanoke, Va., Charles Lee Dickerson, 71, finally married Mrs. Martha Shelton, 70. Her father had frightened him into breaking their engagement fifty-two years earlier.
★ In Paris, Ky., Gallant Fox, holder of horse racing's triple crown—he won the Kentucky Derby, the Preakness, and Belmont Stakes in 1930—died at the age of 27.
DEATHS: ORAN ("HOT LIPS") PAGE, 46. Jazz trumpeter and vocalist, he was one of the first Negroes to play with a white orchestra.
FRED B. SNITE JR., 44. The self-styled "boiler kid", he lived eighteen and a half years in an iron lung following an attack of polio, was married, had three daughters.
DR. ENRICO FERMI, 53. An Italian-born, Nobel Prize-winning physicist, in 1942 he achieved the first nuclear chain reaction in a secret experiment in a University of Chicago court. This success made possible the atomic bomb.

December In Antwerp, Belgium, a soldier, Hendrik Verheyen, was court-martialed and sent to prison for thirteen months for stealing his outfit's cannon.
★ In El Sobrante, Calif., a holdup man forestalled pursuit by forcing his victims, a cab driver and a service-station attendant, to drink a bottle of whisky in six minutes before he took off.
★ In West Berlin, Dr. Fritz Heese complained that he could not collect an overdue bill for $476 from the Soviet government. In the winter of 1953, he had been called to Berlin's Soviet Zone and shown diagnostic reports on Premier Stalin. His verdict: Stalin was near death. (Stalin died a few days later.) Thereafter, Dr. Heese said, he submitted a consultant's bill four times, was four times ignored.
★ In Toppenish, Wash., after his first four months as a fireman, Ron Butler finally got a chance to drive the department's new fire engine. Alone in the station house when the alarm sounded, he jumped to the driver's seat, roared off, neglected to open the station-house door.
DEATHS: WILHELM FURTWÄNGLER, 68. Director of the Berlin Philharmonic Orchestra through most of the Hitler period, he was an outstanding interpreter of Beethoven, Schubert, and Wagner. In 1947 a Big Four commission cleared him of active collaboration with the Nazis.
ARTHUR GARFIELD HAYS, 73. A wealthy attorney, he was a crusader for civil rights, notably in association with the American Civil Liberties Union.
JAMES HILTON, 54. Best-selling British novelist, he wrote the books from which two notable films were made, *Goodbye, Mr. Chips* and *Lost Horizon* (from which "Shangri-La", the term for a Utopian retreat, was taken).

THE ETERNAL MALE turns from past to present. This photo, entitled "Eve", took first prize in interservice photo contest, proving once again that the most popular study of man is woman

TEXT INDEX _____

PICTURE INDEX

Ferrer, Mel: 363
Fontana, Zoe: 357
Forrest, Sally: 335
Frederika, Queen: 162-63
Gabor, Zsa Zsa: 427
Galard-Terraube, Lt.
   Geneviève de: 107
Garbo, Greta: 339
Gardner, Ava: 357
Geva, Tamara: 309
Gleason, Jackie: 364, 366
Glenconner, Lord: 159
Greco, Emilio: 400
Grock: 131
Hajek, Joseph: 436-37
Hampton, Lionel: 302
Haney, Carol: 334
Hardaway, Rose: 138
Harriman, Averell: 41
Hatoyama, Ichiro: 206
Hemingway, Ernest: 417
Hepburn, Audrey: 330, 363
Hepburn, Katharine: 360, 361
Hirohito, Emperor: 213
Ho Chi Minh: 96-97
Hoffman, Harold G.: 89
Hopper, Hedda: 345
Humphrey, George M.: 43
Hutton, Betty: 377
Jackson, Henry Martin: 60-61
Jenkins, Ray Howard: 60, 67
John, Augustus E.: 395
Juin, Marshal Alphonse: 128
Kafka, Franz: 310
Kaganovich, Lazar M.: 178-79
Kapus, Gisella and Eva:
   188-89
Kaye, Danny: 225
Kelly, Gene and Fred: 358-59
Khrushchev, Nikita
   Sergeyevich: 178-79
Killimayer, James: 93
Kilmer, Dorene: 335
Kitt, Eartha: 331
Kosloski, Mary: 292
Landy, John: 382-83
Lane, Mara: 354
Lebron, Lolita: 33
LeClercq, Tanaquil: 303
Lewis, Jerry: 344

Liberace, Wladziu
   Valentino: 365
Lodge, Henry Cabot, Jr.: 43
Lollobrigida, Gina: 255, 348,
   349
Long, H. B.: 84-85
Luce, Clare Boothe: 426
Luce, Henry: 426
Lynn, Mrs. A. D.: 84-85
Magallanes, Nicolas: 303
Malenkov, Georgi M.: 96-97,
   178-79
Mannstedt, Heinz: 434
Mao Tse-tung: 96-97
Marciano, Rocky: 386
Margaret, Princess: 159
Marsh, Reginald: 394
Marx, Groucho: 377
Matisse, Henri: 398-99
Maurois, André: 416
McCarthy, Joseph Raymond:
   59, 61, 65, 71
McClellan, John L.: 60-61, 66
Meek, Joseph T.: 26
Mendès-France, Pierre: 126-27
Mendès-France, Mme. Pierre:
   127
Molotov, Vyacheslav M.: 122
Monroe, Marilyn: 324-25, 355
Moore, Henry: 401
Mundt, Karl E.: 60-61, 67
Naguib, Maj. Gen.
   Mohammed: 228-29
Nasser, Gamal Abdel: 226-27,
   228-29
Neff, Hildegarde: 338
Nehru, Jawaharlal: 117, 220
Neuberger, Richard L.: 31
Neurath, Baron Konstantin
   von: 145
Nixon, Richard M.: 44
North, Sheree: 344
Pahlavi, Shah: 233
Perón, Juan D.: 255
Petrillo, James C.: 25
Petrov, Evdokia: 186, 187
Philip, Duke of Edinburgh:
   152-53, 156-57, 263
Picasso, Pablo: 392, 393
Pleven, René: 128

Potter, Charles E.: 60-61
Potts, Wally: 389
Rhee, Syngman: 202
"Rochester" (Eddie
   Anderson): 375
Rodgers, Richard: 309
Roolaid, V.: 183
"Roxanne" (Dolores
   Rosedale): 372
Rubirosa, Porfirio: 427
Rutherford, Frank: 329
Salem, Maj. Salah: 228-29
Salisbury, Harrison E.: 327
Schaak, Christel ("Miss
   Germany"): 149
Schine, G. David: 61, 64
Seletz, Dr. Emil: 314
Sheppard, Dr. Samuel: 81
Siegel, Paul: 379
Soekarno, Achmed: 214-15
Soraya, Queen: 232
Sperry, Capt. Edward G.: 57
Spring Orchid: 196, 197
Stapp, Col. John P.: 52, 53
Steinberg, William: 304-305
Stevens, Robert T.: 58, 64
Stewart, Elaine: 355
Symington, Stuart: 60-61, 66
Tennant, Colin: 159
Tito, Marshal: 162-63
Toscanini, Arturo: 315
Townsend, Col. Peter: 158
Truman, Harry S.: 24
Truman, Margaret: 370, 371
Tsai, Dr. Loh Seng: 300
Turova, I.: 182
"Vampira" (Maila Syrjaniemi):
   374
Vishinsky, Andrei: 172
Voroshilov, Marshal Kliment
   E.: 178-79
Vries, Volkje and Tjitske de:
   290
Walton, Jack: 56
Welch, Joseph: 58, 70
Wilson, Charles E.: 38
Wolfson, Louis Elwood: 274
Wood, Dee Dee: 334
Young, Robert R.: 270
Zorina, Vera: 308-309

PICTURE SOURCES

ALLIED ARTISTS: 352-3

BERT BEAVER: 404

D. M. BERNAND (France): 131 (tp)

BERETTY-VAN NOPPEN (France): 138

BLACK STAR: 127 (tp-rt), Horvat 217, 406, Hassner 240-1, Heinrich 245, (3 photos) 300-1, Covello 348 and 399, Ted Russell 422

LAMAR BOREN: 389

JOSEPH BRUN (Switzerland): 388

CAMERA CLIX: Kurt Severin 259, 293

CAPITOL RECORDS: 304-5

C.B.S.: 364, 367

COMBINE: 400

CONSOLIDATED PRESS (Australia) from P.I.P.: 187

COORDINATION from GAMMA: 236-7

CULVER: 339

YVES DEBRAINE (Switzerland): 171

EASTFOTO: (2 photos) 174-5, 178-9

EUROPEAN: 196, 197, 310

FOTO-VESPASIANI (Italy): (2 photos) 408-9

FREE LANCE PHOTOGRAPHERS: Florea 354, 375

UNOSUKO GAMO: 203

GRAPHIC HOUSE: Eileen Darby 326-7

THEODORE HECHT: 311, 345

ILLUSTRATED: 152-3, 242-3, 395

INDIANAPOLIS TIMES from WIDE WORLD: 90-1

INTERCONTINENTAL from GAMMA: 184

INTERNATIONAL NEWS PHOTOS: 20, 21, 33, 42 (rt, cn), 43 (cn, lt), 44, 46-7, 57, 58 (tp), 59, 66 (bot), 67 (tp, bot), 71, 75, (Barney Coons) 80, 82, 128, 131 (bot), (4 photos) 136, 142, 143 (tp), 145, 146-7, 151, 169, 172, 182, 186, 192-3, 220, 225, 226-7, 228-9, 246-7, 248-9, 253, 260-1, 263, 282-3, 314, (Per-Olow, 3 photos) 360-1, 386-7, 403, 412 (lt), 426, 427, 438-9, (Major Leslie Wood) 441

KARK-TV: (4 photos) 84-5

KELPIX: Earl Leaf 377

KEYSTONE: 48, 130, 183, 235, 401, 431, 436-7

KEYSTONE PRESS Ltd.: 162-3

LIFE Magazine © Time, Inc.: Front Endpaper (rt) Ralph Morse, George Skadding 26-7 and 74, Burton Glinn 29, Brian Seed 116, Frank Scherschel 124-5, N. R. Farbman 296-7, Allan Grant 357

LOS ANGELES EXAMINER from I.N.P.: 93

LOS ANGELES HERALD EXPRESS: 342-3

RODERICK MACARTHUR: 338

MAGNUM: Robert Capa 110-1 and 330-1, David Seymour 140-1 and 355 (lt), Erich Lessing 144, Homer Page 205, Erich Hartmann 334 (lt), Werner Bischof 334-5, Philippe Halsman 316 and 365, Dennis Stock 358-9, 363 and 374, Elliott Erwitt 366

ALEXANDER MARSHAK: 214, 215

J. NAHON (France): 432-3

N.B.C.: Sy Friedman (2 photos) 315

ARNOLD NEWMAN (Courtesy of LIFE Magazine): 40, 41

NEW YORK DAILY NEWS from GILLOON: 83, 188, 339

NEW YORK HERALD TRIBUNE: Bob Noble 271

NEW YORK JOURNAL-AMERICAN from I.N.P.: 338 (lt)

NEW YORK TIMES from WIDE WORLD: 12-3, 14-5, 96-7

PARAMOUNT: 344

PARIS MATCH from GAMMA: 100, 101, 107, 123, 127 (bot), 135, (4 photos) 170, 191, 221, 278-9, 330, (5 photos) 392-3, 416, 418-9

PENGUIN: 347

PHOTO-REPRESENTATIVES from EAST-WEST: 11, Horace Bristol 190, Takamasa Inamura 206, Takahiro Ono 208-9

P.I.B. from GAMMA: 164

PIX: 156-7, 168, Karsh 267, 290-1, Baron 303, Ullman 398-9, Dungan 414

ALFRED PUHN: 394

RANDOLPH & DELONG: 321 (lt)

RAPHO-GUILLUMETTE: Sabine Weiss 126, Doisneau 137, Sanford Roth 139, Ormond Gigli (3 photos) 308-9, 343 and 320 (lt, rt), André de Dienes 317

REFLEX (London): George Varias 150

A. RULMONT for La Meuse (Belgium): 158

GREG SHUKER: 173

PAUL SIEGEL for THE MINNEAPOLIS STAR AND TRIBUNE: 378-9

RUTH SONDAK: (4 photos) 370

TALBOT: 321 (lt)

UNITED PRESS: (2 photos) 18, 32, 43 (lt), 98 (rt), 104-5, 127 (tp-lt), 159, 161, 165, 202, 232, 292, 372, 417, 423

EDMOND WATKINS: 302

WIDE WORLD: Front Endpaper (3 photos, lt), Back Endpaper (4 photos), 17, 24-5, 36, 38, 42, 52, (3 photos) 53, 56, 58 (cn, bot), 60-1, 61, 64, 65, 66 (tp), 70, 72, 73, 81, 89, 98 (lt), 112-3, 117, 120, 121, 122, 143 (bot), 149, 198, 199, 216, 233, 234, 252, 255, 264, 265, 270, 275, 323, 338 (bot), 349, 371, (8 photos) 382-3, 402, 430, 434

JERRY YULSMAN: 346

Dear Mr. Henslin,

My name is Sydney Conley. I'm a student at Midlands Technical College in Columbia, South Carolina. I'm studying for a test that I have tomorrow in Sociology and I just thought you might like to know that I find your book *Essentials of Sociology* very interesting. Thanks to your book, I'm considering continuing my study of Sociology.

Thanks again
Sydney Conley

Hello Professor Henslin,

My name is Marta Holliday and I am a student at Marymount College in Tarrytown, NY. I am taking Introduction to Sociology at Nassau Community College to earn extra credits and your text was required reading for our class. I just wanted to tell you how much I enjoyed your book. I found the chapters fun and interesting—especially how you opened each with a sketch or a personal vignette.

It was a pleasure to read your work. I felt as though I became acquainted with you through your words.
Sincerely,
Marta A. Holliday

Dear James,

Hey there, my name is Leo Chagolla. I attend the University of Toledo and I am a Pharmacy major. When I registered for classes in the beginning of the fall semester, I was told I would either need to take sociology or psychology as an elective. To tell you the truth, I only took sociology because I had to—and it sounded easier than psychology. What I have discovered is that sociology has become one of the most interesting subjects I have ever studied.

Your book, *A Down-to-Earth Approach*, is marvelously well written and constructed. I seriously believe that reading your book has made me a better person. I am only one chapter away from completing the book—my class was only supposed to read on to chapter 9—but I just cannot stop reading.

Leo Chagolla

Hello,

My name is Margaux Strawn and I have just signed up for Sociology 101. I had taken a course on Sociology in high school many moons ago. I felt very overwhelmed when first reading your textbook, but as I dug into the book, the reading became very easy and interesting. I would like to thank you for helping to produce a book that already has me looking up more information on DuBois.

Sociology potential,
Margaux Strawn

Dear Mr. Henslin,

I would like to take a minute to write you a brief letter expressing my gratitude for your most interesting and enlightening book. I have just begun my exploration into the world of sociology. With the help of your book, and my college professor, you have helped to educate me in a discipline that was foreign to me. I was unaware of the possibilities available to sociology majors, and after researching I have found this is definitely the field for me!

Sincerely,
Katie Bailey